Catastrophes, Confrontations, and Constraints

Catastrophes, Confrontations, and Constraints

How Disasters Shape the Dynamics of Armed Conflicts

Tobias Ide

The MIT Press
Cambridge, Massachusetts
London, England

© 2023 Massachusetts Institute of Technology

This work is subject to a Creative Commons CC-BY-NC-ND license.
Subject to such license, all rights are reserved.

[CC BY-NC-ND]

The MIT Press would like to thank the anonymous peer reviewers who provided comments on drafts of this book. The generous work of academic experts is essential for establishing the authority and quality of our publications. We acknowledge with gratitude the contributions of these otherwise uncredited readers.

This book was set in Stone by Westchester Publishing Services. Printed and bound in the United States of America.

Library of Congress Cataloging-in-Publication Data is available.

ISBN: 978-0-262-54555-6

10 9 8 7 6 5 4 3 2 1

This book is dedicated to Carmen, Walter, Sieglinde, and Kurt.
Thanks for always being there for me. Your sympathy and support have been immeasurable.

Contents

Acknowledgments   xi

1 Setting the Foundation: Disasters and Conflicts   1

Why Study Disasters and Armed Conflicts?   1
The Emergence of Disaster-Conflict Research   5
State of Knowledge   8
Contributions of This Study   12
Goal, Definitions, and Plan   14

2 After the Disaster: Motives, Strategies, and Incentives for Conflict (De-)escalation   19

Grievances   25
Solidarity   27
Opportunity   29
Constraints   32
Costly Signal   33
Image Cultivation   35
Summary   37

3 Cases, Conditions, and Qualitative Comparative Analysis   39

Sample of Cases   39
Data Collection and Analysis   41
Causal Conditions and Theoretical Expectations   48

4 Disasters and Armed Conflict Dynamics: Evidence from 36 Cases   55

Cases of Conflict Escalation after Disasters   55
  Bangladesh 1991: The Chittagong Hill Conflict after Cyclone Gorky   55

  Colombia 1999: Shaking Grounds, Shaking the Peace Process? 57
  Egypt 1994: Floods, Fire, and Fury 60
  India (Andhra Pradesh and Orissa) 1999: The Cyclone as an Opportunity for Naxalite Insurgents 62
  India (Assam) 1998: Floods, Recruitment Opportunities, and Conflict Persistence 65
  Philippines 1990: Earthquake-Related Opportunities for Both Sides 67
  Sri Lanka 2004: Wave of Violence? 71
  Tajikistan 1992: Independence, Civil War, and Floods 74
  Uganda 1999–2001: Drought, Food Insecurity, and Raids 76
 Cases of Conflict De-escalation after Disasters 78
  Bangladesh 2007: Cyclone Sidr and the Maoist Insurgency 78
  Burundi 2005–2006: Drought, Democratization, and the Peace Process 81
  India (Kashmir) 2005: Cross-Border Constraints in the Face of an Earthquake 84
  Indonesia 2004: Wave of Peace? 86
  Myanmar 2008: The Karen Conflict after Cyclone Nargis 89
  Pakistan 2010: Floods Facilitating Conflict De-escalation 92
  Somalia 1997: Flood in the Midst of Chaos 95
  Somalia 2010–2011: Drought and Famine in a Fragile Country 97
  Turkey 1999: Öcalan's Capture, the Marmara Earthquake, and the PKK's Cease-Fire 100
 Cases with No Disaster Impact on Conflict Dynamics 102
  Afghanistan 1998: Remote Earthquakes Did Not Shape Conflict Dynamics 102
  Afghanistan 2008: Freezing the Conflict? 105
  Algeria 2003: Grievances and Opportunities after the Boumerdès Earthquake 107
  India (Assam) 2007: The ULFA's Inability to Exploit Flood-Related Opportunities 109
  Indonesia 1992: No Link between the Flores Earthquake and the East Timor Conflict 110
  Indonesia 2006: Disaster in Yogyarkata, De-escalation in Aceh? 112
  Iran 1990: The Kurdish Struggle after the Manjil-Rudbar Earthquake 114
  Iran 1997: The MEK Insurgency and the Qayen Earthquake 116
  Nepal 1996: Correlation but No Causation between Floods and Armed Conflict Escalation 117
  Pakistan 2005: Escalation after, but Not Related to the Kashmir Earthquake 119
  Pakistan 2015: Turning On the Heat, Turning Off the Conflict? 121
  Peru 2007: High-Intensity Earthquake, Low-Intensity Conflict 123
  Philippines 1991: Storm, Flood, and Conflict De-escalation 125
  Philippines 2013: Super Typhoon, but Few Conflict Implications 127

Philippines 2012: No Link between Typhoon and Conflict Escalation   129
Russia 1995: The Sakhalin Earthquake and the Conflict in Chechnya—Too Far Apart   131
Russia 2010: Triple Disaster Not Linked to Conflict De-escalation   133
Thailand 2004: Tsunami and Conflict Escalation—Correlation but No Causation   135
Summary   137

5   Armed Conflicts in the Aftermath of Disasters: Key Findings   139

General Findings and Their Implications   139
    Armed Conflict Escalation, De-escalation, and Continuation   139
    Motive   145
    Strategy   147
    Communication   152
Disaster Types and Conflict Dynamics   155
When Do Disasters Have an Impact on Conflict Dynamics?   158
Escalation or De-escalation after a Disaster?   166
Summary   174

6   Conflict Implications of the COVID-19 Pandemic   177

The COVID-19 Disaster   177
The Islamic State Conflict in Iraq   183
The Taliban Conflict in Afghanistan   187
The Boko Haram Insurgency in Nigeria   191
The Conflict between the CPP/NPA and the Philippine Government   196
Discussion   200

7   Conclusion   205

Key Findings and Their Implications   205
Where Is the Future?   212
Lessons for Practice and Policy   214
Final Considerations   217

References   219
Index   281

Acknowledgments

This book was written over a period of two and a half years (from October 2019 to May 2022), in two different places (Melbourne and Perth), and while a major pandemic ravaged the world. While this phrase is terribly overused, the book truly feels like the end—and also is the reward—of a long journey.

Like every journey, this one started with the first step (another overused phrase). In late 2018, the Australian Research Council (ARC) awarded me a Discovery Early Career Research Award (DECRA) to conduct a three-year research project on disasters and conflict dynamics at the University of Melbourne. The project moved with me to Murdoch University Perth when I started a new position there in early 2021. This book is a direct result of the DECRA project and would have been infeasible without the continuous support of the ARC, the University of Melbourne, and Murdoch University.

Of course, when the project was awarded to me, I was already embedded in and versed in the research landscape. Credit for this goes to my earlier academic mentors, in particular (in temporal order) to Andreas Osiander, Klaus Roscher, Jürgen Scheffran, and Anja P. Jakobi. Jon Barnett provided invaluable advice on the project from my initial thinking about conflicts and disasters all the way through writing the DECRA application and conducting the research.

I am grateful to Michael Brzoska, Halvard Buhaug, Ken Conca, Ian Kelman, and Patrick A. Mello, who provided feedback on earlier versions of different chapters. Arden Haar was an excellent research assistant collecting literature on the case studies, while Markus Meisner supported me in the processing of the quantitative conflict data. Several colleagues also gave me invaluable advice and feedback on particular case studies, most notably

Bob East, Muhammad Feyyaz, Vanessa Lamb, Lisa Palmer, Sol Santos, Stefan Vandeginste, Christian Webersik, and Katrin Wittig.

Finally, the biggest thank-you goes to my friends and family. We were often unable to see each other while I was writing this book, but being in contact with them helped me get through Melbourne's "mega lockdown," and I very much enjoyed catching up during or after a day at the beach in Perth. My wife Davina and my son Immanuel are particularly noteworthy here. They are truly the light of my life. This book is dedicated to my parents and grandparents, even though this dedication cannot nearly account for all the sympathy and support they provided to me. To paraphrase another popular saying: In the end, a journey is not about the destination but about the company that we keep.

1 Setting the Foundation: Disasters and Conflicts

Why Study Disasters and Armed Conflicts?

Disasters triggered by extreme natural events have devastating impacts on individuals, groups, and societies. Since the year 2000, such disasters have claimed 1.25 million lives. Some past events were even more devastating, such as the 1959 Yellow River flood in China (2 million deaths), the 1965–1967 drought in India (1.5 million deaths), the 1983–1984 drought in Ethiopia (300,000 deaths), and Cyclone Bhola in Bangladesh (then East Pakistan) in 1970 (300,000 deaths). To this one can add the health effects of disasters—for example, injuries, post-traumatic stress, the destruction of housing, health, water, and food infrastructure, and post-disaster disease outbreaks (Makwana 2019; Salazar et al. 2016). Following the 2010 earthquake in Haiti, for example, malaria, dengue fever, and cholera infections increased massively (Enserink 2010). Furthermore, disaster can have devastating economic effects. In the years 2019–2021, disasters caused global economic damage of US$150 billion, $210 billion, and $280 billion, respectively (Munich RE 2021). Taken together, this is more than the annual GDP of countries like Argentina, Belgium, Hong Kong, or Nigeria. Consequently, reducing the risks associated with disasters is an essential component of the sustainable development goals[1] and subject to a separate (yet closely related) agreement endorsed by the United Nations (UN 2015), the Sendai Framework for Disaster Risk Reduction.

1. Particularly by target 11.5: "By 2030, significantly reduce the number of deaths and the number of people affected and substantially decrease the direct economic losses relative to global gross domestic product caused by disasters, including water-related disasters, with a focus on protecting the poor and people in vulnerable situations" (UNDESA 2015).

Because of inconsistencies and uncertainties in the data, trends in disasters are not easy to assess (Visser et al. 2020; Wirtz et al. 2014). However, in the face of climate change,[2] urbanization, the increasing concentration of populations in exposed or vulnerable areas (e.g., urban slums, coastal cities), and persistent poverty,[3] the world will likely experience more frequent and more intense disasters in the coming decades (Cappelli et al. 2021; Franzke and Torelló i Sentelles 2020; Kelman 2020). This finding is corroborated by empirical data. Giuseppe Formetta and Luc Feyen (2019) find clear upward trends for disaster events, fatalities, and economic damage for the period from 1980 to 2016. Likewise, Nicolas Boccard (2021), comparing four global datasets, finds that disaster events and, to a lesser degree, disaster-related economic damage showed clear upward trends between 1970 and 2019. By contrast, the number of fatalities per million people is trending downward, indicating a reduced vulnerability (see figure 1.1).

Just like disasters, armed conflict is a major challenge for humanity in the twenty-first century. The Uppsala Conflict Data Program (UCDP) estimates that since the turn of the millennium, more than 1 million people have died in battles between organized armed groups (Pettersson et al. 2021). Some studies suggest that this estimate can be up to three times higher if the long-term effects of injuries are considered (Obermeyer et al. 2008; Spagat et al. 2009). Destruction of health infrastructure, food and water insecurity, and a lack of public services owing to insecurity further add to the civilian death toll. General life expectancy in Syria, for instance, declined by up to 20 years after the onset of the civil war in 2011 (Guha-Sapir et al. 2018).

Beyond their immediate impacts on health, armed conflicts can have long-lasting impacts on human development. One example of this is lower school enrollment and graduation rates owing to the destruction of school buildings, general insecurity, and participation of youths in military activities (Swee 2015). Fighting also results in massive destruction to the infrastructure, leading to reduced assets and economic opportunities for years to come (Sowers et al. 2017). Valerie Cerra and Sweta Chaman Saxena (2008), for instance, find that civil war onset results in a GDP decline of 6% in the

---

2. Climate change will lead to higher temperatures and more evaporation, which increase the risk of heat waves and droughts. Warmer air can also hold more water, thus making extreme rainfall events (and the associated floods) more likely. Sea level rise is also associated with higher flood risks in coastal areas (Funk 2021).

3. Poor people often lack the resources to prepare for or recover from extreme natural events like earthquakes or tropical storms.

Setting the Foundation

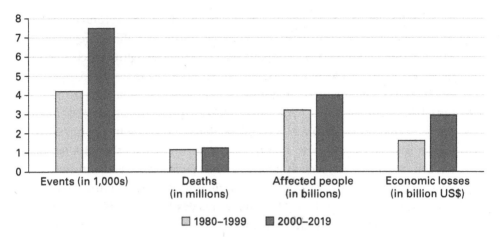

Figure 1.1
Comparison of disaster data for 1980–1999 and 2000–2019.
Source: CRED and UNDRR (2020).

first year. These effects can be even more severe at the individual level. After the Rwandan genocide in 1994, around 20% of the population became impoverished (Justino and Verwimp 2013). Hence, reducing the number of armed conflicts is not only at the core of sustainable development goal 15 (Peace, Justice and Strong Institutions) but also key to achieving other sustainable development goals.

In the light of these insights, it is even more worrisome that the number of active armed conflicts worldwide is at its highest level since World War II. During the Cold War era, this number fluctuated between 17 and 47. After a brief peak in 1991 (53 conflicts), the prevalence of armed conflict declined steadily until 2009 (31 conflicts). However, each single year since 2015 featured more than 50 armed conflicts, and 2019 (55) and 2020 (56) saw the most active armed conflicts since 1946. The large majority (> 95%) of these conflicts take place within countries, usually in the form of civil wars[4] (Pettersson et al. 2021). As a consequence, this book will deal primarily with intrastate armed conflicts, usually between a government and a rebel group (and their respective allies).[5]

---

4. International support for the conflict parties is far from uncommon, however.
5. This is well in line with wider climate-conflict (Scartozzi 2021; von Uexkull and Buhaug 2021) and disaster-conflict research (Brzoska 2018; T. Nelson 2010). Both bodies of work agree that disasters are far more likely to affect intrastate rather than international conflicts.

With the number of armed conflicts at a historically high level and disaster frequency and intensity on the rise, conflict- and disaster-affected regions will increasingly intersect. This is particularly so because fighting increases the vulnerability of a society to disasters as infrastructure is destroyed, poverty increases, and long-term investments in disaster risk reduction are off the table. In line with this, Katie Peters (2017: 10) concludes that "58% of deaths from disasters occurred in countries that are also among the top 30 most fragile states." Likewise, disasters can affect well-established risk factors for armed conflict, such as poor economic performance and anti-state grievances. Since 1989, 73% of the most disaster-affected countries have also suffered from more than 500 battle-related deaths (Ide 2020b).

Not surprisingly, then, decision makers, researchers, and the broader public are increasingly concerned about the intersections of disasters and armed conflicts, and particularly about the impact of disasters on armed conflict risks. More than 1,300 academic studies have assessed the impact of climate change and environmental stress on various forms of conflict, many of which focus on disasters (Sharifi et al. 2021). Some of those studies arrive at far-reaching conclusions, such as that "disasters significantly increase the risk of violent conflict" (Nel and Righarts 2008: 179).

This concern is echoed among policy makers. In a 2021 UN Security Council meeting, French foreign minister Jean-Yves Le Drian argued, "In recent years, droughts, floods, storms, tropical cyclones and extreme temperatures have directly caused nearly 2 million deaths, to say nothing of the human tragedies linked to the conflicts sometimes precipitated by these disasters" (UN Security Council 2021a). Already in 2015, then US president Barack Obama argued that "severe drought helped to create the instability in Nigeria that was exploited by the terrorist group Boko Haram. It's now believed that drought and crop failures and high food prices helped fuel the early unrest in Syria, which descended into civil war in the heart of the Middle East" (The White House 2015).

Other public figures, such as UN secretary general António Guterres, England's King Charles III, and US presidential candidate Bernie Sanders, as well as news media and comic strips, have also linked droughts, floods, and storms to armed conflict risks, including in Syria and Sudan (Selby and Hulme 2015). However, analysts and NGOs also consider disasters as "silver linings" (Renner and Chafe 2007: 16) that can induce enhanced solidarity and peaceful cooperation. When the government and the rebels in Aceh,

Setting the Foundation

Indonesia, signed a peace agreement a few months after the devastating 2004 tsunami, some observers termed the disaster a "wave of peace" (Gaillard, Clavé, and Kelman 2008: 511).

This book analyzes the impact of disasters on the dynamics of ongoing intrastate armed conflicts. Doing so is relevant for the burgeoning research on disasters, environmental security, climate change impacts, armed violence, civil wars, and peace. But it can also have important practical implications. Assume for a moment that we know the conditions under which disasters contribute to conflict escalation or de-escalation (the book certainly offers some insights on this issue). In the best case, this would mean politicians, international mediators, and development agencies would work to create the conditions that facilitate conflict de-escalation after disasters, hence saving lives and opening spaces for safe aid delivery and negotiations.

But even when relevant conditions for disaster-conflict linkages are structural and persistent, knowing them is important for designing post-disaster policy measures. If conflict de-escalation is expected, humanitarian aid workers can move into the affected areas to provide disaster- and conflict-related relief. Periods of reduced conflict intensity also provide opportunities to further economic development projects and to (re-)start informal peace talks between the conflict parties. By contrast, if we know that fighting is likely to intensify after a disaster, the evacuation of aid workers, the postponement of development projects, and international pressure on conflict parties to limit the use of violence are likely better options.

The Emergence of Disaster-Conflict Research

Disaster sociology has long been interested in the effects of disasters on conflict and cooperation, broadly conceived. Already during World War II, Pitrim A. Sorokin (1942: 159) wrote on the effects of disasters on individuals and societies:

> Some become brutalized, others intensely socialized. Some disintegrate—morally, mentally, and biologically; others are steeled into an unbreakable unity.... This diversification and polarization of effects upon the mentality and conducts of various units of the population, as well as upon sundry fields of culture, manifests itself in practically any calamity.

Follow-up studies considered the effects of disasters on community coherence and integration (Fritz and Williams 1957), studied local conflicts in post-disaster periods (Quarantelli and Dynes 1976), or analyzed how disasters exacerbate pre-existing cleavages (Cuny 1983). While providing valuable theoretical and conceptual knowledge, disaster sociology focuses mostly on the community level and conflicts with no or low levels of violence. Therefore, this body of research provides only limited insights on the intersections between disasters and organized armed conflicts.

With very few exceptions (e.g., Ember and Ember 1992; Rajagopalan 2006), peace and conflict studies have not dealt with disasters related to natural hazards (e.g., droughts, floods, storms, and earthquakes). During the Cold War, conflict researchers largely focused on the superpower rivalry, arms races, and struggles of independence. After the collapse of the Soviet Union, civil wars and post-conflict peace building emerged as major topics (Richmond 2011; Sambanis 2004), with terrorism being at the top of the agenda since 2001 (Hoffman 2006). Interest in environmental security also increased from the 1990s onward, but focused mostly on the scarcity of renewable resources and the use of high-value resources to finance conflicts (Barnett 2001). Disasters played only a minor role in all these debates, leading Philip Nel and Marjolein Righarts (2008: 178) to diagnose a "tendency by political scientists and other conflict specialists to underestimate the growing importance of geography and environmental factors. Given the growing importance of environmental factors as climate change kicks in and as natural ecologies are stretched to the limit, it becomes all the more important to correct this oversight."

Up until 2008, only three major cross-case studies on disasters[6] and intrastate armed conflict had been available. A. Cooper Drury and Richard Stuart Olson (1998) employed a statistical analysis and found that higher levels of disaster severity increase levels of political unrest in a given country. Dawn Brancati (2007) hypothesized that earthquakes make various forms of intrastate conflict more likely, as they cause resource scarcity as well as funding and recruitment opportunities for armed groups. These assumptions were confirmed by his large-N study.[7] Similarly, Nel and Righarts (2008) concluded that disasters facilitate conflict occurrence, as they cause grievances, competition for scarce resources, and state weakness that can be exploited

---

6. As opposed to environmental factors or climate changes more generally.
7. Large-N studies analyze a larger number (usually hundreds or thousands) of cases, usually based on statistical methods.

by rebel groups. All three studies also identified context factors that make a disaster-conflict nexus more likely, such as widespread poverty, persistent inequality, and anocratic regimes.[8]

However, from the late 2000s onward, academic interest in disasters and armed conflicts within countries increased tremendously. Several factors account for this development.

First, the security implications of climate change emerged as a prominent issue in political and scientific debates. In 2007, Al Gore and the Intergovernmental Panel on Climate Change (IPCC) received the Nobel Peace Prize, and the UN Security Council held its first-ever debate on climate change (McDonald 2021: 44–93). In the same year, the journal *Political Geography* published an influential special issue on climate change and conflict (Nordås and Gleditsch 2007). As discussed above, one of the most worrisome implications of climate change is an increase in the frequency and intensity of disasters like heat waves, droughts, floods, landslides, and tropical storms.

Second, several research streams converged toward an increasing consideration of disaster-conflict interlinkages. Conflict research strongly focused on civil wars and intrastate violence, which are more likely to be affected by environmental factors, including disasters. Studies on environmental security were analyzing how conflict risks are affected by the scarcity of natural resources, which can be facilitated by disasters. Disaster scholars became increasingly interested in how armed conflicts increase communities' vulnerability to disasters. And the literature on disaster diplomacy provided evidence that disaster-related actions may have at least a short-term impact on diplomatic relations between states (Kelman 2006).

Third, three real-world developments increased research interest in—and political demand for knowledge on—the topic. In 2007 and 2008, a massive rise in global food prices increased food insecurity, resulting in riots in more than 20 countries (mostly in the Global South). This triggered intense research on the impact of food prices and food availability on various forms of conflict, while disasters are considered a key driver of harvest failure and food insecurity (Martin-Shields and Stojetz 2019).

An earthquake in the Indian Ocean on December 26, 2004, triggered a massive tsunami, killing over 200,000 people in more than a dozen countries.

---

8. Anocracies are mixed political regimes that are neither full democracies nor full autocracies.

Two of the most heavily affected countries suffered from long-standing civil wars: Indonesia (in particular the province of Aceh) and Sri Lanka. A few months after the tsunami, a comprehensive (and ongoing) peace agreement was signed for Aceh, while the civil war in Sri Lanka escalated heavily. This posed the question of whether and how the tsunami impacted these strongly diverging conflict dynamics (see chapter 4 for further details on these cases). A year earlier, in 2003, a civil war between rebels and the government emerged in the Sudanese region of Darfur, which caught the attention of media worldwide. The onset of the war was preceded by an intense drought, leading analysts to speculate about a disaster-conflict link (De Juan 2015). Then UN secretary general Ban Ki-moon (2007) stated that "the Darfur conflict began as an ecological crisis, arising at least in part from climate change."

Hypothesized links between a major drought in 2007–2008 and the onset of the civil war in Syria in 2011 further fueled interest in disaster-conflict links from 2014 onward (Gleick 2014). Gina Yannitell Reinhardt and Carmela Lutmar (2022) argue that the COVID-19 pandemic has had a similar impact (see chapter 6).

State of Knowledge

Research basically agrees that disasters, while rooted in historical structures and everyday realities, are critical junctures "because during the emergency response phase of a disaster—but usually more significantly during recovery and reconstruction—decisions and choices among alternatives are often stark in their consequences" (Gawronski and Olson 2013: 134). Large-scale disasters accelerate developments, make ongoing trends visible, and often lead to calls for far-reaching actions. This increases the contingency of a situation, making a broader palette of more radical political decisions thinkable and ultimately possible (Birkmann et al. 2010).

But does such increasing room for political maneuver and contestation affect matters of peace and (armed) conflict? There are quite a few studies analyzing such interrelations from a long-term and historical perspective. Peter Neal Peregrine (2019) concludes, on the basis of archaeological data, that climate-related disasters made violent conflict more prevalent in 22 societies prior to written history. Likewise, ancient kingdoms on the Korean Peninsula were more likely to be invaded after large-scale disasters that reduced their defense capability (Jun and Sethi 2021). Disasters are also associated with the onset of civil wars in China between 1470 and 1911 (Lee 2018). While such research is useful in providing a broader historical perspective, the applicability of its insights to the modern, highly technologized and interconnected world might be doubted. Historical data are also not fine-grained enough to discern the specific dynamics of conflicts in the post-disaster period.

Since the mid-2000s, when academic and political interest in the topic increased, a number of studies have dealt with the impact of disasters on armed conflict onset or incidence. By contrast, reduced conflict risks in the wake of disasters have hardly been discussed.

Concerns about the impact of disasters on international wars were quickly refuted, but an intense debate about disasters and civil wars (or similar forms of organized intrastate violence) emerged. As discussed above, the early studies of Brancati (2007), Drury and Olson (1998), and Nel and Righarts (2008) all found a link between disasters triggered by natural hazards and the incidence of political violence within countries. In line with this, Peter Nardulli and colleagues (2015) argue that rapid-onset disasters with high death tolls increase the risk of political unrest. This effect, however, is rather weak, and conditional factors like the economic basis of a society play a major role in conditioning it. There is also evidence that hydro-meteorological and climate-related disasters facilitate armed conflict onset under conditions like low levels of human development or the exclusion of ethnic groups from political power (Ide et al. 2020).

By contrast, several well-executed studies argue that "climate-related natural disasters do not increase the risk of armed conflict" onset (Bergholt and Lujala 2012: 147) or that disasters are not linked to political instability in general (Omelicheva 2011). Rune Slettebak (2012) even argues that armed conflict risks decline after climate-related disasters owing to higher solidarity among the affected groups. Voices that are skeptical about the existence of a disaster-conflict link are a minority position at the moment.

The sample of relevant research increases when one includes studies on specific types of disasters, but the overall picture hardly changes. According to the group around Ramesh Ghimire and Susana Ferreira (Ghimire and Ferreira 2016; Ghimire et al. 2015), floods and flood-related migration increase the risk of armed conflict incidence, but not onset. The 2015 earthquake in Nepal is supposed to have reduced social conflict intensity in a post-conflict context, unless a region received large amounts of disaster-related aid

(De Juan et al. 2020). The literature on drought is extensive and cannot be fully summarized here.[9] Studies like those of Guy Abel and colleagues (2019) or Adrien Detges (2016) conclude that droughts make armed conflict onset more likely, but only during specific time periods or in certain regions (e.g., those characterized by limited road infrastructure). There is also evidence that rainfall deficits and the occurrence of political conflicts are linked through higher food prices (Raleigh et al. 2015). But again, some studies remain skeptical about such a nexus (Buhaug et al. 2015; O'Loughlin et al. 2014).

This divide is also visible in the case-based literature. For the civil wars in Darfur and Syria, some researchers claim that intense drought conditions triggered migration, which in turn increased grievances in the receiving regions and eventually led to violence (Faris 2007; Gleick 2014). Other scholars remain highly skeptical of such claims (Selby et al. 2017; Verhoeven 2011). Recent evidence suggests that the disasters played a minor, yet still discernible, role for the onset of civil war in both areas (Ash and Obradovitch 2020; De Juan 2015).

From this brief overview, I conclude that disaster has an impact on intrastate armed conflict onset and incidence, although such a link is minor and highly dependent on the presence of various context factors. This concurs with a prominent review of the climate-conflict literature stating that "climate variability, hazards and trends have affected organized armed conflict within countries," while "other conflict drivers are much more influential" (Mach et al. 2019: 194).

However, insights on the onset and incidence of conflicts do not necessarily apply to their dynamics. For sure, some of the factors driving conflict onset, like collective grievances and state weakness, can also account for an intensification of violence. But a mismatch remains. State weakness, for instance, increases the risks of armed conflict onset but can also be linked to a de-escalation of a conflict as armed forces retreat from a contested area or lack the capabilities to attack rebel groups. Likewise, studies on armed conflict incidence only focus on whether fighting is taking place (or not), while ignoring the intensity and dynamics of the conflict. The transferability of insights on conflict onset/incidence to the field of conflict dynamics is therefore severely limited (Chaudoin et al. 2017).

9. The reviews by Ide et al. (2016) and Sakaguchi et al. (2017) can be consulted for this purpose.

Setting the Foundation

The same applies to two other streams of study in the broader field of disaster and conflict research. First, several studies find that disasters increase the number of public protests, especially in non-democratic countries (Apodaca 2017; Ide, Rodriguez Lopez, et al. 2021). This is because disasters cause grievances and weaken state capacities. Disasters also facilitate mobilization because they catalyse the construction of a shared identity (as disaster victims) and cause an inflow of NGOs (which act as mobilizers). To counter such protests, governments frequently respond with repression, which is a cheap option for poor and/or disaster-strained states (Pfaff 2020; Wood and Wright 2016). Anti-regime protests and government repression might contribute to an escalation of armed conflicts—for example, those in Libya and Syria during the Arab Spring. But this is certainly not always the case (think about Bahrain and Iran in 2011, for instance), and such a disaster-protest-escalation nexus would need to be backed up by solid empirical evidence.[10] Second, several studies find that droughts increase individual motivations to participate in violent actions if no proper political institutions are in place (Detges 2017; Linke et al. 2018; Vestby 2019) and that disasters result in more hostility toward out-groups (Chung and Rhee 2022). But again, the link between such changed motivations and conflict escalation or de-escalation remains to be established.

There is very little research on the impact of disasters on conflict (de-)escalation as of yet, especially when compared with that on conflict onset and incidence. Some studies do not even distinguish between conflict causes and conflict dynamics (Koubi 2019). In general, environment security research is characterized by the "near complete lack of attention devoted to possible impacts of changing environmental conditions on the dynamics of conflicts" (Wischnath and Buhaug 2014: 12). The few existing studies on the impact of disasters on ongoing armed conflicts within countries use very different data and methods, are hardly comparable, provide limited insights on causal pathways, and arrive at starkly different conclusions.

An unusually dry, wet, or cyclone-intense year in the Philippines (Eastin 2018), agricultural production shocks in India (Gawande et al. 2017; Wischnath and Buhaug 2014), and large inflows of aid related to the 2004 tsunami in Sri Lanka (Kikuta 2019) are all associated with higher conflict

---

10. The studies cited above do not deal with the impacts of protests and repressions on the wider dynamics of armed conflicts.

intensity. In one of the most comprehensive studies so far, Nina von Uexkull and colleagues (2016: 12391) concluded for Africa and Asia: "For agriculturally dependent groups as well as politically excluded groups in very poor countries, a local drought is found to increase the likelihood of sustained violence." Scholars also link disasters to an increase in terrorist attacks, at least in contexts characterized by poverty, few political freedoms, and links to international extremist groups (Berrebi and Ostwald 2011; Paul and Bagchi 2016).

By contrast, other analysts argue that cease-fires (Kreutz 2012) and negotiations (Nemeth and Lai 2022) in civil wars are more likely in the aftermath of a disaster, hence pointing to an at least temporary de-escalation impact of disasters. Researchers also find that conflict intensity is usually higher in areas with high staple food production (Koren 2018) and above-average rainfall (Salehyan and Hendrix 2014). High food availability in the absence of droughts or other disasters makes conquering a region more attractive and provides armed groups with higher capabilities to engage in violence. The case study literature remains divided as well. Some scholars claim that the 2010 floods in Pakistan facilitated recruitment by Islamist groups, and hence their capacity to escalate the conflict with the government (Arai 2012). But Ayesha Siddiqi (2014) contends that this link has not been straightforward as there has been significant local variation in whether support for rebels, the government, or neither of them grew in the post-disaster period.

Contributions of This Study

This book advances existing research in at least eight major ways.

First, disaster-conflict research has emerged as a burgeoning field of study in the past two decades. Because more frequent and more intense disasters can result from climate change and tend to increase the scarcity of renewable resources, the disaster-conflict nexus is also key for wider debates on climate change and conflict and on environmental security. All three fields have so far focused predominantly on intrastate armed conflict onset or incidence, while knowledge on the impact of disasters on the dynamics of ongoing armed conflicts is limited. Such knowledge is of crucial importance given that disaster-affected areas and conflict zones are increasingly likely to intersect in the future.

Second, a recent survey of international peace and conflict studies finds that researchers are focusing mostly on war and armed violence (Bright and Gledhill 2018), while Paul F. Diehl (2016: 1) argues that international relations scholars "should pay greater attention to peace." In line with this, most work on environmental conflict and climate security analyzes whether disasters increase armed conflict risks. This book takes a broader approach by explicitly considering a third possibility: an increase of cooperation and/or a decrease in armed conflict risks after a disaster.

Third, disasters can be considered as external shocks to societies. For sure, disasters are never completely exogenous. Some societies have much better capabilities than others to mitigate the adverse effects of natural hazards—for instance, by enforcing earthquake-resilient building, establishing elaborated dikes to cope with floods, and setting up well-funded insurance and reconstruction programs. However, the magnitude of a drought, storm, or earthquake can make a big difference for two similarly vulnerable societies and is generally beyond human control. My study hence contains valuable insights on the conflict implications of other "external" shocks, such as pandemics, fluctuations in commodity prices, or global economic crises (see also chapter 7).

Fourth, research has so far largely been focused on the existence of a link between environmental stress / climate change / disasters and intrastate armed conflict. By contrast, the "mechanisms of climate–conflict linkages remain a key uncertainty" (Mach et al. 2019: 193). A systematic review of disaster-conflict research found that more than 80% of all studies ask whether disaster affects conflict risks, while less than 20% also analyze the causal pathways connecting disasters to conflicts (Xu et al. 2016). Likewise, previous studies indicated that a disaster-conflict link is dependent on the presence of scope conditions, including agriculture dependence, ethnic discrimination, poverty, and deficient political institutions. Existing small-N studies usually identify a large number of relevant intervening variables, hence making parsimonious theory building difficult, while quantitative approaches consider only a few context factors. Drawing on a variety of data sources and a method well suited to detect complex causal patterns, this book studies whether disasters facilitate the (de-)escalation of intrastate armed conflicts, as well as the pathways and contexts in which they do so.

Fifth, and relatedly, this book also bridges a persistent gap in the peace and conflict research and security studies (including climate security) literature. Frequently, (1) qualitative studies of few cases are considered in a nuanced and context-sensitive way, and (2) large-N statistical studies characterized by high degrees of reproducibility and generalizability exist apart from each other (Ide 2017; Jutila et al. 2008). The qualitative comparative analysis (QCA) employed in this study serves to build further bridges between quantitative and qualitative approaches by combining advantages from both worlds (see chapter 3 for details).

Sixth, the literature on armed conflicts commonly distinguishes between two pathways to the onset (and incidence) of fighting (Taydas et al. 2011): grievances (which motivate individuals and groups to take up arms) and opportunities (for starting violence, such as the availability of weapons, recruits, and hideouts). This book presents one of the first studies to test this framework for armed conflict dynamics. Furthermore, as I will argue in chapter 2, a third pathway has to be considered when explaining conflict escalation and de-escalation because armed groups frequently intensify or restrain from using violence to communicate a message to different audiences (e.g., their opponents, internal rivals, or international supporters).

Seventh, and more generally, the literature on intrastate armed conflict dynamics is just emerging in international relations and security studies (e.g., Chaudoin et al. 2017; Ruhe 2021). This book is one of the first studies on the role of environmental factors in shaping armed conflict intensity.

Eighth, and finally, disaster research has long acknowledged that "violent conflict interacts with natural hazards in a wide variety of ways" (Wisner et al. 2004: 27). There is widespread consensus that the presence of armed violence increases vulnerability and hence the likelihood that a hazard turns into a disaster (Siddiqi 2018; Wisner 2017). However, the intensity of armed conflicts is likely to matter as well. Conflict escalation can result in additional destruction of infrastructure, the politicization of aid, curfew and access restrictions, and the absence of humanitarian actors owing to security concerns. Conflict de-escalation, by contrast, offers a window of opportunity for rescue operations and the delivery of humanitarian aid. This book therefore makes an important contribution to research on disaster vulnerability and response.

Goal, Definitions, and Plan

This book aims to answer three questions: (1) Do disasters influence the intensity of armed conflicts between governments and rebels? (2) Are disasters more likely to facilitate an escalation or de-escalation of armed conflicts? (3) Which pathways and context factors can account for intrastate armed conflict (de-)escalation after a disaster has struck?

Before presenting the plan of this book, I will define some key terms.

In this study, I employ the UCDP definition of armed conflict as "a contested incompatibility that concerns government or territory or both where the use of armed force between two parties results in at least 25 battle-related deaths. Of these two parties, at least one is the government of a state" (Gleditsch et al. 2002: 618–619). The book will only deal with intrastate armed conflicts, of which the principal parties are (1) the government, which controls the state military and security forces and is often supported by non-state armed militias, and (2) a rebel or insurgent group, which uses systematic, armed violence and is often supported by other rebel groups and/or civil society organizations.[11] Unless otherwise noted, I use the terms "conflict," "armed conflict," and "intrastate armed conflict" interchangeably for the sake of simplicity. If an armed conflict within a country causes more than 1,000 battle-related deaths, it reaches the level of a civil war. Armed groups include both government and rebel forces.

In line with the UN General Assembly (2016: 13), I define a disaster as "a serious disruption of the functioning of a community or a society at any scale due to hazardous events interacting with conditions of exposure, vulnerability and capacity, leading to one or more of the following: human, material, economic and environmental losses and impacts." In other words, a disaster is the product of (1) a society being exposed to a hazard and (2) a society being vulnerable to the hazard. In this book, I focus on natural hazards such as earthquakes, floods, droughts, storms, heat waves, and cold spells. Although extreme natural conditions with considerable destructive potential (hazards) can hardly be mitigated at all, disaster prevention is possible by reducing vulnerability before a hazard occurs (Chmutina and von Meding 2019).

Vulnerability refers to the capacity of a society or group to anticipate, prepare for, cope with, resist, and recover from a hazard (Wisner et al. 2004: 11). Vulnerability is a result of continuous and "normal" conditions (often only made visible to broader audiences by the disaster). Early warning systems, building standards, the quality of emergency services, and bank savings all determine vulnerability—that is, how much damage a strong shaking of the ground does and how quickly and comprehensively

---

11. Both conflict parties may use violence against civilians as part of their struggle.

individuals, households, groups, or countries recover.[12] In addition to being more vulnerable, poor and marginalized groups also often have to settle in areas particularly exposed to disasters, such as flood plains or steep slopes.[13]

This book has a modular structure, which makes it suitable for a broad range of readers. This structure also ensures that certain chapters can be read without an in-depth knowledge of the previous content. That said, the three key questions about the existence and direction of, pathways underlying, and context factors relevant for a disaster–armed conflict intensity nexus form the backbone of this study. Consequently, they are addressed throughout the book.

This introductory first chapter provides essential discussions about key definitions, the development of disaster-conflict research, and the current state of the literature. It is therefore highly suitable for students and researchers aiming to familiarize themselves with the research field.

The second chapter develops the theoretical framework of this study. It distinguishes between two conflict dynamics—escalation and de-escalation—as well as three approaches to explaining these dynamics: motive, strategy, and communication. By combining them, six potential impacts of disasters on armed conflict dynamics can be discerned: conflicts escalate because disasters raise grievances among the relevant actors, because disasters provide opportunities for armed groups to stage attacks, or because armed groups seek to send costly signals after a disaster. Alternatively, conflicts may de-escalate because disasters increase local and national solidarity, because disasters provide restraints to armed groups' mobility and capability, or because armed actors seek to cultivate a positive image after the disaster. While building the theoretical framework for my study, chapter 2 also provides a comprehensive overview about wider debates on climate change, environmental stress, disasters, peace, and conflict.

Chapter 3 introduces the sample of cases analyzed in this study, the main method of analysis, and the relevant conditions (or variables). In short, I conduct a qualitative comparative analysis (QCA) of 36 cases of major disasters striking a country with an ongoing armed conflict. All cases

12. Obviously, the timing and strength of an earthquake also determine how much damage is done. Stronger earthquakes that occur when people are inside and/or asleep usually result in a greater loss of lives.
13. Emergency services and shelter may also be less present in these areas.

occurred in the period between 1990 and 2020. QCA is well able to disentangle complex causal relationships, identify relevant context factors, and combine quantitative and qualitative data.

Chapter 4 contains the 36 qualitative case studies on disaster-conflict intersections that form the empirical core of the book. It discusses the conflict background and dynamics, the disaster and its impacts, and the existence and nature of a disaster-conflict intensity link. Evidence comes from 21 countries: Afghanistan, Algeria, Bangladesh, Burundi, Colombia, Egypt, India, Indonesia, Iran, Myanmar, Nepal, Pakistan, Peru, the Philippines, Russia, Somalia, Sri Lanka, Tajikistan, Thailand, Turkey, and Uganda (see figure 3.1 in chapter 3). This chapter also contains relevant insights for specialists working on particular regions, countries, disasters, or rebel groups. As the case studies provide brief overviews about each conflict and disaster as well as a wealth of further references, they are also suitable as illustrative examples (or introductory readings) for students and early career researchers.

Chapter 5 synthesizes evidence from the case studies, quantitative data, and the QCA to answer the key questions of the book: Do disasters have an impact on armed conflict dynamics, and if so, how and in which contexts? I find that disasters have an impact on armed conflict dynamics in 50% of all cases, which are evenly split between escalation (25%) and de-escalation (25%) cases. Two context factors are key for disasters shaping conflict dynamics: a high vulnerability to disasters and a strong disaster impact on at least one conflict party. Armed conflicts escalate either when the rebel group gains power vis-à-vis the government during the disaster or when the rebel group intensifies its activities in reaction to the grievances of the disaster-affected population, while a strong government fights back. Disasters facilitate armed conflict de-escalation by weakening at least one conflict party while the other is unable to capitalize on this weakness.

Taken together, this indicates that while disaster impacts on armed conflicts are rather prevalent, they occur only under specific conditions and might well manifest as conflict de-escalation. Overall, changes in the strategic environment (rather than participants' motivations or communication logics) explain most disaster-conflict linkages, while limiting the use of violence to cultivate a group's image is common after large-scale, rapid-onset disasters. People with a working knowledge of environmental security, disaster impacts, and armed conflicts will be able to read chapter 5 as a stand-alone contribution to existing research (even though I recommend a brief look at the summary section of chapter 2 beforehand).

Chapter 6 focuses on a very recent disaster, the COVID-19 pandemic, and its impact on armed conflict dynamics. After reviewing the existing literature on COVID-19 and conflict, I analyze how the pandemic affected the dynamics of four civil wars during the time period March 2020 to September 2021: the Taliban conflict in Afghanistan, the actions of the Islamic State in Iraq, the Boko Haram insurgency in Nigeria, and the Communist rebellion in the Philippines. The analysis shows that, depending on the political-economic contexts and leadership decisions, rebel groups can scale up violence when the government is preoccupied with the pandemic response, restrain from violence and provide a pandemic response themselves to increase their legitimacy, or be heavily affected by the financial and logistical impacts of COVID-19 and hence unable to wage more violence. This chapter is of interest to anyone working on the societal implications of the COVID-19 pandemic. Readers with a basic knowledge of peace and conflict should be able to easily understand chapter 6 (if you don't have such knowledge, I recommend having a look at chapters 1 and 2).

The seventh chapter concludes the book. It summarizes key insights and demonstrates how they speak to current debates in international relations, peace and conflict studies, environmental social sciences, security studies, climate change research, and political geography. I also reflect on avenues for further research and implications for policy makers.

Disasters triggered by natural hazards and armed conflicts are two of the most important challenges of our time, and their intersections are likely to increase in the years to come. By offering a comprehensive study on how disasters affect armed conflict dynamics, this book offers crucial insights for understanding and addressing these challenges.

2 After the Disaster: Motives, Strategies, and Incentives for Conflict (De-)escalation

This chapter builds the theoretical framework for this book, thereby providing a comprehensive overview of the potential interlinkages between disasters and armed conflict dynamics.[1] As outlined in chapter 1, armed conflict refers to a contested incompatibility between a government and a rebel (or insurgent) group (and their respective allies) involving the systematic use of armed, physical violence. This definition covers violence against civilians as part of an armed confrontation. Most armed conflicts I consider are civil wars.

The framework established here is based on two dimensions (see table 2.1 later in the chapter). First, if disasters influence the dynamics of armed conflict, they might contribute to either its escalation or its de-escalation. An armed conflict escalates if the intensity of the fighting increases, resulting in a higher number of battle-related deaths. Conversely, armed conflicts de-escalate if fewer battle-related deaths occur, hence indicating a lower frequency and/or intensity of battles. The horizontal dimension of the framework refers to the possibilities of armed conflict escalation and de-escalation.

A third possibility is that disasters have no impact on the dynamics of armed conflicts. Mariya Y. Omelicheva's (2011) statistical analysis, for instance, finds no robust link between disaster occurrence and political instability. One reason for this might be that the disaster is not severe enough or occurs far away from locations relevant to the armed conflict (Ide et al. 2020). Another option is that disasters do not affect armed conflict dynamics because other drivers are more important. A recent review of the literature on climate change (including climate-related disasters)

---

1. If arguments from the literature on armed conflict onset are applicable to conflict (de-)escalation, I include them as well.

and conflict concludes that factors "such as low socioeconomic development and low capabilities of the state . . . are judged to be substantially more influential" (Mach et al. 2019: 193). Armed groups usually fight over political power or territorial control rather than disaster impacts. If disasters do not affect the groups' fighting capabilities or revenue streams, they are unlikely to have an impact on their strategic decisions (Blattman and Miguel 2010; Cederman and Vogt 2017). Finally, the different escalation and de-escalation dynamics that disasters can trigger (see below) might equal out. This would imply that disasters do affect armed conflicts, but the net effect in terms of battle-related deaths still converges around zero.

In this study, I primarily seek to explain the dynamics of armed conflict escalation and de-escalation after disasters (which are also more policy relevant; see chapter 1). However, non-escalation occurs rather frequently, and the respective cases are important in the analysis to separate relevant from irrelevant factors.

The second (vertical) dimension of the framework refers to the drivers of armed conflict dynamics. Three approaches can be distinguished here. The first one focuses on the *motive* of actors, typically of combatants, leaders, and supporters of armed groups. Already half a century ago, Ted Robert Gurr (1970) proposed that relative deprivation—people perceiving that they are less well off than they should be, especially vis-à-vis other social groups—is an important source of political conflict. Subsequently, researchers have argued that socio-economic inequalities, political marginalization, and (instrumentally) revived "ancient hatreds" (Kaufman 2001: 3) are important drivers of armed conflict. Confirming these assumptions, more recent cross-case studies find that ethnic polarization (Esteban et al. 2012), low income levels (Chaudoin et al. 2017), and the absence of democratic freedoms (Lacina 2006) tend to increase armed conflict intensity. Ethnic integration, secure livelihoods, and high levels of democracy and human rights protection, by contrast, should reduce conflict risks.

In the early 2000s, Paul Collier and Anke Hoeffler (2004) argued that previous approaches are overly focused on grievances and therefore unable to explain how collective action problems can be overcome. In other words, why should individuals risk participating in armed conflicts to achieve more inclusive political and economic systems if they receive the same public goods when their ethnic or class comrades win the struggle without their support? Instead, Collier and Hoeffler propose that individual greed is driving people to participate in armed conflicts—for example, to gain profits from natural resource incomes captured during a war. There is indeed evidence for high resource rents increasing conflict intensity (Ross 2004). However, greed and grievances are often deeply intertwined (Ballentine and Sherman 2003; LeBillon 2001), and disasters have at best a modest and short-term influence on greed-related factors, such as when they complicate natural resource extraction and trading (Ramsay 2011; Tominaga and Lee 2021).

More important for this framework is that all the approaches discussed essentially agree that human motivations and motives are central to the dynamics of armed conflict. The more aggrieved individuals are, and the more they seek to improve their personal or group's situation, the more likely they are to join an armed group (either the rebels or the government). Further, the larger these groups grow, the more intense the respective violent conflict will be. Similarly, if we conceive armed groups as agents of a certain social group (their constituency or principal), more intense grievances and demands among the members of this group will increase the willingness of the agent to engage in violence (Wucherpfennig et al. 2012). Conversely, if individuals are less aggrieved about their situation and less hostile toward others, armed conflict intensity should decline. In line with these arguments, several studies find that wealth differentials (Buhaug et al. 2014), the political exclusion of ethnic groups (Cederman et al. 2010), and perceptions of unfair disadvantages (Siroky et al. 2020) increase violent conflict risks.

The second approach to explaining armed conflict dynamics is focused on *strategy*, or rather the strategic environment armed groups face. Gurr (1970) already acknowledged the role of governments' repressive or accommodating capacity as well as the challengers' organizational capability. In an influential article, James D. Fearon and David D. Laitin (2003: 75) argue that "not ethnic or religious differences or broadly held grievances but, rather, conditions that favor insurgency" are most powerful in explaining variation in civil war occurrence and intensity. Grievances, as well as greed motives, are far too common to have significant explanatory power. By contrast, the opportunity structures that allow social groups to act on these motives are far more important in shaping civil war risks.

Several empirical studies confirm the plausibility of this approach. Fearon and Laitin (2003) find that, among other factors, state weakness and mountainous terrain increase the prevalence of civil war. Weak states are less capable of suppressing rebel groups, while mountains or other forms of inaccessible terrain provide hideouts and hence increase the capability of insurgents to wage war. In the short term, certain weather conditions such as low visibility (e.g., due to fog or sandstorms) provide opportunities for surprise attacks, thus increasing conflict intensity (Carter and Veale 2013). Similarly, external financial support and revenues from high-value natural resources boost the fighting capacity of armed groups, while high levels of dependence on civilians for financing provide a constraint on violence (Salehyan et al. 2014). According to Samuel Bazzi and Christopher Blattman (2014), rising prices of export goods, among other factors, make civil wars less deadly because the fighting capacity of the state vis-à-vis the rebels is improved.

I label the third approach used in my analysis *communication* (or *violence as communication*). It emerges from several concerns. Armed conflict research, including work on disasters and conflict, is overwhelmingly concerned with armed conflict onset (Chaudoin et al. 2017). From a practical perspective, such a focus is of limited relevance. Although it might help prevent armed conflict onset, it provides little guidance in regard to curbing violence during armed conflicts and building peace afterward (Beardsley et al. 2019; Woodward 2007). More important for this study is the consideration that "determinants of conflict severity seem to be quite different from those for conflict onset" (Lacina 2006: 276; see also chapter 1). This connects to Stathis N. Kalyvas's (2006) prominent argument that a range of factors at various scales account for the dynamics of violence in civil wars, several of which are quite different from the macro-cleavages underlying the civil war and the drivers of the war's onset.

Relatedly, strategy-based approaches conceive armed groups (including government forces and rebels) as reacting in a more or less rational way—depending on the information they have and can process—to their material environment. The latter includes the strength of the opponent, the availability of financing opportunities, and the ability to recruit fighters, among others. But the use and non-use of violence in civil wars can also have an important signaling function—that is, conflict escalation or de-escalation is supposed to convey a message and represents "a mode of information exchange" (Raleigh 2012: 463). This use of violence is also strategic in nature. It is not a direct response to a material environment but indicates the need and/or will to send a message. In the words of Benjamin Lessing (2015: 1504–1505), "Another elemental function of violence is as a signal. In this view, acts of violence—quite apart from their physical, 'battlefield' effects—convey important information about the perpetrator's operational capacity, resolve, internal cohesion, and so on."

This signal or message can be directed toward various audiences. Violence might be a "costly signal" (Kydd and Walter 2006: 50) to the government that rebel groups are still present and ready to fight, which is particularly important if the government declared the respective conflict over or if the government (or some external actor) excluded the specific group from negotiations. Similarly, armed groups can use violence to demonstrate their control of, or at least presence in, an area, hence indicating that disobedience and cooperation with the government will be costly, including for civilians (Boyle 2009; Kalyvas 2004). At the same time, actors might restrain their use of violence against certain actors (e.g., civilians) or during certain periods (e.g., cease-fires) to convey a positive image of themselves, particularly if they are dependent on the support of civilians, democratic states, or the international community (Fortna et al. 2018).

Furthermore, civil wars are rarely dyadic, but often characterized by the competition of multiple groups, on both the government side (e.g., the state military, pro-government militias) and the rebel side (e.g., several rebel factions) (Jentzsch et al. 2015). These groups frequently use violence to demonstrate to their constituency or (civilian) support group that they are capable and determined to fight for their cause, while moderate groups are weak and irrelevant (Boyle 2009; Valentino 2014). This can increase group coherence, which "generates attention and recruits in a competitive environment and hence may convince others to transfer loyalty" (Raleigh 2012: 472). According to Kalyvas (2004), the targeting of civilians (rather than armed forces or military infrastructure) is typical for violence-as-communication because it is "cheap"—that is, associated with few losses and risks.

The logic of communication can complement and even override motives and strategic concerns in conflict situations. For example, even if the government has made concessions, rebel groups might escalate violence to show their continued presence on the ground and to signal to their constituencies that they will not accept compromises. Likewise, even if the strategic environment is conducive to a military offensive, rebels can exercise constraints to improve their reputation among key supporters (e.g., civilians or other states). So far, the communication approach has received very limited attention in research on disasters and armed conflict. Reasons for this include a focus on conflict onset or prevalence rather than intensity

(Hultman and Peksen 2017; Lacina 2006) as well as a largely "positivist–rationalist" orientation of the field (Ide 2016: 69).

In reality, these three approaches are not necessarily mutually exclusive but often overlap with and even reinforce each other. Reduced grievances can provide fewer strategic opportunities for the recruitment of new fighters, while a group with newly gained revenues and recruits can escalate violence to both capitalize on this opportunity and signal its new strength to civilians, opponents, and international actors. Sometimes, studies even draw on the same data to measure different concepts. Low per capita income, for example, has been used as a proxy for the existence of both economic grievances and weak statehood. Alternatively, two or more approaches can be present at the same time and cancel out each other's impacts. A heavy counterinsurgency campaign by the government, for instance, can increase motivations for rebel attacks (owing to the associated human rights violations) and simultaneously undermine the capability for such attacks (as more rebel fighters are killed and captured).

Yet, it is still important to distinguish analytically between these three approaches or logics of violence in armed conflicts for at least two reasons. First, from a practical point of view, it is highly important to know the drivers behind violent conflict (de-)escalation in order to address the associated risks. While conflict de-escalation often falls short of solving the conflict, it saves lives and provides opportunities for mediation and the delivery of humanitarian assistance (Beardsley et al. 2019). In terms of policy, measures to address grievances (e.g., land reform) differ considerably from those tackling strategic environments (e.g., arms embargoes) or violence-as-communication (e.g., providing selective support to moderate groups).

Second, research has highlighted that both climate security and disaster-conflict research lack a decent understanding of the causal mechanisms connecting both phenomena (Buhaug 2015; Reinhardt and Lutmar 2022). However, "we do not have an adequate explanation of the phenomenon under study until we can say why the model works" (McKeown 1999: 172). Put differently, in order to make sure that a correlation or sequence of events is not just coincidental or driven by some unobserved factors but represents a causal relationship, we need to trace the pathways connecting an event (here: a disaster) to its supposed consequences (here: conflict escalation or de-escalation). Approaches that specify different, theoretically plausible causal links support this endeavor.

Table 2.1
Theoretical framework of this study

	Escalation	De-escalation
Motive	Grievances	Solidarity
Strategy	Opportunity	Constraints
Communication	Costly signal	Image cultivation

Table 2.1 combines the two relevant dynamics of armed conflicts after disasters (escalation and de-escalation) with the three approaches to explaining violence in ongoing conflicts (motive, strategy, and communication). The resulting matrix specifies six possible impacts of disasters on conflict dynamics that structure my empirical analysis: grievances, solidarity, opportunity, constraints, costly signal, and image cultivation. The remainder of this chapter discusses these six impacts in greater detail.

Grievances

Disasters can lead to intense grievances among segments of the affected population. Events like earthquakes, storms, and floods often have significant material losses, such as houses, animals, savings, or productive assets. Losses might also be emotional—for example, friends or family members who die or are injured during the disaster. People who believe that state authorities have not done enough to protect them from or support them after a disaster can quickly grow frustrated (Drury and Olson 1998) and lose trust in the relevant authorities (Kang and Skidmore 2018). In the same vein, grievances can also result from a shortage of valuable resources after a disaster, such as food, water, or land (Brancati 2007). High food prices in particular may result from disaster-induced destruction of storage facilities, supply lines, and agricultural assets and are closely linked to political dissatisfaction (Hendrix and Haggard 2015) and armed conflict risks (Koren and Bagozzi 2016).

This is particularly the case when disasters are a product of pre-existing inequalities and power structures and hence lay bare socio-economic fault lines (Albala-Bertrand 1993). Grievances will be particularly intense if certain groups are privileged during disaster preparation, emergency relief, or reconstruction. One should note here that while disasters often reveal and even contribute to existing inequalities, grievances can occur even if this is not the case. It is sufficient for people to perceive that disasters cause or deepen inequalities. According to Ramesh Ghimire and Susana Ferreira (2016: 26), "Individuals commonly blame the government for natural disasters regardless of its responsibility and response, leading to hostility towards the government." If rebel groups control parts of the disaster-affected territory and fail to provide adequate or unbiased support, they will face resentment by the population as well. Perceptions of the distribution of various forms of support—such as rescue operations, food ratios, or financial compensation—after the disaster are particularly contentious owing to their high visibility (De Juan et al. 2020; Rahill et al. 2014).

Government reactions to disasters that do not include the fair distribution of relief and reconstruction aid might also increase grievances. The evacuation of local people from supposedly disaster-prone areas, which are then used for business development or military purposes, has received intense criticism (Klein 2007; Siddiqi and Canuday 2018). Also, in anticipating discontent and protests, especially authoritarian governments tend to increase repression in the aftermath of disasters, such as by arresting activists, blocking NGO access, and breaking up demonstrations (Pfaff 2020; Wood and Wright 2016). Similar measures, which are not very popular in times of grief and need, can be pursued by rebel groups if they control a certain territory or seek to do so (Arjona 2014). Eunbin Chung and Inbok Rhee (2022) even detect a general increase in hostility toward out-groups after disasters.

Furthermore, disasters might increase grievances via migration. In general, migration is an important coping strategy to deal with environmental extremes, including disasters (Black et al. 2011). Getting out of harm's way during, for instance, an earthquake or a storm and returning to an area after it is safe is a rather common short-term pattern with little impact on grievances. But one or several household members might migrate for longer time periods to more prosperous and/or urban areas to earn additional income that helps with post-disaster reconstruction and building resilience to future events. In extreme cases, permanent migration of larger groups of people can occur if livelihoods in a region become unsustainable because of disaster losses (Berlemann and Steinhardt 2017).

Such migration is typically intrastate and of short distances because networks and funds for international migration are lacking (Groth et al. 2020). Yet it can still cause grievances if migrants shift ethnic balances in the receiving region (hence fueling inter-ethnic rivalries), cause competition for scarce resource, or do not receive sufficient government support (Brzoska and Fröhlich 2015; Ghimire et al. 2015). Recurrent storms, floods, and droughts in Bangladesh, for example, amplified migration flows to slums in Dhaka and the Chittagong Hill Tracts in India, thereby increasing resource competition in the former and ethnic tensions in the latter (Reuveny 2007; Saha 2012). Vally Koubi and colleagues (2018; 2021) also find that people migrating after experiencing several extreme weather events are more likely to have severe grievances and to join political movements.[2]

Disaster-related grievances can drive the escalation of armed conflicts in various ways. Aggrieved parts of the population can push the rebel groups fighting for their cause to increase their efforts or even join the rebels themselves. Conversely, if non-state armed groups control a territory but are unable to provide adequate disaster-related "rebel governance" (Walch 2018a: S248), people might turn their support to the government or pro-government militias. Either way, an increase of local support increases the fighting and intelligence capabilities of an armed group, thereby driving conflict escalation. Supporting this approach, Jonas Vestby (2019) finds that droughts have a negative impact on the perceived living conditions, which in turn increases the willingness of individuals to participate in violence. Further, according to Adrien Detges (2017), severe droughts raise the endorsement of political violence among politically dissatisfied parts of the population.

Solidarity

The occurrence of a disaster can also lead to increased solidarity and cooperation, hence facilitating conflict de-escalation. In their review of several case studies, disaster sociologists Charles E. Fritz and Harry B. Williams (Fritz and Williams 1957: 48) concluded the following:

> The net result of most disasters is a dramatic increase in social solidarity among the affected populace during the emergency and immediate postemergency periods. The sharing of a common threat to survival and the common suffering produced by the disaster tend to produce a breakdown of pre-existing social distinctions and a great outpouring of love, generosity, and altruism.

2. However, when studying internal migration in Bangladesh, Kristina Petrova (2021) finds that severe floods increase the likelihood of migration but that such migration does not lead to more protests in the receiving areas.

According to Fritz and Williams, this reaction is a form of psychological coping with disasters at the individual level and functionalistic for community recuperation. Follow-up studies also find that community conflict is notably absent in the first few months after a disaster. This is because the disaster represents a common threat, facilitates identity building through the notion of shared affectedness, and sets clear priorities, goals, and incentives for working together (Quarantelli and Dynes 1976). As a result, social trust and cohesion rise, although this effect is often limited to the immediate post-disaster period (Calo-Blanco et al. 2017; Toya and Skidmore 2014). Once conditions return to normal and/or questions related to the distribution of reconstruction funds emerge, pre-existing conflicts and divisions may return.[3] In line with this, violence against civilians by armed groups also tends to decline in the first few months (and even years) after a disaster (Haer and RezaeeDaryakenari 2022).

The literature on disaster diplomacy builds on these insights while connecting them more thoroughly with questions of high-intensity conflict and peace (Kelman 2012; Streich and Mislan 2014). It hypothesizes that disasters provide opportunities for diplomacy in the forms of negotiation and disaster-related cooperation between hostile parties. Potential reasons for this include increased solidarity between leaders or populations, emerging perceptions of shared external threats, and cooperation between conflicting groups in disaster preparation, emergency relief, or reconstruction. Summing up two decades of research, Ilan Kelman (2018: 175) concludes, "Disaster-related activities do not create new initiatives in achieving peace or reducing conflict, but a diplomatic process with pre-existing conditions can be catalysed or supported," at least in the short to medium term (6–12 months after the disaster).[4] The literature on environmental peace building is slightly more optimistic that shared environmental challenges can contribute to building trust and understanding between parties with tense relations (Ide 2019; Johnson et al. 2020).

Such an increase in solidarity, cooperation, understanding, and diplomacy might reduce the grievances that fuel an armed conflict. Increased

---

3. But note that other studies find a positive effect of disasters on trust one and a half years and more after the onset of the event, contingent on high levels of social capital in the pre-disaster period (Dussaillant and Guzmán 2014).

4. Pre-existing conditions refers to factors like the current absence of high-profile political conflicts, the existence of informal networks, and the willingness of leaders to use the disaster for diplomacy, among others.

community coherence can address local tensions, at least temporarily. This leads to a de-escalation as the settling of pre-existing scores at the community level is an important driver of violence in civil wars (Kalyvas 2006). Solidarity with affected populations in the territories of rival groups and the desire to allow relief provision could also result in fewer armed activities in the aftermath of a disaster. Rune Slettebak (2012) indeed finds that climate-related disasters decrease armed conflict risks, although his study focuses on conflict onset (rather than intensity) and does not test any causal mechanisms. According to Alexander De Juan and colleagues (2020), regions in Nepal that were hit harder than others by the 2015 earthquake experienced a reduction in social conflict. Providing more explicit support for a disaster diplomacy perspective, cross-case research by Joakim Kreutz (2012) indicates that disasters facilitate peace talks and cease-fires.

Finally, disasters provide opportunities for governing actors to demonstrate their skills and responsiveness (Toya and Skidmore 2014). This is the case if disaster prevention and warning efforts are credible, if sufficient resources are mobilized and used fairly and efficiently, and if leaders show compassion toward the affected populations (Olson and Gawronski 2010). If the reputation of the government becomes more favorable, rebels might face less pressure by their constituencies to engage in attacks (and might have a harder time recruiting combatants for such attacks), hence resulting in a de-escalation of violence. But rebel groups can also use disaster response to win the hearts and minds of the local population, thus establishing firm control over a territory. Once a rebel group establishes such control, the intensity of violence usually declines because local scores are settled, government-rebel interactions decline, and there is less need to clear the front lines (e.g., by killing civilians perceived to support the other side) (Balcells 2010).

Opportunity

According to Philip Nel and Marjolein Righarts (2008: 164), disasters provide opportunities for groups to accumulate "collective action resources" that enable them to intensify an armed conflict. This might happen in several ways. First, disasters lower the opportunity costs for participating in armed conflict. Individuals joining such an endeavor face a high risk of capture, injury, and death and therefore tend to seek opportunities in other economic sectors. However, disasters can cause enormous economic disruptions, such as when an agricultural area faces a drought or when production and service businesses are destroyed by storms, floods, or earthquakes. The resulting loss of livelihoods can make it easier for both government militias (Eastin and Zech 2022) and rebel groups to recruit followers as deprived individuals have few legal choices to generate income (Barnett and Adger 2007). Successful disaster governance, particularly by rebel groups, can also increase an actor's prestige and further facilitate the recruitment of followers (Arai 2012).

Enhanced recruitment is often associated with an escalation of armed conflicts. For one, the capabilities of the recruiting armed group to gather intelligence and stage an attack improve. Also, competing groups might well recognize the boost in strength of a competitor, increasingly perceive the respective actor as a threat, and attack it before it can fully capitalize on its newly gained numerical advantage. Political conflict studies have long identified shifts in the balance of power between rival parties and the associated dynamics of over-demanding by the weaker party and preventive aggression by the stronger one as a source of violent conflict (Organski and Kugler 1980). A rebel group reaching a certain level of strength can also choose to abandon guerrilla strategies in favor of open warfare, which causes more casualties (Butler and Gates 2009).

Recruitment is not the only way that disasters can (potentially) shift balances of power in a conflict region. In the aftermath of an extreme event, large amounts of relief and reconstruction support often flow toward the affected region. After the 2010 floods in Pakistan, the 2004 Indian Ocean tsunami, and the 2010 earthquake in Haiti, the United Nations Office for the Coordination of Humanitarian Affairs (UN OCHA 2019) channeled almost US$4 billion of humanitarian aid to the disaster-stroked areas. Acquiring such funds through negotiation or appropriation will boost the strength of an armed group because it can pay more recruits, hire specialists, or purchase additional weapons and equipment.

Consequently, government and insurgent troops will seek to gain control of the disaster-affected territories, usually by force, hence driving conflict escalation. Similarly, rebels might attack these areas in order to sabotage aid projects that are intended to strengthen the social contract between the government and the population (Zürcher 2016). Recent studies find that "areas where aid is being distributed are targeted more heavily [by terrorist groups] than areas without aid distribution" (Nemeth and Mauslein 2020:

382). According to Kyosuke Kikuta (2019), districts with higher reconstruction rates after the 2004 tsunami in Sri Lanka experienced higher levels of violence as armed groups competed for their control. Groups like al-Shabaab in Somalia have also taxed and stolen drought-related food aid for military purposes (Levy and Yusuf 2021).

One of the most frequently discussed causal pathways between disasters and armed conflict is the emergence of a power vacuum or of state weakness (Brzoska 2018; Hollis 2018; Meierding 2013). Disaster can limit the access of state forces to certain areas (e.g., because roads are washed away), thus providing the rebels with an opportunity for military expansion and territorial or organizational consolidation. In such a power vacuum, states might be unable to protect civilians and punish opponents. This reduces the opportunity costs for joining a rebel group (Berrebi and Ostwald 2011). In situations of persistent insecurity, civilians also often turn to non-state armed groups for the provision of public goods like protection from violence or disaster relief (Kalyvas and Kocher 2007).

State weakness is also relevant outside the affected area. Economic growth might decline in the face of intense or recurrent disasters that affect agricultural yields, infrastructure, and productive assets, thereby decreasing the tax base of the state. This, in turn, reduces its military strength and capability to support its population and/or politically relevant elites. Similarly, governments might draw troops and funds to the disaster-affected regions, making other parts of the state territory more vulnerable to rebel recruitment and attacks. In line with this, Peter F. Nardulli and colleagues (2015) find that the positive impact of rapid-onset disasters on civil unrest is even stronger outside the area where the disaster strikes.[5]

However, disasters can also weaken rebel groups, hence providing strategic opportunities for the government to escalate the conflict in order to to achieve gains on the battlefield. Rebel infrastructure and bases might be hit hard, vegetation can be destroyed and no longer serve as a hideout, combatants are perhaps injured or may have been killed in the disaster, and civilian populations could face hardships that make them unable to provide support (such as food, taxes, or information) to the insurgents. Furthermore, assistance provided by the government (most likely amplified by international

---

5. This finding could also provide support for the disaster-migration-grievances pathway discussed above.

actors) likely reduces territorial control of the rebel group, leading to blurred front lines that increases violence in civil wars (Balcells 2010). If the disaster affects rebel strongholds and the government provides relief, improved intelligence gathering by state agencies can further weaken the rebels and pave the way for a military offensive by the government (Eastin 2018).

Constraints

Many of the possible impacts of disasters discussed in the "Opportunity" section might also provide constraints for armed groups, thus facilitating conflict de-escalation. Most obviously, disasters affect transportation infrastructure—for example, by destroying bridges, flooding roads, or rendering secret forest paths impassable due to storm damage. These impacts reduce the troops' mobility and their capability to engage in fighting activities. If agriculture is heavily affected by the disaster, the military, militias, and rebel groups are likely to face food shortages, which reduces their ability to engage in violence, at least over large areas and extended time periods (Bagozzi et al. 2017). Idean Salehyan and Cullen Hendrix (2014) draw on these arguments to explain their finding that drought-induced water scarcity reduces incidences of political violence. In particular, part-time combatants fighting for insurgents or militias at certain times (but who engage in "normal" economic activities at other times) might be too busy with securing their livelihoods and reconstruction work to participate in armed conflict in the post-disaster period (Venugopal and Yasir 2017).

Disasters can also facilitate conflict de-escalation by reducing the capabilities of the warring parties to use violence. This is the case when, for example, military bases, personnel, and equipment are adversely affected by the disaster. The economic damage caused by disasters also reduces the tax base of both the government and rebel groups (particularly if the latter have limited access to outside support or valuable resources), which inhibits their ability to purchase equipment and pay combatants. Governments might also have to re-direct financial and military resources (e.g., troops or machinery) for post-disaster rescue, relief, and reconstruction activities (Kreutz 2012). Further, rebel groups face recruitment constraints that go beyond the (temporary) loss of supply lines and financial assets because "significant state government assistance in collaboration with the international humanitarian actors in rebel areas is likely to lead to a loss of territorial control for the rebel group, making its recruitment activities more complicated and risky" (Walch 2018b: 337). Alternatively, a government or rebel group unable to manage a disaster adequately can suffer from a loss of popular support among the population, reducing its financial and recruitment base.

Going beyond the short-term capabilities of the conflict parties to wage violence, disasters may also affect the more long-term strategic considerations of the conflict parties. Ripeness theory suggests that parties of an armed conflict generally prefer to pursue their goals by unilateral means, usually through the use of violence. However, at some point in time, the parties might conclude that victory is no longer possible and that to continue the conflict would impose considerable costs on them. Such a "mutually hurting stalemate" defines the moment when a conflict is ripe for resolution as the opponents start perceiving peace to be more beneficial than war (Zartman 2000: 228). By weakening the government and the rebel group in both financial and military terms, disasters can contribute to the emergence of ripe moments for conflict resolution, with conflict intensity declining during the exploratory talks and negotiation period.

Kreutz (2012) draws explicitly on ripeness theory in his study on disasters and separatist conflict resolution. He finds that short-term peace talks and cease-fires, but not the conclusion of peace agreements, are more likely after disasters. While an increase in cease-fires fits well with the reduced capabilities explanation discussed above, support for ripeness theory is more limited given the lack of significant findings for peace agreements. Likewise, Stephen Nemeth and Brian Lai (Nemeth and Lai 2022) conclude that negotiations in civil wars are more likely after a disaster that hits both the government and the rebels. They attribute this finding to a general weakening of both sides, reduced expectations of imminent victory, and the need to support civilians.

Costly Signal

Disasters can increase the intensity of violence-as-communication during an armed conflict in various ways. To start with, rebel groups and governments rely on various forms of support. Local populations, for instance, can provide taxes, recruits and a hideout for the rebels but can also supply pro-government troops with food or information. Various external states might channel financial support and military goods to the conflict parties

(Salehyan et al. 2014) or provide legitimacy by backing their demands (Duyvesteyn 2017). The different forms of support are usually contingent on the respective group being perceived as capable and determined to fight for its cause. Should doubts occur that this is still the case after a disaster, or should the armed groups only fear that such doubts might emerge, the groups are likely to stage violent attacks in order to demonstrate their continued presence and strength. More extremist groups might try to outbid their moderate counterparts to gather support (Conrad and Greene 2015). One way to do so is by rejecting disaster diplomacy and relief cooperation while increasing fighting intensity to illustrate their uncompromised stand for a certain cause. State actors can also demonstrate their determination (and distract from their disaster preparation failures) by intensifying military activities (Lee et al. 2022).

Likewise, when a disaster causes a noticeable decline in fighting capability, armed groups might react with a small- to medium-scale offensives to demonstrate their strength to opponents. Attacking civilians could be a particularly "attractive" (yet morally highly problematic) option as they are easy to target, even with reduced military capabilities (Haer and RezaeeDaryakenari 2022). By staging such "symbolic attacks," a conflict party aims to prevent its opponent's offensives during a period of vulnerability. An increase in violence might also send an intimidating signal to the civil population, namely that the armed group is still capable of retaliating against those supporting other conflict parties (Kydd and Walter 2006). This issue is particularly salient for rebel groups facing government (and international) actors moving into their territories to support civilians through relief operations and reconstruction efforts, which could also result in the government collecting information and the population being less loyal to the rebels (Walch 2018b). But Benjamin E. Bagozzi and colleagues (2017) also find evidence that armed groups use violence against agricultural populations during droughts to signal that they do not tolerate resistance against food extraction by the rebels in these areas.

Michael J. Boyle (2009: 268) argues that the intensification of violence frequently results from a "fear of political exclusion." In such situations, a conflict party is not represented at the bargaining table and protests against this exclusion through the use of violent attacks, simultaneously demonstrating its relevance. This could explain conflict escalation in the face of post-disaster moves toward conflict resolution caused by increased solidarity or restraint (see above). Perhaps more relevant, non-state armed groups may aim to underline their territorial control or at least their ability to wage violence in certain places, demonstrating that they at least must be consulted when post-disaster aid is distributed. The safety of aid workers is an important concern among many international organizations and NGOs (Stoddard et al. 2019). However, questions about who distributes aid, and to whom, caused severe disagreements between governments, rebels, and international aid workers in post-tsunami Aceh and Sri Lanka (Harrowell and Özerdem 2019; Zeccola 2011; see also the case studies "Indonesia 2004: Wave of Peace?" and "Sri Lanka 2004: Wave of Violence?" in chapter 4).

In sum, the costly signal pathway assumes that armed groups have good reasons to demonstrate their strength, determination, territorial control, and/or relevance in the aftermath of a disaster. Verbal communication is often inadequate for these purposes, as "talk is cheap" and hardly credible in environments characterized by high levels of insecurity and hostility. A government is unlikely to conclude that an offensive against a supposedly weakened rebel will prove fruitless simply because the rebels claim they still have sufficient military capability, for example. The escalation of violence, by contrast, is a "costly signal" (Kydd and Walter 2006: 50). Put differently: such an escalation is usually too risky and costly to be part of a bluff, and hence more credible.

Image Cultivation

As has been discussed above in more detail, armed groups on both the government side and the rebel side receive support from various groups, including foreign governments, civilians, and local elites. Such (inter-)dependence necessitates communication between an armed group and (potentially) supporting actors, and as with the intensification of violence, restraining from violent actions can also be an effective communication strategy. This is because acting in a certain way is more credible than just making claims or announcing plans for action, particularly if increased grievances or improved opportunity structures after a disaster set incentives for conflict escalation, yet the conflict party limits its use of violence.

Armed groups might opt to de-escalate an armed conflict as a communicative action in two situations. The first one is when an armed group strongly depends on a part of the population that has been heavily affected by the disaster. Rebel groups, for instance, often merge with the civilian population to avoid detection by government intelligence, rely on local taxes and food supplies, or recruit members from a certain constituency. But governments may aim to win the hearts and minds of the population in the course of a counterinsurgency campaign as well, and thus they rely on local support for gathering information or supplies for military troops (Polk 2007). Earthquakes, floods, storms, and droughts can have an enormous effect on the lives and livelihoods of vulnerable populations.

By restraining violence in the face of disasters, armed groups communicate several messages to the (heavily) affected groups. They show their condolence and solidarity (as seeking military gains from tragic events might be perceived as inappropriate), counter accusations of being more interested in winning the war than in supporting people (as resources used for relief work cannot be simultaneously used for military purposes), and demonstrate their support of the population by trying to establish a secure environment for relief and reconstruction. Studies finding that civil war parties are more likely to negotiate (Nemeth and Lai 2022) and conclude a cease-fire (Kreutz 2012) after major disasters support these arguments. Similarly, Kyle Beardsley and Bryan McQuinn (2009) argue that rebel groups that strongly depend on local taxes are more likely to seek peace in post-disaster contexts than rebels with external funding sources.

The second situation during which violence de-escalation as a form of communication is likely to happen is when conflict parties depend on foreign support such as military or development aid. As remarked by Reyko Huang (2016: 104), "Rebels often undertake measures, such as compliance with international humanitarian law, not as part of a coherent military strategy but to please external audiences." Governments face similar incentives. James H. Lebovic and Erik Voeten (2009), for instance, find that negative representations of a country by the United Nations Commission on Human Rights significantly reduce multilateral aid. Governments and rebels can restrain violence after disasters to cultivate an image as reliable and responsible actors.

Particularly when donors have a strong democratic and human rights record, when they have invested large amounts of money in the affected region, and/or when many of their citizens are in the areas devastated by the disaster (e.g., as aid workers), rebels and governments might want to send a strong signal about their reliability by limiting the use of violence

(Fortna et al. 2018). Even countries that are traditionally skeptical about foreign interference and Western human rights norms, like China, pushed for the government of Myanmar to set aside political disputes and accept international aid after Cyclone Nargis in 2008 (Junk 2016). Moral concerns of the international society can therefore also pressure armed groups to signal their goodwill by limiting the use of violence.

To sum up, a "reduction in conflict intensity can be . . . a central signaling device" (Ruhe 2021: 690). The higher likelihood of negotiations and cease-fires after a disaster again provides supportive evidence here (Kreutz 2012; Nemeth and Lai 2022). Regarding the civil war in Aceh, Jean-Christophe Gaillard and colleagues (Gaillard, Clavé, and Kelman 2008: 517) describe how both conflict parties were strongly dependent on local populations and especially international support. They purposefully de-escalated the conflict after the 2004 tsunami in order to cultivate a positive image and ensure sustained assistance: "Many observers agreed that resorting to military solutions to resolve the conflict in a concurrent post-disaster emergency and rehabilitation context would be politically incorrect in the eyes of the wider Indonesian population and international community" (see also the case study "Indonesia 2004: Wave of Peace?" in chapter 4).

In contrast to the other two potential de-escalation impacts of disasters, the decline in violence here is driven neither by increased solidarity nor by material constraints imposed by the disaster. Rather, at least one of the conflict parties restrains the use of violence (even if grievances increase or opportunities emerge) to send a message to one or several actors.

Summary

This chapter laid the theoretical foundation for the book. It combined the two main outcomes of interest (armed conflict escalation and de-escalation) with the three approaches to explaining the dynamics of armed conflict: motive, strategy, and communication. By doing so, I was able to differentiate six potential impacts of disasters on ongoing armed conflicts (or pathways connecting disasters to a change in armed conflict intensity). The impacts can overlap and reinforce or cancel out each other.

Armed conflicts may escalate after disasters because of increased grievances of the affected populations, because armed groups face better opportunities to wage violence (e.g., recruitment of deprived individuals, state weakness), or because armed groups seek to send a costly signal about their continued presence, strength, and determination to relevant audiences. Alternatively, disasters can result in increased solidarity and trust, pose restraints to the mobilization and mobility of armed groups, or provide incentives for actors to cultivate a positive image by restraining from the use of violence, hence leading to a de-escalation of the conflict. Especially the communication approach and its associated pathways (costly signal and image cultivation) are innovative as research on disasters and conflict has so far focused largely on motives and strategic concerns (Brzoska 2018). This chapter represents the first theoretical formulation of the communication approach in the environmental security and climate conflict research field.

3 Cases, Conditions, and Qualitative Comparative Analysis

This chapter elaborates on the cases studied in this book, the methods employed, and the core causal conditions used in the analysis. The main text presents core information in a concise way while various footnotes and the online appendix (available on the MIT Press website) contain further information and data.

Sample of Cases

My analysis focuses on 36 cases in which major disasters triggered by natural hazards overlap with an intrastate armed conflict. A disaster is the "serious disruption of the functioning of a community or a society at any scale" (UN General Assembly 2016) that results from an extreme natural event (a hazard) striking a vulnerable social system. An armed conflict is "a contested incompatibility that concerns government or territory" (Gleditsch et al. 2002: 618) and occurs between a government and an organized, armed rebel group (see chapter 1 for extensive discussions of these definitions).

The unit of analysis of my study is the country.[1] In recent years, research on environment- and climate-conflict linkages has increasingly utilized high-resolution data that allow for subnational analyses (Ide 2017; Koubi 2019). Such a focus on subnational administrative units or small geographical

---

1. The only exception to this rule was made for the Indian cases. India has by far the largest territory in the sample. It is also characterized by a multitude of armed conflicts and major disasters each year. Using the country as the unit of analysis would have been infeasible as multiple large disasters occurred during each year. Instead, I use Indian states—quite large geographical entities by themselves—as units of analysis.

areas allows scholars to study local intersections between disasters and conflicts. However, I focus on the country level because disasters have a wide range of effects that go beyond the area physically affected by the hazard and can have impacts in other parts of the country. For instance, disasters

> may lead to migration to urban areas and increased prices for urban consumers; declining state revenues can lead to strains on public finances and negatively affect public-sector employees across the economy; finally, disaster-affected populations can take their protests and demands directly to the national capital. Causal pathways may be long and far-reaching. (Hendrix and Salehyan 2012: 38)

In order to compose the sample, I first made a list of all armed conflicts recorded by the Uppsala Conflict Data Program (UCDP) Armed Conflict Dataset for the period from 1990 to 2020 (Pettersson et al. 2021).[2] I then compared this list with a record of all disasters causing more than 1,000 deaths as provided by the International Disaster Database (EM-DAT) (Guha-Sapir 2021), focusing on climatological, geophysical, hydrological, and meteorological events.[3] Whenever such a disaster struck a country with an active armed conflict at the time, the case was included in the sample. The threshold of 1,000 deaths makes sure the respective disasters wreaked considerable havoc on infrastructure, economies, and human life and therefore were large enough to have an impact on wider armed conflict dynamics. "Smaller crises or disasters often do not lead to significant changes in societies, institutions, and organizations because the impacts can be managed within existing regulatory regimes" (Birkmann et al. 2010: 637). That said, even small-scale disasters can affect highly localized conflict dynamics or patterns of low-intensity violence. The findings of this book, however, mainly apply to large-scale disasters and high-intensity armed conflicts.

However, I have included five disasters that fell short of causing 1,000 deaths. These five disasters still had considerable societal impacts and allowed me to include countries that were not previously represented (Burundi, Egypt, Nepal, Peru, Uganda) as well as disasters that were under-represented

---

2. For the period prior to 1989, disaster data are less reliable (Hollis 2018), and no monthly information on armed conflict dynamics are available. I could not include 1989 as some variables are time-lagged.
3. EM-DAT is the best available public dataset when it comes to large-scale disasters and the national level of analysis (Huggel et al. 2015).

(droughts) in the sample. Furthermore, no more than four disaster-conflict intersections per country can be present in the sample, primarily to avoid a heavy overrepresentation of India and the Philippines.[4] Overall, there is a slight overrepresentation of rapid-onset events (16 earthquakes and 7 cyclones) compared with medium-onset (7 floods) and slow-onset disasters (3 droughts, 2 heat waves, 1 cold spell) in the sample.

Table 3.1 provides an overview of the 36 cases of conflict-disaster intersections covered by the analysis, and figure 3.1 visualizes this sample.

For an initial assessment of the armed conflict dynamics after the disaster relative to the pre-hazard period, I compiled monthly information on battle-related deaths from the UCDP Georeferenced Event Dataset (Sundberg and Melander 2013).[5] Specifically, the analysis compares the 12-month periods before and after the month during which the disaster took place. For longer time periods, it is increasingly likely that a potential impact of disasters on conflict dynamics vanishes or is superimposed by other factors (Chung and Rhee 2022; Raleigh and Kniveton 2012). I consider an armed conflict to escalate or de-escalate if the growth/decline in battle-related deaths is at least five standard deviations in the post-disaster period as compared with the year before the disaster. This preliminary quantitative assessment is backed up (and corrected in more than one third of all cases) by qualitative, case-study-based evidence for all 36 cases. Figure 3.2 visualizes the change in battle-related deaths for the cases in the sample.

Data Collection and Analysis

This book is based on qualitative and quantitative data for the 36 cases of disaster–armed conflict intersections. Qualitative data were collected through extensive, desk-based case studies. I used literature and web searches[6] to gather relevant information on each disaster, each armed conflict, and the potential interlinkages between them. Furthermore, I consulted with and/or interviewed various experts on the respective cases (see

---

4. I included the disaster with the most deaths for which sufficient data are available.
5. Battle-related deaths are the established measure of conflict intensity in the literature (e.g., Hultman and Peksen 2017; Ruhe 2021) and include those killed during encounters between parties to an armed conflict as well as victims of civilian targeting.
6. With a preference for academic articles and books retrieved via Scopus and Google Scholar.

Table 3.1
Cases studied in this analysis

ID	Country	Disaster	Year	Disaster-related deaths	Conflict Party A	Conflict Party B
1	Afghanistan	Earthquake	1998	7,023	Taliban	UIFSA
2	Afghanistan	Cold spell	2008	1,317	Government	Taliban
3	Algeria	Earthquake	2003	2,266	Government	GSPC
4	Bangladesh	Cyclone	1991	138,866	Government	JSS/SB
5	Bangladesh	Cyclone	2007	4,234	Government	PBCP-J
6	Burundi	Drought	2005–2006	120	Government	PALIPEHUTU-FNL
7	Colombia	Earthquake	1999	1,186	Government	FARC
8	Egypt	Flood	1994	600	Government	IG
9	India (Andhra Pradesh, Orissa)	Cyclone	1999	9,843	Government	PWG
10	India (Assam)	Flood	1998	1,811	Government	ULFA
11	India (Assam)	Flood	2007	1,103	Government	ULFA
12	India (Kashmir)	Earthquake	2005	1,309	Government	Kashmir insurgents
13	Indonesia	Earthquake, tsunami	1992	2,500	Government	Fretilin
14	Indonesia	Earthquake, tsunami	2004	165,708	Government	GAM
15	Indonesia	Earthquake	2006	5,778	Government	GAM
16	Iran	Earthquake	1990	40,000	Government	KDPI
17	Iran	Earthquake	1997	1,568	Government	MEK
18	Myanmar	Cyclone	2008	138,366	Government, DKBA	KNU
19	Nepal	Flood	1996	768	Government	CPN-M
20	Pakistan	Earthquake	2005	73,338	Government	Baloch Ittehad, BLA
21	Pakistan	Flood	2010	1,985	Government	TTP
22	Pakistan	Heat wave	2015	1,229	Government	TTP
23	Peru	Earthquake	2007	600	Government	Sendero Luminoso
24	Philippines	Earthquake	1990	2,412	Government	CPP/NPA
25	Philippines	Cyclone	2012	1,901	Government	ASG
26	Philippines	Cyclone, floods	1991	5,956	Government	CPP/NPA

Table 3.1
(continued)

ID	Country	Disaster	Year	Disaster-related deaths	Conflict Party A	Conflict Party B
27	Philippines	Cyclone	2013	7,354	Government	CPP/NPA
28	Russia	Earthquake	1995	1,989	Government	Chechen Republic of Ichkeria
29	Russia	Heat wave	2010	55,736	Government	Forces of the Caucasus Emirate
30	Somalia	Flood	1997	2,311	USC (Mahdi)	USC (Aideed)
31	Somalia	Drought	2010–2011	20,000	Government	Al-Shabaab
32	Sri Lanka	Earthquake, tsunami	2004	35,399	Government	LTTE
33	Tajikistan	Flood	1992	1,346	Government	UTO
34	Thailand	Earthquake, tsunami	2004	8,345	Government	Patani insurgents
35	Turkey	Earthquake	1999	17,127	Government	PKK
36	Uganda	Drought	1999–2001	115	Government	LRA

the acknowledgments). This information is summarized and fully referenced by the 36 case studies in chapter 4. The qualitative data are complemented by quantitative information on a number of relevant variables (see next section of this chapter) such as agricultural dependence, poverty, and the level of democracy. The online appendix contains a detailed overview of all the quantitative data sources and how they were processed.

In order to make sense of the large and complex qualitative dataset compiled and to combine it with quantitative information, I employ qualitative comparative analysis (QCA). This method is based on Boolean algebra and conceives cases as being members of certain sets, such as the set of democratic countries or the set of countries where rebels are adversely affected by a disaster.[7] QCA then analyzes the relationship between different sets to determine whether a condition is necessary or sufficient for an outcome.

QCA offers several advantages in the context of this book. First, QCA is interested in causal explanations for an outcome, and my research question is specifically why some disasters are followed by conflict escalation,

---

7. Conversely, cases can be non-members (or out of) of certain sets. While fuzzy-set QCA allows for partial-set membership scores, I utilize the crisp-set (or binary) version of QCA as this is recommended when the outcome of the analysis is binary.

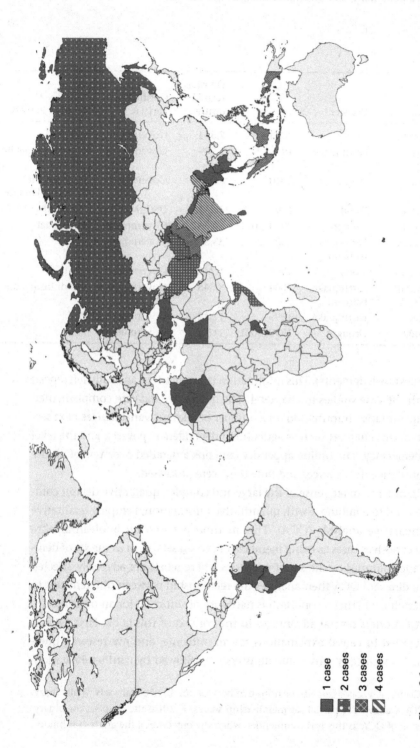

Figure 3.1
Countries covered by the analysis. This map was created with the help of MapChart (https://mapchart.net).

de-escalation, or no change in conflict dynamics. Second, QCA is designed to account for conjunctural causation—that is, it can identify causal relationships characterized by the interaction of various factors (rather than, say, the average effects of individual variables). This fits my assumption that several interacting conditions need to be present for disasters to shape conflict dynamics (Mahoney 2010). Third, QCA is based on the idea of equifinality, implying that it can disentangle various distinct pathways leading to the same outcome. As discussed in chapter 2, there are several rather different potential pathways connecting disasters to conflict (de-)escalation.

Fourth, it is possible that different combinations of conditions are relevant for an outcome (e.g., conflict escalation) and its absence (e.g., conflict de-escalation). QCA is well able to detect such asymmetric causality. Fifth, QCA is geared toward detecting complex patterns in medium-N qualitative datasets like the one presented in this book. Finally, the method allows the integration of qualitative and quantitative data as it requires the calibration of all raw data into (in my case) binary measures of either 1 (case is a member of the respective set of cases) or 0 (case is out of the respective set of cases) (Mello 2021; Schneider and Wagemann 2012). These advantages have resulted in QCA becoming a rapidly emerging method in international relations, security studies, and the environmental social sciences (Groth et al. 2020; Ide and Mello 2022).

After data for all relevant conditions are collected and calibrated, the QCA checks for necessary conditions.[8] In the next step, a truth table is constructed that contains all possible combinations of conditions and the empirical cases that fit the respective truth table row.[9] If such truth table rows "differ in only one causal condition yet produce the same outcome,

8. A condition is necessary if it is present in (almost) all cases where the outcome is present. QCA uses a non-deterministic understanding of quasi-necessity.
9. One truth table row exists for each possible combination of conditions. This means that a QCA with k conditions (k being any number) will include 2^k truth table rows. With a limited set of cases, problems related to limited diversity occur because of the existence of too many logical remainders (truth table rows/combinations of conditions not covered by empirical cases), hence rendering the QCA results unreliable (Marx and Dusa 2011; Schneider and Wagemann 2010). In this study, I follow Patrick A. Mello's (2021) benchmark of using a maximum of one condition for every five cases in the sample.

Chapter 3

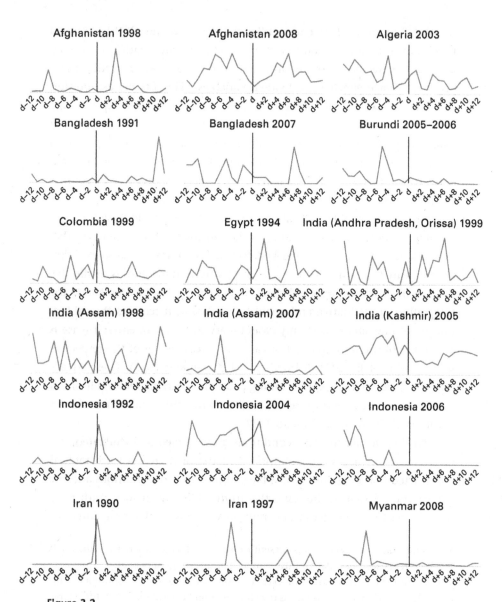

Figure 3.2
Battle-related deaths for the two-year period around the respective disaster. The vertical line marks the month of the disaster.

Cases, Conditions, and Qualitative Comparative Analysis

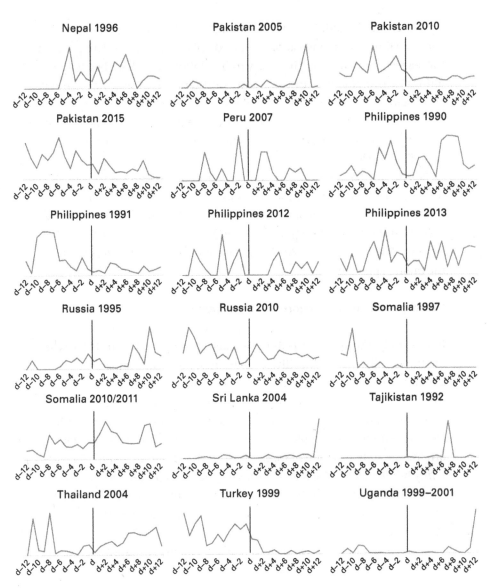

Figure 3.2
(continued)

then the causal condition that distinguishes the two expressions can be considered irrelevant and can be removed" (Ragin 1987: 93). This is called the logical minimization. It results in a solution that describes the conditions or combinations of conditions sufficient for an outcome (Rihoux and Ragin 2009). While different solutions are possible depending on the handling of logical remainders,[10] I focus on the parsimonious solution as it is the most robust and the most straightforward to interpret (Baumgartner and Thiem 2020).

Box 5.1 in chapter 5 provides further information on how to read QCA solutions, including on key indicators like consistency (How well does the solution explain the outcome?) and coverage (How much of the outcome is covered by the solution?). I use the fsQCA 3.0 software to conduct my analysis (Ragin and Davey 2017) and perform various robustness tests (see the online appendix).

Causal Conditions and Theoretical Expectations

In this study, the QCA proceeds in two steps (see figure 3.3). It first focuses on the conditions that facilitate disasters having any impact at all on armed conflict dynamics (stage 1) before investigating why escalation is the outcome in some cases and de-escalation in others (stage 2). This two-stage procedure allows me to test a large number of relevant conditions with a medium-size sample[11] and to account for variable sets of factors driving the different outcomes. (I return to this point in chapter 5.) Here, I only briefly discuss the relevant causal conditions in order to avoid overlaps with chapter 2. Chapter 5 provides an in-depth theoretical discussion of the factors identified as relevant by the empirical analysis and their interactions.

When it comes to the conditions that are causally relevant for a disaster having an impact on conflict dynamics (stage 1 of the QCA), I focused

---

10. See the footnote 9 for a definition of logical remainders. The possible solution types are (1) the parsimonious solution that includes all logical remainders that simplify the solution, (2) the intermediate solution that only includes simplifying logical remainders that are in line with theoretical assumptions, and (3) the conservative solution that includes no logical remainders. All three solutions are perfectly in line with the empirically observed patterns (Dusa 2022; Schneider and Wagemann 2012).
11. This helps to mitigate problems associated with limited diversity (see footnote 9).

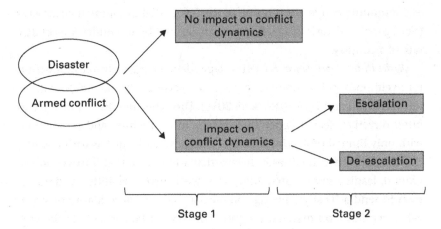

Figure 3.3
Visualization of the two-stage QCA.

on structural as well as dynamic factors. Structural factors make a country or region more prone to conflict escalation and hardly change over time. Dynamic factors, by contrast, occur (and change) within relatively short amounts of time and serve as catalysts or precipitants for conflict (de-)escalation (Hendrix and Glaser 2007; Kaufman 2001). Even though disasters usually make visible and aggravate (rather than discontinue) conditions that prevailed during "normal" pre-disaster times (Wisner et al. 2004), they can cause some rapid developments that influence conflict risks (Brzoska 2019; Gawronski and Olson 2013; see also chapter 2).

I hypothesized the following structural conditions to be causally relevant for a change in conflict dynamics (for good or bad) after a disaster:

Poverty: Widespread poverty is a relevant condition for all pathways connecting disasters to changes in armed conflict intensity. Poor people often have very limited capabilities to deal with and recover from a disaster, which could result in stronger grievances and better recruitment opportunities for armed groups (Barnett and Adger 2007; Drury and Olson 1998). Poverty also implies limited capabilities of the state and/or rebel groups to extract taxes or resources in the wake of a disaster. The associated lack of capabilities could make it more attractive to use the communicative functions of violence to send a signal about fighting capabilities (to opponents) or responsible restraint (to supporters) (Raleigh 2012). Research also points toward the possibility of significant post-disaster solidarity in poor regions, as community cooperation is one of the few available coping mechanisms (Venugopal and Yasir 2017). Poverty is measured by the under-5 mortality rate of a country.

Agricultural dependence: Societies dependent on agricultural production for livelihoods and economic prosperity are particularly vulnerable to disasters (Feitelson and Tubi 2017; Seter 2016). Droughts, floods, or earthquakes often directly affected agricultural assets, infrastructure, and production, with only limited protective measures being available. Just as with poverty, this indicates that the disaster has particularly devastating impacts on the ground, leading to increased grievances, weakened capabilities, and incentives to send a "costly" message but also a rise in local solidarity or stronger dependence on external support. This should be particularly the case when poverty and agricultural dependence are present simultaneously. My preferred measure for agricultural dependence is the contribution of the primary sectors to a country's GDP.

Democracy: Democratic political systems provide channels to articulate disaster-related grievances through legal and non-violent ways, such as protests or elections (Apodaca 2017). In democratic systems, leaders also have incentives to provide disaster risk reduction and relief measures to broad constituencies (Keefer et al. 2011; Sen 1983). This not only reduces grievances but also lessens the impacts of the disaster on the ground, making it more difficult for insurgents to capitalize on the disaster. At the same time, democratic governments can find it hard to prioritize military struggles against rebels vis-à-vis using the resources and (military) manpower for disaster relief. Scholars have argued that political groups tend to use violence more frequently in democracies as governments are more sensitive to public pressure (Chenoweth 2013).[12] The same logic could compel rebels to send a costly signal after disasters—for example, to convey a message about government incompetence in the face of a double disaster (one resulting from a natural hazard and the other from armed violence). In particular, states that have recently democratized and that are dependent on international support could constrain violence after disasters to improve their reputation. Data on democracy come from the Autocratic Regime Dataset (Geddes et al. 2014), but results are robust to using the polityIV dataset (see the online appendix).

12. Empirical support for this proposition is contested, however (see Magen 2018).

Furthermore, the analysis includes the following (disaster-related) triggering factors.

Overlap: There are multiple reasons to suspect that a spatial coincidence between the disaster-affected region and the areas in which fighting takes place is a crucial context factor for a disaster-conflict linkage. To start with, the temporary inaccessibility of an area (owing to destroyed roads and railways, for instance) can provide the rebels with an advantage vis-à-vis the government but also constrain the mobility of all conflict parties (Brzoska 2018). The government might also use relief-provision efforts to gather intelligence (Eastin 2016) in the affected areas. Grievances about disaster preparation and relief efforts can be directed against the government or insurgents (whoever is considered responsible) if their troops are present in the region (Walch 2018a). Likewise, instances of cooperation and solidarity between hostile groups (or even troops) are more likely to occur if both are placed in the affected area (De Juan et al. 2020). Finally, if disasters hit conflict areas and change the power dynamics on the ground, state forces or rebels can feel compelled to send a costly signal about their continued capabilities and determination to fight, or to restrain from violence in order to cultivate their image. These logics should be particularly pronounced in regions characterized by poverty and agricultural dependence. Information on the overlap between disasters and conflict zones is obtained from the qualitative case studies.

Adverse impacts on at least one conflict party: The disaster and conflict areas do not necessarily need to overlap for the former to have an impact on the latter. Disasters can also shape conflict dynamics if they have adverse impacts on the resources, troops, finances, or capabilities of at least one conflict party. Consider, for example, a countrywide drop in support for the government because of its poor handling of a disaster (Katz and Levin 2015). Likewise, rebels might recruit from among the deprived populations in disaster-affected areas and send their new fighters to other areas of the country, while the government faces budgetary constraints and reduced troop availability due to a disaster outside the conflict area (Ide et al. 2020; von Uexkull et al. 2016). Adversely affected conflict parties also often feel a greater urge to use violence as a communicative tool (Kydd and Walter 2006) and can do so in every part of the country where they have a sufficient presence. In this sense, "adverse impacts" is complementary to "overlap" as both conditions feature a very similar underlying logic. I determine the existence of relevant adverse impact based on qualitative information.

Aid: A large inflow of foreign aid after a major disaster could have a significant impact on conflict dynamics in both directions. The aid can be used to alleviate grievances, prevent the weakening of the state apparatus, and increase conflict parties' compliance with the calls of international donors to limit the use of violence during the emergency phase (Bernath 2016; Klitzsch 2014). In this sense, aid could also mitigate grievances caused by poverty, vulnerability, and authoritarianism in the aftermath of disasters. However, the unequal distribution of aid can also lead to grievances, while rebels might violently sabotage government aid projects (De Juan et al. 2020). Both conflict parties could also divert the inflowing aid to boost their military capabilities, particularly if they are adversely affected by the disaster (Kikuta 2019; Levy and Yusuf 2021). The amount of foreign aid entering a country after a disaster (derived from AidData 2016) relative to the GDP indicates a large inflow of foreign aid.

The second stage of the QCA focuses on why in some contexts where disasters shape conflict dynamics the outcome is a rise in fighting intensity, whereas in other cases the outcome is a de-escalation of the conflict. Just as in stage 1, the analysis included a combination of structural and dynamic (or precipitating) conditions. As the first stage already identified the individual or combinations of conditions that make a setting prone to disaster-related changes in conflict dynamics, stage 2 focuses primarily on dynamic factors that shape whether a conflict escalates or de-escalates. These conditions are the following:

Unfair distribution: This condition indicates whether the affected population perceives the preparation for, impacts of, relief efforts related to, and reconstruction measures after the disaster as unfair or biased. Such perceptions result in serious grievances, particularly against state institutions (Ide, Kristensen, et al. 2021). This is because "people often turn to governments when a disaster strikes because governmental organizations have the necessary resources" (Schneider 2018: 552). These grievances might also compel the rebels to send a (violent) costly signal to demonstrate their disagreement with the government. Consequently, the unfair distribution of disaster impacts, relief, and reconstruction is expected to facilitate armed conflict escalation. The case studies provide information on grievances related to unfair aid distribution for each case.

Rebel dependence: I hypothesize that if the rebels depend on the local population in the disaster-affected areas, conflict de-escalation is a more likely outcome. A population occupied with disaster relief and reconstruction is less likely to support a rebel group with information or manpower. If the population is impoverished by the disaster, there is also very limited room for providing money or food to the insurgents, even if the latter resort to forced extraction of such goods (Adano et al. 2012; Bagozzi et al. 2017). Finally, rebels who live in the same area as and have established a social contract with a population tend to reduce fighting activities in order to provide disaster relief (Beardsley and McQuinn 2009; Walch 2014). Qualitative information on rebel dependence on the local population is derived from the case studies.

Impact on conflict parties: For the second stage of the QCA, I determine whether the disaster had a negative impact on the resources, troops, finances, or capabilities of the rebels and/or the government. This is a more nuanced measure than the adverse impacts measure from stage 1 and allows me to specify which conflict parties experienced negative impacts from the disaster. If only one conflict party is adversely affected, I expect a conflict escalation, either because the stronger side pushes for a military advantage or because the weaker side uses increased violence to demonstrate its continued power and determination. If both the rebels and the government are weakened by a disaster, limited capabilities and a call to limit the use of violence (either by more solidaric domestic audiences or by the international public) are expected to result in conflict de-escalation (Brzoska 2018; Raleigh 2012). If no conflict party is weakened by the disaster, further trends in fighting intensity very likely depend on other factors, such as the intensity of local grievances or the inflow of international aid.

The analysis also considers two rather structural conditions in the analysis of conflict escalation and de-escalation after disasters:

Weak rebels: If rebels have very low fighting capacities and few personal and financial resources to draw on (particularly when compared with the state forces), they will likely be unable to exploit state weakness or champion popular grievances. To the contrary, a disaster that has even a moderate impact on their resources or support base could seriously undermine the insurgents' ability to wage violence. Consequently, conflict de-escalation should be present in the aftermath of a disaster if the rebel group is weak (Cunningham et al. 2013; Tominaga and Lee 2021). The Non-State Actor dataset provides information on the capabilities and relative strength of a rebel group (Cunningham et al. 2013).

Capable state: States with an effective bureaucracy and a strong military should be able to promote cooperation and reduce grievances after disasters. Such states are also unlikely to be weakened by a disaster to such a degree that rebels could exploit their (temporary) weakness. They further rely less on violence to signal their (considerable) strength. However, if rebels are weakened by a disaster or if strong grievances combine with an absence of democracy, governments of capable states could intensify their military activities (Hendrix 2010; Selby and Hoffmann 2014). I combine information on government effectiveness, military personnel, and economic extraction capacity to determine the capability of a state.

The online appendix provides detailed information on how data for all conditions were collected and analyzed.

While the cases-to-conditions ratio in stage 1 (6 conditions for 36 cases) is in line with established standards (Marx and Dusa 2011; Mello 2021), stage 2 has slightly too many conditions (6) for the number of cases (18). I mitigate this issue by subsequently running core models containing only the four conditions causally relevant for the outcome, which is in line with established benchmarks and does not affect the results.

4 Disasters and Armed Conflict Dynamics: Evidence from 36 Cases

This is the core chapter of the book in terms of empirical data. It briefly describes the history of the armed conflict and the impacts of the disaster for all 36 cases under study before tracing the potential impacts of the disaster on conflict (de-)escalation for each case. The analysis is guided by the theoretical framework laid down in chapter 2 and will be synthesized in chapter 5. This chapter is reserved for qualitative studies of the 36 instances of disaster-conflict intersections covered by my analysis. I start by discussing those cases where disasters had an impact on armed conflict escalation, followed by the cases where disasters facilitated conflict de-escalation, and finally the cases where no disaster-conflict links were present.

Cases of Conflict Escalation after Disasters

Bangladesh 1991: The Chittagong Hill Conflict after Cyclone Gorky

The Chittagong Hill Tracts is a hilly area in southeastern Bangladesh bordering India and Myanmar.[1] It hosts a large and heterogeneous tribal population known as Pahari or Jumma. More than 500,000 out of a total population of close to 950,000 people in 1991 identified as Pahari (BBS 1994). After Pakistan gained independence in 1947, the Chittagong Hill Tracts lost the special administrative status they had during British rule. Among the consequences were migration to the area from other regions of then East Pakistan as well as the political, economic, and cultural marginalization of the tribal communities. This process of migration and marginalization accelerated when Bangladesh became independent in 1971. The

---

1. The area comprises the three districts of Bandarban, Khagdachhadi, and Rangamati.

new government explicitly rejected demands for autonomy or the constitutional acknowledgment of the tribal people of the Chittagong Hill Tracts.

As a consequence, the Chittagong Hill Tracts People's Coordination Association (JSS) was established in 1972 to forward claims to autonomy. An armed wing, the Peace Force (SB), emerged shortly afterward and started to confront the Bangladeshi military from the mid-1970s onward. The JSS/SB largely waged guerrilla warfare. Despite significant troop deployments, a large resettlement program initiated in 1979, and the emergence of militias, the government was unable to achieve a military victory. Peace negotiations were ongoing during the late 1980s, leading the government to implement unilateral measures to increase the autonomy of the Chittagong Hill Tracts in 1989 (Ahmed 1993). These measures were welcomed by more moderate elites and younger people, who benefited from the development schemes implemented since the 1970s, but they faced fierce resistance by the JSS/SB. As a consequence, the armed conflict intensified while previously high popular support for the JSS/SB vanished, forcing it to rely more strongly on its bases in India (Uddin 2008).

A devastating cyclone (sometimes referred to as Gorky) and associated storm surges struck Bangladesh and especially the Chittagong Hill Tracts in late April 1991. It caused around 139,000 fatalities and massive destruction, including estimated economic damage of US$3 billion (Haque and Blair 1992). While the losses were enormous, two factors limited the eruption of severe anti-government (or anti-settler) grievances in the Chittagong Hill Tracts. First, within Bangladesh, the cyclone was largely framed as a natural and inevitable event, especially given the country's track record of severe disasters (Dove and Khan 1995). Second, while poor and marginalized groups were the most severely affected by the cyclone (Chowdhury et al. 1993), its impact did not reflect the socio-political divides that were at the core of the conflict. Muinul Islam (1992) reports that people who had relocated to the area with government support since the 1970s were most vulnerable to the disaster.

Yet, the post-disaster period saw a significant intensification in violence, with 76 battle-related deaths in the 12 months prior to the cyclone and 268 fatalities in the subsequent year. A minor spike in violence occurred in the immediate aftermath of the disaster and a second, much larger spike in April 1992. This conflict intensification was largely driven by violence against civilians, mostly by pro-government forces: 242 of the 268 deaths in the post-disaster period were civilians. The conflict has long been characterized by civilian victimization as the JSS/SB targeted (perceived) supporters of the government while government troops, militia, and some newly arrived (ethnic Bengali) settlers targeted (supposed) rebel supporters during counterinsurgency. According to Ala Uddin (2016: 326), "Many incidents of massacre, attack, and reprisal, indiscriminate arrest, torture, judicial and extrajudicial torture, killing, rape, sexual violence ... and abduction took place." But such an upsurge of civilian victimization was still unusual (Amnesty International 1992).

The grievance pathway is unable to account for this conflict escalation given that the impact of the disaster on grievances was minimal and the intensification was mainly driven by government actors. Likewise, from an opportunity perspective, using violence against civilians rather than against the weakened military apparatus of the rebels made little sense. By contrast, the government of Bangladesh and its allies were concerned about the possibility of popular grievances fueling anti-Bengal resistance and hence support for the JSS/SB after the disaster. Memories of the devastating 1971 cyclone, which facilitated anti-Pakistan resentments and ultimately fuelled the Bangladeshi independence struggle, likely served as a cognitive point of reference in this context (Hossain 2018). The government was determined to avoid repeating this scenario in 1991. It is thus very plausible that conflict escalation was due to a preemptive costly signal by the government, which intended to demonstrate its determination in the struggle against the JSS/SB as well as its willingness to quell unrest and opposition among civilians.

Colombia 1999: Shaking Grounds, Shaking the Peace Process?
Following a decade of violent clashes between the conservative government of Colombia and liberal political groups (1948–1958), the government started to perceive Communist groups as the bigger threat and took a repressive stake toward them in the late 1950s. Around the same time, Communist movements in Colombia grew more organized and violent. In 1964, the Southern Bloc Guerrilla (SBC) was formed out of various self-defense groups with the explicit goal of overthrowing the government. In 1966, the SBC changed its name to Revolutionary Armed Forces of Colombia (FARC). The FARC was successful in quickly establishing control over rural areas and in financing its insurgency through coca cultivation and

the drug trade. However, struggles for political control and fundamental reforms of the unequal socio-economic system remained the bottom line of the conflict.

The 1980s saw a complex peace process that eventually failed along with (and partially due to) the emergence of right-wing paramilitary groups killing (supposed) FARC leaders and supporters (Molano 2000). While these groups received military support and shared the government's anti-FARC stance, the government had very limited control over them (Serres 2000).[2] The intensity of the conflict increased throughout the 1990s despite a democratization process in 1991, with the rebels expanding their territorial control. In 1998, newly elected president Andrés Pastrana initiated another peace process with the FARC (Bejarano 2003; Chernick 2001).

Shortly after the official inauguration of the peace talks on January 9, 1999, a 6.1-magnitude earthquake affected the departments of Quindío and Risaralda in western-central Colombia on January 25 (Hashimoto and Miyajima 2002). The earthquake resulted in around 1,200 deaths and immediate economic losses of US$1.9 billion, with large cities like Pereira and especially Armenia being heavily affected. The earthquake hit shortly before the start of the harvesting season in a major coffee-growing area (coffee being a major export good of Colombia). Earthquake-induced landslides destroyed parts of the Andean highway, substantively affecting imports and exports via Colombia's main port (Sanchez-Silva et al. 2000). As a consequence, Colombia's economy "shrank by nearly 6 percent in the first quarter of 1999" (Brancati 2007: 724). Meanwhile, the slow recovery of the water supply systems, a lack of national relief coordination, and the delayed arrival of rescue teams increased the hardship of the earthquake victims. Widespread looting and aid appropriation in particular caused significant local grievances (Restrepo and Cowan 2000).

In the remainder of 1999, peace negotiations between the Colombian government and the FARC stalled and violence escalated. The number of battle-related deaths (mostly non-civilians) increased from 915 in the 12 months prior to the earthquake to 1,295 in the subsequent year.

Scholars have linked this conflict escalation to several factors, including the desire of the rebels to use military victories to improve their negotiating

---

2. In fact, fighting between paramilitary and government troops was far from uncommon.

position. The United States provided significant support to the Colombian government from late 1999 onward,[3] leading the military to believe it could win the war with renewed offensives (Chernick 2001; Richani 2005; Villaveces 2003). Other authors argue that the demilitarized zone established at the start of the peace process—characterized by an absence of government police and military personnel—enabled the FARC to increase its fighting capabilities and stage new attacks (Bejarano 2003). However, these arguments do not hold up when it comes to explaining the escalation of the conflict in the first months of the year 1999—that is, in the months after the earthquake. The FARC had numerous incentives to stage attacks before the peace process and would have needed some time to capitalize on the opportunity of the demilitarized zone. Further, the main source of US funding for the government, the Plan Colombia, was not approved until 2000 (Bejarano 2003; Richani 2005). Finally, the establishment of a demilitarized zone also reduced encounters between government and FARC fighters (Villaveces 2003).

The earthquake interacted with the above-mentioned factors and facilitated an escalation of the conflict, particularly in 1999. The grievances and costly signal pathways cannot account for this. The Quindío department, which was the most affected by the disaster, was never a rebel stronghold. Despite significant grievances, the Georeferenced Event Dataset (GED) of the Uppsala Conflict Data Program (UCDP) registers no conflict events in a 100-kilometer radius around the area that suffered the most destruction in the period from 1998 to 2000. Increased recruitment by FARC and progovernment groups or the use of violence as a communication strategy is also not reported.

Three opportunity factors account for the conflict escalation after the 1999 earthquake in Colombia. First, the loss of government income due to the recession undermined the army's fighting capabilities, at least until Plan Colombia kicked in during the year 2000 (Brancati 2007; LADB 1999). The link between the loss of coffee revenues and the higher armed conflict intensity via lower state capacity in Colombia is well established in the literature (Dube and Vargas 2006). Second, large investments in reconstruction[4] (coupled with lower revenues) forced the government to scale down "plans

---

3. US$2.04 billion between 1999 and 2002 alone, at least 81% of which was used for purchasing weapons.
4. Reconstruction costs were more than US$100 million.

to outflank the rebels and win over their base of support in other areas of the countryside" via investments in public services and infrastructure (Rother 1999). Third, the Ministry of Defence sent an additional 6,000 military and police personnel to the affected region in order to stop the looting and restore public order. This reduced the state's presence in other areas (Rother 1999; Venturini 2012). The FARC capitalized on the weakness of the state to launch additional attacks in the post-earthquake period (Richani 2005).

Egypt 1994: Floods, Fire, and Fury

During the 1960s, tensions between socialist-secularist nationalism (dominant in the government) and political Islam (repressed by the state) increased in Egypt. In the mid-1970s, the Islamic Group (IG)[5] was formed by students to campaign for an Islamic form of government. In contrast to similar groups (like the Muslim Brotherhood), IG pursued a radical pathway, including the use of violence against government representatives. Despite prominent individual attacks,[6] the group conducted only limited activities throughout the 1980s. This changed in the early 1990s. Aggrieved by harsh repression and supported by veterans who fought against the Soviet Union in Afghanistan, IG launched a guerrilla-style insurgency against the Egyptian state (Matesan 2020b).

IG received external support from Iran, Sudan, and al-Qaeda and was able to access training camps in Afghanistan. This enabled the group to exploit grievances from impoverished urban youths and religious extremists. By 1992, IG had established strongholds in Upper Egypt[7] and even temporarily took control of the Imbabah neighborhood in Cairo (Mubarak 1996; START 2015). The rebels killed hundreds of people during terrorist attacks, mostly Coptic Christians, police forces, and foreign tourists. Negotiations between the Egyptian government and the IG failed in 1993, and the government decided to increase violent countermeasures (Kepel 2002: 276–298; Matesan 2020a; Schuck 2016).

Very early on the morning of November 2, 1994, torrential rain struck Upper Egypt, resulting in heavy flooding along the Nile in the area between

---

5. The group is perhaps better known under its Arab name, al-Gamaa al-Islamiyya.
6. Including IG's involvement in the assassination of President Anwar Sadat in 1981 by Islamic jihad.
7. Comprising the governorates of Assiut, Minya, and Sohag.

Luxor and El Minya. The disaster caused around 600 deaths, affected more than 100,000 people, and resulted in economic damage of US$140 million. The area surrounding IG stronghold Assiut suffered the worst damage. The flood almost completely destroyed several villages and towns. A wave of "burning water" killed several hundred people in the town of Durunka when oil from a derailed tank car mixed with floodwater and ignited (Murphy 1994). Improper urban planning and a lack of flood preparedness by authorities contributed to the disaster's impact (El-Batran and Arandel 1998). Aid was slow to arrive and was perceived to be insufficient by many affected people in areas with high poverty rates (perhaps also due to limited international support), leading to local grievances and protests. Ten days after the floods, many victims were still without temporary accommodations (Ayeb 1995; Lancaster 1994; UN DHA 1994).[8]

In the aftermath of the flood, conflict intensity increased significantly from 155 to 235 battle-related deaths (12 months before and after the disaster, respectively). The escalation was even more intense in the two governorates most affected by the disaster, Assiut and Minya, where the number of deaths rose from 79 to 184. One reason for this was certainly strategic decisions by the Egyptian government to scale up the counterinsurgency, and by IG to react to such repression with more open violence. However, these processes had started in late 1992 and can hardly explain a conflict escalation two years later (Hamzawy and Grebowski 2010; Schuck 2016).

It is plausible that flood-related grievances played a role in the conflict escalation. The lack of sufficient preparation and particularly the government's slow and under-resourced response to the disaster contributed to local grievances, including in IG strongholds. This was particularly true for the young, urban poor, who were the key constituency of the IG (Kepel 2002: 293–294). President Hosni Mubarak did not even travel to the worst affected areas during his post-disaster visit, and "Prime Minister Atef Sedki was confronted by angry survivors" (Martone 1994). Islamic political groups (mostly the Muslim Brotherhood, but also the IG) filled the void by providing relief in a quick and unbureaucratic way (Ayeb 1995), powerfully illustrating the deficits of the Egyptian state and the "good intentions" and capabilities of the IG. According to several observers, this increased the

---

8. President Hosni Mubarak's failure to visit the worst-affected areas during his post-disaster visit further raised these grievances.

motivation of locals to support radical Islamic groups (Berman 2003; Lancaster 1994). In other words, flood-related grievances and the provision of relief likely increased local support for IG, enabling the rebels to intensify the conflict with the Egyptian government.

India (Andhra Pradesh and Orissa) 1999: The Cyclone as an Opportunity for Naxalite Insurgents

In 1967, grievances about poverty, land inequality, and a lack of government support triggered a peasant revolt in the village of Naxalbari, West Bengal. The protests spread quickly, and the Communist Party of India (Marxist-Leninist) joined forces with the rural peasants to form the Naxalite movement. The Indian state crushed the revolt by force. In the late 1970s, the Naxalites were reduced to small numbers and highly fractionalized (Mehra 2000). However, starting in the 1980s, the movement experienced a sustained growth in size and military strength. The group most strongly associated with this growth is the People's War Group (PWG),[9] formed in April 1980. In line with the larger goals of the Naxalite movement, the PWG sought to overthrow the Indian government and to establish a socialist, anti-imperialist state by military means. It quickly built a considerable base of support among peasants, laborers, members of lower castes (*Dalits*), tribal groups (*Adivasis*), and women in the economically underdeveloped, heavily forested areas of Andhra Pradesh (Chandra 2014; Gupta 2007).

The capabilities of the PWG continued to increase throughout the 1990s. It purchased or seized modern weapons, expanded its military apparatus, and gained influence in new areas (most notably Orissa[10]) (Kujur 2008; Ramana 2006). Neoliberal economic policies by the central government (including the promotion of export-oriented agriculture and food subsidy cuts) had a negative impact on many people in India's poverty-ridden east, which further strengthened support for the Naxalites. The PWG was also able to exercise territorial control in its core areas, enforcing minimum wages, providing jurisprudence, and collecting taxes. The group earned further revenues by extortion, drug cultivation, and appropriation of government funds

9. The official name of the group is the Communist Party of India—Marxist-Leninist (People's War). It split from the Communist Party of India (Marxist-Leninist) but remained part of the Naxalite movement.
10. Just like Andhra Pradesh, Orissa is a federal state of India.

(Mahadevan 2012; Scanlon 2018). Several states, including Andhra Pradesh, reacted to these developments by extending the legal powers of the police and by forming militia-style police units (so-called greyhounds) to confront the insurgents (Ahuja and Ganguly 2007; Dubey 2013; Mehra 2000).[11]

In October 1999, the eastern coast of India was ravaged by two powerful cyclones. The first one caused relatively minor damage and 84 deaths in Orissa and Andhra Pradesh between October 17 and 19. The second cyclone, by contrast, brought wind speeds of up to 350 km/h, massive rainfall, and tidal surges as high as seven meters from October 28 to 30. Described by local inhabitants as the worst storm they had ever experienced, the cyclone resulted in 9,843 fatalities and economic damage of US$2.5 billion. The mostly agricultural livelihoods of the region were devastated; entire harvests, up to half of all cattle, and tree plantations vital for local livelihoods were lost. Damage to infrastructure, commercial facilities, and fishing equipment was widespread as well. Poor hygiene conditions in the immediate aftermath of the storms caused outbreaks of diseases—in particular, cholera (BBC News 1999).

The coastal areas of Orissa suffered the brunt of the cyclone, but considerable destruction was observed up to 60 kilometers landward as well as in northern Andhra Pradesh. The government of Orissa was criticized for launching insufficient early warnings, not providing enough shelters, and acting too slow regarding relief provision and infrastructure reconstruction (Dash 2002). Andhra Pradesh, by contrast, performed these tasks relatively effectively (and could even provide relief to Orissa). Considerable international and particularly national aid was provided to Orissa, but its impact was limited by corruption, a lack of coordination, and the inaccessibility of many areas (K. Das 2002; Panigrahi 2003; Thomalla and Schmuck 2004; UN OCHA 2000).

The intensity of the PWG insurgency increased slightly after the cyclone. While the previous 12-month period saw 95 battle deaths, this number rose to 111 in the subsequent year. This increase was caused by combatant as well as civilian deaths and falls short of passing the significance threshold (five standard deviations) established earlier. One reason for the rising number of casualties might be the increasing cooperation between the different Naxalite groups, as the PWG merged with the Party Unity in 1998

---

11. The Indian military is not directly involved in the Naxalite conflict.

and also started negotiating with the Maoist Communist Centre (MCC) in the late 1990s[12] (Kujur 2008; Ramana 2006). The PWG's capability to fight the government also increased owing to the formation of local armed units in areas controlled by the group (Scanlon 2018).

That said, the cyclone also played a role in escalating the conflict. While the most disaster-affected district of Jagatsinghpur saw no conflict events during the relevant time period, the PWG was active in areas that experienced large-scale destruction in southern and eastern Orissa as well as in northern Andhra Pradesh (Mohanty 2010). The PWG "primarily survives on poverty, disparity and discontent among the masses" (Dubey 2013: 2) to recruit fighters and followers (Mehra 2000), and the cyclone had a major impact on rural livelihoods in a region that was already among the poorest in India. More than three years after the storm, many areas were economically worse off than before the cyclone struck, particularly in the agricultural sector (Pareeda 2002). In line with this, Kishore Gawande and colleagues (2017) find that land productivity shocks in agricultural areas tend to increase Naxalite conflict intensity (see also Eynde 2018). Furthermore, as a consequence of the cyclone, "food security of many households was severely endangered" (K. Das 2002: 4785). Statistical studies indicate that reduced food production (and hence food insecurity) increases conflict intensity in India by enabling rebel groups to recruit new followers (Wischnath and Buhaug 2014).

The post-disaster situation provided further opportunities to the PWG to escalate the conflict. Considerable national and international aid flows entered the affected regions, and Naxalite groups developed schemes to appropriate such funds by founding or infiltrating NGOs (Mahadevan 2012). Although such practices were widespread, there is no concrete evidence that this happened with cyclone-related funds. In addition, riots and looting (undertaken mostly by desperate survivors) occurred in the first few weeks after the disaster, requiring the deployment of additional police and military personnel (BBC News 1999; Jayasekera 1999). This provided the insurgents with additional room for maneuver. These opportunities diminished over time, and correspondingly, the increase in conflict intensity is limited to the first six months after the disaster (see figure 3.2). Solidarity and cooperation across socio-economic (including caste) divides, by

---

12. The PWG and the MCC eventually merged in 2004.

contrast, occurred in some local instances but had no impact on the wider conflict dynamics (Pareeda 2002). Rather, the PWG was able to exploit opportunities related to recruitment, pre-occupation of security forces, and possibly financing, enabling it to escalate the conflict with the government.

India (Assam) 1998: Floods, Recruitment Opportunities, and Conflict Persistence

The emergence of the United Liberation Front of Assam (ULFA), founded in 1979, is closely tied to the Assam movement, which demanded the expulsion of non-indigenous groups from the federal state of Assam between 1979 and 1985 (and vanished afterward). However, unlike the Assam movement, the ULFA sought to unite people with different ethnic backgrounds living in Assam to gain independence, or at least autonomy from India (Baruah 2012). The group heavily criticized the centralized political decision making, the indifference of the Indian state toward development problems in Assam, and the unfair exploitation of the state's natural resources (in particular, oil, timber, and tea). Initially, the ULFA enjoyed broad public support, was able to generate income through local taxes and extortions (Bhaumik 2009: 252–258), had good relations with the Assam Gana Parishad (AGP) government in the state, and received weapons and training from other armed groups[13] as well as from the Pakistani Inter-Services Intelligence (ISI). The rebels grew to formidable strength. Reacting to this threat, the Indian government (supported by a newly elected state government) ordered several military offensives against the ULFA between 1990 and 1992 but was unable to quell the unrest.[14] The ULFA also shifted some of their bases to neighboring Bangladesh and Bhutan, making it harder for the Indian state to target them (Kotwal 2001).

However, a combination of intense military pressure, a reduction in public support due to atrocities committed, and high incentives set by the Indian government triggered the surrender of a significant number of ULFA cadres to the government from the mid-1990s onward. By March 1997, more than 5,000 fighters had left the group. The resulting Surrendered ULFA (SULFA) organization provided information to the military and

---

13. Notably, the Nationalist Socialist Council of Nagaland and the Kachin Independence Army.
14. Talks between ULFA leaders and the Indian government also took place in 1992 but yielded no results.

sometimes even engaged in battles with the ULFA. After a failed assassination attempt on AGP chief minister Prafulla Mahanta in 1997, government violence against the ULFA escalated (Mahanta 2013). Starting in 1996, and intensifying in 1998, multiple disappearances and direct killings of ULFA members or supporters and their relatives occurred (Baruah 2007; A. Dutta 2014; Saikia 2015).[15]

In August 1998, Assam experienced an extreme flood event that affected all districts of the state (Avinash 2014; D. Das 2014). The Brahmaputra, one of the world's largest rivers, flows through the state and swells during the monsoon season. As a result, a degree of flooding occurs every year in Assam, and the local population has generally adapted to this. However, the 1998 floods were the worst in decades. Several embankments of the Brahmaputra broke, leading to sustained destruction of agricultural land due to the deposit of river sediment. Authorities failed to issue an early warning. The floods resulted in 1,811 deaths, the destruction of at least 5,500 hectares of fertile land, and the need to resettle several villages, hence severely affecting the economic development of the already poor region (Goyari 2005; Kipgen and Pegu 2018; Varma and Mishra 2017). As Assam is a peripheral state and floods occur rather frequently, support for the flood victims by the Indian state and the international community was limited (Mukhim 2014).

On first view, the flood seems to have had little impact on the conflict dynamics as the number of battle-related deaths in the 12 months before and after the floods remains constant (71). However, qualitative evidence suggests that the flood played a minor role in preventing a de-escalation of the conflict, hence shaping its intensity. The ULFA faced a more organized Indian state in the late 1990s with a unified command structure (integrating police and military forces) and had lost the support of the AGP state government. At the same time, popular support for the rebels declined owing to several assassinations conducted by the ULFA, a large number of fighters surrendered, and the targeted killings took a further toll (Baruah 2007; Mahanta 2013). Why, then, was the ULFA able to sustain its armed activities at a similar level?

The 1998 floods facilitated the ULFA's recruitment of new followers and fighters in two ways. First, it increased grievances. Improper flood control characterized by corruption and top-down solutions as well as insufficient

---

15. It is suspected that SULFA members, acting with permission of the government, were behind these killings.

compensation for flood victims (especially if they had no land titles) had fueled sentiments of neglect against the Indian state for quite a while, and the 1998 floods further strengthened this perception (Gohain 2007; Varma and Mishra 2017). The ULFA, by contrast, gained local sympathies by supporting the construction of embankments and dikes (Baruah 2007; U. Dutta 2008). Second, the ULFA recruited mostly poor or unemployed (yet educated) youths, among others, by offering a monthly salary of 1,500–2,000 rupees.[16] The 1998 floods had a remarkable impact on poverty and unemployment rates (Hrishikeshan 2003; Kotwal 2001), hence increasing the pool of potential recruits. In the words of Partha Das and colleagues (2009: 22), there was a "growing frustration and unrest in the youth from flood-affected families. There are instances of unemployment, impoverishment, and grievances against bad governance leading some youths to join insurgent groups: such groups try to recruit young men and women from poor families."

The ULFA also profited financially from taxing—and in some cases even being involved in—companies building embankments after floods (Mukhim 2014).[17] But while demand for such embankments grew after the 1998 floods, this revenue source remained marginal overall for the ULFA (Bhaumik 2009). That said, the ULFA still benefited considerably from improved recruitment opportunities.

Philippines 1990: Earthquake-Related Opportunities for Both Sides

The Communist Party of the Philippines (CPP) was founded in 1968 in Central Luzon. It split from the Philippine Communist Party, which had carried the armed, pro-land-reform Huk movement during the 1950s (but was defeated militarily by the government). The Maoist CPP formed an armed wing, the New People's Army (NPA), in 1969.[18] Initially a rather small group, the NPA was successful in recruiting students in urban areas and particularly inhabitants of poor, rural regions characterized by inequality and corruption. The CPP's demand for land reform was particularly appealing to the latter. When the government of President Ferdinand Marcos declared a state of emergency in 1972, support for the CPP and NPA increased further.

16. Equivalent to US$35–50 in October 1998.
17. Activist Sanjoy Ghose, who campaigned for community-based solutions rather than embankments constructed by companies, was killed by the ULFA, causing a public outcry in Assam.
18. It also established an umbrella for supporting mass organizations like unions in 1973: the National Democratic Front of the Philippines.

The NPA reached its heyday in the mid-1980s, when its ranks were filled with well-educated students, and it could draw on wide support networks in rural areas for its guerrilla warfare. At the same time, the state had to cope with a deteriorating economy and was fighting on two fronts: against the CPP/NPA insurgents and against separatist groups in Mindanao (Santos and Santos 2010b).

The situation changed when the CPP refused to participate in the snap elections of 1985 and the subsequent protests against election fraud, which resulted in the ousting of Marcos in 1986. New president Corazon Aquino started peace negotiations with the rebels, but when those failed in 1987, she declared a total war against the Communists. The NPA quickly lost ground: between 1987 and 1991, its fighters were decimated from 25,200 to 14,800 (P. Santos 2010). Reasons for the success of the government troops include a series of internal NPA purges to identify government agents, a change to more effective military strategies involving fewer human rights violations by the Philippine army, the possibility to articulate grievances non-violently after the regime change in 1986, and some agrarian reform efforts (Marks 1993; P. Santos 2010; S. Santos 2005; Timberman 1991). The emergence of local militias—called Citizens Armed Forces Geographical Units (CAFGUs)—supported by the army since 1987 further weakened the NPA in rural areas (de Guzman and Craige 1991).

On July 16, 1990, a 7.8-magnitude earthquake struck the island of Luzon, which at the time was still a CPP/NPA stronghold. It caused 2,412 deaths and resulted in total economic costs equivalent to US$1.5 billion (Booth et al. 1991). While the capital city of Manila suffered some damage, the area north of it around the cities of Baguio, Dagupan, Cabanatuan, and San Jose was most heavily affected. Analysts described the government response to the disaster as "disorganized, uncoordinated, slow, inadequate, unprepared, and ill-equipped" (Tayag and Insauriga 1993: 377). This was partly due to road damage that had cut off routes to many of the heavily hit regions (Casis 2008; Quinn 1991). Local communities, NGOs, and parts of the Philippine military stepped in to fill the void left by the insufficient government response (Bankoff 2004; Cola 2003). Despite coordination problems and with some delay, these relief works proceeded relatively well.

Nevertheless, the poorer inhabitants of Luzon suffered substantial medium- to long-term negative effects (Benson 1997; Cola 2003). Only

6% of the residents whose houses were damaged received repair assistance (Tayag and Insauriga 1993). Furthermore, the earthquake affected agricultural land and irrigation structures, which had a substantial effect on food production. This combined with the destruction of the transportation, mining, and manufacturing infrastructures put an additional toll on the Philippine economy, which already suffered from high foreign debt, price declines of export goods, and a lack of investor confidence (Timberman 1991). At least in Luzon, "people who barely noticed the seismic event have felt their standard of living decline in its aftermath. The earthquake has increased food prices, unemployment and pressure on the national balance of payments" (Booth et al. 1991: 87).

After the earthquake, the NPA declared a unilateral cease-fire to allow for relief and rehabilitation (Lane 1991). However, the government did not declare a cease-fire in response, and eventually the NPA broke the cease-fire (de Guzman and Craige 1991). Both sides escalated the conflict considerably after the earthquake. Countrywide, the numbers of battle-related deaths increased from 991 in the 12 months before the disaster to 1,691 afterward. The increase is even more remarkable in the most heavily affected central and northern parts of Luzon,[19] which witnessed an increase from 84 to 301 deaths. The clear majority of casualties was combatants.

There is evidence that this increase in conflict intensity can be attributed to improved opportunity structures for the NPA and the Philippine army. The Philippine military struggled with providing disaster relief to a large area with crucial transportation infrastructure damage (Hall 2004). Together with the very limited state access to certain (especially remote rural) regions, this allowed the weakened NPA to extend its sphere of influence. Furthermore, the earthquake further deteriorated the already dire economic situation, hence creating additional recruitment opportunities. In particular, the NPA recruited heavily from the rural poor. "For many of them, there [was] no other alternative to survive or get away from economic deprivation" (S. Santos 2005: 21), particularly in the context of the economic hardship caused by the earthquake. Several NGOs and faith-based organizations, many of which were among the first providers of disaster relief, have a history of supporting CPP and NPA recruitment (usually indirectly by promoting pro-rebel discourses) (Eastin 2017).

19. Specifically, the provinces of Cagayan Valley, Central Luzon, Cordillera Administrative Region, and Ilocos Region.

On the side of the Philippine government, the CAFGUs gained military importance since the late 1980s and numbered around 70,000 persons in 1990. Like the NPA, the Philippine army recruited many CAFGU members from poor, rural groups. With few livelihood alternatives available, especially in a post-disaster landscape, benefits like a regular paycheck, educational programs, and health insurance were very attractive (de Guzman and Craige 1991). This is corroborated by a recent study finding that after high-impact disasters and bad harvests, people are more likely to join the CAFGU (Eastin and Zech 2022). Further supporting the recruitment argument, there is statistical evidence that lower rice harvests increase civil war intensity in the Philippines (Eastin 2018), and the earthquake reduced rice production in central and northern Luzon (Booth et al. 1991).

Joshua Eastin (2017, 2018) also finds that disasters provide opportunities for the Philippine military to gather information in the affected areas during relief and reconstruction measures. In the case of the Luzon earthquake, the military was indeed heavily involved in relief operations, and the UCDP-GED records several attacks of government troops on rebel hideouts in the subsequent year. There is no direct evidence, however, for a relationship between post-disaster assistance, intelligence gathering during the disaster response, and more targeted attacks in the aftermath of the Luzon earthquake.

Communication-based explanations are unlikely in this case because (1) the declining strength of the CPP/NPA was obvious, and (2) both conflict parties only infrequently attacked easy targets like civilians. In addition, (3) a spike in conflict intensity is visible only six months after the disaster, which is very late to use violence to send a message, but sufficiently long to translate information, recruitment, and territorial gains into fighting capability. Grievances may have played a role as well—for example, by boosting the rebels' rank with earthquake survivors frustrated with the government response. The latter was delayed and corruption-ridden (Tayag and Insauriga 1993)—a point the CPP also highlighted prominently in its outreach (Liwanag 1991). However, with disasters partially conceived as acts of God (Bankoff 2004), some external aid flowing to Luzon, and no reports of major protests against the government's disaster response, the opportunity pathway is far more plausible for the government-CPP/NPA conflict after the Luzon earthquake.

Sri Lanka 2004: Wave of Violence?

Sri Lanka gained independence from Great Britain in 1948. The new state was home to a majority Sinhalese, Buddhist population (74%) as well as several minorities, the largest being the Hindu Tamils (18%).[20] From independence onward, Tamils expressed concerns about their marginalization by Sinhalese political elites. The new state indeed prioritized pro-Sinhalese politics, thus also significantly reducing the number of Tamils in professional, administrative, and military jobs as well as in higher education institutions. Neoliberal policies from the 1970s onward increased existing economic inequalities. In 1956, Sinhala became the official language of the state, and in 1972, Buddhism became the quasi-official religion, hence further increasing tensions. In 1976, the Liberation Tigers of Tamil Eelam (LTTE) emerged to pursue an independent state of Tamil Eelam in northeastern Sri Lanka through military means. Following ethnic riots in 1983, the conflict escalated into a full-blown civil war (Goodhand 2001).

With initial support from India and from (forced or voluntary) diaspora contributions since the 1990s, the LTTE quickly emerged as a highly sophisticated rebel army (Beardsley and McQuinn 2009; van de Voorde 2005). The Sri Lanka military also greatly increased its forces and provided support to paramilitary groups. Grievances in the Tamil areas remained high, owing to issues of economic disparities and ethnic discrimination, among others. Intense fighting continued until 2000, with several interruptions during (ultimately unsuccessful) negotiations.[21] Prospects for a peace process increased in the early 2000s, with both sides showing a willingness to negotiate. A cease-fire agreement was concluded in February 2002, and peace talks started seven months later. However, the process stalled because of internal rifts within the LTTE,[22] the election of hardliner Mahinda Rajapakse as Sri Lankan prime minister in April 2004, and a stockpiling of arms by both sides during the negotiations (Goodhand and Klem 2005; Nieto 2008).

In the middle of this tense situation, a massive tsunami triggered by a 9.3-magnitude earthquake in the Indian Ocean hit Sri Lanka on December

---

20. There is also a significant and frequently marginalized Muslim population, but I do not discuss this group here.
21. Negotiations took place in 1985, 1987, 1989–1990, and 1994–1995.
22. The Tamil Makkal Viduthalai Perani, led by Colonel Karuna, separated from the LTTE in March 2004, resulting in fights between the groups.

26, 2004. Waves up to 10 meters high devastated two-thirds of the country's coastline, leaving more than 35,000 people dead and producing total economic damage of US$1.4 billion. The disaster affected the northern and eastern parts of the country—the heartland of the LTTE—most severely. This is to some extent due to the civil war, which increased the vulnerability of communities to the tsunami. Compared with the LTTE, which provided immediate emergency relief in the areas it controlled, the government was initially slow to respond to the disaster. However, Sri Lanka's health system was well prepared for the disaster. Local solidarity networks (across political divides) as well as the arrival of unprecedented amounts of international aid workers and funds quickly eased the situation (Yamada et al. 2006). Overall, the emergency relief phase is "widely considered a remarkable success" (Athukorala 2012: 221).

Despite enormous international financial contributions of more than US$3.5 billion, the reconstruction phase was not implemented smoothly. Reasons for this include a lack of coordination between government agencies and international donors, the implementation of measures that were insensitive to the local context (Korf et al. 2010; Rajasingham-Senanayake 2009), and the slow delivery of the financial aid commitment by the international community (Athukorala 2012; Haigh et al. 2016). Disputes between the government and the LTTE about who could distribute aid in the LTTE-controlled areas in the northeast further aggravated the situation (Silva 2009). As a result, discontent about the reconstruction process was widespread. This controversy exacerbated the already deeply rooted ethnic divisions and resentment against the government, in particular in northeastern Sri Lanka (de Silva 2009; Yamada et al. 2006).

The conflict between the government of Sri Lanka and the LTTE escalated significantly in the year after the tsunami. Battle-related deaths increased to 98, up from 24 in the 12 months prior to the disaster, with a particularly sharp spike in December 2005 (64 deaths). "By the time the tsunami struck, the talks in Sri Lanka had already collapsed, and preparations for war were already underway" (Tunçer-Kılavuz 2019: 723). Even before the disaster, tensions were high as neither side was ready for political compromise. But the tsunami facilitated the path toward conflict escalation.

Grievances are an important part of the story here. The LTTE insisted on distributing tsunami aid in the areas it controlled, while the government claimed responsibility for the disaster response in all parts of Sri Lanka

(Uyangoda 2005). After a six-month negotiation process that undermined trust on both sides, the conflict parties agreed on a joint Post-Tsunami Operational Management Structure (P-TOMS) to distribute aid (Goodhand and Klem 2005). Weeks later, the Supreme Court suspended P-TOMS, ruling it unconstitutional; this further intensified grievances and mistrust, particularly among the LTTE (Le Billon and Waizenegger 2007). Likewise, the resulting delay (and in some cases, lack) of reconstruction funds aggravated popular resentment against the government in the northeastern parts of the country. In the Sinhalese-dominated areas, by contrast, perceptions about preferential treatment of the northeastern, conflict-ridden regions also fueled discontent (Enia 2008; Klitzsch 2014). Thus, the tsunami contributed to grievances among political elites and popular constituents on both sides.

The communicative aspect of violence played a role as well. The LTTE suffered from an internal split in March 2004, and the government believed the rebels had been considerably weakened by the tsunami. As a result, the LTTE staged several attacks over the course of 2005 to show its continued military and political relevance (Le Billon and Waizenegger 2007; Uyangoda 2005). Similarly, the government lost a major coalition partner over its agreement to P-TOMS, and important political parties[23] accused the LTTE of re-arming in the post-disaster period (Enia 2008; Tunçer-Kılavuz 2019). This increased the pressure on newly elected hardliner president Mahinda Rajapakse to take a tough, military stand toward the rebels.

The opportunity pathway was less relevant in this case. The tsunami undermined the capacity of both sides to go to war temporarily. This potentially explains the absence of conflict escalation in the first months after the disaster. However, both sides were still strong enough to engage in violent confrontations (Uyangoda 2005). Kyosuke Kikuta (2019) finds that higher housing reconstruction rates after the tsunami are positively related to more violence from 2006 to 2009, suggesting aid appropriation for military purposes as a potential mechanism. But overall, international aid had a limited effect on both sides' fighting capabilities and had a greater influence on determining where rather than when attacks took place (Goodhand and Klem 2005). In sum, the 2004 tsunami facilitated an escalation of the government-LTTE conflict in Sri Lanka, mostly through the grievances pathway, but also through the costly signal pathway.

23. For example, the People's Alliance and the People's Liberation Front.

Tajikistan 1992: Independence, Civil War, and Floods
When Tajikistan became an independent state in September 1991, three struggles overlapped and erupted into open political (and later armed) conflict. First, a coalition of liberal democratic and Islamist parties[24] that had formed during the Gorbachev period in the Soviet Union opposed the continued political dominance of the old Communist elites in Tajikistan. This opposition movement later became known as the United Tajik Opposition (UTO), the principal opponent of the government in the civil war. Second, and relatedly, the Communist elites rejected emerging claims for more Tajik (ethnic) nationalism voiced by the opposition. These claims were also perceived as a threat by the Uzbek (around 24% of the total population) and Russian (around 7%) minorities (Atkin 1997).

Third, long-standing clan and regional rivalries became salient. Tensions were particularly significant between groups from the Leninabadi[25] and Kulyab regions (from which elites in the Soviet era were recruited and which formed the backbone of the Communist Party) and inhabitants of the Gorno-Badakhshan and Garn regions (which, largely excluded from political power, predominantly supported opposition parties). After the escalation into a civil war, political elites linked regional identities to ethnic identities in their rhetoric, resulting in several massacres along these lines (Gretsky 1995; Rubin 1994).

The election of Rakhmon Nabiyev of the Communist Party to the presidency in November 1991 fueled discontent by the opposition parties, which did not accept the results. When Nabiyev claimed emergency powers in April 1992 and increased repression of the opposition, the latter staged a series of protests in the capital city Dushanbe. The situation escalated into violent protests and skirmishes not only in Dushanbe but also in other parts of the country in May 1992. Despite various rounds of negotiations and the temporary formation of a coalition government between the Communist Party and the UTO, violence between rebels and pro-government militias (such as the Popular Front) quickly escalated in 1992 and 1993 (Tunçer-Kılavuz 2011). Initially, the UTO was rather successful owing to

---

24. The most important ones were the Islamic Rebirth Party, the Democratic Party of Tajikistan, the nationalist Rastokhez coalition, and the regionalist Lali Badakhshon party.
25. Also known as Khujant.

its regional support, good organizational basis, and weapon supplies from Afghanistan. However, the tide turned when Uzbekistan and Russia decided to support the Tajik government in late 1992 (Lynch 2001; Rubin 1994).

During the height of political turbulence and contestation in mid-May 1992, constant and heavy rainfall triggered the most severe floods in the history of the country. The floods left more than 1,300 people dead and caused around US$500 million of direct damage (World Bank and GFDRR 2016). The follow-up economic costs were enormous owing to the destruction of infrastructure, agricultural land, and irrigation systems, with an estimated GDP loss of up to 90%. The disaster affected the areas along the Yakhsu River (especially north of Kulob) as well as along the Kyzylsu and Vakhsh Rivers (especially the Kus-Abad area south of Dushanbe) most heavily (Brilliant et al. 1992: 54; CAREC 2006).

While the groups had previously engaged in minor quarrels,[26] the Tajik civil war erupted in May 1992 (with 75 battle-related deaths) and remained intense in the year after the flood (with an average of 303 deaths per month). The floods were not a contributing factor to the onset of the civil war. The main fighting activities had already started in Dushanbe several days before the floods struck. Further, the factors that fueled the escalation of tensions were not flood-related, such as competition for political power as well as regional and ethnic grievances (Tunçer-Kılavuz 2011). There are also no reports about unfair aid distribution or significant strains on the (already weak) state after the floods (Ghasimi 1994).

By contrast, it is very likely that the floods influenced the intensity of the conflict, as the event created opportunities for UTO recruitment. After the collapse of the Soviet Union, Tajikistan was very poor and strongly dependent on agriculture (Foroughi 2002), with subsistence agriculture being an important means to sustain livelihoods (Lynch 2001). The flood had a strong negative impact on agriculture, particularly in the relatively densely populated southwest of the country, making the recruitment of deprived individuals by armed groups easier. Location- and region-specific patronage networks facilitated the recruitment of impoverished people (Tunçer-Kılavuz 2011). In line with this, a substantial part of the fighting in the 12 months after the floods took place in or very close to the disaster-affected regions, in particular along the Vaksh and Kyzylsu Rivers, in and

26. The UCDP does not record these events, however.

around Dushanbe, and south of Kulob. Major support for the opposition came from the Garn region, which was also strongly affected by the floods along the Kyzylsu River (Ghasimi 1994). The flood facilitated the recruitment of deprived individuals (particularly by the rebels), hence being one (but not the most important) driver of conflict escalation.

Uganda 1999–2001: Drought, Food Insecurity, and Raids

The conflict in Uganda's north emerged from political competition between several southern groups (particularly the Buganda tribe) and the Acholi people in the north. From 1980 onward, the National Resistance Army (NRA) violently contested the ruling government, which enjoyed support from the Acholi. In 1986, the NRA, which represented the interests of groups in southern Uganda, was able to oust President Tito Okello. Yoweri Museveni became the new head of the Ugandan state. Parts of the former national army regrouped as the Uganda People's Democratic Army (UPDA) in the Acholi homelands but signed a peace agreement with the government in 1988. Another Acholi group resisting Museveni's rule out of fears of political-economic marginalization and revenge killings, the Holy Spirit Movement (HSM), was defeated militarily in 1987. Subsequently, Joseph Kony formed the Lord's Resistance Army (LRA) from the remainders of the UPDA and HSM.[27] The LRA integrated various groups keen to defend Christianity, to promote Acholi spiritualism, and to overthrow the Musevini regime (Kisekka-Ntale 2007; van Acker 2004).

Despite very limited local support (which further declined over time owing to the LRA's extensive violence against Acholi civilians), the LRA managed to hold its own against the NRA.[28] During the 1990s, its strength grew considerably because of support from Sudan, mostly in the form of weapons and safe havens beyond the Ugandan borders (Faulkner 2016).[29] The LRA further increased its ranks by large-scale forced recruitment, particularly of children (Haer et al. 2011). Peace negotiations in 1993 and 1994 failed to end the conflict, as did efforts by the NRA to confine the Acholi population in northern Uganda to camps, to set up self-defense militia,

27. The LRA was previously known as the Liberation Army (1987–1988) and the Uganda People's Democratic Christian Army (1988–1992).
28. The NRA became Uganda's national army after the successful 1986 coup. In 1995, it changed its name to the Uganda Peoples' Defence Force.
29. The LRA was mostly active in the Gulu, Kitgum, and Pader districts of Uganda.

and to win the conflict through large-scale offensives in 1991 and 1997 (Branch 2005; van Wyk 2017; Vinci 2007). Corruption, a lack of competence, and vested interests in the NRA prevented military success against the LRA (Espeland and Petersen 2010; Feldman 2008).

With the LRA conflict ongoing, a severe drought shattered Uganda's north in the late 1990s. While the exact start and end dates are hard to delineate, August 1999 through July 2001 is a solid estimate for the period during which drought conditions prevailed on the ground.[30] The drought affected the Karamoja region in northeastern Uganda most severely, but the Acholi regions also experienced considerable impacts, including harvest loss and food price increases of up to 100% (ACT 1999). The drought undermined the livelihoods of at least 300,000 people, rendered more than 200,000 food insecure, and caused 115 fatalities.

Besides the combination of high temperatures and low precipitation, the immense vulnerability of northern Uganda explains these severe impacts: years of armed violence between the NRA and the LRA as well as intense communal conflict destroyed the agricultural systems of the already poor region (WFP 2004).[31] The situation was further aggravated by a large number of internally displaced people (IDP), insufficient infrastructure, and a dependence on an almost completely agricultural economy. International aid was rather low when compared with amounts provided for similar disasters, and the government was both unable and unwilling to conduct large-scale relief operations (ACT 2003; Adams 2002; van Acker 2004). On the national level, the drought had moderate economic impacts because it was mostly confined to the peripheral northern regions (MFPED 2001; MWLE 2002).

In the aftermath of this disaster, Uganda experienced a slight escalation in conflict intensity. The trend is remarkable, yet below the five standard deviations threshold for military fatalities, which increased from 140 during the pre-drought year to 317 in the 12 months after the drought. However,

---

30. EM-DAT provides a start date (August 1999) but only an end year for the drought (2001). According to the Weighted Anomaly Standardized Precipitation (WASP) index (IRI 2011) used by EM-DAT (Below et al. 2007), May 2001 was the last month that saw drought conditions in some areas of northern Uganda. Precipitation was above average in July 2001 and afterward; no major droughts were reported for the rest of the year.
31. In the Kitgum district, for example, the cattle population declined from 156,667 in 1986 to 3,239 in 1998, while country-wide, cattle stocks grew significantly during the same period (van Acker 2004: 343).

the increase in civilian deaths, which went from 40 to 171, is significant and attacks by the LRA largely account for this rise.[32]

The slight rise in military fatalities can hardly be attributed to the drought. The disaster did not affect the fighting capability of the NRA. To the contrary, the government troops launched Operation Iron Fist in March 2002, confronting the LRA in northern Uganda and (in the context of improved relations between the Sudanese and the Ugandan government) in southern Sudan. LRA groups reacted by retreating from southern Sudan and moving to the Acholi and Karamoja regions in Uganda, hence increasing violent confrontations there (Dunn 2004; Espeland and Petersen 2010).

By contrast, there is ample evidence that from the early 2000s onward, the LRA increased attacks on villages, humanitarian convoys, and IDP camps to loot food (UNSCN 2003). While looting was always an important source of income, the loss of its bases in Sudan as well as the drought (and the associated food scarcity) increased the LRA's dependence on such attacks (Vinci 2007). This is well in line with an increase of international food aid during and in the immediate aftermath of the drought (WFP 2004), and with reports about the LRA's inability to secure proper food supplies for its members during this time period (Bevan 2008; Haer et al. 2011). In other words, the strategic environment the LRA faced in the wake of Operation Iron Fist and the drought required the utilization of additional sources of food. The LRA thus resorted to increased levels of violence against civilians to extract food and other resources from the local population, refugee camps, and (drought-related) humanitarian relief operations.

Cases of Conflict De-escalation after Disasters

Bangladesh 2007: Cyclone Sidr and the Maoist Insurgency

In 1968, the Purbo Banglar Communist Party (PBCP) split from the Communist Party of Bangladesh because of the former's commitment to Maoism and to illegal/violent methods. The group conducted several attacks throughout the 1970s, 1980s, and 1990s, but overall it remained fairly limited in its activities. Its financial and organizational bases were weak, because Maoism in Bangladesh remained highly fractionalized with a larger

---

32. In fact, violence against civilians by NRA forces declined, although data availability is very limited in this regard.

number of competing groups (Amin 1985). From the early 2000s onward, the struggle between the Communist rebels and the government intensified for two reasons. First, in 2001, several hundred surrendered PBCP fighters and cadres were released from prison, many of whom were still committed to armed struggle. Second, the Janajuddha Faction (PBCP-J) splintered from the PBCP in 2003 and decided to intensify armed conflict activities, as well as become the dominant Maoist group in the country (South Asia Terrorism Portal 2018). As a result, the number of guerrilla attacks and clashes with the Bangladeshi army increased in various parts of the country.

On November 15, 2007, Cyclone Sidr made landfall in southwestern Bangladesh. While its strength was similar to that of Cyclone Gorky in 1991 (see the case study "Bangladesh 1991: The Chittagong Hill Conflict after Cyclone Gorky" later in this chapter), improved evacuation procedures and shelter availability along with other factors[33] greatly reduced the death toll. Nevertheless, Sidr caused enormous damage and left more than 4,000 people dead,[34] along with economic damage of around US$1.7 billion (Paul 2009). Poor people were disproportionately affected as the storm struck economically less developed parts of the country. The sub-standard buildings inhabited by poorer families could not withstand the storm. Further, there is documented evidence of unequal distribution of reconstruction funds in favor of wealthier households (Nadiruzzaman and Wrathall 2015). Similarly, Rabiul Islam and Greg Walkerden (2014: 287) find that in the immediate post-disaster period, "60% of households exchanged mutual support with neighbours and friends." But in the months after the disaster, solidarity vanished and conflicts over access to relief occurred.

When comparing the one-year periods before and after Cyclone Sidr, there is a small yet remarkable decline in both the frequency (11 down from 17 incidents) and the intensity (11 down from 22 deaths) of encounters between the PBCP-J and government forces. Civilians play no role in this dynamic, as not a single death of a non-combatant is reported for the 25 months under study. This de-escalation of the conflict coincided with a general decline in political violence in Bangladesh as a temporary, non-partisan

33. Sidr struck less populated and physically less exposed areas during a period of relatively low tides. It also did not last as long as Gorky.
34. I use the EM-DAT estimate here, whereas government data state a death toll of 3,406.

caretaker government took power to prepare the next elections and banned most political activities. However, this cannot account for a de-escalation of the conflict between the PBCP-J and the government. This is because the caretaker government assumed power more than 11 months prior to the cyclone and its ban mostly affected violence related to elections and competition between political parties, rather than the insurgency-style violence of the PBCP-J (Suykens and Islam 2015).

Explanations based on the solidarity pathway or constraints on rebel groups also cannot account for the reduction of violence after the disaster. As discussed above, initial solidarity among cyclone victims vanished quickly and community relations even turned contentious over relief distribution (Islam and Walkerden 2014). Also, while some core areas of the PBCP-J in southwestern Bangladesh were among the most severely affected districts,[35] violent encounters also took place much farther north (Haque and Jahan 2016). The PBCP-J's connections to the local population were too weak and its operational presence in the region too insignificant for Sidr to affect its fighting motives or capabilities (South Asia Terrorism Portal 2018). Relatedly, the Maoist insurgents could not capitalize on the reinforced socio-economic grievances and class cleavages after the cyclone.

A plausible explanation for the de-escalation of the conflict is strategic constraints on the government forces, and particularly on the police units responsible for fighting the PBCP-J, like the notorious Rapid Action Battalion (RAB). Access to and intelligence gathering in the worst affected regions (several of which hosted PBCP-J cells) were limited after the cyclone. Further, the Bangladesh government deployed more than 40,000 personnel to the affected area, including police and military units (IFRC 2007a). There are no reports of units like the RAB taking part in this operation, but the latter frequently supported or substituted for regular police units. Therefore, the capabilities of the police to hunt down and engage with Maoist rebels certainly declined in the wake of Sidr. This was especially the case as additional capabilities were already required to enforce the ban of political actions introduced by the caretaker government. According to the UCDP dataset, the conflict de-escalation pattern is also mainly driven by a decline in police raids against the PBCP-J. Available evidence therefore

35. In particular Bagerhat, Khulna, Pirojpur, and Satkhira.

indicates that a temporal reduction in government strength and capability caused by the cyclone was a major cause of the conflict de-escalation.

Burundi 2005–2006: Drought, Democratization, and the Peace Process

Following Burundi's independence in 1962, struggles between the Hutu and Tutsi population groups were a key component of Burundian politics.[36] While the majority of the population was Hutu,[37] the Tutsi dominated the government and the military. In 1972, Hutu groups launched an invasion from neighboring Tanzania, leading to a violent backlash by the Tutsi elite and the deaths of between 100,000 and 200,000 Hutu. This consolidated the political and military dominance of the Tutsi. Several pro-Hutu parties emerged in the subsequent years, often having their bases in neighboring countries to which many Tutsi fled after the 1972 massacre. Among these was the Party for the Liberation of Hutu People (PALIPEHUTU), which emerged in 1980 in a refugee camp in Tanzania and established its armed wing, the National Liberation Forces (FNL), in 1985. The return to democracy through elections in 1993, a coup attempt in the same year, and the assassinations of prominent Hutu politicians sparked a civil war between the Burundian military (dominated by Tutsi and opposing a stronger Hutu influence after the elections), Tutsi militia, and several Hutu rebel groups (Boshoff et al. 2010; Lemarchand 2009; Vandeginste 2009).

Negotiations under external pressure and South African mediation resulted in the 2000 Arusha Agreement, which initiated a process of political transition and peace building in Burundi. Initially not a party to the agreement, the largest Hutu rebel group—the National Council for Defense of Democracy–Forces for the Defense of Democracy (CNDD-FDD)—joined it in 2003 and won the first elections under the new constitution in 2005. The PALIPEHUTU-FNL, by contrast, radicalized and continued its violent struggle against the government and, from 2003 onward, also against the CNDD-FDD (Alfieri 2014). Peace negotiations initiated in January 2004 failed only eight months later (Boshoff et al. 2010; Nimubona et al. 2012; Vandeginste 2009).

36. It is important to avoid primordialist and essentialist assumptions, because ethnic differences were frequently manipulated and instrumentalized in power struggles between political elites in Burundi (Wittig 2016).
37. Today approximately 85% of the population is Hutu, while 14% is Tutsi.

Northeastern Burundi experienced low rainfalls from 2000 onward, and in early 2005 the situation worsened and evolved into a severe drought.[38] While the region was formerly considered the breadbasket of the country, years of armed conflict had taken a significant toll on the agricultural capacity of the northeast, as well as on the assets (e.g., cash and seed reserves) of its population. At the same time, agriculture and pastoralism were the main sources of livelihoods. Disaster vulnerability was thus very high (Baramburiye et al. 2013; IFRC 2007b).

Within months, food security in the region declined sharply, and until mid-2006, around 2.2 million people in Burundi (out of a total population of 7.5 million) required food assistance. The government and international agencies channeled money and food aid to address the drought. But overall, insufficient resources, the ongoing civil war, and the very limited road infrastructure inhibited relief work. As a consequence, at least 120 people died and many more migrated internally or to Tanzania (FAO 2005; IRIN News 2006; The New Humanitarian 2006).[39] The economic damage of the drought is hard to assess, but the World Bank (2018: 37) estimates that the drought led to a decline in Burundi's GDP growth from 4.8% (in 2004) to 0.9% (in 2005). The drought ended in January 2005, but famine conditions persisted until May 2006 (USAID 2006).

Toward the end of the drought, and particularly in its aftermath, the conflict de-escalated significantly. Fighting between the government of Burundi and the PALIPEHUTU-FNL resulted in 590 deaths in the 12 months before the drought but only 106 deaths in the year after the drought, with clear downward trends of both combatant and civilian casualties. These trends are largely driven by wider political developments. Joint initiatives by the Burundian military and the CNDD-FDD had already weakened the PALIPEHUTU-FNL in 2004, and the deployment of 5,000 UN peacekeepers from June 2004 onward further limited the insurgents' room for maneuver (Rodt 2012).[40] The new (Hutu-led) government in power since 2005 also prioritized the negotiated resolution of the PALIPEHUTU-FNL conflict,

---

38. The province of Kirundo was hit the hardest, but a state of emergency or famine was also declared for Muyinga, Cankuzo, Ngozi, and Rutana.

39. The exact numbers of refugees are unknown, but the Red Cross (IFRC 2007b) estimates 15,000 migrants to Tanzania in 2005 alone.

40. The UN peacekeepers replaced a smaller African Union mission active in Burundi since 2003.

resulting in a peace agreement in 2006 (El Abdellaoui 2009). Furthermore, the peace agreements with other armed groups forced the PALIPEHUTU-FNL

> to moderate its position and to enter into negotiations from early 2004 onwards. With the agreed ethnic parity in the defence and security forces and the representation of Hutu at all levels of the state, in particular after the 2005 elections, the movement had lost much of its ideological *raison d'être*. (Vandeginste 2009: 80)

From the information that is available, it is very likely that the drought played a contributing role toward the conflict de-escalation. The political developments between 2000 and 2005 discussed above are certainly the main drivers of the decline in conflict intensity (Alfieri 2016; Boshoff et al. 2010). The regions most affected by the drought in northeastern Burundi do not coincide with the stronghold of the PALIPEHUTU-FNL in 2005 and 2006, the Bujumbura Rurale province in the west of the country (Alfieri 2014; Rodt 2012).

However, the PALIPEHUTU-FNL was active in northern Burundi during the drought (Project Ploughshares 2011), while the drought-induced spike in food prices (up to 100%) affected its strongholds in other parts of the country (FAO 2005). The group was highly reliant on local contributions to fund and staff the insurgency (Alfieri 2016; Wittig 2016), while Burundi's rural population was characterized by poverty, land scarcity, and a strong dependence on agriculture (Baramburiye et al. 2013; Lemarchand 2009). Therefore, the drought affected the PALIPEHUTU-FNL's finances (owing to an impoverishment of the supporting population), ability to recruit members (as locals struggled to secure their livelihoods), and supply lines (because higher food prices made it more expensive to feed troops). Taken together, the drought diminished the group's fighting capability. This is well in line with evidence that reflects an increase in forced recruitment and extortion (as compared with voluntary contributions) during and after the drought (Alfieri 2016).[41]

The significant GDP loss associated with the drought and the necessity to redirect resources to drought aid might also have influenced the CNDD-FDD government's decision to negotiate with the PALIPEHUTU-FNL, thus abandoning its initial preference for a crackdown strategy that

---

41. However, this can also be explained by a reduced ideological attractiveness of the group to its Hutu constituency in the face of the democratization process and the inauguration of a Hutu-led government in 2005.

would have likely resulted in conflict escalation (Wittig 2016). But even if direct evidence of this is missing, the drought still contributed to conflict de-escalation by weakening the PALIPEHUTU-FNL rebels.

India (Kashmir) 2005: Cross-Border Constraints in the Face of an Earthquake

The Kashmir region has been a source of dispute between India and Pakistan from the time both countries partitioned in 1947. Pakistan claims the Indian part of Kashmir (the Jammu and Kashmir state, J&K) as part of its territory, among others, due to the predominantly Muslim population (around 80%). The J&K has remained economically weak, and the special status that was promised by the initial Indian constitution was progressively undermined, leading to local frustration, particularly in the Kashmir valley (a sub-region of the J&K). Local protests against this situation emerged in the 1960s. In the context of rigged state elections in 1987,[42] anti-Indian protests and armed resistance erupted in the J&K. The conflict between the Indian government and various Kashmir insurgent groups quickly escalated into a civil war. With the support of Pakistan and other militant Islamic groups (such as Afghanistan war veterans), the insurgents quickly grew to considerable strength. Religious and pro-Pakistani groups like Hizb-ul-Mujahedeen and Lahkar-e-Toiba gained the upper hand vis-à-vis secular and pro-independence factions.[43] The Indian government's efforts to resolve the conflict through repression were unsuccessful owing to broad Kashmiri and external support for the insurgents (Ganguly 2001; Sharma 2015).

From 2003 onward, the conflict declined in intensity but remained unresolved. Kashmir's population was war-weary at the turn of the millennium given that the insurgents had achieved very little. Disenchantment with external, Pakistani groups was growing because of human rights violations and because most locals favored independence over unification with Pakistan. State elections in 2002 were considered open and fair (Samii 2006). A cease-fire agreement between India and Pakistan in 2003, followed by peace talks in 2004, reduced conflict between both states, and hence Pakistan's

---

42. The elections were rigged by the ruling National Conference party to the disadvantage of political groups more critical of India.
43. Such as the Jammu and Kashmir Liberation Front (JKLF), which suffered heavily from the Indian counterinsurgency and played little role after 1995.

support for the insurgency. Improved Indian control over the border further limited external support for the rebels (Bose 2007: 154–203; Snedden 2013; Staniland 2013).

On October 8, 2005, a 7.8-magnitude earthquake shattered the Kashmir region. The epicenter was located on the Pakistani side of the border, and Pakistan also suffered the brunt of the damage with more than 73,000 deaths and direct economic damage of US$5.2 billion (Halvorson and Hamilton 2010; see also the case study "Pakistan 2005: Escalation after, but Not Related to the Kashmir Earthquake" later in this chapter). Indian Kashmir was heavily affected as well, experiencing 1,309 deaths. Just like the direct economic damage (US$359 million), the "impact of the earthquake on livelihoods has been moderate" (ADB 2006: 39). Livelihoods in the J&K were largely based on self-sufficient agriculture, and at the time the disaster struck, fields had been harvested and animals were out of their barns. Infrastructure destruction was heavy, especially in the health, transportation, and medical sectors. The remote location of and security situation in Indian Kashmir, along with a lack of preparation and (at least initially) coordination, complicated the relief and reconstruction efforts. But overall, disaster-related operations of the Indian military (in conjunction with international supporters) proceeded smoothly, despite local distrust of the Indian armed forces. There were occasional reports of unfair aid distribution along ethnic and political lines (Nabi 2014; Renner and Chafe 2007).

In the aftermath of the earthquake, hopes were high that pragmatic cooperation could enhance Indian-Pakistani reconciliation, which would have most likely diminished the insurgency in the J&K as well. Despite India delivering aid to Pakistan, the re-establishment of cross-border phone lines, and the opening of the border at five posts in Kashmir, the underlying cleavages between India and Pakistan proved too strong to be addressed by disaster diplomacy (Akcinaroglu et al. 2011; Kelman et al. 2018). There was, however, a notable decline in conflict intensity in the J&K, from 1,388 battle-related deaths in the year before the disaster down to 870 deaths in the post-earthquake period.

Part of this de-escalation can certainly be ascribed to a general downward trend in conflict intensity since 2003 that was driven by improved Indian-Pakistani relations, lower local support for the insurgents, and tighter border controls. However, the de-escalation was particularly pronounced in the first six months after the earthquake. There are two plausible pathways connecting the disaster to this trend. First, the Kashmir insurgency was strongly driven by groups with bases across the border in Pakistan. This area was the most affected by the earthquake. Lahkar-e-Toiba, for instance, lost at least 70 fighters during the disaster, in addition to its training camps being damaged. Pakistani-based groups were occupied with other tasks: "In many cases the first to arrive on the scene to assist in post-earthquake rescue and relief efforts were members of Islamist groups, including militant jihadi organisations" (Wilder 2010: 416). The Indian military, likewise occupied with relief and reconstruction, could not escalate the conflict in spite of its opponents' weakness, particularly since the rebels could retreat to Pakistani territory (ADB 2006; Nabi 2014). In short, both conflict parties faced strategic constraints in the first months after the earthquake.

Second, pro-Pakistani extremists in Indian Kashmir also restrained from using extensive violence in order to prevent a deterioration of theirs and Pakistan's image in the aftermath of the disaster. Pakistan faced strong international pressure, particularly by the United States, to stop its support of terrorist groups in the aftermath of 9/11. The London bombings three months before the earthquake intensified such pressures, because terrorism was very high on the international agenda again. After the earthquake, the world focused its attention on Kashmir. For example, military contingents from 19 countries participated in the relief and reconstruction operations (Cosgrave and Herson 2008: 194), with the United States being strongly involved (Wilder 2010).

In such a situation, an escalation of violence by Pakistani-backed groups would have sent a devastating message to the international community and Pakistan's allies, which would have interpreted this as a sign of Pakistan supporting international terrorism (Samii 2006; Staniland 2013). Image cultivation hence played a role in the conflict de-escalation as well. This is further supported by a strong decline in civilian casualties in the first five months after the earthquake (27, as compared with 137 in the five months before the disaster) because the international community is particularly sensitive to violence against civilians.

Indonesia 2004: Wave of Peace?

The Aceh region in northwestern Indonesia had a tense relationship with the central government since Indonesia achieved independence in 1949. Reasons for this include a history of Aceh as a strong and independent sultanate, the Muslim population's opposition to secular policies of the government, the loss of autonomy status in 1950 and again in 1967, and tensions about the distribution of revenues from Aceh's rich natural resources (in particular, oil and gas). An early rebellion in Aceh supporting Darul Islam[44] took place between 1953 and 1959 but was defeated by the government. In 1976, the Free Aceh Movement (GAM) staged another rebellion, this time for an independent Aceh. The Indonesian military quickly quelled the resistance, but the GAM remained active in Aceh (Schulze 2003; Sulistiyanto 2001).

From the late 1980s onward, the GAM again increased its activities.[45] The Indonesian military reacted with heavy repression, including counterinsurgency measures (Aspinall 2007). In the wake of the 1997 financial crisis, and particularly the democratization process (*reformasi*) in 1998, the GAM gained further strength. It was able to take control of substantive areas in Aceh, thus broadening its revenue and recruitment base. Peace negotiations in 2000 and 2002–2003 failed, each time followed by an escalation of the conflict. In May 2003, the government declared martial law in Aceh, closed the province to the outside world, and carried out a heavy military campaign. In October 2004, newly elected Indonesian president Susilo Bambang Yudhoyono and vice president Jusuf Kalla re-started back-channel negotiations with the GAM.

Shortly after the re-start of the negotiations, and with intense counterinsurgency activities ongoing, a 9.3-magnitude earthquake occurred off the west coast of Aceh. Massive damage in coastal Aceh was caused by the ground shaking, but even more damage was caused by the subsequent tsunami with wave heights between 4 and 30 meters. At least 165,000 people died, partially due to a lack of tsunami awareness and the human security implications of the conflict (Gaillard, Clavé, Vibert, et al. 2008).[46] Productive losses and infrastructure destruction amounted to US$8.2 billion (Mahdi 2006). Roads and bridges collapsed or were washed away, significantly hampering emergency aid. Oil transfer facilities and port infrastructures in Aceh were also damaged, which in turn increased the financial burden for the Indonesian government (Ghobarah et al. 2006). However,

---

44. A rebel group fighting for the establishment of an Islamic state in Indonesia, mostly during the 1950s.
45. Partially because Libya trained 700–800 GAM fighters.
46. The large majority of Acehnese did not know what a tsunami is. Conflict-related displacement, poverty, insecurity, and injury complicated evacuation efforts.

due to the end of martial law and massive international support, emergency relief and recovery operations have generally been considered successful (Klitzsch 2014; Zeccola 2011).

As indicated by figure 3.2, Aceh experienced a spike in conflict intensity in the first month after the disaster, with a monthly average of 79 battle-related deaths in the year before the earthquake/tsunami and 131 casualties in January 2005. This escalation was mainly due to the Indonesian army extending its presence in the disaster-affected areas. However, as both conflict parties started formal peace negotiations on January 23 and concluded a peace agreement in August, the conflict rapidly de-escalated. Overall, the number of deaths in the post-disaster 12-month period (222) is significantly lower than in the previous year (947).

Two factors were crucial in setting the stage for this conflict de-escalation and the associated peace negotiations. First, political leaders on both sides, and especially Yudhoyono and Kalla, were committed to the peace process and were willing to accept a compromise. Second, the capabilities of both actors were significantly reduced, producing a mutually hurting stalemate that neither side could evade by military means. The Indonesian state was still coping with the impacts of the political changes and the economic turbulence of the late 1990s as well as with international pressures to resolve the conflict peacefully. The GAM had lost up to two-thirds of its members during the period of martial law and received little international support for its independence claims (Aspinall 2005; Schulze 2007).

The tsunami accelerated this de-escalation process in two major ways and one minor way. The first major pathway relates to constraints faced by the government and the GAM. The Indonesian state mainly controlled the coastal areas of Aceh. It experienced significant losses of personnel, infrastructure, and equipment owing to the disaster, including 2,698 security forces and 60% of its civil servants in the provincial capital Banda Aceh (Ghobarah et al. 2006; Le Billon and Waizenegger 2007). But the GAM also lost important support bases along the coast and was unable to provide relief in the territories it controlled without access to external (usually government controlled) aid (Enia 2008; Schulze 2007). In other words, the disaster exhausted the capabilities of both conflict parties even further and contributed to the mutually hurting stalemate (Kingsbury 2007).

The second major pathway from the earthquake/tsunami to conflict de-escalation was image cultivation. There was a general sense that "resorting to military solutions to resolve the conflict in a concurrent post-disaster emergency and rehabilitation context would be politically incorrect in the eyes of the wider Indonesian population and international community" (Gaillard, Clavé, and Kelman 2008: 517). The Indonesian government and especially the GAM strongly sought international backing for their positions. A GAM negotiator stated quite explicitly, "What we need is international support" (Schulze 2003: 265). At the same time, the international community made clear that reconstruction support was conditional on conflict de-escalation and advances in the peace process (Harrowell and Özerdem 2019). Also, both the Indonesian government (after the recent democratization) and the GAM (fighting guerrilla warfare dependent on local support) could hardly allow themselves to lose popular support. De-escalating the conflict and committing to peace talks was therefore crucial to cultivate a positive image among key audiences for both parties (Le Billon and Waizenegger 2007; Tunçer-Kılavuz 2019).

Finally, micro-level instances of cooperation between combatants and supporters from both sides increased local support for the peace process (Gaillard, Clavé, and Kelman 2008). Along with a general sense of "there has been enough suffering in Aceh" among the Indonesian public, this allowed leaders on both sides "to assume the high moral ground in seeking peace" (Kingsbury 2007: 104). However, local cooperation was minor and short-lived, while expressions of solidarity would have been unlikely to facilitate the peace process beyond the initial negotiation period (Enia 2008). This reduces the explanatory power of the solidarity pathway as compared with the constraints and image cultivation pathways.

Myanmar 2008: The Karen Conflict after Cyclone Nargis

Tensions between the dominant Burmese (or Bamar) and the minority Karen ethnic groups date back to the colonial area, as the British colonial administration privileged the Karen over other ethnic groups. When Myanmar became an independent country (known as Burma until 1989) after World War II, the Karen demanded a separate state. However, the new government turned down this plea as well as requests for a special status of the Karen ethnic group. As a result, the Karen National Union (KNU) was founded in 1947 to pursue Karen interests. When negotiations failed in the wake of communal conflicts and provocations by both sides, the political conflict escalated into a full-blown civil war in late 1948.

Over the next six decades, the conflict continued with changing fortunes and several splits and alliances on the side of the rebels. The KNU and its military arm, the Karen Nation Liberation Army, frequently formed alliances with organizations representing other ethnic groups as well as with the Burmese democracy movement. At various times, the rebels controlled larger territories in eastern Myanmar. But the KNU also faced significant setbacks when the Democratic Kayin Buddhist Army (DKBA) split away from the group and fought alongside the government in 1994,[47] and when the Karen National Union–Peace Council (KNU-PC) separated in January 2007 to sign a peace agreement with the government. Already with the fall of its headquarters in Manerplaw and a decline of lucrative black-market trade along the Myanmar-Thai border in the 1990s, the KNU had to increasingly rely on guerrilla tactics rather than open confrontations (O'Hara and Selling 2012: 27–33). The process of losing territorial control that had begun in the 1980s accelerated with government and DKBA offensives between 2004 and 2009 (Core 2009).

On February 9, 2008, the military government announced a constitutional referendum in May 2008 that would be followed by general elections in 2010. This decision was contested by a wide range of opposition and civil society groups because of (1) a lack of prior consultation (including with representatives of ethnic minorities), (2) several features of the new constitution that would ensure the continuation of military rule, and (3) doubts about the fairness of the announced elections. While several Karen groups eventually participated in the elections, many Karen remained skeptical and the KNU was hostile to the process (South 2011).

During this politically turbulent period, Cyclone Nargis made landfall in Myanmar on the night of May 2, 2008. Owing to a lack of preparation, unfortunate timing (during high tides and at night), and the topography of the affected region, destruction was enormous: the storm caused 140,000 deaths and destruction of property worth US$1.75 billion. To make matters worse, the government responded slowly to the disaster and initially refused international aid because of fears of foreign interference. Later, it mobilized more resources and accepted international support, but only from "friendly" countries and only if the foreign helpers obtained the respective visa.

47. The split was mainly caused by frictions between Christian and Buddhist factions in the KNU.

Despite calls to do so, the government did not postpone the constitutional referendum, except in the worst-affected regions. Nargis caused the most destruction in the Irrawaddy region of southern Myanmar, but the Kayin (Karen) state (the core KNU territory) was affected as well, with the Karen group being overall heavily affected (Howe and Bang 2017; South 2008).

In the 12 months after Nargis, the intensity of the government-KNU conflict declined remarkably, with 67 battle-related deaths compared with 321 deaths in the year before the cyclone. This de-escalation is almost exclusively driven by less civilian targeting (down from 256 to 26 victims) by pro-government forces. This is surprising given the restrictions of political freedoms after Nargis as well as during the run-up to the 2008 referendum and 2010 elections.

The solidarity pathway can hardly explain this development as the cyclone rather hardened political front lines. Delayed relief efforts and the rejection of international support fueled discontent with the government. At the same time, relief and reconstruction activities increased government suspicions of political activism and foreign interference (Than 2009). Constraints on armed government activities were also not significant. Conflict data report no drop in armed confrontation directly after Nargis, and the government's military access to the Kayin state was hardly affected, especially given the local DKBA presence. In addition, Ashley South (2011: 40) reports offensives by the military and DKBA, both of which frequently targeted civilians, in 2008 and 2009.

Rather, the conflict de-escalation was driven by the Burmese regime's efforts to cultivate its image toward external constituencies. In the wake of the critique of its disaster response, the upcoming constitutional referendum, and the planned elections, the government was eager to avoid further deterioration of its image. South (2008) argues that the government rejected Western disaster aid to obscure human rights violations from the international public during a politically sensitive time, further demonstrating that concerns about the state's image played a role in government considerations. Regional powers with more friendly relations to Myanmar, particularly China, urged the government to accept international aid. By doing so, they set incentives to limit other practices that may shed an unfavorable light on the Burmese rulers, such as military violence against civilians, at least temporarily (Junk 2016). This was particularly relevant as the government eventually allowed a number of foreign aid workers into the country. In sum, there is evidence that image cultivation by the government of Myanmar resulted in conflict de-escalation via a reduction in civilian targeting in the wake of Cyclone Nargis.

Pakistan 2010: Floods Facilitating Conflict De-escalation

The Pakistani Taliban, named Tehrik-i-Taliban Pakistan (TTP), emerged in December 2007 as an alliance of smaller and regional Islamist groups. Its various members share three central goals: introduce the *sharia* in Pakistan, resist the influence of the United States and other Western powers in the region (particularly in neighboring Afghanistan), and push back the Pakistani state from their areas of control. The state of Pakistan traditionally supported Islamist militant groups to gain a stake in Afghanistan since the 1980s, but it has curtailed their influence (including through military means) since 2001 under US pressure to support the war on terror. Once established, the TTP quickly expanded existing strongholds in the politically and economically marginalized North-West Frontier Province (NWFP) and Federally Administered Tribal Areas (FATA),[48] but also had an operational presence in the other regions of Pakistan. Owing to the inclusion of existing militant groups, the possession of modern weapons, and an international supply of weapons, fighters, and funding (e.g., from Afghanistan, the Gulf states, and Uzbekistan), as well as local support networks,[49] the TTP posed a significant challenge to the Pakistani state (Biberman and Turnbull 2018; Feyyaz 2016; Sheikh 2016; Siddique 2010).

Initially, the government of Pakistan reacted with a mixture of military repression and accommodation, including support for pro-government factions of the Pakistani Taliban and negotiations with the TTP (Khan and Wei 2016). However, after the TTP increased its territorial influence in northern Pakistan and conducted terrorist attacks in other parts of the country, the military launched several large-scale offensives against the TTP during 2009. Heavy fighting occurred, but the Pakistani armed forces were able to procure and control significant amounts of territory, thereby severely weakening the TTP. However, the rebels remained capable of initiating localized offensives (in northwestern Pakistan) and major terrorist attacks

---

48. Since 2018, both areas are part of the Khyber Pakhtunkwa province.
49. Taliban-style groups resisting the state-like Tehreek-e-Nafaz-e-Shariat-e-Mohammadi (TNSM) emerged as early as 1992. They gained currency after the US invasion of Afghanistan in 2001, and again with US drone strikes in Pakistan since 2004.

(countrywide). The military offensives also created grievances among the local populations with the potential to further fuel the insurgency (Akhtar 2010; Akhtar 2019; M. Nelson 2010).

A few months after the peak of the Pakistani military's offensive, a devastating flood of the Indus River, triggered by heavy rains, occurred in July and August 2010. Close to 20% of Pakistan's territory became inundated. The total death toll from the flood is estimated at 1,985, with direct economic damage of US$9.7 billion and around 20 million displaced persons. Agricultural land, infrastructure, and assets were destroyed on a large scale. While all provinces were severely affected, northwestern Pakistan—including TTP strongholds like the FATA—suffered the most from the floods. The heavy rains affected the region directly, giving it little time to prepare for the disaster. The northwest of Pakistan was also highly vulnerable to the disaster owing to its remoteness, the destruction and displacement caused by the conflict, and the predominance of agricultural livelihoods (Arai 2012).

State agencies were ill prepared to respond to the floods, but the military, local NGOs, and international supporters provided rapid and effective relief operations (Deen 2015). Food insecurity was nevertheless high, particularly in rural areas (Doocy et al. 2013). Reconstruction proceeded slowly in the first year after the floods, especially for poor and significantly affected households in Pakistan's northwest (Kurosaki 2017). Consequently, significant anti-government resentments emerged, including among the FATA, owing to a perceived lack of state support after the floods (Arai 2012; K. Khan 2019; Siddiqi 2013).[50]

The flood triggered concerns that the TTP might use anti-state grievances and material deprivation to expand its support base and recruit new followers (Kazim 2010; Küstner 2010). However, the intensity of the conflict was reduced by more than 50% in the year after the disaster, with the number of battle-related deaths declining from 6,297 to 3,006. This decline was mostly driven by fewer battle events and military encounters. The number of terrorist attacks, a tactic widely used by the TTP, only declined from 151 to 143, with a slight increase in deaths from such attacks: 763 in the year before the floods, and 903 in the year after the floods (START 2018).

50. According to Siddiqi (2013), several state measures such as the distribution of Watan cards (pre-charged ATM cards) were actually rated very positively by the flood victims, yet not identified as services provided by state agencies.

While the army offensives in 2009 are an important reason for the subsequent decline of the conflict between the Pakistani state and the TTP, the flood also played a role because its impacts constrained both parties. In late 2010 and well into 2011, the Pakistani army could not extend its operations (or maintain their high level of intensity as seen in 2009) because it was "overstretched with flood relief and military operations" in other areas (Fair 2011: 104). The floods in combination with the territorial losses in 2009 also reduced the capabilities of the Taliban rebels. They were busy to some degree with relief work,[51] while their income from local taxes, donations, and ransom kidnapping declined (Feyyaz 2011; Siddique 2010). Given the large flooded areas, including in heavily contested regions like the Swat Valley in Khyber Pakhtunkwa, both conflict parties also faced heavy logistical challenges to wage battles against each other (Fleiss et al. 2011). This is consistent with the available data on violent confrontations: the number of large battles, which demand manpower, finances, and logistics, declined, while the frequency of terrorist attacks by the TTP (which can be conducted by small sub-groups with fewer resources) remained almost constant.

Concerns that the TTP would use the floods to extend their sympathies and boost recruitment did not materialize. The Taliban delivered only a limited amount of disaster-related relief and services, particularly when compared with the extensive support provided by the Pakistani military in many areas (Arai 2012; Deen 2015). Further, relief provision (or the lack thereof) hardly translated into sustained political support for the TTP or the government (Fair et al. 2017; Siddiqi 2014). Likewise, other explanations for the decline in conflict intensity are implausible: there are no reports of instances of solidarity or cooperation between the Pakistani government and the TTP after the floods, and the Taliban were not concerned with image cultivation after the floods (to the contrary, they continued terrorist attacks on civilians and publicly threatened international relief workers) (Feyyaz 2020; Masood 2010). The constraints pathway is the relevant link between the 2010 floods and a de-escalation of the conflict between the Pakistani government and the TTP.

51. The extent is contested, with some authors claiming an important role for Taliban groups in post-disaster charity work (Kazim 2010; Siddique 2010), while others consider them "low key as providers of disaster relief" (Arai 2012: 58) at best (see also Biberman and Turnbull 2018).

Somalia 1997: Flood in the Midst of Chaos

Major General Siad Barre assumed power in Somalia in 1969. Originally, his regime integrated all major clans, but with growing economic stress and critique about the lost war with Ethiopia in the late 1970s, Barre's rule was increasingly based on repression. Several clans[52] and political groups started to engage in violent resistance against the government, leading to Barre's overthrow by the United Somali Congress (USC) in 1991. USC's Ali Mahdi then became president of Somalia, but the new government was heavily contested. A breakaway faction of the USC led by Mohammad Farrah Aideed (and supported by the Somali National Alliance as well as the Ethiopian government) became one of the key challengers of the very weak government (supported by the Somali Salvation Alliance).[53] Several other armed groups with political, economic, and religious goals also participated in various armed struggles in Somalia (Vinci 2006). I will focus on the struggle for political power between the Madi and the Aideed factions of the USC.

Despite major peace negotiations in 1993, 1994, 1996 (after Hussein Aideed replaced his deceased father), and 1997, the conflict continued throughout the 1990s. UN and US interventions between 1992 and 1995 also failed to restore peace. However, since 1995, armed conflict, while still persistent, generally became less intense and widespread (Menkhaus 2006). While fronts shifted fast and ambush attacks were common, most fighting took place either in Mogadishu or in the agriculturally (and thus economically) important regions in southern Somalia (Bakonyi and Stuvøy 2005; Pham 2011).

In October and November 1997, an El Niño event triggered heavy rain in southern Somalia. Combined with the lack of maintenance of dikes and flood channels (also due to the ongoing civil war), this caused devastating flooding along the Juba and Shebelle Rivers—that is, in Somalia's breadbasket region. The disaster caused the loss of over 2,000 lives and widespread devastation of agricultural livelihoods owing to the destruction of fields, infrastructure, and assets. Approximately 21,000 livestock, as well as 90% of the maize and 50% of the sorghum production, were lost (FAO 1997; WFP

---

52. In Somalia, clan identities, while an important source of political mobilization and economic solidarity, are also fluid and changing (Duyvesteyn 2000).

53. Key allies of Aideed were the Somali National Alliance as well as the Ethiopian government, while the Somali Salvation Alliance was a key supporter of the Mahdi government.

1998). This event is considered the worst flood in Somalia's history, especially as it damaged two important export goods: cattle and bananas. The floods facilitated the spread of Rift Valley fever among local cattle, leading to import bans by Kenya and Saudi Arabia (two key importers of Somali cattle). The disaster also undermined banana production by flooding and destroying plantations (Little et al. 2001; Little 2003; Webersik 2005). Cases of malaria and cholera also multiplied (UNCU 1998).

During and after the floods, conflict intensity declined dramatically. According to the UCDP-GED data, 252 battle-related deaths occurred in the year before the disaster, none during the two months of the flood, and only 16 in the year after the disaster. But the validity of these data is questionable given that Somalia was a failed state during this time period, making data gathering difficult, and that the UCDP recognizes no government side for the period 1997–2000, hence recording fewer events.[54] To further validate this information, I use data on all armed conflict events from another widely used conflict dataset—ACLED (Raleigh et al. 2010)—for the nine months before and after the disaster in the most flood-affected areas.[55] Again, we can see a clear decline, from 12 events and 41 fatalities before the disaster to 6 events and 1 fatality during and after the floods. Qualitative accounts further confirm this conflict de-escalation (de Sousa 2014).

While a general decline in violence (particularly by clan-based groups like both USCs) had been recognized in Somalia since 1995 (Menkhaus 2006), the floods accelerated this trend by providing constraints on armed conflict activities. Most fighting between the USC factions during that time took place either in and around Mogadishu or in the agricultural regions of southern Somalia. In the latter, mobility was severely constrained by the floods, hence making troop movement almost impossible.

The prices of maize (+530%) and flour (+110%) in the local markets skyrocketed between October 1997 and January 1998 (Little et al. 2001: 153), making it harder to recruit and feed fighters. This was especially the case

---

54. That is, no confrontations between the government and the USC are recognized, although events involving their respective sub-groups and allies are on record. In addition, this should bias data only for November and December 1996 and is unlikely to drive the downward trend in battle-related deaths.
55. These areas are Lower Jubba, Middle Jubba, Gedo, and Lower Shebelle. I use a time period of 9 rather than 12 months before and after the disaster because ACLED only goes back as far as 1 January 1997.

because the armed groups could not rely on loyal supporters and hence had to pay freelance gunmen (*mooryaan*) as soldiers in the mid-1990s (Vinci 2006). Strong declines in cattle exports and banana production further reduced the purchasing power of Mahdi's and particularly Aideed's forces (Webersik 2005). The relevance of food production and revenues from the flood-affected areas for war efforts in other parts of Somalia is well established: "Access to power at the state level (whatever its basis) is intimately intertwined with access to—and ultimately use of—productive resources in rural southern Somalia" (Cassanelli and Besteman 1996: 202). Providing logistical and financial constraints on both conflict parties, the 1997 floods facilitated a conflict de-escalation in Somalia.

Somalia 2010–2011: Drought and Famine in a Fragile Country

As discussed in the previous case study, the overthrow of Major General Siad Barre in 1991 marked the start of several rounds of armed conflict between different political groups competing for power in Somalia. External interventions by the African Union, the UN, and the United States, as well as various peace negotiations were unable to end the hostilities. While a relatively stable (but internationally not recognized) state of Somaliland was established in northern Somalia during the 1990s, the central government in Mogadishu remained extremely weak and had little power outside of the capital (Pham 2011).

In 2004, a new government, the Transnational Federal Government (TFG), was formed based on an agreement between several major warring factions. However, several local Islamic courts (especially in the south of Somalia) that had already formed in the 1990s to maintain local order resisted the new government. They joined forces under the Islamic Courts Union (ICU)[56] and were quickly able to control significant parts of the country. The ICU suffered major military defeats by an alliance of government and intervening Ethiopian forces in late 2006 and early 2007, but Islamic resistance remained vibrant. Later in 2007, al-Shabaab (Arabic for "The Youth") emerged as the strongest Islamist rebel group and main competitor of the government and its allies.[57] The goal of the Islamist group was to gain control over Somalia

---

56. Also known as the Council of Islamic Courts.
57. The main government allies were Ethiopia (which withdrew in 2009) and the African Union Mission to Somalia (AMISOM, established in 2007).

and turn it into an Islamic national state free of secular influences (Solomon 2014). Al-Shabaab was able to conquer vast amounts of territory in south and central Somalia as well as areas of Mogadishu until 2010 (Hansen 2013; Mueller 2018).

In the middle of al-Shabaab's rise to power and struggle with the TFG, a severe drought affected southern and central Somalia in 2010 and 2011. The main *gu* rains in spring 2010 were already below average, and the *deyr* rain season (September–December) saw a 50-year low in precipitation. The 2011 *gu* rainfall record was very low as well. Together with higher global food prices, declining agricultural incomes, weak infrastructure, low government capabilities, and prevalent insecurity and internal displacement, the stage was set for widespread agricultural collapse and food insecurity. International responses to the disaster were slow until the UN declared a famine in June 2011. Al-Shabaab's refusal of food aid and general resistance to international aid further complicated relief efforts (Maxwell and Pitzpatrick 2012).[58] The drought affected around 4 million people and caused at least 20,000 casualties (with some sources stating numbers above 100,000), most of which came from groups with low socio-economic statuses and/or limited ability to wage violence (Lindley 2014; Menkhaus 2012).

At first glance, the enormous negative impacts of the drought on livelihoods and the agricultural economy seem to have increased the intensity of the conflict.[59] The average number of battle-related deaths per month increased from 133 in the year before the drought, to 172 during the drought, to 238 in the year after the drought, making Somalia one of the cases with the largest standard deviations in conflict intensity (+13.5).[60]

However, this impression of a drought-conflict escalation nexus is misleading. The conflict escalation had already started two months prior to the

---

58. The United States and other Western countries added al-Shabaab to the list of foreign terrorist organizations in 2008, which led to a decline in international food and development support for southern Somalia owing to legal concerns.
59. This would be in line with Jean-François Maystadt and Oliver Ecker (2014), who find that below-average rainfall increases armed conflict risk in Somalia. However, the results are hardly comparable, as their study focuses on conflict incidence (rather than onset), includes low-intensity conflicts (rather than just high-intensity violence), and uses data from 1997 until 2009 (rather than for the 2009–2012 period).
60. Civilian victimization played only a very small role, with more than 98% of the battle-related deaths occurring in fights between armed groups.

Disasters and Armed Conflict Dynamics

end of the drought when Kenya intervened in southern Somalia in October 2011 to combat the growing influence of al-Shabaab along the Kenyan-Somali border (Mueller 2018). Shortly after, Ethiopia staged another offensive in favor of the Somali government (February/March 2012), while the number of TFG forces (due to financial support by the European Union [EU] and the United States) and AMISOM troops (due to a new mandate) grew significantly (Hansen 2013: 118–119). In other words, the end of the drought coincided with significant external action against al-Shabaab and increased support of the Somali government, and the latter two factors were the key drivers of the conflict escalation.

Rather, the drought had a de-escalating impact on the conflict. Given that this drought was a very slow-onset, long-term disaster, conflict dynamics should have already changed during the 23-month period of the drought. Indeed, the five-month moving average of battle-related deaths declined from 238 in June 2010 to 102 in August 2011 (just weeks before the Kenyan intervention). Also, if the drought is roughly divided into two 10-month periods,[61] the conflict intensity is more than five standard deviations lower in the second period.

These trends are well in line with qualitative evidence. Both al-Shabaab and the TFG looted disaster-related aid, but the amount was not significant enough to boost their fighting capabilities. Al-Shabaab actively resisted the operation of relief agencies in its territory, thereby "driving away a lucrative source of funding" (Menkhaus 2012: 31), with other income streams (e.g., taxes, charcoal trade) being much more important. The TFG controlled only around 5% of the drought-affected territory, and the looted aid was often used for political patronage (Menkhaus 2012; Pham 2011). Similarly, the collapse of agricultural livelihoods increased the number of marginalized and destitute people who could be recruited by armed groups. At the same time, the lack of a food supply, loss of income, and discontent about drought responses impeded recruitment efforts (Kfir 2017).

Overall, al-Shabaab was significantly weakened by the drought due to two factors. First, internal rifts increased over the denial of access for many humanitarian relief agencies. Second, al-Shabaab lost considerable popular support because of its disaster mismanagement, including the lack of

---

61. Ignoring the first months of the drought, when impacts were hardly felt, and the last two months, when the Kenyan intervention was already ongoing.

support in the affected areas, the expulsion of relief agencies, forced restrictions of the drought victims' mobility, and the taxation of the local population in the face of the disaster. The TFC forces were too weak to exploit this situation, leading to a conflict de-escalation that was mostly due to strategic constraints (Hansen 2013; Pham 2011).

Turkey 1999: Öcalan's Capture, the Marmara Earthquake, and the PKK's Cease-Fire

Kurds constitute a significant minority population of around 15 million in Turkey, especially in the southeastern region of Anatolia. Grievances about the lack of an independent Kurdish state as well as economic, political, and cultural marginalization have been significant at least since the foundation of the Republic of Turkey in 1923. Pro-Kurdish activism grew particularly in the 1960s and 1970s. In 1978, the Kurdistan Worker's Party (PKK) was founded to advocate for an independent, socialist state of Kurdistan.[62] It quickly gained influence and popularity in the southeast owing to its uncompromising stand against landlords, its reinforcement of widespread Kurdish grievances, and its support from external actors like the Soviet Union, Iraqi Kurds, and Syria (Tezcür 2015). In 1984, the PKK initiated a violent conflict with the Turkish state by launching guerrilla attacks on army units. Despite its considerable resources, the Turkish military was unable to quell the insurgency, which increased in intensity throughout the 1980s and early 1990s (Roth and Sever 2007).

However, by 1995, the military had gained the upper hand over the insurgents by undertaking a number of controversial yet effective counterinsurgency measures (e.g., training village militias, forced evacuation of villages in the southeast, large offensives in 1992 and 1995). Afterward, the insurgency continued with lower intensity and changed tactics of the PKK, including bombings in western Turkey. The 1998 Ardana Agreement between Turkey and Syria, which resulted in the expulsion of the PKK from its safe retreat and training areas in Syria, dealt the PKK another major blow. In February 1999, PKK founder and leader Abdullah Öcalan was captured by Turkish forces. From prison, Öcalan called on the PKK to abandon armed struggle, enter a cease-fire, and retreat into Iraq. Despite some dissent, the PKK mostly obeyed this call (Gunther 2000; Marcus 2007a; Ünal 2012).

62. The PKK dropped references to socialism in the 1990s.

A few months after Öcalan's capture, a 7.4-magnitude earthquake devastated the Marmara region in northeastern Turkey on August 17, 1999. The region was Turkey's economic center and comprised 23% of its population as well as 33% of its GDP at the time. More than 17,000 people died in the earthquake, and a conservative estimate of the total damage is US$4–10 billion, or 2%–4.5% percent of Turkey's GDP (World Bank 1999). Important transportation, electricity, and water infrastructure (including in Istanbul) also experienced major damage. While international actors and local civil society organizations were quick to act after the disaster, it took state institutions several days (and in some cases, weeks) to conduct proper relief work (Çetin 2013). In a survey of the earthquake victims, only 10.3% of all respondents stated that they received aid from the state (R. Jalali 2002). The inadequate enforcement of building codes, corruption, and a lack of disaster preparation caused a surge of public criticism of the Turkish government. The latter reacted by repressing media and NGO operations in the affected area and by scaling up its earthquake response (Jacoby and Özerdem 2008; Pelling and Dill 2010).

After the earthquake, grievances and protests against the government and the army were widespread but did not turn violent (Arlidge 1999). The rebels could not capitalize on them, as the earthquake occurred far from the Kurdish regions in southeastern Turkey where the PKK had its social basis (R. Jalali 2002; Marcus 2007b). Rather, the conflict between the Turkish state and the PKK de-escalated significantly after the disaster. The UCDP-GED registered 1,777 battle-related deaths in the year before the Marmara earthquake, and only 206 in the subsequent 12 months.[63] The main drivers of this de-escalation were certainly the general weakening of the PKK since the mid-1990s, the Ardana Agreement, and the capture of Öcalan. In line with this, two strong declines in battle-related deaths had already occurred before the earthquake: in December 1998, when Syria started to implement the Ardana Agreement, and in June 1999, after Öcalan called for the cessation of violence (Gunther 2000; Ünal 2012).

By contrast, the earthquake played a minor role in the third major decline in conflict intensity between September (85 deaths) and October (10 deaths) 1999. In September, the PKK declared a unilateral cease-fire and

---

63. Civilian deaths account for less than 2% of the total numbers and show a similar declining trend.

largely retreated into Iraq (Ünal 2012). While Öcalan had ordered these moves, his call was not uncontested. But the "earthquake gave his PKK a political opportunity to endorse this appeal" (Walker 2000: 73) by portraying the cease-fire and retreat as a gesture of goodwill. This was particularly important during a time when both Turkey and the PKK struggled to gain international support for their respective positions.[64] According to a statement by the PKK, "To unilaterally stop the war at this time of heavy disaster is the greatest support to the state and people of Turkey" (Associated Press 1999).[65] Similar to Greek-Turkish reconciliation after the same disaster (Akcinaroglu et al. 2011; Ganapati et al. 2010), the Marmara earthquake provided the PKK leadership with a justification and a strategic rationale to claim solidarity toward the Turkish state, even though the decline in attacks was driven by other political and military concerns (Gunther 2000). While of limited relevance to the conflict dynamics overall, the Marmara earthquake provided some incentives for the PKK to engage in image cultivation, hence playing a minor role in the decline in battle-related deaths.

Cases with No Disaster Impact on Conflict Dynamics

Afghanistan 1998: Remote Earthquakes Did Not Shape Conflict Dynamics

The decades-long period of war in Afghanistan started with a military coup in 1978, bringing the Communist Popular Democratic Party (CPDP) of Afghanistan to power. In the subsequent year, the Soviet Union intervened militarily in Afghanistan to support the Communist regime and quell resistance against it. This set the stage for a civil war between the Afghan government and Soviet troops, on the one side, and several rebel groups commonly known as the *mujahedin*, supported by Pakistan, the United States, Iran, and Saudi Arabia, on the other side. When the Soviet army left Afghanistan in 1989, the CPDP government of Mohammed Najibullah was able to remain in power, owing to, among other reasons, an increasing fragmentation of the rebels. After the final defeat of Najibullah's forces in 1992, this fragmentation increased. Several armed groups established strongholds

---

64. The PKK aimed to prevent being labeled as a terrorist organization by European states and the United States, while Turkey sought to strengthen its bid for EU membership.

65. Öcalan also announced from prison that the PKK would start the retreat earlier—in mid-August rather than early September—due to the earthquake.

in different parts of the country and fought for control over the capital city of Kabul.

In 1994, another armed faction emerged in southern Afghanistan: the radical Islamist Taliban, led by Mullah Mohammad Omar. The group received considerable financial and military support from Pakistan,[66] gained the backing of the Pashtun population[67] seeking to re-establish its pre-1978 dominance, and resonated well with indigenous calls to end the widespread insecurity and fragmentation of the country. Therefore, the Taliban were able to gain ground quickly. They conquered Kabul in 1996, pushed farther north in 1997 (Magnus 1998), and by 1998 controlled 90% of Afghanistan's territory (Rubin 2000). The other main rebel groups[68] joined their forces under the label United Islamic Front for the Salvation of Afghanistan (UIFSA), otherwise known as the Northern Alliance. Supported by Iran, Russia, Uzbekistan, Tajikistan, and India, UIFSA was able to consolidate strongholds in northern Afghanistan (Gossman 2001; A. Jalali 2001; Khalilzad 1997).

In the first half of 1998, two strong earthquakes shook the Rustaq region in the northeastern borderlands of Afghanistan, which at the time were controlled by the UIFSA. During the night of February 4, a 6.1-magnitude earthquake hit the area, followed by a 6.9-magnitude earthquake on May 30. The disasters killed 2,323 and 4,700 people, respectively. No comprehensive damage assessment was possible,[69] but several villages were completely destroyed by landslides and there was extensive damage to the fragile, mud brick houses. The May earthquake also did considerable damage to harvests and water-related infrastructure in a region that was already characterized by poverty (Strand et al. 2000). There are reports of the UIFSA providing help to disaster victims, but its capacities were insufficient, and the group therefore called for international assistance (McFadden 1998).

66. As well as from transnational Islamist networks, many of which were linked to Saudi Arabia.
67. The Pashtun are the largest and traditionally politically dominant ethnic group in Afghanistan. The armed groups controlling Kabul in the mid-1990s were predominantly of Tajik and Uzbek ethnic origin.
68. Most important are the armed groups led by Rashid Dostam, Ahmad Shah Massoud, and Burhanuddin Rabbani, who previously fought each other over control of Kabul.
69. This was due to the remoteness of the region, a lack of infrastructure, and the absence of government institutions.

Remoteness of the affected region, bad weather, and a lack of infrastructure seriously complicated external relief after both disasters. It took two days for news about the February earthquake to reach the outside world, and several weeks for larger amounts of relief goods to arrive. Combined with the cold weather and the shortage of food, this led to local despair and grievances, including threats to aid agencies (Bird 1998; Emerald Insight 1999). However, once the relief operations reached the areas, aid delivery was well coordinated and perceived to be fair (Hardcastle and Chua 1998; UN OCHA 1998). The networks and knowledge built during the disaster in February accelerated the response to the May earthquake. For both disasters, the overall amount of international aid was moderate but not insufficient, owing to the rather small number of affected people in the sparsely populated area (Barr 1998; Benini 1999; CNN 1998).

In the 12 months after the May earthquake, 12,158 casualties were recorded for the conflict between the Taliban and the UIFSA. This reflects an increase in both civilian and military casualties when compared with the year before the first earthquake (7,284 deaths), but the increase falls short of reaching the significance threshold introduced in chapter 3 (five standard deviations). More importantly, the increase was caused by a massive summer offensive by the Taliban in July, August, and September 1999, which was unrelated to the earthquake. The offensive had the strategic goal of capturing UIFSA strongholds in the northwestern provinces of Bamian, Balkh, Faryab, and Jowzan, all of which were far away from the earthquake-affected area. The offensive took place in the context of Kyrgyzstan and Uzbekistan withdrawing support for the UIFSA, while Pakistan provided strong backing to the Taliban (Akimbekov 2002; Christia 2012: 57–83; Khalilzad and Byman 2000).

Neither earthquake had any impact on the capabilities or strategic objectives of the UIFSA. They took place in a remote area with a small population living off subsistence agriculture. These areas hardly contributed to the war economy (Benini 1999; Rubin 2000). There was no fighting in Rustaq in the late 1990s. Furthermore, neither the UIFSA nor the Taliban had the resources or territorial control to provide significant relief to the earthquake-affected population (Popham 1998). In order to support rescue efforts after the February earthquake, "Mullah Mohammad Omar ... was reported to have ordered his forces to halt all military operations against the alliance on the Takhar Province front" (McFadden 1998). However,

UCDP data show no decline in conflict intensity in this province after the disasters, but rather an increase related to the 1998 summer offensive. In sum, the two earthquakes had no impact on the dynamics of the Taliban-UIFSA conflict.

Afghanistan 2008: Freezing the Conflict?

The previous case study provides a brief overview of the history of the conflict until the late 1990s. In 1999 and 2000, the Taliban consolidated their power over Afghanistan and made further military progress, confining the UIFSA to a small territory in the northeastern corner of the country. Following the terrorist attacks of September 11, 2001, a multi-national coalition led by the United States joined forces with UIFSA. Within three months, the Taliban lost all their strongholds and an interim government led by Hamid Karzai was established. The new administration included many former prominent UIFSA members and was backed by the strong international coalition on the ground. This coalition included the US-led Operation Enduring Freedom and the UN-sanctioned, multi-national International Security Assistance Force (ISAF). The remaining Taliban suffered major defeats during the rest of the year and in 2002 (Giustozzi 2007).

The situation changed from 2003 onward, however, with the Taliban re-grouping and conducting attacks against Afghan security forces and international coalition troops, particularly in southern Afghanistan.[70] Profits from the opium trade, support from international jihadi networks and local religious authorities, and safe recruitment and training areas in the Pakistani borderland supported this resurgence. The Taliban also regained control in certain areas in the south of the country and procured their public support in these areas. This was possible due to grievances about corruption, political exclusion (particularly of Pashtuns), and civilian casualties caused by the international coalition and Afghan security forces (Qazi 2010; Weigand 2017). By 2006, the Taliban started to selectively engage foreign troops in open battles (even though guerrilla-style attacks remained their predominant mode of operation). As a reaction, international forces increased from 15,400 in 2003 to 58,100 in 2008, but they were unable

70. Giustozzi (2007) labels the post-2002 movement "neo-Taliban" as it overlaps only partially with the old Taliban movement of the 1990s and represents a much more heterogeneous coalition of Pashtun warriors, Pakistani extremists, international jihadists, local warlords, and criminal groups.

to defeat the Taliban (Zyck 2012). Consequently, violent confrontations steadily increased from 2003 to 2007 (Giustozzi 2019; Sperling and Webber 2012; Thruelsen 2010).

From early January to mid-February 2008, northern, western, and central Afghanistan (and especially the province of Herat) experienced an extreme cold spell, with temperatures below −30°C (−22°F) and more than 250 centimeters of snow (Leithead 2008). The cold spell caused 1,317 deaths due to pneumonia, frostbite, and avalanches. No reliable estimate of the economic impact is available, but the deaths of 316,000 cattle dealt a heavy blow to the agricultural economy of the region (Peikar 2008). Existing shelter was often inadequate to protect people, and several hundred houses were destroyed during the disaster. The snowfall made many roads impassable, preventing aid from reaching several remote areas. This resulted in a doubling of prices for heating fuel (mostly wood and coal) and food in the affected areas (Welthungerhilfe 2008). Locals as well as members of parliament voiced discontent about the weak response of the Afghani state, but the latter had too few resources to arrange for a rapid, large-scale response (The New Humanitarian 2008). International actors as well as ISAF troops provided relief, but this was perceived to be too little and too slow, hence preventing any chance of a popularity boost for the government or the international coalition (Associated Press 2008; Deutsche Welle 2008).

In the aftermath of the cold spell, the conflict between the government (supported by the international coalition) and the Taliban continued unimpaired. One can observe only a small, insignificant reduction of battle-related deaths from 6,951 to 5,885 when comparing the 12-month periods before and after the disaster. This is well in line with other accounts stating that after escalating between 2003 and 2007, conflict intensity plateaued between 2007 and 2009. Neither side was able to make a major breakthrough or was forced or willing to back down (Giustozzi 2019; Zyck 2012). The disaster had little effect on the recruitment or financing sources of the insurgents (located in southern Afghanistan and the Pakistani borderland rather than in the areas affected by the cold spell) and the Afghani government (which received strong international support) (Giustozzi 2019; Rynning 2012). The conflict intensity was very low during the cold spell, but this is in line with a general seasonal pattern of violence in Afghanistan characterized by limited fighting during harsh winter conditions followed by spring and summer offensives (Eriksen and Heier 2009; Leithead 2008; O'Loughlin et al. 2010). The 2008 cold spell hence had no impact on conflict intensity in Afghanistan.

Algeria 2003: Grievances and Opportunities after the Boumerdès Earthquake

Algeria remained an economically weak and politically repressive country for most of the time since gaining independence in 1962. As a consequence of popular protests and opposition, multi-party elections were held for the first time in 1990. However, after Islamic parties won the first round of the election, the military canceled round two, seized power, and banned the most successful opposition party (the Islamic Salvation Front). In the light of this, more radical groups like the Armed Islamic Group (GIA) formed to violently overthrow the government and establish an Islamic state. From the mid-1990s onward, several groups split from the GIA, owing to its frequent use of violence against civilians. The GIA quickly became irrelevant politically and militarily (Martinez 2004).

The most prominent of these splinter groups is the Salafist Group for Preaching and Combat (GSPC), which formed in 1998 and quickly emerged as the strongest rebel group. In general, however, violence declined in Algeria during the late 1990s and the GSPC was not an existential threat to the survival of the government. It conducted guerrilla-style attacks in northern Algeria but also had a stronghold in the southern, Sahel region of the country. Due to its weak social base, an amnesty offer by the government in late 1999, and a government offensive in 2002, the GSPC largely retreated from northern Algeria between 2000 and 2004 (Cronin et al. 2004: 100–101; Gyves and Wyckoff 2006). During the same time, it also grew more committed to global jihad than to the struggle in Algeria (Gray and Stockham 2008; S. Harmon 2010).

On May 21, 2003, a 6.8-magnitude earthquake hit northern Algeria. Massive building destruction resulted in more than 2,200 casualties and a total economic loss of around US$65 billion. The towns of Zemmouri and Boumerdès in the Boumerdès province were most strongly affected (Meslem et al. 2012). It quickly became apparent that insufficient implementation of building codes and a low quality of state-built housing blocks (especially if designed for working- and middle-class households) were the main reasons for the excessive destruction (Lekkas and Kranis 2004).

Despite international support, the affected people considered the relief operations delayed and inadequate, resulting in significant anti-regime protests (Housego 2003; C. Smith 2003). When President "Bouteflika travelled to Boumerdès to survey the damage an angry crowd kicked and stoned his car" (Evans and Phillips 2007: 273). Islamic groups reportedly tried to provide aid to the survivors, but the government prohibited such efforts, and it remains unclear whether the GSPC tried to or was able to provide some relief (Reppert-Bismarck 2003).

The province most affected by the earthquake—Boumerdès—was also an operational focus of the GSPC and saw most attacks of the group between 2003 and 2006. Therefore, the stage was set for various pathways of conflict escalation: the GSPC could have drawn on the grievances of the disaster victims to gain new supporters and recruits, and both government and the rebels could have used violence to signal their continued presence/strength in the area after the earthquake. Similarly, state control was limited by the destruction, and up to "10,000 members of the army and police were helping rescue workers" (Reppert-Bismarck 2003). The police station of the city of Boumerdès was destroyed, presenting the GSPC with ample opportunities to intensify its violent campaign. It indeed used a period of chaos during an aftershock a few days later to kill a police officer (Gyves and Wyckoff 2006).

However, the UCDP data indicate that neither grievances nor opportunities nor signaling logics were important enough to change the dynamics of the GSPC-government conflict significantly. The year before the earthquake saw 593 battle-related deaths, compared with 534 in the subsequent 12 months. This picture does not change when only the Boumerdès province or an alternative conflict dataset (ACLED; see Raleigh et al. 2010) is considered. Three factors can explain this: First, the GSPC had little popular support in the disaster-affected region. Second, its military capabilities were rather weak, with a total of 300–500 fighters, while the government received increasing international support in the context of the war on terror (Cronin et al. 2004: 101; Gray and Stockham 2008: 94). Third, the GSPC was in the process of shifting its operational bases to southern Algeria, and international attacks (e.g., in Iraq or Mali) were becoming more relevant than the struggle at home (Filiu 2009; S. Harmon 2010). Overall, the Boumerdès earthquake caused significant grievances but had no impact on the conflict dynamics.

India (Assam) 2007: The ULFA's Inability to Exploit Flood-Related Opportunities

I discuss the emergence and development of the struggle between the ULFA and the Indian government from the late 1970s to the late 1990s in the case study "Assam (India) 1998: Flood, Recruitment Opportunities, and Conflict Persistence" earlier in this chapter. Waves of targeted assassinations and army offensives against the ULFA as well as counter-attacks by the rebels continued until the early 2000s. After 2001, however, the ULFA faced various problems. Popular support vanished further, and the government of Bhutan took a stronger stance against the group. After losing its hideouts in Bhutan and having several of its cadres captured by joint operations of the Bhutanese and Indian armies in 2003 (Kotwal 2001), the ULFA agreed to peace negotiations. Facilitated by the People's Consultative Group (PCG),[71] several rounds of talks took place in 2005 and 2006 but yielded no substantive results. This sparked another round of violence from September 2006 onward (Baruah 2007; Mahanta 2013; Saikia 2015).

Shortly afterward, a major disaster occurred in Assam. Extreme rainfall and the failure of multiple embankments caused the Brahmaputra River to flood more than 2,000 villages and large areas of agricultural land in July 2007, causing 1,103 deaths. Thirteen percent of the state's population was directly affected by the disaster, with no early warning issued by authorities. Relief efforts proceeded slowly because many streets were flooded and inaccessible (Hill 2007). During "the flood in 2007 a complete breakdown in the agricultural system occurred when a large area of agricultural land was affected by sand deposits" (Das et al. 2009: 13). As a consequence, food insecurity and poverty increased in the affected areas along the Brahmaputra, and the relocation of several villages was necessary (Kipgen and Pegu 2018). As in 1998, government reactions to the flood were considered slow and inadequate, and the flow of aid from international actors into the region was limited as well (Mukhim 2014). However, strong social networks at the local level and adaptation strategies like labor migration of youths mitigated the impact of the floods to some degree (Das et al. 2009).

The 12-month period after the floods experienced a significant de-escalation of the conflict between the Indian government and the ULFA.

---

71. A group of prominent Assam civilians sympathetic to the ULFA tasked by the rebels to set the ground for direct talks with the government.

The UCDP-GED records only 143 battle-related deaths for this period, which represents a clear decline compared with the previous year (273 deaths). However, factors not related to the flood were the main drivers of this de-escalation trend. The significant decline of public support the ULFA experienced between 2001 and 2007 reduced its ability to recruit or draw support from the local population. Hideouts in Bhutan (and, from late 2008 onward, in Bangladesh) were no longer easily available. Finally, surrenders continued, with the capitulation of two powerful companies of its 28th battalion in mid-2007 hitting the ULFA particularly hard. Under these circumstances, the capability of the rebels to initiate further attacks diminished considerably (A. Dutta 2014; Misra 2009).

Without a doubt, the 2007 floods caused significant hardship, poverty, and grievances among the population of Assam (Das et al. 2009; Singh 2008). But unlike in 1998, the ULFA was in no position to exploit them. The group had lost the support of large parts of the Assamese people. It had also largely stopped addressing flood-related (and other development) problems in local communities by the mid-2000s,[72] reducing its ability to present itself as a better alternative to the government (Mahanta 2005; Misra 2009). Finally, the ULFA was accused of prioritizing economic motives and foreign interests over the grievances of the people in Assam (Mahanta 2013)[73] and was severely weakened by the increasing number of surrenders.

Indonesia 1992: No Link between the Flores Earthquake and the East Timor Conflict

When Portugal instigated the decolonization process in East Timor in 1974, the Revolutionary Front for an Independent East Timor (FRETILIN)[74] quickly emerged as the strongest political party. FRETILIN started as a movement of urban elites but quickly gained wide support owing to its support for rural communities. After successfully resolving a coup by competing parties, FRETILIN declared East Timor's independence on November 28, 1975. Ten

---

72. Including through the welfare organizations associated with the ULFA, such as the Jatiya Unnayan Parishad.
73. The support of Pakistan during the Kargil War in 1999 and its cooperation with Bangladesh drove this impression.
74. Armed combat operations were performed by its armed wing, the Armed Forces of National Liberation of East Timor (FALINTIL). In 1987, FALINTIL became the armed force of the National Council of the Maubere Resistance.

days later, Indonesian forces invaded and occupied the country. FRETILIN continued to control significant territory and to fight the Indonesian military but suffered tremendous losses until late 1978 because of the power of the (US-supplied) Indonesian military and the brutal occupation regime. Afterward, it had to resort to low-intensity guerrilla warfare with no territorial control (Niner 2000).

Resistance against the Indonesian occupation grew again in the late 1980s and early 1990s owing to various developments. In 1988, several rebel groups joined forces under the National Council of the Maubere Resistance (CNRM) (Myrtinnen 2009). FRETILIN remained as the dominant group in the council. At the same time, increasing international attention as well as non-violent protests in East Timor and Indonesia increased pressure on the Indonesian government. Despite this, the Indonesian military continued its firm control of East Timor (Fernandes 2010; Salla 1997). A series of violent crackdowns as well as the capture of important rebel leaders between November 1991 and November 1992 further strengthened its position (Niner 2019; Pinto and Jardine 1997).

On December 12, 1992, a 7.5-magnitude earthquake occurred on the northern coast of Flores Island, located in Indonesia's southernmost province, East Nusa Tenggara, the poorest region of Indonesia. The earthquake was followed by several tsunamis (with wave heights up to 4 meters) and a series of aftershocks (with magnitudes up to 6.0) (Kawata et al. 1995). Because many inhabitants lived close to the coast and many buildings had weak structures, around 2,500 people were killed during the disaster. "The damage to homes and public infrastructure ... is estimated at US$273.5 million," and the predominantly agricultural livelihoods were devastated by a loss of livestock, farming equipment, boats, and fishing gear (Pribadi and Soemardi 1996: 2). Despite rapid interventions by the government, the destruction of roads and communication infrastructure delayed the response (JICA 1992). However, the general reception of the Indonesian government's three-stage coping plan, involving significant domestic and international financial resources, was positive (World Bank 1993). There are reports of an insufficient consideration of local authorities and cultural norms, but this did not cause protests or widespread grievances (Boen and Jigyasu 2005).

Conflict intensity in East Timor saw very moderate changes after the earthquake/tsunami disaster, with 13 battle-related deaths in the year before and 25 deaths in the subsequent 12 months. The disaster is not linked to the conflict dynamics in any way. East Timor was not affected by the earthquake. Flores Island is separated from East Timor by hundreds of kilometers of land and sea, and even on the island, disaster-related grievances were not a major political factor. The Indonesian government did not send additional troops to Flores Island, and external funders covered around 79% of the direct post-disaster reconstruction costs (US$148.7 million in total) (World Bank 1993: 2). Especially given the highly unequal military balance between the Indonesian military and FRETILIN (Fernandes 2010), the disaster provided no incentives, opportunities, or constraints for the armed groups. The minor escalation of the conflict[75] can rather be explained by an increase in crackdowns of pro-independence demonstrations and operations by the Indonesian military to capture FRETILIN leaders (Niner 2019; Pinto and Jardine 1997).

Indonesia 2006: Disaster in Yogyarkata, De-escalation in Aceh?
Please consult the case study "Indonesia 2004: Wave of Peace?" (earlier in this chapter) for a general introduction to the conflict. In August 2005, the government of Indonesia and the GAM signed a comprehensive peace agreement. Provisions included, among others, a far-reaching autonomy of Aceh, the withdrawal of all "non-organic" Indonesian military and security forces,[76] an amnesty and reintegration fund for GAM members, the demobilization and disarmament of GAM troops, and the deployment of an external monitoring mission (Aspinall 2005; Schulze 2009).

Sporadic violent clashes between the Indonesian military and small, pro-government militias on the one hand and the GAM on the other still occurred after the agreement, including some violence against civilians. However, the overall level of violence was significantly lower.[77] Tensions between the conflict parties remained, regarding, for example, the exact distribution of revenues from Aceh's natural resources, the ability of the central government to overrule local regulations, and reintegration funds for GAM members (Aspinall 2009). But overall, popular and elite support

---

75. Which is below the five standard deviations threshold introduced in chapter 3.
76. That is, generally speaking, all forces that were stationed in Aceh in excess of normal (peacetime) contingents, as indicated by the presence of security forces in other Indonesian provinces.
77. The UCDP registers 5 battle-related deaths in the six months after the peace agreement, compared with, for instance, 133 fatalities in January 2004 alone.

for non-violent, democratic politics remained high (Törnquist 2010), and "GAM commanders expressed satisfaction with what they had gained along with the peace" (Sindre 2010: 246).

While the post–civil war peace-building process in Aceh was still ongoing, a 6.3-magnitude earthquake struck the southern central region of the Indonesian island of Java on May 27, 2006. The Bantul district and the city of Yogyakarta, both characterized by high poverty rates, were the most affected. The earthquake caused 5,778 deaths (Matsuoka and Yamazaki 2006), and the economic damage was estimated at US$3.1 billion, resulting in a 23% decline of the local economy. Damage to buildings was extensive, owing to poor construction, while public infrastructure suffered less damage and was quickly restored (Consultative Group on Indonesia 2006).[78] Experts and the local population generally considered relief and reconstruction efforts to be successful, not at least because of significant national and international support. Except for occasional delays resulting in some public protests (*Jakarta Post* 2006), business and house recovery support were widely available and unbureaucratic (Leitmann 2007; Resosudarmo et al. 2012). The government promoted an inclusive and participatory approach. Solidarity and mutual support were generally high in Bantul and Yogyakarta despite the poor being more heavily affected. "The high level of public participation in the recovery phase minimised potential conflict . . . and hastened recovery" (Kusumasari and Alam 2012: 361).

The conflict in Aceh de-escalated significantly after the Yogyakarta earthquake. Battle-related deaths decreased by more than 12 standard deviations from the pre-disaster period (30 deaths) to the post-disaster 12-month period (0 deaths). However, for three reasons, this de-escalation cannot be attributed to the earthquake. First, the disaster and the conflict locations are roughly 2,000 kilometers apart. The earthquake did not affect the relative capabilities of the Indonesian state, particularly given the local solidarity around Yogyakarta, the international disaster support, and the weakened GAM (Leitmann 2007; Schulze 2007). Second, the conflict had already started to de-escalate with the signature of the peace agreement eight months before the earthquake, and violent clashes had ceased completely three months before the disaster.

---

78. With the partial exception of the education sector, which the earthquake affected heavily.

Third, several other factors can explain the conflict de-escalation very well. After the peace agreement, there was considerable "commitment by both GAM and the Indonesian government to make the peace process work" (Schulze 2009: 30). The majority of the local population in Aceh supported the peace process as well (Törnquist 2010). Many former GAM commanders earned significant amounts of money, particularly in the natural resources and construction sectors,[79] boosted by large peace-building and post-tsunami reconstruction funds flowing into Aceh (Aspinall 2009). The Aceh Monitoring Mission (September 15, 2005–December 15, 2006), sponsored by the EU and some members of the Association of Southeast Asian Nations overseeing the implementation of the peace agreement, was very effective in supporting the cessation of armed hostilities (Schulze 2009). Finally, GAM candidates won the post of governor and 7 out of 19 district head positions in the December 2006 elections, marking a transformation from an armed conflict to a democratic struggle (Aguswandi and Large 2008; Palmer 2010).

Iran 1990: The Kurdish Struggle after the Manjil-Rudbar Earthquake

The Kurdish Democratic Party of Iran (KDPI) was formed in 1945 with the goal of creating an autonomous Kurdish region in western Iran. In January 1946, it declared the Republic of Kurdistan (also known as the Republic of Mahabad), which was not recognized internationally and was recaptured by Iranian military forces in the following 12 months. The conflict continued at a low level in the following decades, with the KDPI recruiting mostly from urban middle classes and tribal areas. Despite popular support, the Kurdish rebels remained weak and were unable to re-establish territorial control.

While the KDPI initially supported the 1979 revolution in Iran, relations with the new, autocratic, and Islamist regime quickly deteriorated. During this time, the KDPI also adopted a secondary goal of turning Iran into a democratic state. The rebel group was able to establish significant territorial control in late 1979 and again during the early phase of the Iran-Iraq War in 1980 and 1981. This control quickly vanished once the Iranian army was able to mobilize troops into the region (especially between 1981

---

79. GAM commanders often increased their business positions through neo-patrimonial or predatory means.

and 1983) (Entessar 1984; B. Smith 2009). In the following years, and in particular after the end of the war with Iraq in 1988, the Iranian government established firm military control over the Kurdish region. The KDPI was significantly weakened as a result of struggles between various factions and with other rebel groups, as well as the assassination of its leader Abd al-Rahman Qasimlu in 1989 (Ahmadzadeh and Stansfield 2010; McDowall 2004: 272–283).

The Manjil-Rudbar earthquake struck the area northeast of the capital Tehran, close to the coast of the Caspian Sea, on June 21, 1990, with a magnitude of 7.3. The disaster affected the cities of Manjil, Rudbar, and Lowshan along with around 1,000 villages in the Zanjan and Gilan provinces. Particularly due to its occurrence late at night (12:30 a.m.) and the extensive damage to health and transportation infrastructure, the number of fatalities (40,000) and injured (60,000) was very high (Ibrion et al. 2015). Over 100 landslides triggered by the earthquake further amplified the scale of the disaster. Direct economic losses amounted to US$7.2 billion (Berberian 2005). Unemployment rates increased to 36% after the earthquake, resulting in an increase of poverty and crime. Although Iran has frequently been struck by seismic activities, its preparation and responses were insufficient. The country also had improper building and infrastructure construction, poor shelter policies, reconstruction teams unfamiliar with the local culture and language, and insufficient reconstruction financing. Hosseini et al. (2013) thus reported a drop of confidence in the Iranian government after the disaster.

Despite this public discontent, the earthquake had no discernible impact on conflict dynamics in Iran. The intensity of the government-KDPI conflict was already very low (1 death before the disaster), and it increased only moderately during the earthquake month (23 deaths)[80] and in the year after (7 deaths). This is hardly surprising as anti-regime sentiments in the affected provinces were very low, with no rebel groups operating in the area. The earthquake did not affect the Kurdish areas in western Iran, because the major Kurdish cities of Kirmanshan, Mahabad, and Sanandaj were hundreds of kilometers from the epicenter. Consequently, the ability of the military to access the areas in which the KDPI operated was not restricted, despite the vast destruction of the infrastructure caused by the

80. The majority of the 23 deaths occurred during a KDPI guerrilla campaign that started three weeks before the earthquake (MAR 2010).

earthquake. While the Iranian military participated in the rescue and relief operation around Manjil and Rudbar, it remained present and far stronger than the weakened and divided insurgents in the western part of the country (Entessar 2010: 15–66; McDowall 2004: 272–283).

Iran 1997: The MEK Insurgency and the Qayen Earthquake

The People's Mujahideen Organisation (MEK) is an offshoot of the Liberal Movement (LM), a party that aimed to overthrow the shah and establish a national and democratic regime in Iran. After a failed uprising in 1963, the LM collapsed and the MEK emerged, advocating more religious, leftist, and anti-American sentiments as well as more violent strategies than its predecessor organization. Backed mostly by members of the middle class, the MEK remained weak throughout the 1960s and 1970s and was able to stage only a few guerrilla attacks, also due to internal struggles. In 1979, Ayatollah Khomeini assumed power in Iran during an Islamic revolution and started violently repressing all opposition parties, including the pro-democratic MEK. The resulting struggle was characterized by armed confrontations between the government's Revolutionary Guards and the MEK as well as a number of targeted assassinations. The MEK quickly lost ground. However, it was able to survive with the help of Iraq and, from 1986 onward, staged attacks from Iraqi territory. Due to its support of Iraq in the Iran-Iraq War (1980–1988), the MEK lost popularity in Iran (Ostovar 2016: 73). Despite this, it remained able to engage in minor clashes with the Iranian government as well as to conduct targeted assassinations and bombings during the 1990s (Cafarella 2005; Duncombe 2019; Norris 2008).[81]

On May 10, 1997, a major earthquake struck the Khorasan Province in northeastern Iran, close to the border with Afghanistan. Given the high magnitude (7.1) of the earthquake, the death toll of 1,500–2,000 was rather moderate. This is mostly because the earthquake took place at noon, when few people were inside their houses. Damage to residential and commercial buildings, by contrast, was extensive because standard buildings in the affected region (adobe houses with lightweight walls and heavy roofs) were very vulnerable to ground movements. The loss of many sheep as well as the destruction of road and irrigation infrastructure negatively affected the rural economy.

---

81. Mostly through its 1987 funded military arm, the National Liberation Army (NLA).

The negative impacts of the Qayen earthquake (named after a heavily affected town) were significantly stronger in the southern part of the Khorasan than in northern Khorasan. A previous earthquake in 1979 in the latter had led to higher building standards and improved settlement zoning. The response of the Iranian government was generally considered adequate, with rapid repair of electricity, water, and telephone lines, support for international aid providers, and extensive emergency and reconstruction operations (Hakuno et al. 1997; Valinejad 1997).

Around the time the disaster struck, the Iranian government and the MEK rarely engaged in armed encounters. Conflict intensity barely changed between the pre-disaster period (25 battle-related deaths) and the post-disaster period (18 deaths), with no civilian casualties reported. This is not surprising, as the Qayen earthquake affected a poor and rural region in the east of Iran, while the MEK had its operational bases in Iraq and most battles during this time occurred along the western border of Iran. No relevant constituencies of either conflict party were affected. And while the Iranian state devoted significant efforts to post-disaster rescue and reconstruction (Associated Press 1997), this could not alter the highly unequal balance of power between the Iranian military (around 650,000 active front-line personnel) and the MEK (no more than 10,000 fighters in 1997) (Andrews 2015: 32; Razoux 2015: 544).[82] Therefore, the earthquake had no impact on the conflict dynamics in this case.

Nepal 1996: Correlation but No Causation between Floods and Armed Conflict Escalation

In 1960, King Mahendra Bir Bikram Shah Dev imposed the Panchayat system on Nepal, essentially abolishing democracy and making the monarch the center of the political system. Several democracy movements challenged this move over time, and in 1990 the Jana Andolan movement eventually restored democracy in Nepal. However, the new political system did not meet the expectations of a significant portion of Nepalis. Frequent government changes and continuing political repression alienated many people from the ruling parties despite a decent macro-economic

82. The decision by the United States to include the MEK on its list of terrorist organizations in July 1997 had a more severe impact on the MEK than did the disaster, as it limited its overseas funding opportunities (Cafarella 2005).

performance (Srivastava and Sharma 2010). At the same time, widespread poverty and livelihood insecurity produced significant grievances among Nepal's rural peasants and laborers. Caste, cultural,[83] and gender hierarchies added a large number of frustrated lower-caste members (*Dalits*), ethnic minorities, and women to the picture (Bownas 2015; Upreti 2004).

The Communist movement, which has traditionally been strong in Nepal and attempted an uprising in 1971, mobilized in response to these grievances. In 1990, the Maoist Communist Party of Nepal–Unity Center (CPN-UC) emerged. It participated in the 1991 elections but renamed itself as CPN-Maoist (CPN-M) in 1995 and decided to challenge the government by violent means. After a list of 40 demands was ignored by the government, the Maoists initiated a guerrilla war with attacks on police stations in February 1996. In the first years of the insurgency, only the police (and not the military) responded to these attacks. Due to years of ideological work and strong grievances among disadvantaged groups, the CPN-M could build on a considerable base of support, particularly in remote rural areas where state presence was weak (Lawoti 2009; Subedi 2013).

In June 1996, a few months after the onset of the civil war, a massive monsoon rainfall triggered a serious flood event that resulted in the loss of 768 lives. The disaster had a major effect on the agricultural sector, which provided livelihoods to the vast majority of Nepal's rural population, with at least 6,000 hectares of cropland devastated (IFRC 1996b). While the flood hit several parts of the country, eastern Nepal (and particularly the districts of Jhapa, Morang, and Sunsari) suffered the most damage (UPI 1996). The government partnered with international organizations like the World Food Programme and the Red Cross to deliver relief, but did not consider the disaster serious enough to launch an appeal for international assistance (UN DHA 1996). A limited number of soldiers and police officers from the affected regions also assisted in the disaster relief, but overall, the flood had a limited impact on state capabilities (IFRC 1996a). There are no reports of large-scale local protests related to the flood.

The Maoist conflict intensified significantly after the flood, with 39 battle-related deaths in the year before and 73 in the subsequent 12-month period. This escalation was driven mostly by long-standing poverty and

---

83. This refers to the exclusion of ethnic languages from the education sector and the dominance of the Hindu religion, among others.

inequality, frustration about the outcomes of the democratic transition, and the CPN-M's strategic decision to respond to these grievances with violence. Further relevant factors included the split between moderate and radical Communist groups as well as neoliberal reforms during the 1990s (Hachhethu 1997; Subedi 2013). In addition, rural poverty was an important driver of the conflict escalation (Deraniyagala 2005; Do and Iyer 2010), and the flood certainly increased such poverty. Providing people in flood-affected areas with adequate relief was also on the list of the 40 demands that the CPN-M sent to the government before launching the insurgency (Bhattarai 1996).

However, especially in the first years of the civil war, the conflict was highly localized, with the Maoists running recruitment campaigns and attacking state agents solely in their strongholds (Adhikari and Samford 2013; Joshi 2013). The most conflict-affected districts in 1996 were in the midwestern hills[84] and thus far from the areas in eastern Nepal where the flood caused major havoc (IFRC 1996a). Hence, the insurgents could not benefit from disaster-related grievances or poverty (e.g., for recruitment purposes). Because the flood had a limited impact on the capabilities of both conflict parties, the opportunity and costly signal perspectives are implausible as well. The 1996 flood did not affect the conflict dynamics in Nepal.

Pakistan 2005: Escalation after, but Not Related to the Kashmir Earthquake

Balochistan only reluctantly and under force joined newly independent Pakistan in 1947. The southernmost province remained the economically most under-developed part of Pakistan in the subsequent decades. Centralized decision making and the dominance of non-locals in Balochistan's bureaucracy (as well as in the military) further added to popular grievances. Revolts against Pakistani rule were suppressed by the military in 1948, 1958, and 1962. In the mid-1970s, another, larger-scale armed uprising erupted when the central government disbanded a Baluchi ethno-nationalist government. The guerrilla warfare ended with a cease-fire in 1977 (Aslam 2011; Grare 2013).

In the early 2000s, grievances again intensified in Balochistan. The province continued to experience high levels of poverty, and the rigged regional

---

84. Namely, Rolpa, Rukum, and to a lesser degree Jajarkot.

elections in 2002 demonstrated the continued political marginalization of the region by the center. Revenues from its rich natural resources, like gas, coal, copper, and gold, largely benefited other parts of Pakistan. Large-scale infrastructure projects, including the Gwadar port, accelerated this unequal distribution of benefits and triggered concerns about shifts in the demographic balance (disfavoring ethnic Balochis) caused by immigration (Bansal 2008). The military government of Pervez Musharraf chose repression over negotiation to address these grievances. In response, the Baluchistan Liberation Army (BLA) was formed around 2000 and started to attack army posts and infrastructure (Tariq 2013). The group acquired advanced weapons and sufficient ammunition through links to the Afghan arms and drug markets. Despite this, the conflict remained at a low level until the eruption of large-scale protests in early 2005 further boosted the Baluchi autonomy/independence movement (A. Khan 2009; Samad 2014).[85]

Only months after these protests, Pakistan experienced one of the worst disasters in its history. A 7.8-magnitude earthquake hit the northern regions of the country,[86] leaving more than 73,000 people dead. Infrastructure losses amounted to US$5–6 billion, with the water, power, and transportation sectors most severely affected. The lack of preparation and disaster-related knowledge as well as the inaccessible terrain complicated relief operations. Public opinion about the disaster response varied, ranging from severe criticism of the slow, top-down, and inadequate state reaction to beliefs that the earthquake was an act of God, to satisfaction with the efforts by the Pakistani military and foreign NGOs (Benini et al. 2009; Cosgrave and Herson 2008; Halvorson and Hamilton 2010). The military clearly led the disaster response, particularly during the relief period (Özerdem 2006).

In the aftermath of the earthquake, the conflict in Baluchistan escalated significantly. When comparing the pre- with the post-disaster 12-month period, battle-related deaths increase more than fivefold, from 40 to 216. However, while the conflict was heavily localized in Baluchistan, the earthquake occurred in a different part of the country, which renders grievance- and recruitment-based explanations implausible. The Pakistani military sent an additional 60,000 troops to the earthquake-affected areas, but not

85. This movement contained various groups with heterogeneous goals and structures, including Baluch Ittehad and the Baluch Republican Party.
86. The Northwest Frontier Province and particularly Azad Jammu and Kashmir.

from Baluchistan, where its presence remained strong (Aslam 2011; Cosgrave and Herson 2008). The grievance, opportunity and costly signal pathways are hence implausible.

Rather, the escalation trend was driven by two spikes of violence (visible in figure 3.2) unrelated to the earthquake. In December 2005, the military started a fully fledged offensive against the BLA. "The operation, which had long been coming, was delayed due to the earthquake that hit Pakistan on October 8, 2005" (Bansal 2006: 52). In August 2006, the army killed Baluch leader Akbar Bugti, triggering a new (and more intense) wave of guerrilla warfare by the BLA and its allies (Samad 2014). The 2005 earthquake, by contrast, did not impact conflict intensity.

Pakistan 2015: Turning On the Heat, Turning Off the Conflict?

The analysis in the case study "Pakistan 2010: Floods Facilitating Conflict De-escalation" (earlier in this chapter) describes the struggle between the TTP and the Pakistani state until 2011. The conflict between the Pakistani government and the TTP remained active throughout the early 2010s. After the TTP leader Hakimullah Mehsud was killed in a drone strike in November 2013, the group increasingly broke into smaller factions (Mahmood 2015). Peace negotiations re-started in the same year. However, large-scale TTP attacks on the Karachi airport in June 2014 and the Peshawar Army Public School in December 2014 changed the mood of the government and the general public. The Pakistani army conducted several large-scale military offensives[87] in the second half of 2014 and early 2015, killing over 1,100 Taliban fighters and gaining control over TTP strongholds like North Waziristan (Shah and Asif 2015). As a result, the security situation improved considerably in early 2015, although the TTP still carried out attacks (Akhtar 2019; Khan and Wei 2016; Kugelman 2017).

Between June 18 and June 24, 2015, an unusual combination of warm air (up to 45°C or 113°F), high humidity, and weak winds led to an intense heat wave in Sindh, southern Punjab, and parts of Baluchistan in southern Pakistan. The felt air temperature peaked at 66°C (151°F) and averaged more than 50°C (122°F) during this period, leading to intense heat stress. These meteorological conditions affected the power and water supply, fasting during the holy month of Ramadan, and laborers continuing to work outdoors

---

87. Most notably Operation Zarb-e-Azb, which started in June 2014.

(Salim et al. 2015).[88] The heat wave resulted in 1,229 deaths, with the megacity of Karachi suffering the brunt of the impact (Clark 2015; Hanif 2017).

In a comparison of the year before and after the heat wave, the government-TTP conflict de-escalated remarkably. Battle-related deaths declined from 3,422 to 1,274 in Pakistan as a whole, and from 231 to 72 in Sindh, the province most affected by the disaster.[89] The heat wave indeed triggered several developments relevant to the political conflicts. State, provincial, and city officials as well as parts of the private sector (e.g., energy companies) blamed each other for insufficient responses to the disaster, such as a lack of early warnings and power cuts. Public protests against the mismanagement of the crisis emerged in and around Karachi (Iyengar 2015b; Pakistan Today 2015). Furthermore, the TTP threatened the company responsible for the power supply (and cuts) in Karachi. The TTP stated that it "considers K-Electric fully responsible because of undue load shedding and greed for profits. . . . Tehreek-e-Taliban Pakistan will not hesitate to take proper steps against K-Electric" if the situation does not improve (Nauman 2015).

However, none of these developments were severe enough to trigger a major change in conflict dynamics between the government and the TTP (and if so, grievances, protests, and threats would have more likely facilitated an escalation rather than the observed de-escalation of the conflict). The Pakistani military deployed troops for disaster response purposes to Karachi, but the operation was too small and short-lived to affect its capabilities (Iyengar 2015a). The economic consequences of the heat wave were also mild and offset by a strong performance of the Pakistani economy in 2015 and 2016. And while local cooperation occurred, its small scale and the non-participation of the TTP render solidarity-based explanations for conflict de-escalation implausible (Salim et al. 2015). The military offensives in 2014, by contrast, significantly reduced the capacity of the TTP to launch further attacks. After the end of the offensives in early 2015, the activities of the Pakistani army returned to a "normal" level (Kugelman 2017; Shah 2016). These two factors—rather than the impacts of the 2015 heat wave—convincingly account for the conflict de-escalation.

88. Many Muslims do not eat or drink during the daylight hours of Ramandan, making their bodies particularly vulnerable to heat stress and dehydration during periods of high temperatures.
89. The numbers are almost exclusively driven by conflict events in Karachi (231 and 71 deaths, respectively).

Peru 2007: High-Intensity Earthquake, Low-Intensity Conflict

In 1968, Abimael Guzmán founded the Maoist Communist Party of Peru—commonly known as Sendero Luminoso (Shining Path)—in the southern Peruvian region of Ayacucho. Appealing to Marxist university students and staff members as well as indigenous peasants, he slowly built a strong political (and armed) organization. Local grievances about decades of marginalization by the state, endemic poverty, and ethnic discrimination of indigenous groups facilitated these efforts.[90] In 1980, Sendero Luminoso started to challenge the Peruvian state with guerrilla attacks. Despite active counterinsurgency measures from 1983 onward, the civil war escalated quickly, and by 1991, fighting was present in 88% of all departments (McClintock 1984; Taylor 2017).[91]

Various developments in the early 1990s caused the tide to turn against Sendero Luminoso. The rebels lost support among their peasant base owing to excessive violence against civilians and forced recruitment. Consequently, local self-defense groups (so-called *rondas campesinas*) formed and were armed by the Peruvian state. At the same time, the latter improved its counterinsurgency efforts by, among other things, focusing less on human rights concerns and by improving its intelligence capabilities.[92] In 1992, Guzmán and other senior leaders of the rebels were captured. After Guzmán called for peace negotiations in 1993, the rebels split into rival factions: one remaining loyal to him and one ruling out any possibility of a peaceful solution. By the late 1990s, Sendero Luminoso was confined to the small areas of the Upper Huallaga Valley and the Apurimac–Ene River Valleys (VRAE), and observers considered the group virtually defeated (Masterson 2010; Mealy and Austad 2012; Taylor 2017).

However, with the newly elected president Alejandro Toledo turning his attention to other problems and a few hundred hard-to-trace rebels still active in vast jungles, Sendero Luminoso was able to survive and regroup. The group improved its relationship with the (still marginalized) peasants in the areas it operated, intensified its involvement in the coca business

---

90. Interestingly, the southern highland of Peru experienced a severe drought in 1983, which deprived peasants of their livelihoods and increased the willingness to support Sendero Luminoso.
91. From the mid-1980s onward, Sendero Luminoso was able to extract considerable benefits from coca production and trade to sustain its armed struggle.
92. For instance, by founding a special intelligence unit (GEIN).

to raise funds, and started to forge connections with the FARC rebels in Colombia. From 2006 onward, it increased its guerrilla activities in the Upper Huallaga Valley and VRAE, resulting in backlashes from the Peruvian military (Hyland 2008; Koven and McClintock 2015; Mealy and Austad 2012; Palmer and Bolívar 2012; Sanchez 2003).

On August 15, 2007, a 7.9-magnitude earthquake occurred, its epicenter located off the Peruvian coast. The earthquake resulted in 600 deaths and massive destruction (US$450 million, associated with a GDP loss of at least 0.3%), mostly in the western provinces of Ica, Pincho, Canete, and Chincha (IFRC 2007c). The destruction of houses and civilian infrastructure was massive, but major transport routes suffered only minor damage. A large amount of international aid was released in the immediate aftermath of the earthquake facilitating relief and reconstruction efforts. However, local response capabilities were insufficient, and rather than supporting those efforts, President Alan Garcia created a centralized parallel system. This resulted in a lack of coordination, corruption, and delays related to bureaucratic hurdles. A month after the earthquake, several remote areas still had not received any government support, and reconstruction efforts (particularly for poorer households) were slow (Milch et al. 2010). As a consequence, several large demonstrations by disaster victims took place (BBC News 2007; Elhawary and Castillo 2008), while support for Garcia (−20 to −40%) and the democratic political system (−30%) dropped considerably in the affected areas (Katz and Levin 2015; Taucer et al. 2007).

In the two-year period around the earthquake, the conflict between the Peruvian government and Sendero Luminoso essentially remained at the same (low) intensity, with 23 battle-related deaths in the 12 months before the disaster and 24 deaths in the subsequent year. The earthquake did not affect the conflict dynamics in any meaningful way. The Upper Huallaga Valley and VRAE area were not affected by the disaster, meaning that the rebels could not capitalize on increased grievances or aid inflows, and their activities were not impeded by the earthquake. Further, while the Peruvian military supported the disaster relief efforts to a considerable degree (Elhawary and Castillo 2008), the overall military balance was too uneven for this to have an impact: approximately 200,000 Peruvian military and security forces faced around 900 Sendero Luminoso cadres (Mealy and Austad 2012; Sanchez 2003).

Philippines 1991: Storm, Flood, and Conflict De-escalation

The case study "Philippines 1990: Earthquake-Related Opportunities for Both Sides" (earlier in this chapter) provides a general introduction to the CPP/NPA conflict. While fighting activities increased after the Luzon earthquake, this effect was temporary and started to vanish around April 1991, reversing back to the long-term downward trend in conflict intensity between the Philippine government and the NPA. One reason for this was the general decline of the CPP/NPA due to internal purges, changed government strategies, and the post-1986 democratization (Marks 1993). At the same time, the government was still struggling with significant challenges, including the ongoing economic crisis, insurgencies by the NPA, Mindanao separatists and right-wing extremists, high levels of corruption and patronage, and disasters like the eruption of Mount Pinatubo (Brillantes 1992).

Between November 5 and November 8, 1991, Tropical Storm Thelma (locally often referred to as Typhoon Uring) moved over the Visayas, a group of large islands in the central Philippines. The storm killed at least 6,000 people and caused direct economic damage of US$28 million. The provinces of Leyte and Negros Occidentale were severely affected, but the disaster caused the majority of damage in the riverine parts of the city of Ormoc (Leyte province). Many people died in floods caused by sudden, intense rainfall, with the poorer populations who had settled on vulnerable islands and riverbeds being disproportionately affected (Brillantes 1992; Mahmud 2000). Consequently, Thelma caused considerable losses in assets, employment, and income, especially among the poor (Predo 2010). A major reason for the severity of the floods was extensive deforestation in the surrounding hills; after the storm, many locals demanded a logging ban (Benson 1997; EESC 1992). The government response to the disaster was delayed by a lack of preparation and the interruption of communication lines. But once the response started, it was rather comprehensive owing to much media attention and the local concentration of damage (De Leon and Laigo 1993).

In the year after Tropical Storm Thelma, the conflict between the Philippine government and the CPP/NPA de-escalated significantly. Battle-related deaths dropped to 465 (down from 1,570 in the previous year). However, for a number of reasons, the de-escalation was not related to the disaster. The impacts of Thelma and particularly the associated floods were strongly concentrated in the city of Ormoc. As a consequence, there were no vast, heavily affected rural areas that the rebels could use for recruitment or that the government could access for intelligence gathering. Relief and reconstruction efforts were handled relatively well, owing to high NGO support, the relatively low economic damage, and the geographical concentration of heavy destruction. There was no articulation of major grievances related to the disaster (Alders 2017; Bankoff 2004). It is also worth noting that the disaster-stricken region was not a CPP stronghold in the early 1990s. The decrease in violence intensity was far less significant in the provinces of Leyte and Negros Occidentale (47 deaths in the year before and 28 deaths in the 12 months after the storm[93]) than in the country overall.

In line with this, a range of other factors can account for the conflict de-escalation very well. To start with, the CPP and NPA had been in decline since 1987, reducing their ability to engage in armed confrontations with the Philippine army (see the case study "Philippines 1990: Earthquake-Related Opportunities for Both Sides" earlier in this chapter for further details) (Marks 1993). Two additional external developments reduced the appeal of and support for the CPP. First, shortly before Thelma, the Philippine Senate decided in September 1991 that US military bases would have to be removed from the country—an issue around which the CPP had mobilized for decades (Brillantes 1992). Second, six months after the storm, Fidel V. Ramos was elected president of the Philippines. Among his first actions in office were the legalization of the CPP and preparations to re-start peace negotiations (Brillantes 1993). Perhaps more important, however, was the emergence of a split within the CPP in late 1991 and 1992 over its future strategic orientation. The "reaffirmists" preferred to re-expand control of the countryside and continue the armed struggle, while the "rejectionists" envisioned a greater role for elections and negotiations. Distracted by internal issues and facing a loss of members as many rejectionists left the party after the reaffirmist faction prevailed, the CPP/NPA further reduced its armed activities (P. Santos 2010; S. Santos 2005). Tropical Storm Thelma, by contrast, played no role in the conflict de-escalation.

93. This equals a reduction of 3.7 standard deviations, which is below the threshold of 5.0 usually applied in this analysis.

Philippines 2013: Super Typhoon, but Few Conflict Implications
I describe the development of the CPP/NPA conflict until the early 1990s when discussing the case studies "Philippines 1990: Earthquake-Related Opportunities for Both Sides" and "Philippines 1991: Storm, Flood, and Conflict De-escalation" (earlier in this chapter). From the mid-1990s onward, the CPP/NPA re-gained ground. It was able to recover part of its organizational strength and support base, particularly in remote regions. The population had become increasingly disappointed with the persistent inequality and corruption after democratization in 1986, while the CPP increased its efforts to build a base in rural areas. The campaign to ouster President Joseph Estrada in 2001 also strengthened the connections of the CPP to the broader left-wing and pro-democratic movement. Peace negotiations started again in the early 2000s but were suspended after a number of Western countries blacklisted the CPP and NPA as terrorist organizations. President Gloria Macapagal-Arroyo then declared an all-out war against the Communists in 2006 (P. Santos 2010). The CPP/NPA proved resilient, however, and increased its strength in the late 2000s (even though it did not come close to its peak strength during the mid-1980s).[94] Revolutionary taxes levied from the Philippines' booming mining sector boosted the group's finances (Holden and Jacobson 2007). Another round of peace negotiations started in 2011 but collapsed in early 2013 (Heydarian 2015; Quimpo 2014, 2016).

Less than a year after the peace process eventually failed, Typhoon Haiyan (locally referred to as Yolanda) hit the country. With wind speeds of more than 300 km/h and storm surges up to 6 meters high, it was the strongest typhoon ever recorded. Haiyan left 7,354 people dead, affected around 15 million others, and caused an economic impact of US$10 billion (around 4% of the Philippines' GDP at this time). Tacloban city and the provinces of Cebu, Eastern Samar, Iloilo, Leyte, and Samar were the most heavily affected. Several of these provinces—Leyte and Samar in particular—were NPA strongholds in 2013 (Wasiak 2014).

While considerable international aid flew into the country, "the Philippine government's handling of the post-typhoon crisis was widely derided as lackluster and ineffectual, in terms of logistical response, crisis management,

---

94. The number of NPA fighters was only around 4,000 to 5,000 in 2010, compared with around 25,000 in 1987.

and public relations" (Sidel 2014: 70). Political feuds between the central government and the mayor of the most-affected area (Tacloban) complicated relief efforts. The delivery of emergency aid and the reconstruction of infrastructure were slow owing to a lack of preparation, top-down management, and the precarious security situation (Sidel 2014). It took more than 10 months for a recovery plan (and the associated money) to pass legislation. As a consequence, a movement called People Surge formed around Tacloban to protest the government's handling of Haiyan, along with a lack of compensation and the establishment of a no-build zone along the coast. Two months after the disaster, People Surge mobilized 12,000 people in Tacloban (Salazar 2015; Yamada and Galat 2014; Yee 2018). There were various reports of people looting food, water, and medicine out of desperation and poor post-disaster living conditions (Marshall and Grudgings 2013).

The intensity of the conflict between the Philippine government and the CPP/NPA hardly changed after Haiyan. In the year before the typhoon, there were 175 battle-related deaths, compared with 190 in the 12 months after the typhoon. The NPA attacked military convoys on the Visayas to loot relief goods (government perspective) or prevent counterinsurgency measures, including information gathering (rebel perspective), but this hardly changed the overall dynamics of the conflict (Wasiak 2014).

While grievances against the government developed during the disaster, they were articulated by the non-violent and non-Communist People Surge movement, giving the CPP limited room to mobilize around this issue (Yee 2018). Colin Walch (2018b) finds that the typhoon hampered local NPA recruitment efforts, as it destroyed rebel camps, caused a military presence in the region (in order to distribute aid), heavily affected supportive communities, and interrupted communication lines (hence complicating rebel coordination). Many NPA fighters were locals and had to cope with the impact of the storm on their family's livelihood themselves, leaving them with less time to engage in political/armed activities.[95] At the same time, the impacts of Haiyan were not strong enough to trigger a local de-escalation of violence, particularly as the conflict was already at a very low intensity: the most disaster-affected provinces[96] experienced only two battles (three

95. According to Joshua Eastin (2017), disasters in poor regions provided recruitment opportunities for the CPP/NPA in other instances.
96. Cebu, Eastern Samar, Iloilo, Leyte, Samar, and Tacloban.

deaths) before and two battles (two deaths) after Haiyan (in the respective 12-month time frames).

The NPA declared a two-month cease-fire after the disaster, but this move was strategically motivated (given its own weakening by Haiyan) and not reciprocated by the government (Walch 2018b; Wasiak 2014). Opportunities to build solidarity in the wake of the disaster were thus slim. The typhoon was also not significant enough to affect conflict dynamics beyond the region it struck. The CPP/NPA had other strongholds and was particularly active farther south in Mindanao. The government remained stronger than the NPA, particularly in the areas of solid economic growth, international support, and an ongoing peace process with other rebel groups (Sidel 2015). There is also no evidence of signaling dynamics between the conflict parties related to Haiyan. In other words, despite its heavy impact and the insufficient disaster relief and recovery process, the typhoon had no impact on armed conflict intensity.

Philippines 2012: No Link between Typhoon and Conflict Escalation
Mindanao is the large, southern island of the Philippines. Characterized by Islamic culture and religion, it was never properly controlled by the Spanish colonizers or the US protectorate. When the Philippines became independent in 1946, Mindanao remained politically and economically marginal to the Christian-dominated state. This marginalization, combined with cultural differences and resistance to state-induced migration from northern islands, facilitated calls for an independent Moro[97] nation-state. Between 1968 and 1972, the Moro National Liberation Front (MNLF) emerged to fight for independence through diplomacy and armed struggle. In 1984, the Moro Islamic Liberation Front (MILF) split from the MNLF.[98] The MNLF concluded a peace agreement with the government in 1996, while peace negotiations with the MILF were successful in 2014 (S. Santos 2010).

The Abu Sayyaf Group (ASG),[99] another MNLF breakaway faction, emerged in 1989. Influenced by Afghanistan veterans and (until 1995) al-Qaeda funding, it promoted a radical version of Islam. Unlike the MNLF at

97. Moro is the name of the local Muslim population, coined by the Spaniards and referring to the Moor Muslims in the Mediterranean region.
98. The MILF opposed the peace negotiations and secular politics of the MNLF. Power struggles between different ethnic allegiances also played a role for the division.
99. Also known as Al-Harakatul Al-Islamiyya.

this time, the ASG rejected peace negotiations and proposals for an autonomous (rather than independent) Mindanao. Its extremist ideology and violence against civilians prevented the group from gaining island-wide popular support or the strength of the MNLF or MILF. Yet, it remained able to recruit from poor or ideologically committed youths in rural western Mindanao and was able to carry out significant attacks during the 1990s and 2000s (Banlaoi 2010; Santos and Santos 2010a).

The development of the ASG can be described in three phases (Schuck 2021). It emerged as a rebel group formed by religious extremists and disgruntled MNLF cadres. From the late 1990s onward, the group lost its ideological commitment and frequently engaged in for-ransom kidnappings. This was partially due to financial difficulties and partially because of criminals joining the ASG. However, bombings in major cities remained part of the group's strategy (Santos and Dinampo 2010). The third phase started around 2006 and saw an increasing fragmentation of the ASG into various criminal and Islamist branches (Abuza 2010; East 2013; Katagiri 2019; O'Brien 2012).

On December 4, 2012, Typhoon Bopha (locally termed Pablo) made landfall on the east coast of Mindanao. Torrential rain triggered excessive landslides, while high wind speeds destroyed infrastructure and agricultural systems. The total death toll was 1,901, while economic damage amounted to more than US$1 billion (Rodolfo et al. 2016). The storm caught large parts of the population unprepared, as the typical cyclone route runs farther north and early warnings were frequently not heard or were ignored. The affected area already suffered from poverty and a population that, owing to the legacy of armed conflict, was vulnerable to the disaster. International aid was slow to come in, and only 35% of a UN appeal was funded. Combined with heavy losses in the agricultural sector[100] and transport routes to remote regions rendered inaccessible, Bopha led to worsened poverty and food insecurity in Mindanao (Bamforth 2015). The lack of adequate shelter was also an issue, particularly as reconstruction funds were only available to those with land titles—a relatively well-off minority in the region (Barber 2014; UN OCHA 2013).

Looking at the UCDP data, one can conclude that the conflict dynamics remained relatively stable after Typhoon Bopha. Confrontations involving

---

100. Tom Bamforth (2015: 202–203) reports a production decline of 33%–50% after the typhoon, with staples such as maize (80% of all crops affected) and cash crops like coconut (73%) or banana (72%) being hit hardest.

the ASG accounted for 79 deaths in the year before and 55 in the year after the storm. But according to Bob East (2013: 98), ASG-reported conflict events suffer from significant gaps and biases. The Global Terrorism Database (START 2018), for instance, recognizes a strong rise in ASG activities in the 12-month period after Bopha (32 attacks, up from 20 attacks in the year before[101]), which is confirmed by qualitative accounts (O'Brien 2012). This increase can largely be attributed to an increasing fragmentation of the group, giving individual factions a free hand in using violence, combined with the radicalization of parts of the movement and support from new allies like the Bangsamoro Islamic Freedom Movement (Katagiri 2019).

In theory, Bopha could have boosted ASG membership, as the group recruited predominantly from the rural poor (Loesch 2017). However, in 2013, the group was active only on the islands of Basilan and Sulu. Both are located west of Mindanao and were not affected by the disaster (Eugenio et al. 2016; Rodolfo et al. 2016). With only 400–500 ASG members at that time, the involvement of the Philippine army in the post-disaster relief operation was unlikely to have shifted the military balance in favor of the rebels (Banlaoi 2010). When the armed forces of the Philippines declared a unilateral cease-fire after the typhoon, it explicitly excluded the ASG, leaving little room for diplomacy (*Bangkok Post* 2012). Therefore, Typhoon Bopha had no impact on the government-ASG conflict in the Philippines.

Russia 1995: The Sakhalin Earthquake and the Conflict in Chechnya—Too Far Apart

Russia started to conquer Chechnya and incorporate it into its empire in the early eighteenth century. Local struggles against Russian dominance remained active on a low level during the Tsarist and Soviet times. This resistance was met with fierce repression, including large-scale deportations in the 1820s and particularly in 1944.[102] The experience of collective suffering facilitated notions of Chechen solidarity and identity while also fueling resistance against the central state. After its restoration in 1957,[103] the Chechen-Ingush Autonomous Soviet Socialist Republic (CI-ASSR) received little financial

---

101. This equals more than seven standard deviations.
102. Under the Stalin regime, around 400,000 Chechens were deported to Central Asia, and almost a quarter of them died during or after the deportation.
103. The CI-ASSR already existed between 1934 and 1944.

support from the political center. Despite the presence of oil reserves, it was among the poorest of the Soviet republics. Consequently, the unemployment rate in the early 1990s was around 40% (Bakke 2015; Evangelista 2002).

The combination of economic and political grievances (Fayutkin 2006) and the local elites' hunger for power culminated in strong demands for an autonomous Chechnya during the glasnost[104] period in the late 1980s and the dissolution of the Soviet Union in the early 1990s. Radical nationalist forces led by Dzhokhar Dudayev demanded secession, quickly started dominating Chechen politics, and armed themselves (Tishkov 1997). Dudayev's forces ousted the interim governing council of the CI-ASSR on October 1, 1991, won the election that they organized only 27 days later, and declared Chechnya an independent state in November. The Russian Parliament declared these moves illegal. Between 1991 and 1994, the Russian government pursued a combined strategy of negotiations, a blockade on external aid and financial flows to Chechnya, and support for intra-Chechen opposition to oust Dudayev. None of these measures proved successful. During the early 1990s, several violent quarrels between Russian-supported and pro-Dudayev forces occurred (Bakke 2015; Evangelista 2002; Hughes 2001).

On May 28, 1994, a 7.5-magnitude earthquake shook Sakhalin Island in the far east of Russia, resulting in 1,989 deaths and total economic damage of around US$1 billion. In the most affected town of Neftegorsk, 1,995 of the 3,139 inhabitants perished due to the unfortunate timing of the earthquake (in the middle of the night), a lack of early warning or disaster preparation, and the collapse of weakly constructed buildings. Relief measures by the Russian state (with some international support) were generally adequate (Thomas 1995) but severely delayed owing to the remoteness of Sakhalin Island and the destruction of infrastructure (Reuters 1995). The military involvement in these efforts was minimal. Local inhabitants conducted a few small-scale protests about insufficient rescue operations and a lack of resettlement or reconstruction schemes (Mark Johnson 1998; Porfiriev 1996, 2012).

The conflict in Chechnya saw a remarkable escalation after the earthquake, with 1,242 battle-related deaths in the 12 months before and 2,822 deaths in the subsequent year. The escalation occurred almost exclusively from December 1994 onward (that is, seven months after the earthquake).

---

104. Glasnost refers to Mikhail Gorbachev's policies to increase openness and transparency in the Soviet Union from 1985 onward.

This was the very same month that the government of President Boris Yeltsin launched a large-scale military operation in Chechnya. The Russian military was quickly able to capture the capital Grozny but subsequently was stuck in a persistent and rather intense struggle with Chechen guerrilla fighters.

The Russian military intervention was completely unrelated to the earthquake, which occurred far from Chechnya (more than 6,700 kilometers of direct distance) and hardly affected the Russian state, economy, or military. Rather, the major drivers behind the military offensive include concerns about Yeltsin's popularity in the face of neoliberal reforms, presidential advisers with a clear preference for military intervention, Chechnya's neighboring republics pressuring the Russian government to limit anarchy, and the growing political division in Chechnya[105] (Bakke 2015; Evangelista 2002; Hughes 2001; Rigi 2004). The Sakhalin Island earthquake had no effect on the conflict dynamics.

Russia 2010: Triple Disaster Not Linked to Conflict De-escalation

The war between Russia and Chechnya[106] ended with a cease-fire in 1996, paving the way for further negotiations but de facto leaving Chechnya an independent state. In 1999, Russia started another military offensive (the second Chechen War). This time, it was more successful, taking over Chechnya's capital Grozny and inflicting serious losses on the rebels between 1999 and 2002. Afterward, low-intensity violence persisted between the Russian-installed regime in Grozny and the Chechen rebels, with little peace building and reconstruction taking place. During the same period, the rebellion transformed. While clearly driven by nationalist goals in the early and mid-1990s (Bakke 2015), repression targeted against religious groups, support from transnational jihadist networks, and generational change among its cadres facilitated a gradual Islamization of the separatist movement (Sagramoso 2012; Wilhelmsen 2005).[107]

---

105. These divisions occurred between radical pro-independence elements, which also carried out attacks on Russian territory, and a more moderate movement criticizing Dudayev's lack of concessions to Russia. Both factions also undermined the Chechen-Russian negotiation process.
106. See case study "Russia 1995: The Sakhalin Earthquake and the Conflict in Chechnya—Too Far Apart" earlier in this chapter.
107. Whether this development was driven mostly by instrumental reasons and local grievances or was part of a global jihadist movement remains contested among experts; yet, the majority supports the former position (Hahn 2014; Ratelle 2014).

During the early 2000s, violent resistance against the Russian state also emerged in other parts of the North Caucasus, such as Dagestan, Kabardino-Balkaria, and Ingushetia. Political and religious repression, unemployment, poverty, and corruption were key drivers of this resistance. In October 2007, the then leader of the Chechen rebellion, Doku Umarov, established the Caucasus Emirate. This group united the various regional insurgent groups in a loose fashion and strived to establish an independent Islamic state in the North Caucasus. Bolstered by the support of international jihadist networks[108] and experienced veterans from previous wars in Chechnya, local armed units (*jamaats*) of the Caucasus Emirate quickly escalated violence in the North Caucasus, mostly through guerrilla attacks. The group was also able to conduct large-scale attacks in other parts of Russia, including the bombing of Moscow subway stations in early 2010 (al-Shishani 2014; Ratelle 2014; Souleimanov 2011).

From June to August 2010, Russia experienced a combined heat wave and drought, which also resulted in a series of forest fires. The country's main agricultural areas south of Moscow were the hardest hit. This triple disaster resulted in over 55,000 deaths and economic losses worth US$15 billion. Drought devastated over 13 million hectares of grain crops and reduced gain production by 30% (Vasquez 2011). Consequently, food prices increased countrywide even though the government implemented a grain export ban and released grain reserves. Fires burned 0.5 million hectares and caused haze hazards in Moscow and other areas. Despite severe omissions like the dismantling of forest protection services or the inability to prevent food hoarding and speculation, the national government's popularity grew during the disaster (Lazarev et al. 2014).[109] This was the case because state agencies provided considerable financial support to the drought-affected farmers (Wegren 2011; Welton 2011) and fire-affected households (Bobylev 2011). Prime Minister Vladimir Putin also displayed excellent crisis communication skills (Busygina 2012).

Conflict intensity in the North Caucasus decreased significantly after the heatwave, drought, and forest fires, with 673 deaths in the year before

---

108. The financial viability of the group was also secured through links to organized crime.
109. There were significant grievances, however, among some environmental activist groups. Local government officials in the affected areas also faced public backlash because they were blamed for the dire situation by the national government (Brooke 2010; Szakonyi 2011).

and 517 deaths in the 12 months after the triple disaster. However, this conflict de-escalation was unrelated to the triple disaster. The capability of the Caucasus Emirate to engage in violence declined from 2010 onward owing to several other factors. Russian security forces killed important leaders[110] (al-Shishani 2014). In addition, the resignation of Umarov on August 1, 2010, followed by the revocation of this decision only three days later, triggered intense struggles between regional commands as well as between Islamist and nationalist forces. The Caucasus Emirate was only able to resolve them in mid-2011 (Souleimanov 2011; West and Goodrich 2010). By then, however, support of the group from transnational jihadist networks had declined, as they redirected funds and fighters (including Caucasian militants) to the Syrian civil war (Youngman 2019). In line with this, the decline in conflict intensity was almost exclusively driven by fewer rebel attacks (Radio Free Europe / Radio Liberty 2010).

Furthermore, media reporting of the disaster did not focus on the North Caucasus, and the Russian military did not relocate troops from the region to fight the forest fires (Kirilenko 2010). The North Caucasus was only moderately affected by the drought. In fact, it was the only Russian region that experienced higher grain harvests in 2010 compared with previous years, although food prices still increased (SPA 2010; Wegren 2011; Welton 2011). Therefore, neither the Russian state nor the Caucasus Emirate faced logistical constraints or incentives for image cultivation during the disaster.

Thailand 2004: Tsunami and Conflict Escalation—Correlation but No Causation

The Patani are an ethnic group living in southern Thailand. The region they inhabit has been under the control of the Siam and later Thai state since the early twentieth century. Particularly in the provinces of Narathiwat, Pattani, and Yala (the core Patani region), the vast majority of people are Muslim and speak Malay, while in all other parts of Thailand, Thai is the dominant language and Buddhism the dominant religion. After becoming independent, the Thai state initiated efforts to promote the Thai culture and language in the Patani region, but these efforts had limited success and were met with resistance. The latter included various waves of popular uprising and armed resistance, most notably in 1948 and between 1959 and 1981. These conflicts remained on a low intensity level. From the early

---

110. Such as Anzor Astemirov and Said Buryatsky.

1980s onward, a more accommodative policy by the Thai state—including an amnesty program and an increase of development projects—caused a sharp drop in violence. However, the Patani region remained one of the poorest in Thailand.

In the early 2000s, several groups joined forces and established a coordinated military structure in order to pursue an independent Patani state.[111] These groups (called Patani insurgents here) started to initiate guerrilla attacks against the Thai military and government representatives (e.g., teachers, police officers) in 2003 and particularly in 2004. The main reasons for this upsurge of violence included efforts by Prime Minister Thaksin Shinawatra to rearrange political and security institutions in the south for his own political purposes (McCargo 2006), the growing influence of more radical interpretations of Islam (Albritton 2005), and grievances about the historical marginalization of Malay Muslims (ICG 2005). The Thai state reacted by deploying more military personnel to the Patani region and by conducting harsh counterinsurgency operations (Croissant 2007; Harish 2006).

In the middle of this tumultuous situation, a 9.3-magnitude earthquake in the Indian Ocean caused an enormous tsunami that hit the southern coastal areas of Thailand on December 26, 2004, with wave heights up to 11 meters. In the six affected provinces,[112] the tsunami killed 8,345 people and destroyed the tourism, fishing, and agricultural economies near the coast. While damage to health, transportation, water, and electricity infrastructures was minimal, economic loss is estimated to have been well above US$1 billion (Rossetto et al. 2007). Despite significant international assistance, discontent about the government's preparation and response efforts quickly surfaced in the affected areas. "Locals continued to complain that they lacked adequate shelter and relief" (CFE-DM 2006: 16), that distribution of relief was delayed, bureaucratic, and biased, and that the government had not promoted disaster preparedness. Disputes about land ownership and permission to rebuild communities close to the coast also emerged (Sato 2010). Poor inhabitants and, at least in some areas, Muslims were the most vulnerable to the tsunami (Steckley and Doberstein 2011). On the national level, however, perceptions of a successful response to the

---

111. These groups included the National Revolutionary Front-Coordinate, the New Patani United Liberation Organisation, and the Islamic Mujahideen Movement of Pattani, among others.

112. These provinces are Krabi, Phang Na, Phuket, Ranong, Satun, and Trang.

Disasters and Armed Conflict Dynamics

tsunami increased the popularity of Prime Minister Thaksin Shinawatra prior to the elections in February 2005 (Albritton 2006).

The conflict in southern Thailand has always been characterized by military encounters and civilian victimization, and both dynamics increased after the tsunami. The total number of casualties jumped from 303 (160 military, 143 civilians) in the pre-tsunami year to 491 (215 military, 276 civilians) in the subsequent 12 months. However, this upsurge is part of a general conflict escalation that started in 2003 and continued until 2007, mostly driven by better organization and more radical attitudes of the Patani insurgents as well as heavy-handed military responses of the Thai government (Albritton 2006; Croissant 2007; LaFree et al. 2013).

The tsunami, by contrast, played no role in the conflict escalation in Thailand for several reasons. First, the provinces belonging to the Patani region—where 79% of all violent incidents occurred (LaFree et al. 2013: 85)—were not affected by the tsunami at all (the disaster hit only neighboring provinces). Although a minority Muslim population lived in the tsunami-affected area and was particularly vulnerable to the disaster, they had little connection to the rebel groups. Furthermore, pro-social behavior and risk aversion increased among tsunami survivors, making a contribution to armed struggle less likely (Cassar et al. 2017). Second, there are no hints that either the government or the Patani insurgents aimed to convey any message related to the tsunami. Military considerations as well as urges to react to attacks or public threats by the other side shaped each conflict party's activity patterns (ICG 2005). Third, while the government moved around 5,000 military personnel to the tsunami-affected area, it did not relocate the 15,000 troops deployed to Narathiwat, Pattani, and Yala (CFE-DM 2006). In the aftermath of the 2004 tsunami, none of the grievances, costly signal, and opportunity impacts manifested themselves in Thailand.

Summary

This chapter presented a wealth of qualitative evidence on how disasters do and do not shape armed conflict dynamics. Following long-standing calls in environmental security research (Adams et al. 2018; Gleditsch 1998), I studied a broad range of geographical locations, armed conflict types, political-economic contexts, and conflict outcomes, including cases where disasters had no impact on conflict dynamics. From the qualitative descriptions, one can conclude that disasters have a discernible impact on both armed conflict escalation and de-escalation in some cases, while disaster-conflict linkages are absent in the majority of cases.

The answer to the first guiding question of my study (Do disasters influence the intensity of armed conflicts between governments and rebels?) is hence a qualified yes. The fifth chapter will synthesize the insights from chapter 4 in order to provide further nuance and to answer the second (Are disasters more likely to facilitate an escalation or de-escalation of armed conflicts?) and third (Which pathways and context factors can account for intrastate armed conflict (de-)escalation after a disaster has struck?) key questions of this book.

5 Armed Conflicts in the Aftermath of Disasters: Key Findings

This chapter summarizes and analyzes the key insights derived from the comprehensive case study evidence presented in the previous chapter. It also contextualizes the findings within wider debates on peace and conflict, disasters, climate change, environmental stress, and security. To do so, the chapter proceeds in three steps. First, I present summary statistics on armed conflict dynamics in the aftermath of disasters. Second, I conduct a qualitative comparative analysis (QCA) to identify which conditions or combinations of conditions can explain why disasters affect conflict dynamics in some cases but not in others. The final part of the chapter disentangles the different pathways connecting disasters to either conflict escalation or de-escalation.

General Findings and Their Implications

Armed Conflict Escalation, De-escalation, and Continuation

Within the analytical framework of this book, disasters can interact with armed conflicts in three broad ways: they can, in combination with other factors, facilitate conflict escalation or conflict de-escalation or have no impact on conflict dynamics. As indicated in figure 5.1 later in the chapter, in 50% of the cases studied here, disasters did not shape armed conflict dynamics in any meaningful way. The reasons for this can be multifold, but often include one or several of four factors.

First, other military, political, and economic drivers of conflict dynamics can be more important than the disaster. Long-standing grievances and exclusions rather than the floods in the same year drove the conflict escalation in Nepal in 1996, for example. Similarly, a rapid intensification of the conflict in Baluchistan coincided with the 2005 earthquake, but long-planned offensives by the Pakistani military were the main reason for higher conflict intensity. Likewise, the conflict between the Philippine government and the Communist Party of the Philippines / New People's Army (CPP/NPA) de-escalated in 1991 and 1992 owing to a more accommodative policy by the newly elected president and a (related) rift among CPP members, rather than Tropical Storm Thelma. This reinforces the claim of Katherine J. Mach and colleagues (2019: 194) that compared with environmental and climatic factors, "other conflict drivers are much more influential." In the 18 cases where disaster had an impact on armed conflict dynamics, they interacted with (often more important) non-disaster-related factors.

Second, disasters do not shape armed conflict dynamics if they occur far away from the areas relevant to the conflict. The latter includes territories that are contested between the parties, serve as hideouts and recruitment bases for rebels, or provide important military or economic support to the government. In the sample studied in this book, such a "distance effect" is most pronounced for the 2006 Yogyakarta earthquake in Indonesia (more than 2,000 kilometers from civil-war-ridden Aceh) and the Sakhalin Island earthquake in Russia (around 6,500 kilometers from the armed conflict in Chechnya).

Third, if the disaster does not strain the resources of the conflict parties significantly, an impact on conflict dynamics is unlikely. This might be the case because massive external aid provides relief, because the disaster's impacts are too limited to pose a serious challenge to the conflict parties, or because the rebels and/or the government do not feel committed to provide relief to the disaster-affected populations. Despite its devastating impacts, the 1997 Qayen earthquake did not affect Iran's powerful military apparatus (around 650,000 active personnel), particularly when compared with the People's Mujahideen Organisation (MEK) rebels (10,000 fighters at maximum). Another example is the 1998 Rustaq earthquake in the case study "Afghanistan 1998: Remote Earthquakes Did Not Shape Conflict Dynamics" in chapter 4. Neither the government nor the insurgents devoted many resources to assist the survivors and rebuild the disaster-ridden area. Finally, external funders covered up to 80% of the direct reconstruction costs related to the 1992 Flores earthquake in Indonesia.

Fourth, the inability of a conflict party to exploit opportunities, draw on popular grievances, or send costly signals related to the disaster also makes conflict escalation implausible. After the 2003 Boumerdès earthquake, for instance, the Algerian government faced massive grievances and had to re-direct considerable amounts of resources and security personnel to the affected area. However, by that time, the Group for Preaching and Combat (GSPC) rebels had lost popular support, maintained only a minimal presence in northern Algeria, and were unable to benefit from the situation. This also indicates that the effect of one disaster impact (grievances) can be canceled out by another impact (constraints). When it comes to conflict de-escalation, the government has little incentive to negotiate with very weak rebel groups in the wake of a disaster, and the infrastructure of such groups is often too limited to be seriously affected by an extreme event. Examples of this include the United Liberation Front of Assam (ULFA) after the 2007 floods in India, Sendero Luminoso after the 2007 Peru earthquake, and the Philippine Abu Sayyaf Group after Typhoon Bopha in 2012.

Of the remaining 18 cases, 50% display evidence for armed conflict escalation linked to the disaster, while I find evidence for a disaster-related de-escalation in the other 50% of cases. Seven of the nine escalation cases display rather strong evidence for a disaster-conflict link, as do seven of the nine de-escalation cases, while in the remaining four cases, the disaster-conflict link was either indirect or relatively minor (see table 5.1 and figure 5.1). This is an important finding in at least two respects.

On the one hand, my analysis indicates that major disasters facilitated armed conflict escalation in one of four cases (see figure 5.1). This is in line with claims that disasters can trigger a change in large-scale, complex systems and can therefore have important security implications (Gawronski and Olson 2013). Indeed, several studies find that disasters increase the risk of armed conflict onset (e.g., Gleick 2014; Ide et al. 2020; Nel and Righarts 2008) and incidence (Arai 2012; Ghimire and Ferreira 2016; von Uexkull et al. 2016). The relatively frequent association of disasters with conflict escalation indicates that such security concerns should also include conflict intensity.

This also has implications for wider debates. Given that climate change increases the frequency and intensity of disasters (IPCC 2018), a warmer world is likely characterized by more spikes in armed conflict intensity. Such spikes, in turn, accelerate infrastructure destruction, increase human insecurity, add credibility to irreconcilable narratives of the other party as evil, complicate access for humanitarian aid providers, and further increase

Table 5.1
Overview of cases, conflict dynamics, and detected disaster impacts.

Case	Dynamic	Impact
Afghanistan 1998	None	None
Afghanistan 2008	None	None
Algeria 2003	None	None
Bangladesh 1991	Escalation	Costly signal
Bangladesh 2007	De-escalation	Constraints
Burundi 2005–2006	De-escalation	(Constraints)
Colombia 1999	Escalation	Opportunity
Egypt 1994	Escalation	(Grievances)
India (Andhra Pradesh & Orissa) 1999	Escalation	Opportunity
India (Assam) 1998	Escalation	Opportunity, (grievances)
India (Assam) 2007	None	None
India (Kashmir) 2005	De-escalation	Constraints, image cultivation
Indonesia 1992	None	None
Indonesia 2004	De-escalation	Constraints, image cultivation, (solidarity)
Indonesia 2006	None	None
Iran 1990	None	None
Iran 1997	None	None
Myanmar 2008	De-escalation	Image cultivation
Nepal 1996	None	None
Pakistan 2005	None	None
Pakistan 2010	De-escalation	Constraints
Pakistan 2015	None	None
Peru 2007	None	None
Philippines 1990	Escalation	Opportunity
Philippines 1991	None	None
Philippines 2012	None	None
Philippines 2013	None	None
Russia 1995	None	None
Russia 2010	None	None
Somalia 1997	De-escalation	Constraints
Somalia 2010–2011	De-escalation	Constraints
Sri Lanka 2004	Escalation	Grievances, (costly signal)
Tajikistan 1992	Escalation	(Opportunity)
Thailand 2004	None	None
Turkey 1999	De-escalation	(Solidarity), (image cultivation)
Uganda 1999–2001	Escalation	Opportunity

Note: Parentheses in the "Impact" column indicate that the impact was indirect or played only a minor role.

Armed Conflicts in the Aftermath of Disasters 143

disaster vulnerability (Mena and Hilhorst 2021). At the same time, we have to conceive disasters not just as a result of climate change but also of multiple structural inequalities and problematic trends, such as poverty, exclusion, corruption, urbanization, and poorly designed institutions (Formetta and Feyen 2019; Wisner et al. 2004). Measures to promote inclusivity, improve education systems, and reduce poverty and inequality could hence have positive effects not only in their respective domains but—if properly designed (Ide 2020a; L. Peters 2021)—also on disaster risk reduction and armed conflict risks.

On the other hand, a considerable proportion of cases (25%) in my sample experienced an armed conflict de-escalation linked to a major disaster (see figure 5.1). So far, debates have revolved prominently around whether disasters (or climate change or resource scarcity) amplify armed conflict risks or not, with the third possibility of decreased conflict risks being almost entirely ignored. Only the research on disaster diplomacy (Kelman 2012)—which is largely marginalized in wider debates on environmental or climate security—and a few statistical analyses (De Juan et al. 2020; Slettebak 2012; Tominaga and Lee 2021) address this shortcoming.[1] This "conflict bias" indicates "an ontology of social relations as inherently agonistic" (Barnett 2019: 930) as it excludes the possibility of more peaceful social relations in the aftermath of disasters.

Such a conflict-focused ontology is problematic for several reasons. It reduces our knowledge of peaceful reactions to extreme events and environmental stress, and even of peace processes in general. Scholarship in the fields of peace and conflict studies (Bright and Gledhill 2018), international relations (Diehl 2016), and environmental security (Ide 2018) has been widely recognizing this insufficient attention to peace (when compared with conflict). As a consequence, researchers are less capable of providing policy advice on how to restore (and sustain) peace in disaster-ridden contexts. In the worst case, geopolitical imaginations of looming mass migration and violence in the face of climate change could justify militarized policies to keep refugees out and ensure autocratic state stability in the Global South (Dalby 2020; Hartmann 2014). These considerations, along with the significant

---

1. The literature on environmental peace building is another example of research focusing on the impact of environmental issues on conflict de-escalation and peace (Ide, Bruch, et al. 2021; Johnson et al. 2020). However, environmental peace-building scholars have so far paid little attention to disasters.

number of disaster-related conflict de-escalation cases in my sample, highlight the importance of complex approaches that overcome conflict-centered ontologies and account for a range of conflictual and peaceful outcomes (S. Ali 2007; Peters and Kelman 2020; Scheffran et al. 2012b).

Before discussing relevant pathways between disasters and conflict (de-)escalation, let me briefly address a wider issue related to data reliability. Concerns about the validity and representativity of information on armed conflicts are not new. Political incentives to over- or underreport conflict events (e.g., in order to exaggerate or play down a threat) as well as challenges to gather data in remote or highly insecure regions (Eck 2012; Hendrix and Salehyan 2015; Ide and Scheffran 2014) fuel these concerns. In my analysis, I first classified all 36 cases as disaster-related escalation, de-escalation, or no change of conflict intensity based on quantitative data on fatalities. Afterward, I revisited those classifications in the light of qualitative evidence. When comparing both sets of data, the overall picture does not change tremendously: when relying just on quantitative evidence, de-escalation would be considered more widespread (13 cases as compared with 9 when considering qualitative insights). To a lesser extent, the same is true for escalation (11 vs. 9 cases), while no change of conflict dynamics would be a less prominent category (12 vs. 18 cases).

That said, one should keep in mind that based on quantitative data alone, 13 cases—or more than 36% of the sample—would be classified incorrectly. These include four false positives for armed conflict escalation, five false positives for de-escalation, three false negatives for escalation, and one completely wrong classification.[2] My results are hence a reminder of the importance of qualitative information when checking the validity of quantitative data and quantitative analyses. The triangulation of quantitative and qualitative information is a key strength of the methodological approach underlying my study.

2. False positives for escalation (disaster-related escalation indicated by quantitative data but not confirmed by the case studies): Nepal 1996, Pakistan 2005, Russia 1995, and Thailand 2004. False positives for de-escalation: India (Assam) 2007, Indonesia 2006, Pakistan 2015, Philippines 1991, and Russia 2010. False negatives for escalation (disaster-related escalation indicated by case studies but not quantitative data): India (Andhra Pradesh, Orissa) 1999, India (Assam) 1998, and Uganda 1999–2001. Wrong classification: Somalia 2010–2011 (indicated as escalation by quantitative data, but de-escalation by qualitative data).

Armed Conflicts in the Aftermath of Disasters

Next, I discuss the six potential impacts of disasters on (or pathways connecting disasters to) armed conflict dynamics outlined in chapter 2 in the light of the empirical evidence from the 36 case studies. This discussion is structured along the three relevant theoretical approaches: motive, strategy, and communication (figure 5.1 provides a visual summary).

Motive

The first thing to note is the relatively weak analytical power of the motive approach: disaster-related grievances played a major role for armed conflict escalation only after the 2004 tsunami in Sri Lanka (where costly signals were a relevant factor as well). Grievances were of minor causal relevance in Egypt during the 1994 floods (where political decisions were key drivers of violence escalation) and in Assam after the 1998 floods (where the opportunity pathway has higher explanatory power). On first look, this finding is surprising given that grievances after disasters can be intense—for example, the protests against the government's disaster preparation and response in the cases of Algeria 2003, Egypt 1994, Pakistan 2015, Peru 2007, and Turkey 1999 (see chapter 4). The grievance pathway is also very prevalent in

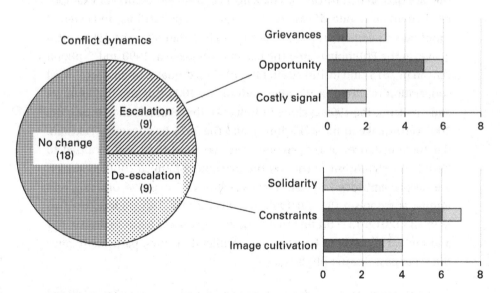

Figure 5.1
Overview of the armed conflict dynamics and disaster impacts detected (light gray bars indicate that disaster impacts played only an indirect or minor role).

existing theoretical accounts of disasters and conflict risks (e.g., Nel and Righarts 2008; Pfaff 2020).

However, as Sara McLaughlin Mitchell and Elise Pizzi (2021: 588) argue, "it is not clear that these grievances necessarily result in violent conflict." This links to the general arguments that grievances are simply too widespread (and resistance against powerful state actors too difficult) to account for changes in armed conflict risks (Fearon and Laitin 2003). The case evidence presented here as well as that of other studies on the issue (Apodaca 2017; Ide, Rodriguez Lopez, et al. 2021; Koubi et al. 2021) suggests that if a disaster is (perceived to be) mismanaged or aid is (perceived to be) distributed in an unfair way, people will protest. But there is little reason to believe that from there they take the personally risky and morally problematic route of supporting or joining an armed group. Those grievances relevant to conflict escalation are usually tied to long-standing divides that facilitate mobilization, such as political and economic marginalization of ethnic groups (Buhaug et al. 2014).

Likewise, increased solidarity after disasters has little impact on wider conflict dynamics. On the one hand, spikes of empathy and cooperation in the face of a shared threat (or challenge) certainly do occur. For example, rebel groups announced cease-fires to allow local populations and external supporters to cope with the disaster in Afghanistan after the 1998 earthquake, in the Philippines after the Luzon earthquake in 1990 and Typhoon Haiyan in 2013, and in Turkey after the 1999 earthquake. Intense local-level cooperation occurred in the aftermath of the 2004 tsunami in Indonesia and Thailand, the 1999 cyclone in India (Andhra Pradesh and Orissa), the 2005 earthquake in India (Kashmir), and the 2015 heat wave in Pakistan. But these instances of cooperation were too short-lived and localized to have had a significant impact on the dynamics of armed conflicts, which are deeply embedded in discursive structures of negative othering and mutual antagonism (Bar-Tal 1998; Kaufman 2001). This underscores Ilan Kelman's (2012: 131) finding that "disaster diplomacy tends to display few and limited success" in transforming conflict dynamics, particularly once the acute post-disaster phase is over.[3]

3. This is corroborated by earlier findings from disaster sociology (Quarantelli and Dynes 1976) and civil war studies (Kreutz 2012).

Strategy

The strategy approach has the highest explanatory power in the sample under study. A change in opportunity structures related to the disaster plays a causal role in six of the nine conflict escalation cases, and in five of them, the disaster-conflict link was strong. The cases come from a diverse set of countries and include fast- as well as slow-onset disasters (see table 5.1). Several recent studies indicate that disasters increase armed conflict onset risks through a change in opportunity structures rather than by increasing grievances (Ide et al. 2020; Salehyan and Hendrix 2014). The case studies presented in the previous chapter confirm this finding for conflict intensity.

What opportunity structures change, exactly, and for whom? Rebel groups benefited in all six cases of opportunity-related conflict escalation from the disaster (see figure 5.2). They were able to recruit more followers in four cases (India [Andhra Pradesh and Orissa] 1999, India [Assam] 1998, Philippines 1990, Tajikistan 1992), to exploit the occupation of government security forces (and resources) with disaster relief in three cases (India [Andhra Pradesh and Orissa] 1999, Colombia 1999, Philippines 1990), to appropriate disaster-related aid in one case (India [Andhra Pradesh and Orissa] 1999), and to exploit the limited mobility of government troops in one case as well (Philippines 1990). Uganda from 1999 to 2001 is an outlier

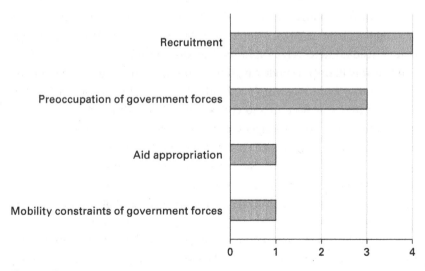

Figure 5.2
Disaster-related opportunities for rebel groups.

case, as the drought did not provide strategic advantages to the Lord's Resistance Army (LRA); instead, in combination with the loss of its bases in Sudan, it forced the group to loot larger amounts of food, hence increasing civilian casualties.

These patterns are remarkable in at least four regards. First, disasters very rarely provide opportunities for government troops to escalate the conflict. Second, a disaster usually has to affect several aspects of the strategic environment in order to open favorable windows of opportunity for rebel groups. This might be due to the considerable strength of state security forces[4] and could be one reason opportunity-driven conflict escalation is rather rare (6 out of 36 cases): disasters frequently affect opportunity structures but are not significant enough (or are significant in different ways) to give insurgents a relevant advantage vis-à-vis the government. Third, and relatedly, in none of the six cases did the rebels gain a significant long-term advantage over the government because of the disaster. Hence, we should put claims that climate change and disasters increase the risk of state failure or government overthrow under critical scrutiny.

Fourth, scholars frequently identify the inflow of additional aid as a potential link between disasters and armed conflicts—for instance, because the aid can be diverted for military purposes or because terrorist groups target aid workers (Kikuta 2019; Paul and Bagchi 2016). This coincides with quantitative evidence that foreign aid inflow increases levels of violence (Jadoon 2018; Nemeth and Mauslein 2020). However, in the sample studied here, rebels appropriated disaster-related aid in a conflict-relevant way in only a single case (and in no case did the government benefit militarily from receiving such aid). A potential explanation for this is offered by Oscar Becerra and colleagues (2014): while official development aid increases on average by 18% after large disasters, it is barely significant when compared with the affected country's overall economy and typically covers only 3% of the damage done by the disaster. Given that the conflict parties can divert only a fraction of this already rather small amount of aid, they are unlikely to benefit substantially from disaster-related aid.

The constraints pathway—the result of pairing the de-escalation outcome with the strategy approach—likewise has a high explanatory value.

---

4. This is true even in many so-called failed or fragile states (Call 2008).

It explains seven out of the nine de-escalation outcomes, and the disaster-conflict links are strong in six of those cases. Consequently, the strategy approach explains 13 out of 18 changes in conflict dynamics after disasters overall.

A disaster imposed serious constraints on the government in five cases and on the rebels in six cases. At least when it comes to the ability to maintain fighting activities and military infrastructure, it thus seems that disaster has an effect on rebels that is equal to or worse than that for state forces. This echoes Michael Brzoska's (2018: 325) claim that "major disasters reduce the capabilities of rebels to escalate violence" and Colin Walch's (2018b) analysis of how typhoons temporarily weakened the CPP/NPA rebels in the Philippines. At the same time, this finding challenges what one may call a state bias in research and policy discussions on disaster-conflict links. Analyses of cases as diverse as Mali (Mbaye 2020; Vivekananda et al. 2019), Sudan (Ban Ki-moon 2007; Welzer 2012), and Syria (Femia and Werrell 2017; Werrell et al. 2015) suggest that disasters fuel state weakness and fragility. They do so by igniting communal tensions over resources, reducing taxable incomes, and over-stretching the already strained resources of the state by necessitating relief operations, among others. By contrast, the adverse impacts of disasters on groups that challenge the state—while far from uncommon—are not taken into account.

Which constraints affect conflict parties in the aftermath of disasters? As illustrated by figure 5.3, in three cases, rebels suffered from financial trouble inflicted by the disaster, mostly because of a loss of revenue options and because a deprived local population can provide less support (Burundi 2005–2006, Pakistan 2010, Somalia 1997). This constraint is most common in the sample, which supports recent quantitative evidence suggesting that rebel groups strongly reliant on natural resource extraction are more likely to collapse following rapid-onset disasters (Tominaga and Lee 2021). To quote Idean Salehyan and Cullen Hendrix (2014: 240–241),

> Violence becomes easier to sustain when resources are available and looting becomes more profitable. Militant organizations do not grow their own food, but depend on voluntary or coerced contributions from the population. Drought depresses rural incomes via reduced agricultural production making it more difficult to find willing donors.

Further relevant constraints for rebels include limited troop mobility due to infrastructure destruction or the territory becoming inaccessible

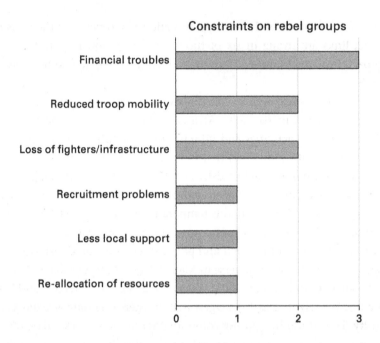
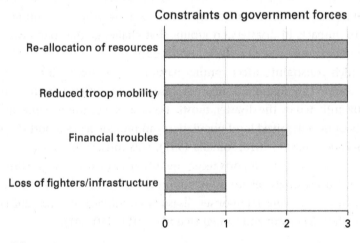

Figure 5.3
Disaster-related constraints on armed conflict parties.

(Pakistan 2010, Somalia 1997), the loss of fighters and infrastructure due to the disaster (India [Kashmir] 2005, Indonesia 2004), and a reduced ability to recruit from a population that is preoccupied with the disaster response (Burundi 2005–2006). In line with the literature on rebel governance (Florea 2020), there is also evidence that if rebel groups control territory, they engage in disaster response efforts, and the population expects them to do so. After the Kashmir earthquake in 2005, jihadi groups redirected resources toward relief efforts, while the mismanagement of the 2010–2011 drought reduced local support for al-Shabaab in Somalia.

The most frequent disaster-related constraints for the government side are the involvement of military and security forces in the response efforts (Bangladesh 2007, Burundi 2005–2006, Pakistan 2010) and limited troop mobility due to the havoc caused by the disaster (Bangladesh 2007, Pakistan 2010, Somalia 1997). Also relevant are the loss of revenues from a disaster-ravaged economy, making it harder to sustain the armed conflict (Burundi 2005–2006, Somalia 1997), and the loss of fighters and military infrastructure (Indonesia 2004) (see figure 5.3). It is worth noting that in all cases where disasters posed significant constraints on government forces, the respective state either was very weak or had only a limited presence in the disaster-affected region. While weak statehood is commonly conceived as a factor increasing environmental and climate conflict risks, this shows that weak states struck by a disaster can be less capable of inflicting violence, at least temporarily. This ties in well with Jan Selby and Clemens Hoffmann's (2014) claim that the climate-conflict literature often assumes that strong states are able to guarantee order and prevent violence, while ignoring the at times excessive amounts of violence conducted by state actors.

Analyzing the instances of conflict escalation and de-escalation covered by the strategy approach reveals an interesting pattern. In three out of four cases where only the government suffered strong adverse impacts and the rebels hence increased their relative strength due to the disaster,[5] fighting intensity increased, and this increase was driven by more rebel attacks. The only exception to this is Bangladesh after Cyclone Sidr (2007), where a combination of military weakness, little popular support, and at least some disaster impacts on rebel capabilities prevented the Purbo Banglar

5. These cases are Colombia 1999, Philippines 1990, and Tajikistan 1992.

Communist Party–Janajuddha Faction (PBCP-J) from capitalizing on the government weakness.

By contrast, in five of the six cases where both rebels and government forces were negatively affected by a disaster, the conflict intensity decreased,[6] as both parties lacked the capabilities to sustain the fighting at previous levels. Uganda 1999 is the exception to this pattern, as the LRA rebels increased violence against civilians to extract more resources and recruit fighters in a more adverse strategic environment.

In two of the three remaining cases, no conflict party suffered strong adverse impacts, but the rebels benefited from increased recruitment and financing opportunities vis-à-vis the government, allowing them to escalate the conflict (India [Andhra Pradesh and Orissa] 1999, India [Assam] 1998). In Somalia 2010–2011, only the rebels suffered from adverse disaster impacts. The Transnational Federal Government lacked the resources to exploit al-Shabaab's weakness during the drought prior to the increase of international support in late 2011, resulting in conflict de-escalation.

Overall, this suggests that if disasters negatively affect the capabilities of the government only, armed conflict intensity is likely to increase, whereas if both rebels and governments suffer from the disaster, conflict intensity tends to decrease. If the rebels face more adverse impacts of the disaster, further developments depend on the capacity of the government to exploit this weakness. This finding suggests that humanitarian relief delivery and conflict mediation efforts are most promising in the aftermath of disasters that negatively affect both conflict parties. By contrast, such efforts are less promising and even outright dangerous (in the event rebels are able to loot aid) if the government bears the brunt of the disaster impacts.

Communication

In this study, the communication approach has slightly higher explanatory power than the motivation approach but is clearly weaker than the strategy approach. Overall, the communication approach can account for six changes in conflict dynamics. In four of those cases, the respective disaster-conflict link is rather strong (see figure 5.1). However, one should note that while scholars have long identified the communicative function of

---

6. These cases are Burundi 2005–2006, India (Kashmir 2005), Indonesia 2004, Pakistan 2010, and Somalia 1997.

violence (e.g., Boyle 2009; Hoffman and McCormick 2004), this book provides the first explicit application of this approach to the field of disaster-conflict interlinkages, or even to environmental security research more broadly. Compared with the more common motivation- and strategy-based approaches, evidence for the communication approach might therefore be underreported in the literature on which the case studies rely.

Costly signal is the least prevalent impact of disasters on armed conflict dynamics. It played a minor role in the escalation of the Sri Lankan civil war after the 2004 Indian Ocean tsunami. Both the Liberation Tigers of Tamil Eelam (LTTE) rebels and the government faced pressures to demonstrate their strength and determination in the post-disaster period, and they did so by staging additional attacks. Bangladesh after Cyclone Gorky (1991) is the only occasion where costly signaling is a major, and simultaneously the only, pathway connecting a disaster to conflict escalation. In this case, specific local memories about disaster-related grievances and the Bangladeshi independence in 1971 combined with fears of the government that the cyclone could catalyze similar developments in the Chittagong Hill Tracts. This resulted in heavier government repression against civilians to convey a warning to the local population.

The communication approach scores better in regard to conflict de-escalation, where four instances of image cultivation occurred. Remarkably, all four cases are characterized by considerable international media attention: the 2004 Indian Ocean tsunami in Indonesia, as it affected many internationals and attracted large amounts of aid; Cyclone Nargis in Myanmar, because of controversies about international aid delivery; the 2005 Kashmir earthquake, owing to the wider geopolitical context characterized by the India-Pakistan rivalry and the war on terror' and the 1999 Marmara earthquake, owing to the prominent role played by Turkey in European political discussions[7] at the time. Furthermore, the first three disasters are among the four deadliest events in my sample,[8] while the Marmara earthquake had grave economic impacts and also a high death toll (17,127), hence attracting further international attention. This makes sense from a theoretical

---

7. Most discussions were in regard to Turkey's potential membership in the European Union and the future of the Kurdistan Worker's Party (PKK) conflict.

8. Indonesia 2004 saw 165,708 disaster-related casualties, Myanmar 2008 saw 138,366 casualties, and India 2005 saw 74,647 casualties (combined number for the Indian and Pakistani side).

point of view: the more media outlets, foreign governments, and international (non-governmental) organizations focus on a conflict zone, the stronger the incentives for conflict parties to limit violence and cultivate their image. As outlined by research on rebel diplomacy, particularly groups involved in separatist conflicts have incentives to present themselves as politically capable and responsible actors (Huang 2016).

One might assume that because rebel groups are usually weaker than the government and more reliant on international support, they are also more likely to engage in image cultivation (Bob 2005). But contrary to this expectation, three rebel groups (the Free Aceh Movement [GAM] in 2004, Kashmir insurgents in 2005, and the PKK in 1999) as well as two governments (of Myanmar in 2008 and of Indonesia in 2004) engaged in image cultivation in the face of disasters. Particularly since Pakistani state agencies (most notably the Inter-Services Intelligence [ISI]) influenced the decision of the Kashmir insurgents to restrain from violence, this suggests that both government and insurgent actors engage in conflict de-escalation to send a message to broader audiences. This is particularly noteworthy when considering that with the exception of the Kashmir insurgents, none of the respective conflict parties depended heavily on international support to perpetuate their struggle. However, one should keep in mind that these insights are derived from a rather small sample of cases that attracted extraordinary amounts of international attention.

The case studies indicate that patterns of violence as communication after disasters differ with regard to which audience is addressed. Fighting escalation as a costly signal was mainly directed at domestic audiences: the population of the Chittagong Hill Tracts, the Sri Lankan government, and the LTTE. By contrast, when armed groups restrained from using violence to cultivate their image, they usually were addressing an international and more diffuse audience.[9] This makes sense from a strategic point of view. Parties to a civil war usually have no opportunities to pressure international constituencies by using extensive violence. Therefore, they tend to "play the good guy" and de-escalate the conflict to convince a global public of their benign nature. This very logic underpins practices of human rights

9. Some specific addressees could be identified, however, such as the United States in the case of the 2005 Kashmir earthquake or China during Cyclone Nargis in Myanmar 2008.

monitoring and "naming and shaming" by NGOs and international organizations (Bob 2005; Risse et al. 2013). By contrast, hostile conflict parties or civilian populations with which armed groups have a tense relation are unlikely to react positively to such restraint. Therefore, the groups have to—and are usually able to—resort to costly signals to convey a message.

Finally, it is worth underscoring that armed groups do not just react to a strategic environment that is "out there" in a rational manner. Rather, they also act on socially constructed perceptions and discourses that align only loosely with material realities (see also Ide 2016; Jabri 1996). The Bangladeshi government's concerns about Cyclone Gorky catalyzing a broad pro-independence sentiment in the Chittagong Hill Tracts, for example, were grossly exaggerated. Likewise, governments and rebel groups have agency and are not just constrained by structural factors. Cyclone Gorky in Bangladesh 1991 and the Indian Ocean tsunami in Sri Lanka 2004 were devastating events and accompanied by a large amount of international attention and support. Yet unlike in Indonesia 2004 or India (Kashmir) 2005, the majority of the involved actors decided to escalate fighting regardless of the implications for their reputation.

Disaster Types and Conflict Dynamics

Researchers and practitioners often distinguish between slow-onset disasters, which unfold over weeks, months, or even years, and rapid-onset disasters, which occur abruptly and (almost) instantaneously. Droughts are a good example of a slow-onset disaster, while earthquakes are rapid-onset events. Different types of disasters might have different impacts on conflict dynamics. Rapid-onset events, for instance, leave societies less time to prepare, which can result in fewer grievances (as the event seems "natural" and beyond political control) but stronger adverse impacts. Slow-onset events might provide conflict parties and their constituencies with more time to prepare for and cope with the disaster, but they also require the investment of resources or the suffering of adverse impacts over sustained time periods (Koubi et al. 2021; Lee et al. 2022; Mitchell and Pizzi 2021).

In order to account for these arguments, I classify all cold spells, droughts, and heat waves in the sample as slow-onset disasters, and all cyclones, earthquakes, and tsunamis as rapid-onset disasters. For floods, I determine for

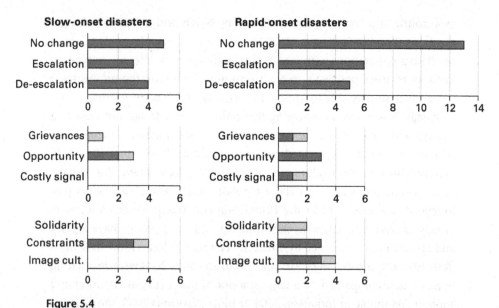

Figure 5.4
Overview of disaster impacts on conflict dynamics by disaster type (light gray bars indicate that disaster impacts played only an indirect or minor role).

each individual case whether the event has a slow or rapid onset. Figure 5.4 compares key findings for both disaster types.

My sample contains 24 rapid-onset disasters and 12 slow-onset disasters. When it comes to determining whether disasters had an effect on armed conflict dynamics, slow-onset disasters facilitate conflict escalation (three times) and de-escalation (four times) almost equally. The same is true for rapid-onset disasters (six escalations and five de-escalations). However, while no change in conflict dynamics accounts for 42% of all cases in the slow-onset sample, this pattern is more prevalent (54%) in the group of rapid-onset events. This is a surprising finding given that most of the literature considers rapid-onset disasters to be more relevant for armed conflict risks (e.g., Nardulli et al. 2015; Nel and Righarts 2008).[10]

Several potential explanations for this finding exist. Floods, which are most often associated with mobility limitations (an important constraint

---

10. One should note, however, that arguments for a greater relevance of rapid-onset events are mostly derived from studies on conflict onset and incidence, and that several studies find an association between drought and conflict (e.g., Couttenier and Soubeyran 2013; Maertens 2021; von Uexkull et al. 2016).

on armed groups; see figure 5.3), are almost always considered slow-onset events in this study.[11] This is a disputable decision as floods normally unfold in a matter of days or weeks. If all floods are considered rapid-onset disasters, the percentage of no-impact cases in the slow-onset (3 out of 6) and rapid-onset (15 out of 30) samples is exactly the same. Alternatively, one can argue that disaster impacts like financial troubles, the reallocation of resources for disaster purposes, and recruitment problems (see figures 5.2 and 5.3) are more severe if they are present over longer periods of time. In the Philippines, for instance, the Maoist rebels were quickly able to continue their operations after Typhoon Haiyan in 2013, while the PALIPEHUTU-FNL had a hard time coping with 13 months of drought in Burundi in 2005 and 2006.[12] The finding that slow-onset disasters are more frequently related to changes in conflict dynamics definitely requires further attention.

When considering how disasters affect conflict dynamics, there are very few differences when it comes to the motivation and strategy approaches. The opportunity and constraints pathways are prevalent among slow- and rapid-onset disaster cases, while grievances and particularly solidarity have limited explanatory power.

The performance of the communication approach (comprising the costly signal and image cultivation pathways) shows strong variation across the sub-samples. It covers only one case (8%) of a slow-onset disaster. Among the rapid-onset disasters, by contrast, the communication approach can explain seven cases (29%), hence narrowly defeating the strategy approach (six cases). Image cultivation is the most frequent pathway in the rapid-onset sample (four cases). This finding does not change fundamentally when all floods are considered rapid-onset events.[13]

How can we make sense of this? When it comes to the escalation of violence, conflict parties like the government of Bangladesh (1991) or the government of Sri Lanka and the LTTE (2004) fear quick changes or a

11. Only Egypt 1994 is considered a rapid-onset flood.
12. PALIPEHUTU-FNL is the Party for the Liberation of Hutu People–National Liberation Forces.
13. In this case, the communication approach applies to 0 out of 6 slow-onset cases but to 6 out of 30 rapid-onset cases. The image cultivation pathway (four cases) is almost as common as the constraints pathway (five cases), but the costly signal pathway (two cases) is outperformed by the opportunity pathway (five cases).

reputation of being weakened after rapid-onset disasters and hence deploy violence to send a message. During slow-onset events, signaling strength is less urgent and can be achieved by other, less costly means. Moreover, rapid-onset disasters often cause immediate and widespread destruction, resulting in considerable national and international attention. This provides a clear incentive for the conflict parties to limit the use of violence. "In contrast to that, in the shadow or the periphery of the public interest, remain slow-onset disasters which involve incremental and cumulative debilitation" (Porfiriev 2015: 187). Slow-onset events hence provide a less supportive context for image cultivation.

When Do Disasters Have an Impact on Conflict Dynamics?

It still remains to be explained why disasters have an impact on conflict dynamics in some cases but not in others and why the outcome is sometimes escalation and sometimes de-escalation. To do so, I draw on the method of QCA as outlined in chapter 3. QCA, like all other methods, has to deal with problems related to limited diversity. Applied to my study, this means that while there is a large number of factors potentially relevant for disaster-conflict links, not all of them can be tested simultaneously with a limited number of cases (36). Otherwise, there is a risk of model overfit and unreliable results (Achen 2005; Marx and Dusa 2011).

I therefore employ a two-stage procedure (see chapter 3 for details). In the first stage, I analyze the conditions under which disasters have any type of impact on armed conflict dynamics. Subsequently, in stage 2, I investigate why some of those cases experience an escalation of fighting dynamics, while in others, fighting intensity declines. This allows me to test a smaller set of variables that are more closely tied to the outcome in each step.

So why do disasters trigger a change in conflict dynamics (for better or worse) in some cases but not in others? I first analyze potential necessary conditions for an impact of disasters on conflict dynamics (*impact*). As discussed in further detail in chapter 3, I focus on structural conditions that make a country more sensitive to disaster impacts on conflicts: *poverty* (indicated by a high under-5 mortality rate), a strong dependence on the primary or agricultural sector (*agridep*), and a democratic political system (*democracy*). In addition, the analysis includes three more dynamic, disaster-related factors: the geographical coincidence between the disaster-affected area and the armed conflict zone (*overlap*), whether at least one

Table 5.2
Necessity analysis for disaster having an impact on conflict dynamics (*impact*)

Condition	Consistency	Necessary (≥0.9)
adverse	0.83	No
agridep	1.00	Yes
aid	0.67	No
democracy	0.67	No
overlap	0.72	No
poverty	0.89	Almost

conflict party experienced significant adverse impacts due to the disaster (*adverse*), and the inflow of large amounts of foreign *aid* in the year after the disaster occurrence.

Table 5.2 reports the results of the necessity analysis.[14] Using the commonly accepted consistency threshold of 0.9 (Mello 2021), the analysis shows that agricultural dependence is a necessary condition for impact, while poverty is almost a necessary condition (see box 5.1 for details on the interpretation of QCA results).

Table 5.3 summarizes the results of the truth table analysis for sufficient conditions. These findings do not change when running a wide range of robustness tests (see the online appendix on the MIT Press website), and all paths have a perfect consistency of 1.00, well above the recommended threshold of 0.8 (Mello 2021; Schneider and Wagemann 2010). The three paths can be read as follows:

1. The simultaneous presence of agricultural dependence, adverse impacts of the disasters on at least one conflict party, and a democratic political system is sufficient for a disaster to affect conflict dynamics.
2. The combination of agricultural dependence, an overlap between the conflict area and the disaster area, and a non-democratic political system is sufficient for *impact*.
3. The combination of high poverty rates, an overlap between the conflict area and the disaster area, and a non-democratic political system is sufficient for *impact*.

14. In crisp set QCA (csQCA), the consistency scores for the presence and absence (~) of a condition add up to 1.00. I therefore report only the higher of the two scores in the tables. In table 5.2, for instance, the score for *aid* would be 0.33.

Table 5.3
Results of the sufficiency (truth table) analysis for *impact*

Path #	1	2	3
Path	agridep * adverse * democracy	agridep * overlap * ~democracy	poverty * overlap * ~democracy
Consistency	1.00	1.00	1.00
Raw coverage	0.56	0.33	0.33
Unique coverage	0.56	0.00	0.00
Cases covered	<u>Bangladesh 1991</u> <u>Bangladesh 2007</u> <u>Burundi 2005–2006</u> <u>Colombia 1999</u> <u>India (Kashmir) 2005</u> <u>Indonesia 2004</u> <u>Pakistan 2010</u> <u>Philippines 1990</u> <u>Sri Lanka 2004</u> <u>Turkey 1999</u>	Egypt 1994 Myanmar 2008 Somalia 1997 Somalia 2010–2011 Tajikistan 1992 Uganda 1999	Egypt 1994 Myanmar 2008 Somalia 1997 Somalia 2010–2011 Tajikistan 1992 Uganda 1999
Solution	agridep * (adverse * democracy + overlap * ~democracy) + poverty * overlap * ~democracy → impact		
Consistency	1.00		
Coverage	0.89		
Cases not covered	India (Andhra Pradesh, Orissa) 1999, India (Assam) 1998		

* = and   += or   →= sufficient for   <u>underlined</u> = case is only explained by this path.

All three solution paths contain one condition indicating a high vulnerability to disasters. This is agricultural dependency in paths 1 and 2, and poverty in path 3. Disasters tend to affect the agricultural sector more strongly than manufacturing or service provision, owing to harvest failures. Likewise, people working in the primary sector usually have less access to social security services. States relying on the agricultural sector to raise tax revenues will be negatively affected by a disaster that destroys harvests (Aryal et al. 2020). Poverty reduces the amount of resources and time that households and states can spend on disaster preparation and recovery. Poor people are therefore more likely to be exposed to, die from, and unable to recover from disasters (Winsemius et al. 2018), and poor states have limited capabilities to provide disaster relief and reconstruction support (Al-Dahash et al. 2019). In line with this, agricultural dependence is a perfect necessary condition and poverty is an almost necessary condition (see table 5.2), again highlighting how important disaster vulnerability is for disaster-related changes in conflict dynamics.

Armed Conflicts in the Aftermath of Disasters

Box 5.1
Interpreting QCA Results

> QCA studies the relationship between (combinations of) conditions and an outcome. Following established conventions, I use + to indicate a logical OR, * to indicate a logical AND, → to indicate a relationship of sufficiency, and ← to indicate a necessary condition.
>
> QCA results are called <u>solutions,</u> and individual configurations of conditions within the solutions are called <u>paths</u>. The solution displayed in table 5.3, for example, consists of three paths, each of which is sufficient for the outcome (or rather a subset of the outcome cases).
>
> Solutions and paths come with two primary measures of fit.
>
> <u>Coverage</u> indicates how many cases with a certain outcome in the sample are explained by the solution (similar to the coefficient size in quantitative studies). In the crisp-set variant of QCA used here, a coverage of 0.8 indicates that 80% of the outcome is explained by the QCA. The <u>raw coverage</u> tells us the total amount of cases (relative to all outcome cases) that are covered by a path, while the <u>unique coverage</u> tells us the number of cases that are covered only by this path (and not contained in any other path). While no threshold for coverage exists, values below 0.6 indicate a rather low explanatory power of the solution (Legewie 2013).
>
> <u>Consistency</u> indicates whether a QCA solution is free of contradictions and necessary or sufficient for the outcome. It measures the fit between the empirical data and the assumed set-theoretic relationship (and thus bears some resemblance to the significance measure in statistical analyses). If, for example, a combination of conditions is present in 10 cases and 9 of those display the outcome, the consistency of this path/solution would be 0.9 in a cris-set (cs) QCA. The commonly accepted threshold for consistency is 0.9 for a necessary condition and 0.75 to 0.8 for sufficient conditions.
>
> When reading a solution, terms in brackets are resolved first, followed by logical ANDs, and finally logical ORs.

It is plausible that in cases with a higher vulnerability to extreme events, disasters are more likely to shape armed conflict dynamics. In general, high levels of agricultural dependence and poverty increase the risk of food insecurity after a disaster. Researchers have associated food insecurity with increased conflict risks (e.g., due to grievances and recruitment opportunities [Koren and Bagozzi 2016]) but also with lower conflict risks (e.g., because of logistical challenges for the conflict parties [Landis 2014]). More specifically, a high disaster vulnerability can lead to

- intense grievances by seriously affected groups unable to cope with the disaster and disappointed about a lack of state or rebel support, as in Egypt 1994 or Somalia 2010–2011;
- disaster-related cooperation owing to the scale of the challenge posed by the disaster, as in Indonesia 2004 or Pakistan 2015;
- reduced fighting and revenue-generating capabilities by state forces and insurgents, as in Colombia 1999 or Somalia 1997, but also enhanced opportunities for recruitment among deprived groups, as in India (Andhra Pradesh and Orissa) 1999 or Tajikistan 1992; and
- increased domestic and/or international attention, hence making the (non-)use of violence as communication by armed groups more likely—for instance, to signal continued determination and capacity to fight (as in Sri Lanka 2004) or to portray oneself as a benign actor (as in Turkey 1999).

High disaster vulnerability is only one part of the story, however.

Each of the three solution paths displayed in table 5.3 also contains a condition indicating that the disaster has a direct impact on either one conflict party, both conflict parties, or the strategic environment in which they operate. Path 1 contains the most direct measure of this: adverse impacts of the disaster on at least one conflict party. Paths 2 and 3 include an overlap between the disaster-affected area and the region in which the fighting took place. This is likely to go along with at least some disaster effects on the troops stationed in this area. Such an overlap can also result in changes to the physical environment that groups have to take into account (e.g., destroyed infrastructure, flooded roads) or in impacts on the population with which government forces and rebels interact (e.g., stronger grievances, increased cooperation, impoverishment).

These direct and indirect effects of the disaster on the groups in conflict can influence the dynamics of ongoing conflicts because they result in

- a need to react to sentiments of the local population, such as frustration about the government's disaster response (as in India [Assam] 1998) or reduced feelings of hostility and threat (as in Indonesia 2004);
- opportunities to capitalize on the disaster-induced weakness of an opponent to stage additional attacks (for instance, in Colombia 1999 or the Philippines 1990) but also severe constraints on military activities (for instance, in Bangladesh 2007 and Burundi 2005–2006); and

- (perceived) shifts in power between the conflict parties that motivate the state or rebels to send a costly signal about their military capability (as in Bangladesh 1991 and Sri Lanka 2004) but also to restrain from using violence to gain (international) public support (as in Indonesia 2004).

Theoretical considerations and case study evidence therefore strongly indicate that the interaction of (1) disaster vulnerability (as expressed by *agridep* and/or *poverty*) and (2) a disaster impact on the conflict parties (as indicated by *adverse* and/or *overlap*) results in a change of conflict dynamics. Furthermore, the case studies have identified a large distance between the conflict and disaster areas as well as the disaster not straining the resources of the conflict parties as important explanations for a non-impact of disasters on conflict dynamics.

The findings also align well with other recently published studies. Regarding vulnerability, Nina von Uexkull (2014) finds that droughts increase the risk of civil war incidence in areas with high agricultural dependence. Likewise, analyses suggest that low levels of human development (another indicator of poverty) increase armed conflict risks in the aftermath of climate-related disasters (Ide et al. 2020). When it comes to disaster impacts on conflict parties, the disaster studies literature has shown how large-scale disasters can overstretch government resources (Cooper and Block 2006; Noy 2009). But Colin Walch (2018b) has also pointed out that disasters limit rebel groups' recruitment efforts, while Yasutaka Tominaga and Chia-Yi Lee (2021) provide evidence that disasters deprive insurgents of funding sources.

A third factor present in all three solutions is democracy, either as a present condition (path 1) or as an absent condition (paths 2 and 3). Theoretically, this is not implausible. Researchers associate democracy with lower vulnerability to disasters because leaders have electoral incentives to invest in disaster mitigation and relief spending to win support among a broad group of voters. Autocratic leaders, by contrast, may provide disaster support only to those constituencies crucial for them staying in power, such as urban populations or regions with strong local leaders backing the regime (Keefer et al. 2011; Lin 2015; Sen 1983). High levels of democracy could therefore be associated with lower post-disaster grievances and well-developed state capacities, among others, while the absence of democracy could result in public discontent and (temporary) state weakness.

However, there are three problems with this interpretation. First, more recent studies suggest that democracy decreases disaster vulnerability only in states with high institutional quality, and might even lead to worse disaster impacts in countries characterized by high levels of corruption and government failure (Persson and Povitkina 2017). In my sample, few states are characterized by high institutional quality (at least relative to members of the Organisation for Economic Co-operation and Development [OECD]). Second, there is very little evidence in the case studies that the (non-)democratic nature of a political system is causally linked to conflict (de-)escalation after disasters.[15] Third, there is no clear empirical association between path 1 (where democracy is present) and conflict de-escalation or between paths 2 and 3 (where democracy is absent) and conflict escalation. Contrary to the expectations, conflict escalation after disasters is slightly more common in democratic countries.[16]

Another potential interpretation relates to the U-shaped relationship between democracy and armed conflict. While highly democratic states are able to mediate grievances before they erupt violently (not least because non-violent forms of action to achieve political goals are available, such as elections or organizing demonstrations), highly autocratic states can effectively repress any form of opposition. States with mixed political systems (so-called anocracies) have neither adequate democratic mechanisms nor strong repressive capacities in place, making them more vulnerable to armed violence (Hegre et al. 2001). But again, there are problems with this interpretation. The U-shaped relationship has high explanatory power when it comes to conflict onset, but it tells us very little about the relationship between democracy and conflict dynamics (Trinn and Wencker 2021). Furthermore, the qualitative case studies still reveal no evidence of a link between the presence or absence of democracy and a disaster impact on conflict dynamics. As a consequence, I consider the presence of *democracy* and *~democracy* in the QCA solution as an artifact of the data and not as indicating a causal relationship.

15. Contrary to theoretical assumptions, massive grievances about the disaster response occurred in democracies like Colombia (1999), the Philippines (2013), and Sri Lanka (2004), while authoritarian states like Iran (1997) and Russia (2010) handled the disasters rather well (and the Russian government even increased its popularity).
16. Path 1 (containing *democracy*) covers six escalation and four de-escalation cases (60% escalation rate), while paths 2 and 3 (containing *~democracy*) cover three escalation and three de-escalation cases (50% escalation rate).

Armed Conflicts in the Aftermath of Disasters

Overall, the QCA indicates that a high level of disaster vulnerability in combination with a disaster effect on one or both conflict parties is an important (and quasi-sufficient) condition for a change of armed conflict dynamics after a large-scale disaster. This conjunction of disaster vulnerability and disaster impacts on conflict parties is present in 20 cases of my sample, 17 of which display a significant conflict (de-)escalation (resulting in a consistency score of 0.85). By contrast, it is present in only 1 of the 16 cases without a change in conflict dynamics (see box 5.2 for further details). The coverage of this conjunction is hence 0.94.

Box 5.2
Changes in Conflict Dynamics: Contradictory and Unexplained Cases

> There are three contradictory cases that display a combination of high disaster vulnerability and an impact of the disaster on at least one conflict party, yet no significant change in conflict dynamics: India (Assam) 2007, Iran 1990, and Pakistan 2005.
>
> In the latter two cases, there was no overlap between the disaster area and the conflict area, but the respective earthquakes had a clear negative effect on the state owing to high economic losses and a preoccupation of the military. However, given the overwhelming strength of the Irani and Pakistani military apparatus as compared with the very weak Kurdish Democratic Party of Iran (KDPI) and Baluchistan Liberation Army (BLA) rebels, these disaster impacts were negligible. In India (Assam) 2007, the floods did not affect either conflict party but did overlap with the conflict area. However, the ULFA was considerably weakened and in no position to react to the floods in a meaningful way. In fact, then, all three cases are characterized by the absence of a relevant impact of the disaster on at least one conflict party, and hence in line with the identified solution (see chapter 4 for further details).
>
> There is one unexplained case that experienced a significant change in conflict dynamics yet no impact of the disaster on one or both conflict parties: India (Andhra Pradesh, Orissa) 1999. Again, this outlier is caused by the way the conditions are calibrated rather than by a deviation from the causal pattern indicated by the QCA. Although the cyclone did not affect the area in which fighting took place, it caused tremendous devastation in an area in which the People's War Group (PWG) was present and engaged in education and recruitment activities. This allowed the rebels to recruit followers from among the disaster victims and divert a part of the incoming aid. In other words, despite a lack of geographical overlap and adverse effects on a conflict party, the 1999 cyclone facilitated conflict escalation by benefiting the Naxalite insurgents.

Escalation or De-escalation after a Disaster?

For the second stage of the QCA, I reduce the sample to the 19 cases where disasters had an impact on armed conflict dynamics and ask, Why do disasters facilitate conflict escalation in some cases but de-escalation in others?

As discussed in chapter 3, I expect these outcomes to be far more driven by dynamic factors related to the disaster impact and the conflict parties' decisions, and consequently include fewer structural conditions in the analysis. The latter conditions include the presence of a capable state with an effective government bureaucracy and a large military (*capablestate*) as well as the rebels having only very limited military strength, financial resources, and territorial control (*weakrebels*). The more dynamic conditions are a dependence of the rebel group on the disaster-affected population for supplies, shelter, and recruitment (*rebeldependence*); perceptions of an *unfair* distribution of disaster impacts, relief, and reconstruction support; a significant adverse impact of the disaster on the capabilities of the government (*impactgovernment*) or rebels (*impactrebels*); and a large inflow of international *aid* after the disaster.[17]

Tables 5.4 and 5.5 show that there is no necessary condition for armed conflict escalation and only one almost necessary condition for de-escalation: an adverse impact of the disaster on the government. This supports initial expectations that a disaster-related conflict (de-)escalation only occurs in certain contexts characterized by a complex combination of conditions.

Tables 5.6 and 5.7 summarize the truth table analyses for sufficient conditions for both armed conflict *escalation* and *de-escalation*. Both solutions are robust to a number of alternative operationalizations (see the online appendix), have a perfect consistency (1.00), and are characterized by a high coverage of 0.78.

The solution for *escalation* consists of two paths that can be verbalized as follows:

1. The absence of perceptions of unfairness related to the disaster in combination with the absence of adverse disaster impacts on the rebels is sufficient for an escalation of the armed conflict.

[17] While 7 conditions are too many for a sample of 19 cases (Marx and Dusa 2011; Mello 2021), I run several truth table analyses with different combinations of conditions and report the model that fits the empirical data best and is robust to alternative specifications.

Table 5.4
Necessity analysis for a disaster facilitating armed conflict *escalation*

Condition	Consistency	Necessary (≥0.9)
aid	0.67	No
capablestate	0.78	No
impactgovernment	0.67	No
~impactrebels	0.78	No
rebeldependence	0.78	No
unfair	0.56	No
~weakrebels	0.78	No
democracy	0.67	No

Table 5.5
Necessity analysis for a disaster facilitating armed conflict *de-escalation*

Condition	Consistency	Necessary (≥0.9)
aid	0.67	No
~capablestate	0.67	No
impactgovernment	0.89	Almost
impactrebels	0.78	No
rebeldependence	0.78	No
~unfair	0.67	No
weakrebels	0.33	No
democracy	0.67	No

2. The simultaneous presence of perceived unfairness, the rebels' dependence on the disaster-affected population, and a capable state is sufficient for conflict escalation.

In the first path for *escalation*, the absence of adverse disaster impacts on rebel groups is the key factor. All three cases covered by the path saw no perceptions of unfair disaster preparation, relief, and reconstruction measures, but the absence of these perceptions played no causal role. In both Philippines 1990 and Tajikistan 1992, the earthquake/floods undermined livelihoods, hence facilitating recruitment efforts by the insurgents that could offer impoverished people a salary. However, this was contingent on the rebel groups being in a position to increase their recruitment of followers. The insurgents could only do this, in turn, because, despite some geographical overlap of the conflict and/or recruitment area with the disaster-affected area, they themselves were not strongly affected by the disaster.

Table 5.6
Sufficiency analysis for armed conflict escalation

Path #	1	2
Path	~unfair * ~impactrebels	unfair * rebeldependence * capablestate
Consistency	1.00	1.00
Raw coverage	0.33	0.44
Unique coverage	0.33	0.44
Cases covered	<u>Bangladesh 1991</u> <u>Philippines 1990</u> <u>Tajikistan 1992</u>	<u>Egypt 1994</u> <u>India (Andhra Pradesh) 1999</u> <u>India (Assam) 1998</u> <u>Sri Lanka 2004</u>
Solution	~unfair * ~impactrebels + unfair * rebeldependence * capablestate → escalation	
Consistency	1.00	
Coverage	0.78	
Cases not covered	Colombia 1999, Uganda 1999–2001 (see box 5.3)	

*= and   += or   →= sufficient for   <u>underlined</u>= case is only explained by this path.

In the case of the Philippines 1990, the rebels benefited from the government forces' preoccupation with disaster-related tasks and limited mobility, while they themselves hardly suffered from such disaster impacts. In the case of Bangladesh 1991, the government was also weakened by the disaster and concerned that the insurgents were keen and capable to exploit this weakness. As a result, government forces intensified violence against civilians to send a message to the broader population in the Chittagong Hills. Grievances (or their absence), by contrast, played no role for conflict escalations.

The logic behind this path implies that the disaster changes the balance of power in favor of the rebels (although the government forces are overall still more powerful), either for real or at least in the eyes of some key actors. This causes either an increase in attacks by insurgents trying to exploit this opportunity or more violence by government forces trying to deter rebels from capitalizing on their (perceived) advantage. Obviously, this path is strongly tied to the strategy and communication approaches, and particularly to the opportunity and costly signal impacts. The path is also well in line with qualitative evidence (presented above) that in the context of the opportunity pathway, it is mostly the rebels escalating violence after the government suffers adverse impacts from the disaster. These patterns also

Box 5.3
Conflict Escalation: Unexplained Cases

> Two cases remain unexplained by (and hence decrease the coverage of) the solution for armed conflict escalation (see table 5.6).
>
> Colombia 1999 clearly belongs to path 1. The government was temporarily yet severely weakened by the Quindío earthquake. The Revolutionary Armed Forces of Colombia (FARC), by contrast, experienced few negative impacts from the disaster and hence aimed to use this opportunity by scaling up its attacks. The condition *unfair* was present in this case, which excluded Colombia 1999 from path 1 during the truth table analysis. However, as explained above, the absence of grievances related to unfair disaster impacts and relief is not causally relevant for this path. This is particularly so in Colombia, where the insurgents were hardly present—and certainly not active—in the regions where inhabitants expressed disaster-related grievances.
>
> Uganda 1999–2001 is a bit of an outlier case in the whole sample as the LRA reacted to adverse disaster impacts on its capabilities with an upscaling of forced extraction, looting, and violence against civilians. Yet, there is a fit with the logic underlying path 2. In their struggle against a capable government, the rebels depended on the drought-affected population to supply them with recruits and resources (e.g., food). In this case, the condition *unfair* (which was absent) is functionally equivalent to another condition (that was present): lack of popular support. Because the LRA could not draw on increased grievances (and hence increased support) by the population to sustain its war against a capable government (particularly during a drought and the associated stress), it had to raid civilians in order to secure resources and (forcibly) recruit fighters (see chapter 4 for further details).

bear some resemblance to the results of a recent study by Tackseung Jun and Rajiv Sethi (2021), who find that ancient Korean kingdoms weakened by extreme weather events faced more frequent invasions.

Before I discuss the second path, two intertwined issues are worth highlighting. First, conflict escalation in the aftermath of disasters is less about the absolute weakening of one actor (usually the government side) but rather about a relative change of power and capabilities between the conflict parties. This aligns with bargaining theory, which expects that armed conflict parties react to sudden shifts of the balance of power with increased violence to maintain (or regain) their relative position (Kikuta 2019). Second, and related, disasters might cause a security dilemma in which the relative gains of one group are perceived as security threats by another (competing) group (as in Bangladesh 1991), even when the first group has no intention or capacity to capitalize on this gain (Herz 1950; see also Kahl 2006: 44–50). This underscores the importance of qualitative and constructivist research on environmental security issues able to take such intersubjective perceptions into account.

The second path for conflict escalation after disasters covers the cases where rebels strongly depend on the disaster-affected population for recruitment, supplies, or hideouts. At the same time, this population is aggrieved due to unfair and/or insufficient disaster preparation, relief, or reconstruction by government actors. As a consequence, the rebels scale up their attacks, either because they benefit from increased support by the population (e.g., in terms of information, support, or manpower) or because they feel they must act on behalf of their aggrieved constituencies (the ethnic, political, or social group in whose name they were fighting). In fact, in all four cases covered by this path, the rebels were a driving force of the conflict escalation (and in all but Sri Lanka 2004, the government did not initiate additional attacks). This increase in rebel attacks is met by a capable state able to stand up to the challenge and retaliate (even in the face of a major disaster), hence causing an increase in battles and battle-related deaths.

My findings are in line with the wider literature on civil war highlighting that rebel groups—particularly if they emerge from, are connected to, or depend on the local population—can act on behalf of the grievances shared by this population (Ottmann 2017; Sorens 2011). One can thus conceive the armed insurgents, at least to some degree, as a principal acting on behalf of their constituency or agent (Miller 2005). Research suggests, for instance, that droughts increase conflict prevalence even if the drought does not hit the conflict area but rather the region inhabited by the group on whose behalf the rebels claim to fight (von Uexkull et al. 2016).

Strategic incentives furthered the escalation of violence in two of the four cases covered by path 2. In India (Assam) 1998 and India (Andhra Pradesh and Orissa) 1999, the disasters facilitated rebel recruitment. In the latter case, the PWG could also loot aid and benefit from the occupation of government forces with disaster relief. Communication played a role only in Sri Lanka 2004, where LTTE rebels increased attacks to send a message about their military capabilities not being weakened by the disaster. In all four cases, the disaster resulted in significant anti-government sentiments on which the rebels could partially capitalize (or even feel they had to act on). Consequently, this path is more closely tied to the motivation approach and particularly the grievances impact. However, in line with their general high relevance, opportunities (for rebel groups) play a considerable role for this path as well.

The solution for armed conflict de-escalation facilitated by a large-scale disaster is summarized in table 5.7. The two paths it contains read as follows:

1. An adverse impact of a disaster on the rebels in conjunction with the absence of a capable state is a sufficient condition for *de-escalation*.
2. The simultaneous presence of an adverse impact of the disaster on the government forces and a weak rebel group is sufficient for disaster-related conflict de-escalation.

Both paths are complementary as they are underpinned by the same logic. One conflict party is weakened by the disaster (rebels in path 1 and government forces in path 2), and the other conflict party is not capable of exploiting this weakness, either because the government has a low capability (path 1) or because the rebels are very weak (path 2). In six of the nine de-escalation cases, the disaster had adverse impacts on both conflict parties,[18] hence reducing their capability to continue fighting at pre-disaster levels, at least in the short to medium term. This finding for *de-escalation* is strongly driven by the strategy approach and in particular the constraints impact, which is present in six of the seven cases covered by the QCA solution and eight of the nine de-escalation cases (Myanmar 2008 is the notable exception, characterized only by the impact of image cultivation). This result is further corroborated by qualitative evidence (presented above) that if both conflict parties are adversely affected by a disaster, conflict intensity tends to decline.

Despite their functional equivalence, there are some differences between the two paths. For the second path (*impactgovernment*weakrebels*), the communication approach is more important, as it is present in two out of three cases (by contrast, the communication approach is present in only two of the five cases covered by path 1). Likewise, the role of the government in reducing fighting intensity is more pronounced in path 2. In Bangladesh 2007 and Myanmar 2008, the government forces drove the conflict

18. These cases are Burundi 2005–2006, India (Kashmir) 2005, Indonesia 2004, Myanmar 2008, Pakistan 2010, and Somalia 1997.

Table 5.7
Sufficiency analysis for armed conflict de-escalation

Path #	1	2
Path	impactrebels * ~capablestate	impactgovernment * weakrebels
Consistency	1.00	1.00
Raw coverage	0.56	0.33
Unique coverage	0.33	0.22
Cases covered	<u>Indonesia 2004</u> Myanmar 2008 <u>Pakistan 2010</u> <u>Somalia 1997</u> <u>Somalia 2010</u>	<u>Bangladesh 2007</u> <u>India (Kashmir) 2005</u> Myanmar 2008
Solution	impactrebels * capablestate + impactgovernment * weakrebels → de-escalation	
Consistency	1.00	
Coverage	0.78	
Cases not covered	Burundi 2005–2006, Turkey 1999 (see box 5.4)	

* = and   + = or   → = sufficient for   <u>underlined</u> = case is only explained by this path.

de-escalation. The rebels restrained their activities in Kashmir 2005, but this move was encouraged by Pakistani state actors that provided funding and shelter to the insurgents. In path 1, by contrast, government forces (4) and rebels (4) drive conflict de-escalation equally often.

Taken together, this indicates that when a disaster hits a vulnerable area where a weak rebel group is present, high levels of international attention cause the government forces to restrain violence in order to cultivate their image. This communication logic is best exemplified by the cases of India (Kashmir) 2005 and Myanmar 2008. It is also partially true for the case of Indonesia in path 1, where the GAM rebels already struggled before the tsunami, while the inflow of international observers and aid was massive. All three disasters are also rapid-onset events, providing additional support for the finding that the image cultivation impact is more relevant for rapid-onset disasters as they attract more attention.

While already important for path 2, the strategy approach (and particularly the constraints pathway) is dominant in path 1, as it is present in four of the five de-escalation cases. The only outlier is Myanmar 2008, which is the only case also explained by path 2. In 60% of the cases covered by path 1, constraints on the rebels is the only causal link between disasters

Box 5.4
Conflict De-escalation: Unexplained Cases

> While the solution presented in table 5.7 is free of contradictions (and hence has a perfect consistency), it cannot account for two conflict de-escalation cases (resulting in a coverage of 0.78).
>
> Burundi 2005–2006 was characterized by a disaster-induced weakening of the PALIPEHUTU-FNL rebels but the presence (rather than absence) of a capable state. However, one can argue that a certain weakness of the government was still present. The drought significantly affected the capability of the state (with a relative GDP loss of 3.8%, among other effects). Furthermore, the disaster struck the northern regions of the country, where control of the government apparatus was low compared with other parts of Burundi. Hence, the government forces were unable to exploit the disaster-induced weakness of the insurgents. The case thus fits path 1 very well.
>
> When it comes to Turkey after the 1999 earthquake, the disaster-conflict link is rather indirect, with solidarity and image cultivation having played minor roles for the armed conflict de-escalation. Here, the disaster affected a capable state but not a weak rebel group—a pattern that does not fit either of the two paths. There is some resemblance, however, to the communication approach discerned in path 2. The PKK leadership expressed solidarity with the affected communities and used this to both justify its retreat into Iraq (which was rather driven by the capture of its leader) and improve its image among the international community (see chapter 4 for more information).

and armed conflict de-escalation. In line with this, in all cases covered by path 1, the rebels are dependent on the local population for support, making an adverse impact of the disaster on their capabilities even more plausible. The government forces, in turn, usually did not have the capability to exploit this weakness.

The findings for de-escalation confirm that disaster can lead to a decline in armed conflict risks by weakening governments as well as rebel groups. This has two important implications for the literature on environmental conflicts and climate security. First, contrary to one-sided narratives about environmental-conflict links, disasters can also decrease armed conflict intensity. Second, climate change and disasters not only and not necessarily facilitate state fragility (although this happens sometimes) but also put significant pressure on the resources and capabilities of insurgents.

Summary

This section briefly summarizes the main empirical insights presented in the chapter. A more detailed discussion of how the results inform research and policy is provided throughout this chapter and also in the conclusion.

Figure 5.5 visualizes several key insights. To start with, the links between disasters and armed conflicts are far from deterministic or unidirectional. In 50% of the cases in my sample, disasters had no relevant impact on the dynamics of armed conflicts, while conflict escalation (25%) and de-escalation (25%) are equally prevalent. This suggests that disasters—and by extension, climate change, food insecurity, and resource scarcity—can contribute to reduced conflict risks and that any impact of environmental factors on conflict dynamics is dependent on (complex combinations of) scope conditions. That said, large-scale disasters are associated with higher conflict intensity in one of four cases in my sample. Disasters are neither the only nor usually the most important drivers of changes in armed conflict dynamics. Rather, they intersect with a broad range of political and economic developments.

The upper part of figure 5.5 provides information on the conditions (or contextual factors) for conflict (de-)escalation after disasters.

My analysis suggests that two factors need to be present simultaneously for disasters to have an impact on armed conflict dynamics (for good or bad): a high vulnerability to disasters (which is also a necessary condition) and a relevant impact of the disaster on at least one conflict party. In the absence of one or both of these conditions, local populations, rebels, and state forces do not operate in a context where disasters make them reconsider their attitudes and strategic considerations regarding the armed conflict.

But why do disasters facilitate conflict escalation in some cases and de-escalation in other cases where both a high vulnerability and impacts on one or both conflict parties are present? Two conjunctions of conditions explain an increase in armed conflict intensity. Either the rebel group remains largely unaffected by the disaster and exploits a disaster-induced weakening of government forces, or the rebel group intensifies its activities in reaction to the grievances of the disaster-affected population, which is met by resistance of a capable state. Conflict de-escalation, by contrast,

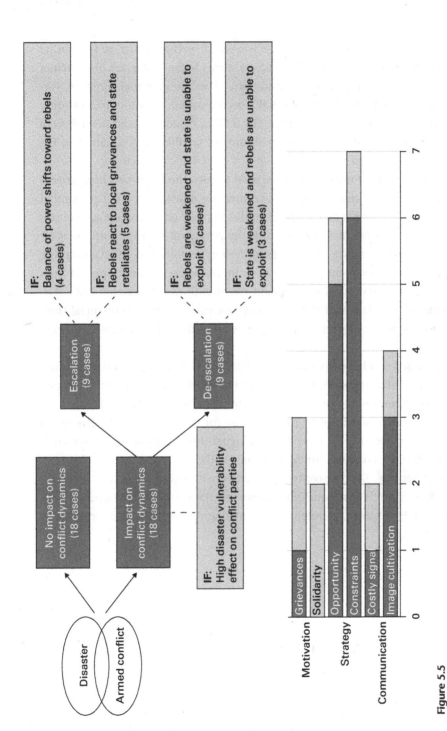

Figure 5.5
Overview of the empirical argument.

occurs when one conflict party is weakened by the disaster and the other side is unable to exploit this weakness, either because of a lack of capacities or because it is under the close scrutiny of an international audience. Furthermore, fighting intensity usually declines if both conflict parties suffer negative impacts from a disaster. The level of democracy and the inflow of international aid are causally irrelevant for conflict (de-)escalation in the wake of disasters.

Rather than focusing on contextual factors, the lower part of figure 5.5 focuses on the causal pathways connecting disasters and armed conflict dynamics. It shows that changes in the strategic environment account for most disaster-conflict intensity links, by providing either opportunities for or constraints on the conflict parties. When it comes to conflict escalation, rebel groups frequently benefit from increased recruitment opportunities or a preoccupation of government forces with disaster-related tasks. Relevant constraints that cause conflict de-escalation include financial troubles, reduced troop mobility, and a re-allocation of resources to disaster relief.

Armed conflict parties also frequently use violence as a form of communication after disasters, mostly to cultivate their image (usually among an international audience) by refraining from the use of violence. This pattern is far more relevant for rapid-onset than for slow-onset events. The use of increased violence to send a costly signal (usually to domestic actors) is much rarer. Likewise, the motivations of the local populations play only a minor role. Disaster-related grievances mattered in some cases and also occur as a relevant condition in one escalation path. Post-disaster solidarity, by contrast, is usually too limited and short-lived to affect conflict dynamics.

6 Conflict Implications of the COVID-19 Pandemic

The COVID-19 Disaster

The outbreak of the new severe acute respiratory syndrome coronavirus 2 (SARS-CoV-2) occurred in the Chinese city of Wuhan in December 2019. While there are rumors that the virus was manufactured in a laboratory, the large majority of experts agree that it spilled over from an animal (such as a bat or a pangolin) to humans. The new coronavirus, commonly referred to as COVID-19, is highly infectious and can be transmitted through the air as well as via contaminated surfaces. Consequently, it quickly spread within China and around the world. While on January 22, 2020, only six countries had reported cases of COVID-19, by March 22 the virus was present in 171 countries. On March 11, the World Health Organization (WHO) declared COVID-19 a pandemic.

As of May 1, 2022, at least 514 million people have suffered from SARS-CoV-2 and more than 6.2 million have died from the disease (Ritchie et al. 2022). These numbers likely do not reflect the actual number of cases, because detection and testing rates in low- and middle-income countries have been rather low. Despite effective vaccines becoming available in late 2020 and many countries quickly initiating ambitious vaccination campaigns, the COVID-19 pandemic is still ongoing. Limited vaccination access in poor countries and remote regions coupled with the occurrence of new, more contagious mutations of the original virus have complicated the struggle against COVID-19 (Zhou 2022). The pandemic hence fits the definition of a disaster employed in this book and the wider literature: a natural hazard (the mutated coronavirus) affected a vulnerable society (due to global interconnectedness, opposition to initial containment measures, insufficient hospital capacities, etc.), resulting in adverse outcomes on a massive scale (Wang et al. 2021). However, in contrast to the disasters discussed in chapter 4, the pandemic is still ongoing, of global (rather than national or regional) scale, and very long term in nature.

After hospitals in several heavily affected regions, such as parts of Italy or New York City, could no longer cope with the additional inflow of patients and death rates increased quickly, many governments took harsh measures to limit the spread of COVID-19. These included travel restrictions, mandatory wearing of face masks (and later vaccination certificates or negative COVID-19 tests) in certain public places, limitations on public gatherings, closures of businesses, schools, and workplaces, home schooling and home office requirements, and stay-at-home orders (lockdowns).

Particularly noteworthy examples include the following:

- A nationwide lockdown declared in India on March 24, 2020, ordering more than 1.3 billion people to stay at home and leaving many migrant workers unemployed and far from home (Biswas 2020).
- The closure of schools nationwide in Bangladesh, Kuwait, Saudi Arabia, the Philippines, and Venezuela for more than 18 months, from March 2020 until late 2021. As of March 2022, schools in 23 countries were still fully or partially closed, depriving over 400 million students of basic education (UNICEF 2022; Westfall 2021).
- Australia closing its international borders from March 20, 2020, until November 1, 2021, denying entry to all non-residents and severely limiting the opportunity of citizens to return.

The direct impacts of COVID-19 and the various policy measures to limit the spread of the virus had a devastating impact on the economy and people's livelihoods. In 2020, the global GDP declined by 3.6% (down from an average growth of 2.8% in the previous five years), triggering the worst worldwide recession since 1946 (World Bank 2022). The closure of markets, shops, and offices as well as the collapse of the tourism, hospitality, and event sectors undermined the livelihoods of many households. Scholars estimate that the pandemic increased the number of people living in extreme poverty[1] worldwide by 97 to 150 million people (Gerszon Mahler et al. 2021; Laborde et al. 2021) and set back human development by almost five years (UNDP 2022). The associated reduction in purchasing power together with supply chain interruptions had serious implications for food security (Laborde et al. 2020).

1. That is, people living on less than US$1.90 per day.

Both mortality rates and poverty risks related to COVID-19 were highest among the poor and marginalized segments of the population. These groups often hold jobs that cannot be done from home. They also have limited assets and savings as well as less access to health insurance, state support, and public infrastructure (Bargain and Aminjonov 2021; Whitehead et al. 2021). Women and girls suffer disproportionately from the pandemic. They are more likely to work in jobs involving frequent interactions with (potentially) infected people, such as nursing or aged/elder care. Furthermore, women work more frequently on short-term contracts, have limited access to health care and credit, and are expected to perform additional household duties, such as when schools are closed (Zamarro and Prados 2021).[2] A combination of increased psychological stress and the inability to leave home increased instances of domestic violence by up to 30% in some countries (UN Women 2020).

Before analyzing in further detail how the COVID-19 disaster has influenced the dynamics of armed conflicts (the main analytical focus of this book), I will provide a brief overview of the general links between COVID-19 and conflict. The pandemic has caused, triggered, or affected several types of conflicts:

- At the international level, countries have competed with each other first for crucial medical supplies to manage the pandemic (e.g., face masks) and then for sufficient amounts of vaccination to immunize their populations. In the context of this "vaccine nationalism," rich countries have successfully pursued their national interests, while many middle- and low-income countries have lost out. At the same time, there are concerns about countries like China or Russia using the supply of vaccines to increase their geopolitical influence (Bollyky and Bown 2020; Zhou 2022).

- At the national level, there has been fierce societal contestation about the handling of the pandemic in many countries. In Melbourne, hundreds of workers protested violently against vaccination requirements for the construction sector in September 2021, leading to the deployment of anti-riot police forces (ABC News 2021). Religious groups actively contested restrictions on religious gatherings in countries as diverse as India, Pakistan, and Israel. Anti-lockdown protesters carried firearms in the United States on several occasions in 2020 and torched a COVID testing center in the Netherlands in early 2021 (Beckett 2020; Haddad 2021).

---

2. At the same time, men are 2.4 times more likely than women to die from COVID-19 once infected (Jin et al. 2020).

Particularly right-wing populist (but also some liberal) parties championed such anti-restriction or anti-vaccination sentiments during elections and parliamentary debates. However, governments (particularly those with a record of human rights violations) have also used the pandemic to repress dissent and implement movement restrictions (Barceló et al. 2022).

- At the local level, the pandemic has triggered or intensified several micro-level conflicts. Some of these relate to xenophobia, such as physical assaults of "Asian-looking" people suspected to have spread COVID-19 (Cabral 2021). Other examples include local protests against the establishment of quarantine facilities for citizens returning from China in the Ukrainian town of Konopkivka in February 2020, a protest by staff members of a hospital in Amol (Iran) demanding more protective equipment, or calls by Mexican tourism operators to receive more support from local authorities during lockdowns.[3]

These conflicts are well worth studying, and researchers have already started assessing the conflict implications of COVID-19. Jeffrey R. Bloem and Colette Salemi (2020), for instance, find that the number of protest events worldwide declined sharply around March 2020 owing to limitations on public gatherings but reached pre-pandemic levels as early as October 2020. This trend also holds for countries that had recently experienced significant protest movements, such as Chile, India, and Lebanon. Maciej Kowalewski (2021) evaluates how protest movements have adapted their strategies in response to public health requirements and resource constraints related to COVID-19. Furthermore, Thomas Plümper and colleagues (2021) argue that protests against COVID-19 containment policies occur most frequently in areas with heavy restrictions and low mortality rates.

Likewise, COVID-19 might increase the risk of armed conflict onset by affecting established drivers of conflict risk, such as poor economic growth, weak economic development, ethnic stereotypes, or medium levels of democracy[4] (Trinn and Wencker 2021).

This chapter will analyze the impact of the COVID-19 pandemic on the dynamics of ongoing armed conflicts between a government and a rebel

---

3. These three examples were extracted from the Armed Conflict Location and Event Data Project (ACLED) (Raleigh et al. 2010).
4. Many democratic or semi-democratic states like Australia, Chile, Kenya, or the Philippines have employed increasingly authoritarian measures in the name of reducing infection rates (Barceló et al. 2022).

group. Scholars have argued that grievances related to pandemic containment measures (e.g., lockdowns during religious holidays or bans on public gatherings) or the economic fallout of the crisis can result in anti-government sentiments. Likewise, rebel groups might increasingly recruit economically deprived individuals or attack governments preoccupied with the COVID-19 response. Finally, government forces or pro-government militia could crack down on political opponents under the cover of public health measures and the preoccupation of the international community with the pandemic (Hilhorst and Mena 2021; Ide 2021; Mehrl and Thurner 2021).

But due to the pandemic, rebels (if they control territory) and particularly governments had to invest considerable resources in public health measures. Especially in combination with the COVID-19-induced economic recession, this means conflict parties could lack the capability to engage in intensive armed violence, resulting in reduced armed conflict intensity (Koehnlein and Koren 2022). Likewise, health diplomacy scholars claim that disease outbreak opens a window for negotiation, cooperation, and cease-fires (Chattu and Knight 2019). Already in March 2020, UN secretary general Antonio Guterres called for a humanitarian cease-fire in the face of COVID-19, to which several armed groups responded positively:[5]

> Our world faces a common enemy: COVID-19. The virus does not care about nationality or ethnicity, faction or faith.... That is why today, I am calling for an immediate global ceasefire in all corners of the world. It is time to put armed conflict on lockdown and focus together on the true fight of our lives. To warring parties, I say: Pull back from hostilities.... This is crucial: To help create corridors for life-saving aid. To open precious windows for diplomacy. (UN 2020)

In the remaining part of the chapter, I study the impact of the COVID-19 disaster on armed conflict dynamics based on four case studies. In line with the rest of the book, I focus on battle-related deaths as recorded by the Uppsala Conflict Data Program–Georeferenced Event Dataset (UCDP-GED) (Sundberg and Melander 2013) as an indicator of conflict intensity, while triangulating this quantitative measure with qualitative information. As in chapter 4, the period of analysis starts one year before the disaster onset (March 2019). Because the pandemic is ongoing, I only take events until June 30, 2021, into account. Figure 6.1 summarizes the dynamics of the analyzed conflicts, and figure 6.2 shows the COVID-19 case numbers for the respective countries. Figure 6.3 illustrates the locations of the case studies.

5. Many of these commitments were one-sided and short-lived, however (Rustad et al. 2020).

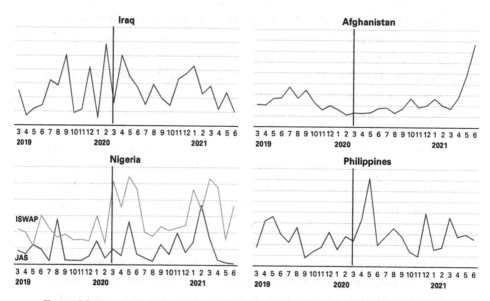

Figure 6.1
Monthly battle-related deaths, March 2019–June 2021. The vertical line represents the onset of the COVID-19 pandemic.

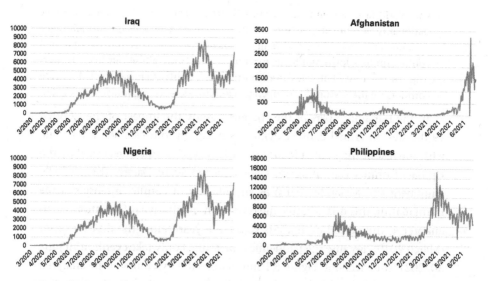

Figure 6.2
Daily new confirmed COVID-19 cases, March 2020–June 2021.
Source: Ritchie et al. (2022).

Conflict Implications of the COVID-19 Pandemic

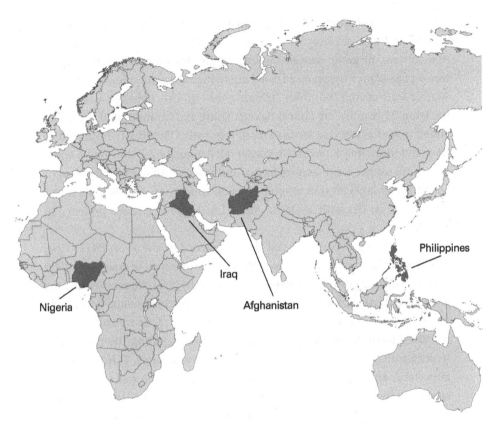

Figure 6.3
Location of the case studies. This map was created with the help of MapChart (https://mapchart.net).

The Islamic State Conflict in Iraq

The group today known as the Islamic State (IS)[6] emerged in Afghanistan in 1999 under the name Jama'at al Tawhid wal Jihad (JTJ). Led by Jordanian Abu Musab al-Zarqawi, JTJ committed to two main ideological principles: Salafism, a very strict and conservative interpretation of Sunni Islam with little tolerance for other belief systems, and offensive Jihadism, the commitment to spread this interpretation of Islam by means of violent action. Despite the

---

6. Other common names are Islamic State in Iraq and al-Sham (ISIS) and Da'ash (or Da'esh).

existence of ideological and strategic disagreements, JTJ initially pledged alliance to and received support from al-Qaeda. Following the US invasion of Afghanistan, the group relocated to Iraq. In the chaos that followed the overthrow of Saddam Hussein by a US-led international coalition in 2003, JTJ—or Islamic State of Iraq (ISI) from 2006 onward—quickly emerged as a powerful actor. By conducting attacks against Shiite and international actors, ISI aimed to fuel a civil war, to drive foreign (mostly US) security forces out of Iraq, and ultimately to establish conservative Sunni rule. However, a coalition of US troops, Iraqi security forces, and tribal militias effectively fought back, and by 2008 ISI had suffered considerable losses. At this time, it had also broken its ties with al-Qaeda. Yet, ISI was able to retain a presence in eastern Iraq.

Three developments catalyzed the resurgence of the IS in 2011. First, the United States started to reduce its military presence in Iraq from 2009 onward, with the complete removal of all troops by 2011, thereby leaving the government less capable to fight insurgents. Second, in the same year, newly elected prime minister Nuri al-Maliki introduced various measures widely perceived to discriminate against Sunni groups, including the removal of senior Sunni leaders from the Iraqi armed and police forces. Third, and most important, anti-regime protests during the Arab Spring and their violent repression by state forces escalated into a civil war in Syria. This provided IS with further opportunities to recruit members, gather weapons, and acquire funds. Long-standing ties with the local population in some parts of Iraq as well as the inflow of foreign fighters (in part due to a well-orchestrated social media campaign) further strengthened IS (Gerges 2016).

Within a few years, IS was able to conquer and control an area of about 1 million square kilometers in Iraq and Syria, including Iraq's second-largest city, Mosul (LeBillon 2022). In Iraq, IS was an "umbrella organisation" (Steed 2019: 9) for former Ba'athist party members who had lost influence during the 2003 regime change, Sunni nationalists, and Islamic fundamentalists. On June 29, 2014, then IS leader Abu Bakr al-Baghdadi declared IS to be a caliphate and de facto state. However, this height of power did not last long. IS's widespread atrocities, international terrorist attacks, and extremist ideology alienated it from the local population, the international community, and (potential) allies. Under attack by other Islamist groups (such as the Al-Nusra Front), airstrikes by a US-led international coalition, Kurdish armed forces, the Russian- and Iranian-backed Syrian military, and Iraqi security forces and militias (supported by Western states), the caliphate collapsed. In 2016, IS lost control over most urban areas in Iraq, and by March 2019 it no longer controlled any territory. Later that year, US forces killed al-Baghdadi (Steed 2019; Vu and van Orden 2020).

Iraq reported its first case of COVID-19 on February 24, 2020, and by September of that year the number of daily new infections had rapidly grown to 5,036. A second wave with up to 8,700 daily cases hit the country in April 2021, and a third wave with up to 13,500 new infections per day followed in July 2021 (figure 6.2).[7] Iraq's war-torn and underfunded health system was highly vulnerable to the pandemic (Calabrese 2020). Furthermore, in early 2020, Iraq was characterized by widespread poverty, unemployment, inequality, and communal tensions—all factors that facilitated the success of IS in the 2010s (H. Ali 2020). During the first months of the pandemic, lockdowns and border closures decreased monthly household incomes by 16%, while 66% of all households reported an involuntary reduction of working days (UNDP 2021).

COVID-19 also had implications for the military capability of the Iraqi government. Due to the pandemic and lingering tensions with Iran, several European nations reduced their troop presence. Likewise, "the U.S. pulled some troops out of Iraq . . . and ordered the troops remaining in the country to stay on their bases—moves that ended most joint missions with local Iraqi and Kurdish troops" (Williams 2020). The Iraqi government cut the military personnel on duty by 50% and sub-divided military units to reduce the spread of COVID-19. Security forces also increasingly took on tasks related to the enforcement of curfews and travel limitations (Abdul-Zahra et al. 2020). However, despite a deepening of the economic crisis (Iraq's GDP declined by more than 10% in 2020), the security forces did not suffer from funding cuts or late salary payments (Brancati et al. 2021).

Initially, IS welcomed the outbreak of the pandemic, describing SARS-CoV-2 as "Allah's smallest soldier" and claiming that faithful Muslims are

---

[7]. As for all cases discussed in this chapter, the actual number of new infections is much higher but underreported because of low testing capacities.

immune to the virus.[8] The insurgents also quickly recognized the reduced military operations of the international anti-IS coalition and the new limitations of Iraq's security forces. Consequently, IS tried to "showcase successes and attribute operations to reduced [W]estern preparedness as a result of COVID-19" (Norlen 2020: 14). In other words, IS perceived the pandemic as an opportunity to gain military ground against a weakened Iraqi state, as its security forces were preoccupied with the pandemic response. Likewise, IS sought to demonstrate to internal audiences (the Iraqi population) and international audiences (mostly the international anti-IS coalition and potential recruits) that it was capable of exploiting the enemy's weakness. The goals behind this were to demoralize its opponents and attract new supporters.

The UCDP data recognize an intensification of the armed conflict between the Iraqi government and IS in the period from February to June 2020, with an average of 66 battle-related deaths, compared with 51 for the entire March 2019–June 2021 period (figure 6.1). This escalation was particularly pronounced in April 2020 (75 deaths). Other sources confirm this trend and attribute it to a higher number of IS attacks (Abdul-Zahra et al. 2020; Brancati et al. 2021; Ide 2021). However, this increase in conflict intensity was not sustained. The number of battle-related deaths reverted back to prepandemic levels in the second half of 2020 and even declined in 2021. Overall, IS was unable to exploit the pandemic to consolidate after (or recover from) its 2016–2019 defeats (UN Security Council 2021b). The year 2021 was therefore the least violent year in Iraq's recent history (*The Economist* 2021).

How do we make sense of this pattern? In the short term, the temporary weakness of the Iraqi government (and its international partners) together with the IS's determination to capitalize on this opportunity (and to send a signal to various audiences) led to an increase in IS attacks and consequently an escalation of the conflict. In the medium to long term, by contrast, IS was weakened by two COVID-19-related developments. The first, and arguably the more important one, related to travel restrictions. Between March 13, 2020, and September 23, 2020, and again from February 18, 2021, until the end of the time period analyzed here (June 30, 2021),

---

8. Later on, this framing was modified, and IS considered COVID-19 alternatively as (1) a sign of the coming apocalypse, (2) a test of faith for Muslims suffering from the disease, and/or (3) Allah's punishment for a sinful world.

the Iraqi government issued and enforced various forms of stay-at-home orders, including curfews. This limited the ability of IS cadres to move around, coordinate, and conduct attacks. The freeze of international travel almost completely stopped the inflow of foreign fighters, which had previously been an important asset for the jihadist insurgents.[9]

Second, voluntary contributions or enforced taxes have been a key source of income for the IS in Iraq (LeBillon 2022). But owing to the COVID-19-induced collapse of the economy, such revenues, as well as the insurgents' ability to collect them during lockdowns, have declined. The same is true for income from contraband and the drug trade, particularly during closures of international borders. With reduced mobility and financial resources, IS was unable to stage further attacks, and pandemic-related challenges and the covert nature of many IS activities prevented the government from exploiting this weakness (Brancati et al. 2021; Norlen 2020; UN Security Council 2021b).

The pandemic had very little impact on local-level conflicts or solidarity. A survey by UNDP (2021: 8), for instance, found that of all interviewed Iraqis, "93 percent reported no change in community tensions."

The Taliban Conflict in Afghanistan

As described in further detail in chapter 4 (see the case studies "Afghanistan 1998: Remote Earthquakes Did Not Shape Conflict Dynamics" and "Afghanistan 2008: Freezing the Conflict?"), the Taliban have their origins in the civil war between the Communist government that claimed power in Afghanistan in 1978 (backed by the Soviet Union) and the nationalist-religious *mujahedin* rebels (supported by Pakistan and the United States). Within the broader *mujahedin* movement, several radically Islamist religious leaders (*mullahs*) started to gather and train students (*taliban*) to join the holy war (*jihad*) against the Communist government during the 1980s. Despite a massive military intervention by the Soviet Union from 1979 onward, the insurgents were able to hold their own against the government. After the departure of the Soviet Army in 1989, the government collapsed in less than three years.

---

9. While IS recruited members from at least 80 countries, battle-experienced jihadists from places like Chechnya, Lebanon, and Palestine were usually much more valuable for the insurgents than recruits from Western countries.

After the fall of the government in 1992, several rebel groups, warlords, and criminal gangs fought for control over various parts of Afghanistan, and particularly of the capital city, Kabul. The Islamist *mullahs* and *taliban* were initially not involved in these struggles. However, with chaos and insecurity spreading, they gathered under the leadership of Mohammad Omar in 1994 to form the Taliban as an organized armed group. Within two years, they had conquered huge swathes of territory, including Kabul. Once in power, the Taliban established a strict Islamic regime to the detriment of women, religious minorities, and more liberal Afghans. Only the Northern Alliance,[10] a coalition of previously competing rebel groups, was able to resist the Taliban and hold some territory in the northern parts of the country (A. Jalali 2001; Rubin 2000; Terpstra 2020).

On September 11, 2001, al-Qaeda staged a series of massive terrorist attacks in the United States. As the group was based in Afghanistan and supported by the Taliban, an international military coalition led by the United States joined the Northern Alliance. Within three months, the alliance defeated the Taliban and established a new government, generously supported militarily and financially by Western states. The Taliban suffered further military losses in 2002 and largely went underground. However, with large profits from the opium trade, support from international jihadi networks (and likely the Iranian government), and safe havens in Pakistani territory, the Taliban consolidated and re-emerged. The insurgents scaled up their guerrilla attacks against Afghan and international security forces from 2003 to 2007 and again from 2010 onward (Giustozzi 2019; Sperling and Webber 2012).

The Taliban were able to grow their manpower, weapons supply, financial basis, and support within some parts of the population over the years. The Afghan state, by contrast, was ridden with political factionalism, corruption, and an inability to address high poverty rates. When the multinational military mission[11] in support of Afghanistan's government ended in 2014 and security became the primary responsibility of the Afghan state, the Taliban used their improved capabilities to attack a weakened opponent. By 2015, the insurgents had increasingly replaced guerrilla warfare with territorial control and open confrontations, soon being actively present in 70% of the country (Sharifi and Adamou 2018).[12] Recognizing that the confrontation

10. Also known as United Islamic Front for the Salvation of Afghanistan (UIFSA).
11. Officially termed International Security Assistance Force (ISAF).
12. Half of Afghanistan's population—around 15 million people—lived in these areas.

could hardly be won militarily, the United States signed a peace deal with the Taliban in February 2020. In essence, both parties agreed that all international troops would withdraw within 18 months, while the Taliban would negotiate with the Afghan government and refrain from supporting terrorism against international actors (Giustozzi 2019; Terpstra 2020).

Five days before the conclusion of the peace agreement, on February 24, 2020, Afghanistan confirmed its first COVID-19 case. The country experienced a first wave of the pandemic from May to July 2020 (with up to 1,241 new infections per day), a very mild second wave in late 2020, and a rapid rise in infections from May 2021 onward (with a peak of more than 3,000 new infections per day on June 17) (figure 6.2). Underfunded and struck by years of violent struggle, Afghanistan's health system was insufficiently prepared for the pandemic, with diseases like cholera, polio, and tuberculosis still being prevalent in the country. Consequently, while Afghanistan experienced few cases in March 2020, the government implemented school and workplace closures, border closures, and stay-at-home orders (which were lifted once infection rates declined). However, during the course of 2020 and again in 2021, the government faced public criticism that it did too little too late, and particularly that it did not coordinate properly with international donors (Furlan 2020).

While restrictive policy measures prevented many deaths, they also had far-reaching socio-economic implications, particularly in combination with the general contraction of the global economy and the ongoing insurgency. COVID-19-related restrictions forced many Afghans to refrain from going to workplaces, agricultural areas, and markets, hence resulting in income losses. In 2020 alone, Afghanistan's GDP declined by 1.9%, while "poverty levels rose from 41.6% to 45.5%, with more than half of the population living under the poverty line" (Sharma 2021). Increased poverty, supply chain disruptions, and closures of the border with Pakistan exaggerated an already fragile food security situation. Estimates suggest the pandemic had negative effects on the food situation of more than 16 million Afghans (Kapur 2021; Quilty 2020).

The Taliban considered COVID-19 a significant threat and reacted accordingly. Specifically, the insurgents conducted awareness workshops, distributed medical equipment (e.g., masks), set up quarantine centers for those arriving from high-risk areas, canceled public events (including mosque visits), sterilized public places, provided medical services in towns without hospitals, and invited international organizations like the WHO and the Red Cross to work in the areas it controlled. From early 2021 on, the Taliban also supported vaccination efforts—for instance, by distributing information or guaranteeing the safety of health workers. This is a significant departure both from earlier policies (when the Taliban actively resisted polio vaccines) and from the actions of other jihadist groups, like IS (in this chapter, see the previous case study, "The Islamic State Conflict in Iraq") or Boko Haram (see the following case study, "The Boko Haram Insurgency in Nigeria").

It is important to note that the Taliban utilized the COVID-19 response as "part of a larger strategy to gain acceptance as a legitimate and responsible actor" (Kapur 2021). The Taliban publicly communicated their efforts to tackle the pandemic and joined public criticism of the government's response efforts. By doing so, they aimed to gain the support of local populations—an important asset for both guerrilla-style warfare and governance tasks[13] (Kapur and Saxena 2020; Shire 2022). As argued by Marta Furlan (2020), in order to increase legitimacy and public support during the COVID-19 pandemic, governments need to handle the disaster well in absolute terms, while insurgents like the Taliban only have to do better than the government in specific areas.

Figure 6.1 shows that in comparison with 2019 (and the previous years), the Taliban did not conduct their traditional spring and summer offensives. After the harsh winter (during which very few battles usually take place), the conflict intensity hardly increased. There are a few reasons for this. First and most important, the Taliban committed themselves to restraint under the terms of the peace agreement with the United States. By conducting a low number of attacks, the Taliban worked toward its goal of all international military forces leaving Afghanistan. Second, the Taliban invested resources and manpower into dealing with the pandemic (and, by doing so, into increasing its legitimacy). The move reduced their capability to stage further attacks. Third, many senior leaders suffering from COVID-19 in mid-2020 caused a leadership vacuum among the Taliban, thereby making it more difficult to plan and coordinate military offensives (Ide 2021;

---

13. In February 2020, the Taliban already controlled 19% of Afghanistan's district. This number increased until they overthrew the government and took full control of the country in August 2021.

O'Donnell and Khan 2020; Polo 2020). The Afghan military, in turn, was weakened owing to low soldier morale, the withdrawal of international support, and high rates of COVID-19 infections among its troops. The government side therefore lacked the ability to escalate the conflict (George et al. 2020; Koehnlein and Koren 2022).

The intensity of the conflict between the Afghan government and the Taliban remained relatively low during the winter of 2020–2021, but this was related to adverse weather conditions rather than to the (rather mild) second wave of the pandemic. And while the third wave of COVID-19 coincides with a rapid upsurge in conflict intensity from April 2021 onward, this conflict escalation was driven by the departure of the US military, the collapse of the Afghan army, and the Taliban's determination to overthrow the government in Kabul (Maizland 2021).

The Boko Haram Insurgency in Nigeria

The northern regions of Nigeria have a history of insurgencies against central state control that goes back more than 200 years and is driven mostly by poverty, discrimination and marginalization by state institutions, and intercommunal tensions. During a period of violent political turmoil in northeastern Nigeria in the early 2000s, Mohammed Yusuf formed the Jama'atuAhlis Sunna Lidda'awati Wal-Jihad (JAS).[14] In line with a radical jihadi agenda, JAS aimed to establish an Islamist regime in northern Nigeria— and later in all parts of the country and eventually Africa—governed by *sharia* laws. JAS also condemned Western culture (including secularism and democracy) and particularly Western education, hence becoming widely known as Boko Haram ("Western education is a sin"), but it never used this name itself. Although JAS was involved in only limited amounts of violence, the Nigerian military enforced a heavy crackdown on the group in 2009, killing 800 members, including Mohammed Yusuf.

Many of the remaining members of JAS either melted into the civil population or went to nearby countries (e.g., Algeria or Mali), where they made contact with other terrorist groups. Their grievances and extremist ideology persisted and were even fueled by the 2009 crackdown. Already in late 2010, JAS had regrouped and was able to conduct attacks against security

---

14. The name translates to "People of Sunnah for Preaching and Jihad."

forces. With financial support and training from al-Qaeda in the Islamic Maghreb and (to a lesser extent) al-Shabaab, JAS quickly turned into a formidable fighting force. By 2014, it controlled a territory the size of Belgium in the states of Borno, Yobe, and Adamawa. The insurgents were also able to carry out spectacular attacks, such as the kidnapping of 276 schoolgirls in April 2014.

Initially, the Nigerian military was not sufficiently equipped and lost support among the local population due to the indiscriminate use of force. However, from 2014 on, it was able to fight back JAS effectively, not least owing to backing from neighboring countries, France, and the United States. By mid-2015 the insurgents were severely weakened, but the conflict continued at low intensity (de Montclos 2014; Iyekekpolo 2016).

In March 2015, JAS formalized its alliance with global jihadist forces by pledging alliance to IS and changing its name to the Islamic State's West African Province (ISWAP).[15] Shortly after, in August 2016, long-standing internal rifts caused an effective breakup of the insurgents. An influential faction, backed by IS, disposed Abubakar Shekau and established Abu Musab al-Barnawi as the new ISWAP leader. Shekau and his followers formed another militant organization, using the name JAS again. Although both groups shared similar goals, had their operational bases in northern Nigeria,[16] and are referred to as Boko Haram, they had different capabilities and strategies: ISWAP was the larger and more capable group (not least due to IS support), which focused on winning the local population's hearts and minds (at least until 2019) and on establishing territorial control while mainly attacking security forces. ISWAP was able to achieve and maintain some territorial control in Borno despite military offensives by government forces in 2019. JAS was smaller, was more extremist, frequently attacked civilians (rather than trying to win their support), and engaged mostly in hit-and-run attacks (Amao 2020; Warner and Lizzo 2021; Zenn 2021).

Nigeria recorded its first case of COVID-19 on February 25, 2020. Subsequently, the country experienced two waves of the pandemic until mid-2021: one from June 2020 to August 2020 with a peak of 790 recorded cases per day, and a second, more severe wave from December 2020 to March 2021 with a maximum of 2,464 daily cases (figure 6.2). Apart from the

---

15. Also known as Wilayat Gharb Afriqiyah.
16. JAS had its base in the Sambisa Forest, while ISWAP conducted most operations around Lake Chad.

large cities, the northern regions of Nigeria were the most severely affected by the pandemic due to crowded refugee camps, insufficient public health campaigns, and widespread distrust in the government. While its youthful population suffered relatively few cases with severe symptoms, the underfunded and conflict-affected health system of (particularly northern) Nigeria was ill equipped to deal with the SARS-CoV-2 outbreak. The government quickly implemented a range of measures to limit the spread of the virus, including stay-at-home orders, restrictions on public gatherings, school closures, and border closures.[17]

Besides sickness and mortality, three effects of the COVID-19 pandemic in Nigeria were particularly concerning. First, the global economic recession led to a 60% decline in oil prices. Oil exports accounted for around 8% of Nigeria's GDP and were a main source of income for the government. Second, the decline in oil revenues combined with restrictions on public life caused an economic recession (−1.8% GDP growth), hence increasing already high rates of poverty (40%) and youth unemployment (42%).[18] The Nigerian government estimates that 20% of all workers suffered job losses due to the pandemic (Eboh 2021). Third, movement restrictions during the harvest periods and limitations on pastoralists' mobility—combined with the recession—had adverse impacts on food security. According to one estimate, the number of people urgently needing food assistance increased from 7.9 to 10.6 million in 2020. While economic growth slowly recovered in 2021, food prices remained high. Poverty, unemployment, and food insecurity are particularly acute problems in northern Nigeria (Agbiboa 2020; Onyeiwu 2021; Sahara Reporters 2020; Samuel 2021).

As shown in figure 6.1, the number of battle-related deaths in the conflict between the government and Boko Haram increased significantly in the first four months of the pandemic. Conflict intensity then declined rapidly (along with lower infection rates and fewer restrictions) but increased again during the second wave of the pandemic from December 2020 to March 2021. These trends hold for both government-insurgent clashes and violence against civilians. Parts of these trends can be explained by long-standing political-economic and strategic factors. A growth in (transnational) extremist networks around Lake Chad, for instance, enabled ISWAP

17. Stay-at-home orders remained in place between both waves.
18. As of late 2021.

and JAS to scale up their activities in early 2020. But the pandemic had an impact on the conflict dynamics as well.

The Boko Haram factions reacted in slightly different ways to COVID-19. JAS conceived the virus as a divine punishment for apostates, stated that "true Muslims" (i.e., its followers) would be immune to the disease, and called for the local population to ignore government restrictions on gathering for preaching. ISWAP, while agreeing that the virus is an expression of Allah's will, explicitly highlighted military opportunities. The group "said the virus and subsequent economic downturn would divert government attention, weaken capacity and increase fragility, giving its fighters more inroads" (Bukarti 2020a). Indeed, the Nigerian government suffered from a loss of oil revenues, the general economic crisis, reduced foreign support, and pandemic-related supply problems of military equipment (e.g., drones). Likewise, the already overstretched capabilities of the military were further strained as troops had to enforce stay-at-home orders and travel restrictions.

Both factions of Boko Haram aimed to capitalize on this weakness by upscaling their attacks (in line with its public discourse, ISWAP did so a few weeks earlier). However, fighting Boko Haram was a priority for the military even during the pandemic. When in doubt, Nigerian security forces used resources and manpower for counterinsurgency rather than for implementing public health measures. Hence, government troops were able to fight back Boko Haram offensives. This is well in line with quantitative evidence of a higher conflict intensity during the first months of the pandemic (Bukarti 2020b; Campbell 2020; Oyero 2020; Polo 2020).

The subsequent decline in conflict intensity can be attributed to a number of factors. These include internal disputes (particularly within ISWAP), the onset of the wet season (which offers worse fighting conditions), and Boko Haram's realization that despite being weakened by the pandemic, the Nigerian military is still able to retaliate and cannot be pushed back easily. From mid-2020 onward, local militias also increased their presence in northern Nigeria to support government troops, hence further complicating Boko Haram's operations. Furthermore, the pandemic had at least three adverse impacts on both Boko Haram factions, reducing their capability to wage violence. First, several leaders and commanders of the insurgents (as well as soldiers on both sides) caught COVID-19 (Koehnlein and Koren 2022). Second, lockdown conditions, which persisted until August

2021, impeded the logistics of Boko Haram, particularly around urban areas (Shola et al. 2021). Third,

> the economic consequences of COVID-19 appear to impact Boko Haram / ISWAP by depriving them of income collected from levies on traders and farmers and from those involved in the illicit trade in fish and farming. This has diminished the resources and capacity Boko Haram / ISWAP has to meet promises to recruits, and it has increased hunger and disaffection among recruits due to reduced supplies. (Olawale 2021: iii)

This is particularly true for ISWAP, which provided some health services and aimed to win the support of the local population, even though this strategy was less focused after hardliner Ba Idrisa became the new group leader in 2019 (Oxford Analytica 2020).

A second spike in conflict intensity in late 2020 and early 2021 coincided with the second wave of COVID-19 infections, but the relationship between the two events is less clear. Given the presence of pro-government militias and several constraints for Boko Haram, the insurgents did not expect to gain a significant advantage over the government. Nigerian president Muhammadu Buhari stated in May 2021 that "around the Lake Chad Basin, Boko Haram terrorism [sic] have taken advantage of the pandemic and pushed back into my country," but increased transnational support and porous borders were likely more important factors for this (Toromade 2021).

It is possible that COVID-19 had a longer-term impact on conflict dynamics by fueling grievances and desperation, hence driving more people to join or to support the insurgents. Traditionally, Boko Haram recruits strongly among unemployed or poor young people (de Montclos 2014), while youth unemployment and food insecurity increased significantly owing to the pandemic.[19] Lockdowns, restrictions on religious gatherings, lack of social and medical support, and violence by security forces (while implementing public health measures) also fueled anti-government sentiments among the population, especially in northern Nigeria. Analysts further emphasize increased space for online recruitment of young people when stay-at-home orders were in place (Shola et al. 2021). Finally, the government had to cut funding for infrastructure (re-)construction and former ISWAP fighter reintegration in the northern states because of the economic crisis, causing further grievances and recruitment opportunities for the insurgents.

---

19. School closures further aggravated the situation.

However, both insurgent factions lost financial resources during the pandemic and had to pay higher food prices. It therefore remains unclear whether Boko Haram could capitalize on these COVID-19-induced grievances and opportunities to boost its recruitment to a significant degree (Olawale 2021).

The Conflict between the CPP/NPA and the Philippine Government

Building on earlier Communist and social movements, the Communist Party of the Philippines (CPP) emerged in 1968 with the goal of overthrowing the government and establishing a Maoist-Communist regime in the country. In order to conduct attacks against government institutions and security forces, the CPP established an armed wing, the New People's Army (NPA). Inequality, corruption, and repression by the Ferdinand Marcos government (1965–1986) fueled public support for the CPP. In the mid-1980s, the NPA commanded over 20,000 soldiers and had established shadow government structures in parts of the country. The tide started to turn against the insurgents when a popular movement ousted Marcos and a democratically elected government took power in 1986. Owing to a combination of the democratization, internal purges, and more effective strategies by the military,[20] the CPP and NPA quickly lost ground (C. Harmon 2020; Santos and Santos 2010b).

Despite this progress, the Philippine government was unable to defeat the insurgents and halt their guerrilla warfare. The CPP/NPA retreated to remote regions, capitalized on grievances about the persistence of poverty and corruption under democracy, and established links to broader pro-democracy and social justice movements. Although not reaching its mid-1980s peak again, the NPA recovered and commanded 3,000–5,000 cadres from the late 2000s onward. Neither the legalization of the CPP in 1992 nor various peace negotiations nor a massive government offensive in 2006 could end the conflict (see the case studies "Philippines 1990: Earthquake-Related Opportunities for Both Sides," "Philippines 1991: Storm, Flood, and Conflict De-escalation," and "Philippines 2013: Super Typhoon, but Few Conflict Implications" in chapter 4). In 2016, right-wing populist Rodrigo Duterte became president of the Philippines. Initially, he worked closely

---

20. Including the formation of local militias called Citizens Armed Forces Geographical Units (CAFGUs).

with the left-wing movement to push forward his social welfare agenda and also re-started peace negotiations with the CPP. But this alliance did not last long. In 2017, the Duterte government declared the CPP and NPA terrorist organizations, and in 2019 it unilaterally ended peace talks between both conflict parties (C. Harmon 2020; Quimpo 2014; P. Santos 2010).

The COVID-19 pandemic affected the Philippines rather early, with the first case being officially confirmed on January 30, 2020. Afterward, case numbers rose slowly but steadily, with a first peak of infections in August and September 2020 (with up to 2,900 new cases per day). A second wave hit the country from March to May 2021, peaking at 15,298 new daily infections (figure 6.2). While initially playing down the threat posed by COVID-19, Duterte implemented one of the harshest lockdowns in March 2020, essentially confining people to their homes. For the remainder of the study period, stay-at-home orders were relaxed or tightened, depending on the case numbers, but essentially remained in place. Despite major health reforms in 2019, the Philippine health system was insufficient to cope with the pandemic, with only 0.6 physicians per 1,000 people,[21] not more than 1,500 intensive care units countrywide, and very limited COVID-19 testing capabilities (Cook 2021; Schaffar 2021).

The socio-economic impacts of the pandemic and the strict lockdown policies were devastating. In 2020, the Philippine economy contracted 9.6%. National debt increased by 26.7%. Consequently, the government was only able to provide social support for poor households during the first strict lockdown in early 2020, while experts considered the state's economic stimulus package to be insufficient. Unemployment rates climbed to a record high of 10.3% in late 2020, pushing an additional 3 million Filipinos into poverty. Moderate growth (0.8%) of the agricultural sector, which employs around 25% of the Philippine workforce, in combination with international remittances, alleviated the poverty impacts of the pandemic (Cook 2021). Community tensions increased during the pandemic. The police used excessive (including deadly) violence to enforce the strict lockdown, while an April 2021 survey reports a 52% increase in crime, local tensions, and community violence (Fallesen and Adolfo 2021). Despite this, public support rates for the highly popular Duterte government did not decline (FutureLearn 2021; Ordinario 2020; Schaffar 2021).

---

21. Versus 2.6 physicians in the United States, 3.7 in Australia, and 4.6 in Switzerland.

As shown in figure 6.1, armed conflict intensity in the Philippines fluctuated from month to month but largely remained the same before and during the COVID-19 pandemic. The monthly average of battle-related deaths increased only slightly during the pandemic (12.9) compared with the 12 months before. COVID-19 infections increased strongly in March 2020 (13.9 deaths). The notable exception to this pattern is May 2020, which saw 41 battle-related casualties in the government-CPP/NPA conflict—64% more than in the second most violent month (25 deaths in December 2020).

Both the Philippine government and the CPP took COVID-19 very seriously from March 2020 onward. Consequently, both the government (on March 19, 2020) and the rebels (on March 26, 2020) declared unilateral cease-fires to support the COVID-19 response and minimize human suffering during the pandemic. However, both conflict parties did not extend their respective cease-fires beyond the end of April 2020, accusing each other of not sticking to their commitment. Indeed, the number of battle-related deaths was higher in March and April 2020 than during the same time period in 2019.

Two explanations exist for the subsequent conflict escalation in May 2020. First, the Philippine government used the strict lockdown (and the preoccupation of international attention with the pandemic) to crack down on any opposition, including the CPP. This is well in line with a 50% increase in police killings in the April–July 2020 period (Schaffar 2021: 188). Second, the CPP/NPA aimed to exploit the heavy involvement of the Philippine security forces in the pandemic response to stage additional attacks. Lockdown enforcement patrols were considered to be easy targets and were unpopular among the population. Furthermore, owing to the lockdown and the economic recession, community donations and taxes extorted from businesses declined. Therefore, some NPA units had to raid supplies to secure access to food. It is uncertain which explanation is closer to the truth. Because they are not mutually exclusive, it might be a combination of both explanations that accounts for the spike in violence in May 2020 (Ide 2021; Jennings 2020; Lischin 2020).

Between May 2020 and June 2021 (the end of the study period), COVID-19 affected both conflict parties in various ways, but the cumulative impacts were too minor to cause significant changes in conflict dynamics.

Community tensions increased during the harsh lockdown, but neither did they spill over into larger political conflicts nor did they affect the popularity of President Duterte. The Philippine government suffered from severe fiscal constraints due to the pandemic, but it did not divert funding away from the security forces. In fact, the July 2020 Anti-Terrorism Act, which gave the security forces more power and specifically targeted the CPP/NPA, indicated an increased commitment by Duterte to end the Communist insurgency before the end of his term in 2022. A combination of the strict lockdown policy and intelligence gathering during aid distribution could have helped the Philippine security forces in their struggle against the insurgents, hence offsetting some of the negative effects of the pandemic, like additional enforcement tasks for government security forces (Broome 2021; Cook 2021).

COVID-19 also had diverse—and overall limited—impacts on the CPP and NPA. Many insurgent strongholds were located in remote rural regions or rough terrain, while infection rates were higher and lockdown enforcement was stricter in urban areas.[22] On the one hand, "the apparent increase in NPA recruitment . . . during the pandemic was owed to its capacity to alleviate the economic hardship brought on by quarantine measures through the provisioning of food and salaries" (Lischin 2020). But on the other hand, taxing certain businesses (mostly from the mining and logging sectors) and raising local contributions became harder due to COVID-19-related restrictions, limiting the ability of the CPP/NPA to provide food and money. Some NPA combatants reportedly surrendered because of pandemic-induced hardships, including food insecurity and SARS-CoV-2 infections, but their numbers are rather small, and it remains uncertain whether they later re-joined the rebels. In January 2021, the NPA announced the formation of urban hit squads, indicating its continued commitment to and capability for armed struggle (Broome 2021; Lischin 2020; NDT Bureau 2021).

When the first vaccines against COVID-19 became available in early 2021, an instance of disaster diplomacy (or health diplomacy; see Chattu and Knight 2019) occurred. The CPP/NPA not only encouraged people to get vaccinated but also guaranteed the safe passage of government vehicles transporting vaccines. In the words of NPA spokesperson Marco Valbuena, "It is a matter of principle for the NPA to respect all humanitarian undertakings that benefit the masses. Thus, the NPA will ensure that transportation of COVID-19 vaccines will be provided a humanitarian corridor for safe and unimpeded passage in guerrilla base and zones" (Rosauro 2021).

22. However, access to health care was better in urban areas.

However, soon afterward, disputes emerged about the vehicles transporting the vaccines. The Philippine government insisted that all suitable vehicles be used for these transports, while the CPP argued that the government should rely on only non-military vehicles because military vehicles can be readily used to covertly transport soldiers and gather intelligence. Neither the vaccine diplomacy nor the related dispute had any relevant impact on the dynamics of the larger conflict (Aguilar 2021).

Discussion

The insights presented in this chapter come with two limitations. First, while the four case studies focus on different world regions and conflict types, they can hardly be representative of the 56 armed conflicts that were active in 2020 worldwide (Pettersson et al. 2021). Second, data availability and reliability are limited. At the time of writing, travel restrictions (along with security concerns) prohibit field research on the conflict implications of COVID-19 in many countries. Likewise, quantitative analyses suffer from a lack of subnational data on COVID-19 cases, a heavy underreporting of new infections for political reasons or lack of testing (particularly in the Global South), and problems verifying reports about conflict events during lockdowns and border closures.

In the light of these limitations, what conclusions can be drawn from the case analyses presented above? To start with, as expected from a societal shock of this magnitude, the pandemic had an impact on armed conflict dynamics. However, my results are in line with other studies showing that the COVID-19-conflict link is neither deterministic nor a one-way street (Bloem and Salemi 2020; Brancati et al. 2021; Ide 2021; Mehrl and Thurner 2021). The pandemic had no significant impact on conflict dynamics in some cases (such as the Philippines), and it triggered fighting escalation in some countries (e.g., Iraq) but de-escalation in others (e.g., Afghanistan). This demonstrates the importance of analyzing the intersection of COVID-19 with national and local policy responses, pre-existing socio-economic conditions, and the nature and intentions of the conflict parties. Likewise, it illustrates the advantages of taking into account the possibility of reduced conflict risks after disasters.

The theoretical framework of this book distinguishes between three types of armed conflict drivers (see chapter 2 for details):

- Motivation: If individuals feel aggrieved or deprived by another group, they can join or at least support an armed group, or push their "armed representatives" to take stronger actions. Everything else being equal, this would result in more attacks and fighting. The opposite is true if people feel solidaric or emphatic toward the government or insurgents, hence advocating for a cease-fire, diplomacy, or negotiations rather than pushing for (or conducting) violent actions.
- Strategy: This approach focuses on the strategic considerations of armed groups and the environment they face. An increase in weapon availability and funds, more willing recruits, or a weakening of the other conflict party (e.g., due to financial problems or internal rifts), for instance, will result in more attacks and a higher conflict intensity. But if intense fighting would scare away civilian supporters, the other party is militarily superior, or bad weather (e.g., snow) limits troop mobility, conflict intensity will most likely decline (everything else being equal).
- Communication: Violence can be an effective means for communicating a message, particularly in the context of armed conflicts. Let us assume a scenario in which the capability or determination of a party to an armed conflict (i.e., the government or the insurgents) is doubted by relevant audiences (e.g., supportive populations or international sponsors). In such a scenario, the respective party might stage additional attacks to demonstrate it is still capable and determined, even if grievances remain similar and the strategic environment is worse. Likewise, conflict parties can renounce from military offensives to cultivate a positive image among relevant support groups.

In the four cases studied in this chapter, the communication and particularly the strategy approach have the highest explanatory power. In Afghanistan, COVID-19 weakened the capability of the government and the Taliban to stage attacks against each other because troops were involved in the pandemic response. The Taliban conducted public health measures to portray themselves as a credible and responsible actor among—and to gain the support of—the local population. Likewise, in Iraq, IS perceived the weakening of the government (owing to financial trouble, the resources required for the pandemic response, and the withdrawal of international partners) as a unique opportunity to stage additional attacks (and send a message to its opponents). However, over the long term, stay-at-home orders and the financial impacts of the pandemic eroded IS's capabilities. A similar dynamic can be observed for Boko Haram in Nigeria.

While COVID-19 and the associated policy measures increased hardships and dissatisfaction among the local population, the resulting grievances were either not directed against a conflict party or did not shape the conflict dynamics significantly. The partial exception to this is Nigeria. While strategic opportunities and constraints were more important factors, human rights violations by security forces when enforcing lockdowns as well as restrictions on religious gatherings amplified popular grievances. These were expressed by the #EndSARS protests in late 2020 and fueled the (religious) anti-government sentiments on which Boko Haram thrived (Olawale 2021). No conflict-relevant instances of disaster or health diplomacy (and increased solidarity) occurred, hence further undermining support for the motivation approach.

The key findings of the analysis of COVID-19 and armed conflict dynamics are as follows:

1. Depending on context factors, the pandemic can fuel conflict escalation, facilitate conflict de-escalation, or have no impact on conflict dynamics.
2. COVID-19 affected armed conflict dynamics in societies vulnerable to health crisis and where at least one conflict party was negatively affected by the pandemic. Usually, the insurgents aimed to exploit a (perceived) weakness of the government, or both sides faced serious limitations to their violent activities.
3. The strategic environment of armed groups is most relevant for explaining linkages between COVID-19 and armed conflict dynamics, while the motivation approach has limited explanatory power. These findings are strongly in line with the results of this book's main analysis of disasters and armed conflict (de-)escalation (see chapter 5).

That said, studying the COVID-19 pandemic yielded at least two further relevant insights. First, insurgent groups have agency, and this agency mattered for how they responded to COVID-19. IS and the Taliban shared a similar Islamist-jihadist ideology.[23] But while the former conceived the pandemic primarily as an opportunity to scale up attacks and regain territorial control,

---

23. Even though there was some ideological difference as well as fierce competition between both groups.

the latter reduced attacks and rather engaged in public health measures, even though this was for strategic reasons. Likewise, Boko Haram in Nigeria spread misinformation about COVID-19 and vaccination campaigns, while the CPP/NPA encouraged vaccinations and agreed to abstain from attacking vehicles carrying vaccine supplies. Given that insurgents frequently control some territory or at least influence the worldview of their followers, their behavior can be a key factor for pandemic responses in politically fragile world regions.

Second, analyses of pandemic-conflict (and disaster-conflict) interlinkages have to take temporality into account. Short-term constraints related to extreme events can turn into opportunities in the long term, such as when the Taliban devoted resources to public health measures (rather than their spring offensive) to gain legitimacy among the population. But the reverse sequence is also possible: both IS and Boko Haram were initially keen and able to exploit the government's preoccupation with the pandemic to stage more attacks, but eventually they also suffered from COVID-19 and the associated restrictions. Considering even longer time horizons (going beyond the period considered here), it is well possible that sustained poverty implications of COVID-19 and considerable education gaps due to school closures fuel extremism and recruitment by armed groups.

Analyzing the implications of pandemics for armed conflict dynamics is not just important for deciding how safe the delivery of humanitarian aid is, when to prepare for conflict escalation, and when mediation and negotiation offers are likely to succeed. Armed conflict (escalation) is also a major stumbling block for dealing with infectious diseases for several reasons—for instance, because health infrastructure is underfunded or destroyed, health professionals leave the country, extremist groups disseminate misinformation, international aid cannot reach certain regions (e.g., because of security concerns), trust in authorities is low, and the movement of fighters and refugees further spreads the disease (Daw 2021; Hilhorst and Mena 2021). Addressing armed conflict persistence and escalation would therefore also prepare countries for dealing with future pandemics.

7 Conclusion

With the intensity and frequency of disasters on the rise and a record number of armed conflicts worldwide, the approach and findings of this book will continue to be relevant for years to come. At the time of writing (early 2022), serious droughts are affecting close to 6 million people in war-ravaged northeastern Syria and more than 13 million people in the Horn of Africa, where armed conflicts are active in Somalia, the Tigray region of Ethiopia, and northern Kenya. In India, heavy floods killed 1,083 Indians while the government was fighting Kashmir and Naxalite insurgents. Over 24,000 people were affected by heavy floods in Colombia, where Revolutionary Armed Forces of Colombia (FARC) dissidents still clash with government forces despite the 2016 peace agreement. At the same time, variants of the novel coronavirus like Delta and Omicron spark worldwide concern.

In the light of this, the conclusion will first summarize key findings of the book and discuss implications for wider research areas. Afterward, it will spell out knowledge gaps and pathways for further investigation before providing some tentative policy recommendations.

Key Findings and Their Implications

The comprehensive analysis of armed conflict dynamics after major disasters presented in this book produced seven key findings.[1]

First, theoretically, disasters can result in armed conflict escalation, de-escalation, or no change in conflict intensity. Disasters may affect conflict dynamics (1) by changing the motives of the leaders, members,

1. See also the final sections of chapters 2, 5, and 6 as well as figure 5.5 for summaries of central theoretical claims and empirical insights.

or constituencies of the conflict parties (e.g., through stronger grievances or enhanced solidarity in the post-disaster period), (2) by influencing the strategic environment of armed groups (e.g., by providing opportunities for recruitment or posing logistical constraints), and (3) by providing incentives to conflict parties to communicate a message (e.g., through the use of violence as a costly signal or by restraining their activities to improve their image).

Second, in the sample studied in this book, disasters having an impact on conflict dynamics (18 cases) and having no impact on conflict dynamics (18 cases) are equally likely. Likewise, conflict escalation (9 cases) and de-escalation (9 cases) were observed with the same frequency. Disasters are never the only driver of conflict (de-)escalation; rather, they are just one of several drivers (and rarely the most important).

Third, changes in the strategic environment for conflict parties is by far the most relevant causal pathway connecting disasters to conflict dynamics. The most common mechanisms are enhanced recruitment and a preoccupation of government forces (for conflict escalation) as well as financial troubles, reduced troop mobility, and a re-allocation of resources (for conflict de-escalation).

Fourth, the communication approach has moderate explanatory power. Particularly after very large or rapid-onset disasters that attract considerable international attention, governments and rebels tend to restrain temporarily to cultivate their images. The motivation approach, and especially the solidarity (or disaster diplomacy) pathway, explains few cases. While intense grievances and enhanced solidarity are common after disasters, they are rarely politically salient enough to affect the dynamics of high-intensity conflicts.

Fifth, disasters influence conflict intensity only in settings where (1) the country is highly vulnerable to disasters and (2) at least one conflict party is significantly and adversely affected by the disaster.

Sixth, armed conflicts escalate if the disaster shifts the balance of power toward the rebels and they then scale up their attacks or if the rebels intensify their attacks in the face of disaster-induced grievances and a capable government fights back. De-escalation is the result of at least one conflict party being negatively affected by the disaster and the other being incapable of exploiting this opportunity.

Seventh, as with disasters in general, the COVID-19 pandemic facilitated conflict escalation, de-escalation, or neither, depending on the country contexts and decisions by the conflict parties. Changes in the strategic environment and the desire to send a message through the use of more or less violence were again the most important causal mechanisms.

These findings have important implications for a range of wider academic debates.

Disaster research has long dealt with the intersection of *disasters and conflict*. This book provides a major contribution to debates about whether, how, and when disasters shape the risk of armed conflicts (Drury and Olson 1998; Nel and Righarts 2008) and—by extension—political change (Gawronski and Olson 2013). Unlike many other studies, it explicitly theorizes and considers the possibility of reduced conflict risks after disasters. However, my results confirm Ilan Kelman's (2012: 131) argument that "disaster diplomacy tends to display few and limited successes" at the intrastate level (previously, this argument had been tested mostly at the international level).

A growing literature disentangles how disasters are governed in conflict-affected states. The respective studies point out several problematic developments, such as the promotion of elite interests and neoliberal development, international interventions insensitive to the local context, the marginalization of certain groups, and the deepening of local tensions in the aftermath of disasters (e.g., Desportes and Hilhorst 2020; Matthew and Upreti 2018; Siddiqi 2018; Walch 2018a). The case studies from chapter 4 illustrate how the presence of an armed conflict shapes disaster governance by governments and rebels. After the 2005 earthquake in Kashmir and the onset of the COVID-19 pandemic in Afghanistan, for instance, rebel groups actively engaged in the disaster response in order to build legitimacy and popular support for their struggle against the government. By contrast, the Bangladeshi government increased violence against civilians after Cyclone Gorky in 1991 to quell dissent. In Sri Lanka, tensions and mistrust caused by the civil war prevented effective disaster relief in the heavily affected (and already marginalized) Tamil areas after the 2004 tsunami. This indicates that disaster governance in conflict areas is particularly prone to politicization and securitization.

Climate change and security is a key issue in current academic, public, and policy debates. The UN Security Council has discussed the topic every year since 2018 (Hardt 2021), while in 2020, a group of 26 peace research institutes from various countries identified climate change as the most important research challenge (Miall 2020). The contribution of this book to the climate security debate is fourfold.

First, researchers have long argued that climate-related disasters and extreme events increase the risk of armed conflict onset (e.g., Ide et al. 2020; Maertens 2021; Vesco et al. 2021) or incidence (e.g., Ghimire and Ferreira 2016; Helman and Zaitchik 2020; Petrova 2022), even though skeptical voices remain (e.g., Nardulli et al. 2015; van Weezel 2019). My results confirm such a disaster-conflict risk nexus for armed conflict intensity. When considering only the climate-related events in my sample, there is a causal link between the disaster and conflict escalation in 30% of all cases (6 out of 20).

However, second, it is important not to conceive the climate-conflict nexus as unidimensional. In a significant number of cases—6 out of 20, or 30%, in the sample of climate-related events—disasters facilitated armed conflict de-escalation. At least in the short term, climate-related disasters can also provide windows of opportunity for community recovery, humanitarian assistance, and negotiations. This resonates with wider calls by security studies, international relations, and climate security scholars to pay more attention to peace and reduced conflict risks (Bright and Gledhill 2018).

Third, a prominent assessment of the current literature concludes that "the mechanisms of climate–conflict linkages remain a key uncertainty" (Mach et al. 2019: 193). The book makes a major contribution to reducing this uncertainty by highlighting the relevance of the strategy approach, by developing an innovative communication approach holding explanatory power in several cases, and by demonstrating the limited relevance of the grievances and particularly the solidarity mechanism.

Fourth, we know that climate change is a driver of conflict risks only in contexts vulnerable to extreme events and already prone to violence (Daoudy 2020).[2] While existing work has focused mostly on structural factors like irrigated land, political systems, or ethnic discrimination, my research highlights the importance of more dynamic factors: how the government and the rebels are affected by the disaster, what opportunities and constraints emerge as a result, how power relations between the conflict parties shift, which communicative environment they face, and, to a lesser degree, how the conflict parties channel popular grievances.

While traditionally focused on conflict onset, incidence, and termination, peace and conflict studies have recently paid growing attention to the *dynamics and intensity of armed conflict* (Lacina 2006). Existing work shows

---

2. This is exactly what the frequently used "threat multiplier" metaphor refers to.

Conclusion

that threatened and imposed sanctions, the presence of peacekeepers, and low income levels increase conflict intensity, while external mediation and arms embargoes lead to less fighting (Beardsley et al. 2019; Chaudoin et al. 2017; Hultman and Peksen 2017; Ruhe 2021). So far, this work has considered neither disasters nor environmental factors in general.[3] My book fills this void and demonstrates that how and when disasters occur matter for conflict (de-)escalation.

Furthermore, peace and conflict scholars have been actively debating about *grievances and opportunities as the main drivers of armed conflict risk* (Taydas et al. 2011). There is general consensus that both explanations frequently overlap and are not mutually exclusive—for instance, when rebels face increased recruitment opportunities owing to widespread grievances (a dynamic that could be observed after major floods in Egypt in 1994 and in India [Assam] in 1998). However, identifying the relative explanatory power of these approaches is not just important for improving theories about armed conflict; it is also important for policy interventions. Increased international (disaster) aid, for instance, can mitigate grievances but also provide opportunities for looting. Grievances (and other motives of participants, such as greed) were considered too widespread to hold explanatory power in the early 2000s (Fearon and Laitin 2003). But subsequent studies showed that horizontal inequalities and relative deprivation are crucial conflict drivers (Buhaug et al. 2014; Siroky et al. 2020), thereby reviving the debate about grievances and opportunity.

The insights presented throughout this book speak to this debate in two main ways. First, I find that the strategy approach (comprising the opportunity and constraints pathways) explains far more cases than the motivation approach (which subsumes the grievances and solidarity pathways). This is true for both disaster-related conflict escalation and de-escalation. Second, I outline and demonstrate empirically that when it comes to conflict dynamics (rather than onset), a third explanation needs to be taken into account: armed groups use violence as a form of communication to send costly signals or abstain from violence to cultivate their image.

Disasters can be considered as *external shocks*. They are certainly not completely exogenous as societies can go a long way to reduce (or increase)

---

3. For partial exceptions, see Eastin (2018), Gawande et al. (2017), and Wischnath and Buhaug (2014).

their vulnerability to disasters—for instance, by introducing drought-resistant plants and irrigation systems, by investing in storm shelters, or by enforcing earthquake-resilient building standards (Kelman et al. 2016). Nevertheless, other key elements of a disaster, particularly the magnitude and timing of the natural hazard, are generally beyond a society's control. Consequently, this book can also provide insights on how armed conflict dynamics are shaped by other external shocks (which are not completely exogenous either). Pandemics are perhaps the most relevant example. Chapter 6 provides preliminary evidence that many patterns of disaster-conflict intensity intersections apply to the COVID-19 pandemic as well, hence speaking to wider debates about political conflicts and pandemics like malaria (Bagozzi 2016), HIV/AIDS (Kustra 2017), and Ebola (Oppenheim et al. 2019).

Other forms of external shocks include steep rises or declines of commodity prices, particularly for export- or import-dependent countries (Bazzi and Blattman 2014; Dube and Vargas 2013), and global economic crises (DiGiuseppe et al. 2012). Indeed, as discussed in chapter 4, a decline in income from coffee export in combination with a general GDP decline made the Colombian government more vulnerable to FARC attacks after the 1999 Quindío earthquake. By contrast, reduced income from banana and cattle exports owing to the 1997 floods undermined the ability of both United Somali Congress (USC) factions in Somalia to wage war.

At the end of a book that pays considerable attention to material losses after disasters, insufficient policy responses, and the strategic environment navigated by conflict parties, it is crucial to emphasize the importance of *perceptions*, *norms*, *discourses*, and other "immaterial" or intersubjective factors. This demonstrates that disaster-conflict research can benefit from—but also contribute to—constructivist research on norms (Grech-Madin 2021), symbolic politics (Kaufman 2011), and crises discourses (Larsson 2020) in international relations. Likewise, the political ecology literature has long been highlighting the relevance of social constructions (e.g., of resources as valuable, of landscapes as worth protecting, or of groups as dangerous/invasive) for socio-environmental conflicts (e.g., Bergius et al. 2020; Van Leeuwen and Van der Haar 2016).

In the context of my study, three points are worth highlighting. First, conflict parties' perceptions of a situation can deviate from the situation's material qualities, particularly in highly securitized environments (see also Fischhendler 2015). The Bangladeshi government's concerns about Cyclone Gorky strengthening the Chittagong Hill Tracts independence movement in 1991, for instance, were certainly exaggerated, but were nevertheless a driving force behind escalating violence against civilians. Likewise, the Liberation Tigers of Tamil Eelam (LTTE) staged additional attacks to counter the discourse of a weakened rebel group after the 2004 tsunami in Sri Lanka. Second, one qualitative comparative analysis (QCA) pathway to conflict escalation contains grievances about an unfair distribution of disaster impacts, relief, and/or reconstruction support. In many places, such perceptions of unfairness were fueled not just by material deprivation after the disaster but also by long-standing narratives of exclusion and marginalization (e.g., of urban youths in Egypt, Tamils in Sri Lanka, and poor people in Assam). Third, the prevalence of image cultivation provides clear evidence for the relevance of norms (e.g., protection of citizens/constituencies in emergency situations) and symbolic politics (e.g., portraying oneself as a benevolent actor) for armed conflict de-escalation after disasters.

Finally, a note on *research methods* is due. This book employed a unique multi-method research design that combined 36 case studies with quantitative data via QCA. This approach seeks to bridge the gap between large-N quantitative studies and qualitative case studies in international relations, security studies, and environmental security research (see also de Bruin et al. 2022; Ide, Rodriguez Lopez, et al. 2021; Scheffran et al. 2012a). The benefits of my research design include a good balance between contextual knowledge and generalizability of the results as well as the ability to triangulate information from quantitative and qualitative data.

The analysis yields good and bad news for both dominant methodological camps. Statistical studies of armed conflict increasingly use fine-grained spatial data well below the national level of analysis. I decided against such an approach as major disasters can in theory influence conflict dynamics in other parts of the country—for example, via migration flows or reduced government revenues. But according to the analysis, an impact of disasters on the conflict parties, which is associated with a spatial overlap of the conflict zone and disaster-affected area in 72% of the cases, is a key condition for disaster-related changes in conflict dynamics. The usage of high-resolution conflict data is hence justified in future analysis.

However, the use of quantitative data alone would have caused the incorrect classification of 36% of all conflict dynamics in my sample, including

10 false positives and 3 false negatives. Qualitative, case-specific knowledge therefore remains highly important. That said, rich, small-N case studies can be weak when it comes to the generalization of results. Based on the cases of Egypt in 1994 and Sri Lanka in 2004, for instance, one might conclude that grievances are an important causal link between disasters and conflict escalation even though this mechanism is rather infrequent.

Where Is the Future?

Based on the above considerations, what are promising directions for further research?

To start with, this book focused on major disasters—those that often cause more than 1,000 deaths, much larger numbers of injured and affected people, and national emergencies in the face of wide-reaching destruction. It is well worth testing whether the theoretical framework and empirical results presented here hold for minor disasters, which are more widespread but less devastating. My assumption would be that such disasters still shape the dynamics of armed conflicts but that the impact is weaker, rarer, more localized, and more dependent on the presence (or absence) of context factors. High-resolution, geo-coordinated data, whose availability is rapidly increasing, are helpful to disentangle very location-specific disaster-conflict interlinkages. In this context, it is also worth going beyond the individual disaster-conflict intersection employed in this book and explore the cumulative impacts of several (small- and large-scale) disasters on patterns of conflict (de-)escalation. This would include longitudinal studies that go beyond the 12-to-18-month time frames employed by my analysis.

Furthermore, this study examined the dynamics of high-intensity armed conflicts, often at the level of a civil war. Research on the disaster-conflict nexus and on climate security is increasingly focusing on the onset or incidence of less intense conflicts, such as riots, non-violent protests, and communal violence (e.g., Döring 2020; Ide, Kristensen, et al. 2021; Ide, Rodriguez Lopez, et al. 2021; Koren et al. 2021; Petrova 2021). Disasters might affect the intensity of such low-intensity conflicts. Protests against corruption and economic mismanagement in Lebanon, for instance, started in mid-2019 but were fueled by intense wildfires in late 2019 and the economic impacts of the COVID-19 pandemic in 2020 (Asmar 2020; Maksad 2019). Likewise, Vally Koubi and colleagues (2021) find that migrants affected by extreme

Conclusion

climatic events in their previous location are more likely to participate in social movements, which can fuel protest intensity. By contrast, large-scale protests against inequality and the high costs of living in Chile rapidly declined during the COVID-19 lockdowns in 2020 (Bloem and Salemi 2020).

Just as with small-scale disasters, investigating the impact of (small- or large-scale) disasters on low-intensity conflicts would strongly benefit from the use of high-resolution data. Riots and demonstrations, for example, are often highly localized and rather short term. Geo-coordinated event data with a daily resolution can be crucial to study them. Big data sources such as Twitter can be an important indicator of the presence of disaster-related grievances in this context (see Koren et al. 2021 for an example). At the same time, there is still a great need for in-depth qualitative studies that shed light on the disaster-protest nexus in specific locations and/or over a longer time period (see Fröhlich 2016 for an example).

Going beyond the high-intensity forms of conflict analyzed in this book and lower-intensity conflicts discussed in the previous paragraphs, researchers need to consider other forms of security as well. The most obvious topic in this context is gender. Several studies have found that women and people with transgender identities are more prone to violence and discrimination in emergency shelters and temporary accommodations during and after disasters (Gaillard et al. 2017; Horton 2012). Depending on the cultural and economic contexts, gender identities also shape who is more likely to die during a disaster—for example, if men take higher risks or if women take care of children during evacuations. Furthermore, psychological stress, material deprivation, and the undermining of male breadwinner roles owing to disasters might result in increased intimate partner violence, although evidence for this link is not yet conclusive (Cools et al. 2020; Ide, Ensor, et al. 2021; Thurston et al. 2021). These and other gender considerations are the next frontier in disaster security research.

In recent years, a growing literature has dealt with the role of natural resources and environmental issues in post-conflict peace building (e.g., Ide, Bruch, et al. 2021; McKenzie Johnson 2021).[4] Managing land and water in an inclusive and sustainable way not only alleviates communal tensions over these resources but also provides secure livelihoods, which reduces

---

4. The term "post-conflict" usually refers to countries where civil wars have ended by means of military victory or peace agreement. These societies still often experience high levels of violence and are far from being free of conflict.

the risk of individuals joining armed groups (Blattman and Annan 2016; Krampe et al. 2021). It is plausible that disasters that undermine livelihoods and fuel perceptions of unfairness (or elite indifference or state incompetence) complicate peace-building processes. Conflict-sensitive disaster risk reduction that builds resilience and strengthens livelihoods, by contrast, might well be able to support peace-building efforts (Harrowell and Özerdem 2019; Peters and Peters 2021). With the literature on peace building burgeoning and more than 50 armed conflicts active worldwide (Pettersson et al. 2021), post–civil war peace building will be an important research and policy issue for years to come. Disaster studies can make valuable contributions to our understanding of (successful) peace building.

Finally, drawing on research on armed conflict intensity and violence as communication, I have developed a new theoretical approach in this book that conceives post-disaster conflict (de-)escalation as a form of costly signal or image cultivation. This approach helps explain 17% of the cases analyzed and is particularly relevant for rapid-onset and high-impact disasters. The violence-as-communication approach is thus well worth being tested—and refined—in further studies on climate change, disasters, natural resources, and conflict. Violence against environmental defenders to send an intimidating message (Middeldorp and Le Billon 2019) or government restraint during protests against land grabbing to please external observers (Hennings 2019), for instance, also has important communicative functions. Conceiving violence as a form of communication also has the potential to enrich wider debates about grievances and opportunities in security studies and about norms and discourses in international relations.

Lessons for Practice and Policy

Finally, I will briefly reflect on the lessons that decision makers can draw from the findings of this book. Before doing so, a notion of caution is due: transferring insights from academic research to practice is often not straightforward and depends strongly on the needs, interests, and resources of decision makers. Likewise, there is always a risk that academic insights are used to legitimize neoliberal, exclusionary, or unsustainable projects. Calling for more military spending and border protection in the wake of a (presumed) climate-conflict-migration nexus (Barnett 2009) and conservation projects in violent environments to forward elite interests at the

Conclusion

expense of locals (Marijnen et al. 2020) are just two recent examples. That said, I would like to highlight five broader lessons that can be drawn from this study.

First, if disasters hit conflict-affected countries that are vulnerable to disaster impacts and shift power relations in favor of the rebels, armed conflicts are likely to escalate. In such settings, mediation efforts are less promising. Likewise, risks for humanitarian aid workers (likely to enter the conflict zone after the disaster) increase in the wake of more frequent/intense battles. This means that governments, NGOs, and international organizations need to take additional steps to protect aid workers. In such settings, they should also pay increasing attention to conflict sensitivity (Harrowell and Özerdem 2019) and take additional steps to prevent aid from being misused to finance the conflict, even though this financing source is usually of minor relevance. One way to do so is through (anticipatory) talks with both conflict parties.

Second, the evidence presented here and by other studies suggests that such talks are by no means cheap but can modify the behavior of conflict parties. Reyko Huang (2016) highlights that 39% of all rebel groups fighting in civil wars engage in some form of diplomacy because, among other reasons, they depend on domestic backing and international support. In line with this, in four cases where disasters attracted strong international attention, at least one conflict party decreased its military efforts to cultivate its image. Likewise, the Taliban scaled down their traditional spring offensive in 2020 to cope with the COVID-19 pandemic and increase their reputation among the population.[5] In other words, putting conflict parties' responses to a major disaster under critical scrutiny[6]—from both domestic and international actors—increases the chances that armed conflict intensity does not increase or even declines. This results in a safer environment for relief and reconstruction efforts.

Third, if a disaster adversely affects both conflict parties, or if one conflict party is already weak and the other suffers from impacts of the disaster, conflict intensity is likely to decline in vulnerable countries. This has two

5. By contrast, parties to the civil wars in Libya and Kashmir increased their attacks during the first months of the pandemic because global public attention was preoccupied with COVID-19 (Ide 2021).
6. This can be difficult, however, as states tend to scale up repression in the aftermath of disasters (Wood and Wright 2016).

major implications. For one, the delivery of relief and reconstruction support is safer, even though it still takes place in a dangerous environment. Furthermore, as soon as such a setting becomes apparent, civil society and the international community should initiate or intensify mediation efforts. As Constantin Ruhe (2021) points out, less violence on the battlefield is often associated with increased trust during negotiations. The six months following a major disaster that leaves both conflict parties weak(ened) could hence provide a window of opportunity for cease-fires and peace talks (see also Kelman 2012; Kreutz 2012; Nemeth and Lai 2022).

Fourth, from a narrower perspective, we have seen that if disasters affect power relations between the government and the insurgents in favor of the latter, the government often has to deal with additional attacks. At the same time, disaster risks are frequently increased by long-standing structural problems and inequalities. Taken together, this suggests that measures to promote inclusivity, improve education systems, and reduce poverty not only promote human security but are also beneficial from a national security perspective.

Moreover, militaries usually play key roles in government responses to major disasters (Michaud et al. 2019), and I have shown that the preoccupation of the security forces with such responses are a key opportunity for rebel groups to escalate violence. Scholars have long argued that stronger civilian roles in disaster risk reduction give rise to more effective participatory and anticipatory approaches (Gaillard and Mercer 2012). From a national security point of view, improved civilian capabilities can also make sure the military is able to effectively perform its core tasks even during major disasters.

Fifth, this study reveals that only countries already vulnerable to disasters (owing to high levels of poverty and/or agricultural dependence) are likely to experience disaster-induced changes in conflict dynamics. Furthermore, rebel recruitment of disaster-deprived (and, to a lesser extent, aggrieved) people is a major mechanism connecting disasters to conflict escalation. Again, this suggests that achieving the sustainable development goals and investing in disaster risk reduction not only benefits livelihoods and human security but can contribute to (inter)national security as well.

Final Considerations

The introductory chapter of this book argued that many scholars and decision makers are concerned about increased armed conflict risks after disasters like droughts, earthquakes, floods, or storms, while attention to reduced conflict risks and even peace has been limited. The former is certainly a real possibility: disasters not only result in immense human suffering but frequently also contribute to armed conflict escalation and/or increased violence against civilians. By contrast, disasters rarely facilitate positive and long-lasting forms of peace. They often trigger some short-lived and highly localized solidarity (which is a remarkable achievement of the involved communities), but this does not translate into decreased conflict intensity.

However, under certain circumstances, disasters pose constraints on the conflict parties, hence catalyzing short-term decreases in conflict intensity. These can be used as windows of opportunity for the delivery of humanitarian aid and the initiation of negotiations. Researchers can support such processes and help alleviate the associated risks by furthering our understanding of the disaster-conflict nexus. In the context of many armed conflicts currently going on around the world and of disasters growing more frequent and intense, this is clearly a worthwhile task.

References

ABC News. 2021. Protesters march through Melbourne's CBD in wake of construction industry shutdown. September 21. https://www.abc.net.au/news/2021-09-21/victoria-construction-industry-shutdown-melbourne-protest-police/100478450.

Abdul-Zahra, Qassim, Bassem Mroue, and Samya Kullab. 2020. ISIS extremists step up attacks as Iraq, Syria grapple with virus. *Military Times*, May 3. https://www.militarytimes.com/news/your-military/2020/05/03/isis-extremists-step-up-as-iraq-syria-grapple-with-virus/.

Abel, Guy J., Michael Brottrager, Jesus Crespo Cuaresma, and Raya Muttarak. 2019. Climate, conflict and forced migration. *Global Environmental Change* 54 (1): 239–249.

Abuza, Zachary. 2010. The Philippines chips away at the Abu Sayyaf Group's strength. *CTC Sentinel* 3 (4): 11–13.

Achen, Christopher H. 2005. Let's put garbage-can regressions and garbage-can probits where they belong. *Conflict Management and Peace Science* 22 (4): 327–339.

ACT (Action by Churches Together International). 1999. ACT alert—Uganda 1/99: Drought emergency in Karamoja Region, Northern Uganda. July 30. https://reliefweb.int/report/uganda/act-alert-uganda-199-drought-emergency-karamoja-region-northern-uganda.

ACT (Action by Churches Together International). 2003. ACT appeal Uganda—emergency assistance to IDP's in Katakwi District—AFUG-32. October 30. https://reliefweb.int/report/uganda/act-appeal-uganda-emergency-assistance-idps-katakwi-district-afug-32.

Adams, Courtland, Tobias Ide, Jon Barnett, and Adrien Detges. 2018. Sampling bias in climate-conflict research. *Nature Climate Change* 8 (3): 200–203.

Adams, Mark. 2002. The humanitarian impact of neglect: Uganda's emergencies. Overseas Development Institute, April 3. https://reliefweb.int/report/uganda/humanitarian-impact-neglect-ugandas-emergencies.

Adano, Wario, Ton Dietz, Karen M. Witsenburg, and Fred Zaal. 2012. Climate change, violent conflict and local institutions in Kenya's drylands. *Journal of Peace Research* 49 (1): 65–80.

ADB (Asian Development Bank). 2006. *India, earthquake 8th October 2005, Jammu and Kashmir: Preliminary damage and needs assessment*. New Delhi: Asian Development Bank.

Adhikari, Prakash, and Steven Samford. 2013. The Nepali state and the dynamics of the Maoist insurgency. *Studies in Comparative International Development* 48 (4): 457–481.

Agbiboa, Daniel E. 2020. COVID-19, Boko Haram and the pursuit of survival: A battle of lives against livelihoods. *City & Society* 32 (2): 1–14.

Aguilar, Krissy. 2021. Palace snubs CPP's suggestion to not let military transport Covid vaccines. Inquirer.net, February 9. https://newsinfo.inquirer.net/1393922/palace-snubs-cpps-suggestion-to-not-let-military-transport-covid-19-vaccines.

Aguswandi and Judith Large. 2008. *Reconfiguring politics: The Indonesia-Aceh peace process*. London: Conciliation Resources.

Ahmadzadeh, Hashem, and Gareth Stansfield. 2010. The political, cultural, and military re-awakening of the Kurdish nationalist movement in Iran. *Middle East Journal* 64 (1): 11–27.

Ahmed, Ahmed. 1993. Ethnicity and insurgency in the Chittagong Hill tracts region: A study of the crisis of political integration in Bangladesh. *Journal of Commonwealth & Comparative Politics* 31 (3): 32–66.

Ahuja, Pratul, and Rajat Ganguly. 2007. The fire within: Naxalite insurgency violence in India. *Small Wars & Insurgencies* 18 (2): 249–274.

AidData. 2016. AidData core research release, version 3.1. October 1. https://www.aiddata.org/data/aiddata-core-research-release-level-1-3-1.

Akcinaroglu, Seden, Jon DiCicco, and Elizabeth Radziszewski. 2011. Avalanches and olive branches: A multimethod analysis of disasters and peacemaking in interstate rivalries. *Political Research Quarterly* 64 (2): 260–275.

Akhtar, Aasim Sajjad. 2010. Islam as ideology of tradition and change: The "new jihad" in Swat, northern Pakistan. *Comparative Studies of South Asia, Africa and the Middle East* 30 (3): 595–609.

Akhtar, Shahzad. 2019. Decline of insurgency in Pakistan's FATA: A counterinsurgency perspective. *Asian Survey* 59 (4): 693–716.

Akimbekov, Sultan. 2002. The conflict in Afghanistan: Conditions, problems, and prospects. In *Central Asia: A gathering storm*, edited by Boris Z. Rumer, 69–113. New York: Routledge.

Albala-Bertrand, Jose-Miguel. 1993. *Political economy or large natural disasters: With special reference to developing countries*. Oxford: Clarendon Press.

References

Albritton, Robert B. 2005. Thailand in 2004: The "crisis in the south." *Asian Survey* 45 (1): 166–173.

Albritton, Robert B. 2006. Thailand in 2005: The struggle for democratic consolidation. *Asian Survey* 46 (1): 14–147.

Al-Dahash, Hajer, Udayangani Kulatungab, and Menaha Thayaparan. 2019. Weaknesses during the disaster response management resulting from war operations and terrorism in Iraq. *International Journal of Disaster Risk Reduction* 34 (1): 295–304.

Alders, Theresa M. 2017. *Floodwaters of death: Vulnerability and disaster in Ormoc City, Philippines: Assessing the 1991 flood and twenty years of recovery*. Perth: Murdoch University.

Alfieri, Valeria. 2014. La courte "reconversion" du Palipehutu-FNL: Continuités et ruptures. In *L'Afrique des Grands Lacs, annuaire 2013–14*, edited by Filip Reyntjens, 55–75. Paris: L'Harmattan.

Alfieri, Valeria. 2016. Le Palipehutu-FNL au Burundi: Dynamiques d'ethnicisation et de "désethnicisation." *Politique Africaine* 1 (141): 169–190.

Ali, Hassanein. 2020. The rise and fall of Islamic State: Current challenges and future prospects. *Asian Affairs* 51 (1): 71–94.

Ali, Saleem H. 2007. A natural connection between ecology and peace? In *Peace parks: Conservation and conflict resolution*, edited by Saleem Ali, 1–18. Cambridge, MA: MIT Press.

al-Shishani, Murad Batal. 2014. From Chechen mafia to the Islamic Emirate of the Caucasus: The changing faces of the insurgency-organized crime nexus. In *Conflict, crime, and the state in postcommunist Eurasia*, edited by Svante Cornell and Michael Jonsson, 82–102. Philadelphia: University of Pennsylvania Press.

Amao, Olumuyiwa Babatunde. 2020. A decade of terror: Revisiting Nigeria's interminable Boko Haram insurgency. *Security Journal* 33 (3): 357–375.

Amin, Nurul. 1985. The pro-Chinese Communist movement in Bangladesh. *Journal of Contemporary Asia* 15 (3): 349–360.

Amnesty International. 1992. *Reprisal killings in Logong, Chittagong Hill Tracts, in April 1992*. London: Amnesty International.

Andrews, John. 2015. *The world in conflict: Understanding the world's troublespots*. London: Profile Books.

Apodaca, Clair. 2017. *State repression in post-disaster societies*. New York: Routledge.

Arai, Tatsushi. 2012. Rebuilding Pakistan in the aftermath of the floods: Disaster relief as conflict prevention. *Journal of Peacebuilding and Development* 7 (1): 51–65.

Arjona, Ana. 2014. Wartime institutions: A research agenda. *Journal of Conflict Resolution* 58 (8): 1360–1389.

Arlidge, John. 1999. Troops slouch as Turks starve. *The Guardian*, August 28. https://www.theguardian.com/world/1999/aug/29/turkeyquakes.turkey.

Aryal, Jeetendra Prakash, Tek B. Sapkota, Ritika Khurana, Arun Khatri-Chhetri, Dil Bahadur Rahut, and M. L. Jat. 2020. Climate change and agriculture in South Asia: Adaptation options in smallholder production systems. *Environment, Development and Sustainability* 22 (6): 5045–5075.

Ash, Konstantin, and Nick Obradovitch. 2020. Climatic stress, internal migration, and Syrian civil war onset. *Journal of Conflict Resolution* 64 (1): 3–31.

Aslam, Rabia. 2011. Greed, creed, and governance in civil conflicts: A case study of Balochistan. *Contemporary South Asia* 19 (2): 189–203.

Asmar, Amir. 2020. What's driving Lebanon's midpandemic protests? Council on Foreign Relations, May 21. https://www.cfr.org/in-brief/whats-driving-lebanons-mid pandemic-protests.

Aspinall, Edward. 2005. *The Helsinki agreement: A more promising basis for peace in Aceh?* Washington, DC: East-West Center.

Aspinall, Edward. 2007. From Islamism to nationalism in Aceh, Indonesia. *Nations and Nationalism* 13 (2): 245–263.

Aspinall, Edward. 2009. Combatants to contractors: The political economy of peace in Aceh. *Indonesia* 87 (2): 1–34.

Associated Press. 1997. Earthquake toll in Iran estimated to climb to 2,400. *New York Times*, May 12. https://www.nytimes.com/1997/05/12/world/earthquake-toll-in-iran-es timated-to-climb-to-2400.html?pagewanted=2.

Associated Press. 1999. Turkey's leader attacks press as too harsh on officials. *New York Times*, August 26. https://www.nytimes.com/1999/08/26/world/turkey-s-leader -attacks-press-as-too-harsh-on-officials.html.

Associated Press. 2008. Afghanistan: Bitter winter claims more than 900 lives. *New York Times*, February 16. https://www.nytimes.com/2008/02/16/world/asia/16briefs -cold.html.

Athukorala, Prema-chandra. 2012. Indian Ocean tsunami: Disaster, generosity and recovery. *Asian Economic Journal* 26 (3): 211–231.

Atkin, Muriel. 1997. Tajikistan's civil war. *Current History* 96 (6): 336–340.

Avinash. 2014. Have a look at 9 deadliest floods in Indian history. Oneindia, September 7. https://www.oneindia.com/feature/have-a-look-at-9-deadliest-floods-in-indian -history-1517017.html.

Ayeb, Habib. 1995. Les inondations de novembre 1994 en Égypte: Catastrophe naturelle... ou politique? *Géographies de l'Égypte* 1 (22): 1–19.

Bagozzi, Benjamin E. 2016. On Malaria and the duration of civil war. *Journal of Conflict Resolution* 60 (5): 813–839.

Bagozzi, Benjamin E., Ore Koren, and Bumba Mukherjee. 2017. Droughts, land appropriation, and rebel violence in the developing world. *Journal of Politics* 79 (3): 1057–1072.

Bakke, Kristin M. 2015. *Decentralization and intrastate struggles: Chechnya, Punjab, and Québec*. Cambridge: Cambridge University Press.

Bakonyi, Jutta, and Kirsti Stuvøy. 2005. Violence & social order beyond the state: Somalia & Angola. *Review of African Political Economy* 104 (5): 359–382.

Balcells, Laia. 2010. Rivalry and revenge: Violence against civilians in conventional civil wars. *International Studies Quarterly* 54 (2): 291–313.

Ballentine, Karen, and Jake Sherman, eds. 2003. *The political economy of armed conflict: Beyond greed and grievance*. Boulder, CO: Lynne Rienner.

Bamforth, Tom. 2015. The social impact of typhoon Bopha on indigenous communities, livelihoods, and conflict in Mindanao. In *Disaster's impact on livelihood and cultural survival: Losses, opportunities, and mitigation*, edited by Michèle Companion, 199–210. Boca Raton, FL: CRC Press.

Bangkok Post. 2012. Philippine military calls holiday truce. December 16. https://www.bangkokpost.com/world/326440/philippine-military-calls-holiday-truce.

Ban Ki-moon. 2007. A climate culprit in Darfur. United Nations, June 16. https://www.un.org/sg/en/content/sg/articles/2007-06-16/climate-culprit-darfur.

Bankoff, Greg. 2004. In the eye of the storm: The social construction of the forces of nature and the climatic and seismic construction of God in the Philippines. *Journal of Southeast Asian Studies* 35 (1): 91–111.

Banlaoi, Rommel C. 2010. The sources of the Abu Sayyaf's resilience in the southern Philippines. *CTC Sentinel* 3 (5): 17–19.

Bansal, Alok. 2006. Balochistan: Continuing violence and its implications. *Strategic Analysis* 30 (1): 46–63.

Bansal, Alok. 2008. Factors leading to insurgency in Balochistan. *Small Wars & Insurgencies* 19 (2): 182–200.

Baramburiye, Juvent, Miriam Kyotalimye, Timothy S. Thomas, and Michael Waithaka. 2013. Burundi. In *East African agriculture and climate change: A comprehensive analysis*, edited by Michael Waithaka, Gerald C. Nelson, Timothy S. Thomas, and Miriam Kyotalimye, 55–87. Washington, DC: International Food Policy Research Institute.

Barber, Rebecca. 2014. Localising the humanitarian toolkit: Lessons from recent Philippines disasters. In *Natural disaster management in the Asia-Pacific: Policy and governance,* edited by Caroline Brassard, Arnold M. Howitt, and David W. Giles, 17–31. Tokyo: Springer.

Barceló, Joan, Robert Kubinec, Cindy Cheng, Tiril Høye Rahn, and Luca Messerschmidt. 2022. Windows of repression: Using COVID-19 policies against political dissidents? *Journal of Peace Research* 59 (1): 73–89.

Bargain, Olivier, and Ulugbek Aminjonov. 2021. Poverty and COVID-19 in Africa and Latin America. *World Development* 142 (1): 105422.

Barnett, Jon. 2001. *The meaning of environmental security: Ecological politics and policy in the new security era.* London: Zed Books.

Barnett, Jon. 2009. The price of peace (is eternal vigilance): A cautionary editorial essay on climate geopolitics. *Climatic Change* 96 (1): 1–6.

Barnett, Jon. 2019. Global environmental change I: Climate resilient peace? *Progress in Human Geography* 43 (5): 927–936.

Barnett, Jon, and W. Neil Adger. 2007. Climate change, human security and violent conflict. *Political Geography* 26 (6): 639–655.

Barr, Joe. 1998. Disaster response with a difference: Afghanistan June 1998. *Australian Journal of Emergency Management* 13 (4): 2–6.

Bar-Tal, Daniel. 1998. Societal beliefs in times of intractable conflict: The Israeli case. *International Journal of Conflict Management* 9 (1): 22–50.

Baruah, Sanjib. 2007. *Durable disorder: Understanding the politics of northeast India.* Oxford: Oxford University Press.

Baruah, Sanjib. 2012. The rise and decline of a separatist insurgency: Contentious politics in Assam, India. In *Autonomy and ethnic conflict in South and South-East Asia,* edited by Rajat Ganguly, 27–45. London: Taylor & Francis.

Baumgartner, Michael, and Alrik Thiem. 2020. Often trusted but never (properly) tested: Evaluating qualitative comparative analysis. *Sociological Methods & Research* 49 (2): 279–311.

Bazzi, Samuel, and Christopher Blattman. 2014. Economic shocks and conflict: Evidence from commodity prices. *American Economic Journal: Macroeconomics* 6 (4): 1–38.

BBC News. 1999. South Asia agencies struggle with Orissa tragedy. November 4. http://news.bbc.co.uk/2/hi/south_asia/505021.stm.

BBC News. 2007. Quake survivors berate president. August 19. http://news.bbc.co.uk/2/hi/americas/6954249.stm.

References

BBS (Bangladesh Bureau of Statistics). 1994. *Bangladesh population census, 1991: Analytical report*. Dhaka: Government of the People's Republic of Bangladesh.

Beardsley, Kyle, David E. Cunningham, and Peter B. White. 2019. Mediation, peacekeeping, and the severity of civil war. *Journal of Conflict Resolution* 63 (7): 1682–1709.

Beardsley, Kyle, and Bryan McQuinn. 2009. Rebel groups as predatory organizations: The political effects of the 2004 tsunami in Indonesia and Sri Lanka. *Journal of Conflict Resolution* 53 (4): 624–645.

Becerra, Oscar, Eduardo Cavallo, and Ilan Noy. 2014. Foreign aid in the aftermath of large natural disasters. *Review of Development Economics* 18 (3): 445–460.

Beckett, Lois. 2020. Armed protesters demonstrate against Covid-19 lockdown at Michigan capitol. *The Guardian*, April 30. https://www.theguardian.com/us-news/2020/apr/30/michigan-protests-coronavirus-lockdown-armed-capitol.

Bejarano, Ana Maria. 2003. Protracted conflict, multiple protagonists, and staggered negotiations: Colombia, 1982–2002. *Canadian Journal of Latin American and Caribbean Studies* 28 (55–56): 223–247.

Below, Regina, Emily Grover-Kopec, and Maxx Dilley. 2007. Documenting drought-related disasters: A global reassessment. *Journal of Environment & Development* 16 (3): 328–344.

Benini, Aldo, Charles Conley, Brody Dittemore, and Zachary Waksman. 2009. Survivor needs or logistical convenience? Factors shaping decisions to deliver relief to earthquake-affected communities, Pakistan 2005–06. *Disasters* 33 (1): 110–131.

Benini, Aldo A. 1999. Network without centre? A case study of an organizational network responding to an earthquake. *Journal of Contingencies and Crisis Management* 7 (1): 38–47.

Benson, Charlotte. 1997. *The economic impact of natural disaster in the Philippines*. London: Overseas Development Institute.

Berberian, Manuel. 2005. The 2003 Bam urban earthquake: A predictable seismotectonic pattern along the western margin of the rigid Lut Block, southeast Iran. *Earthquake Spectra* 1 (S1): S35–S99.

Bergholt, Drago, and Päivi Lujala. 2012. Climate-related natural disasters, economic growth, and armed civil conflict. *Journal of Peace Research* 49 (1): 147–162.

Bergius, Mikael, Tor A. Benjaminsen, Faustin Maganga, and Halvard Buhaug. 2020. Green economy, degradation narratives, and land-use conflicts in Tanzania. *World Development* 129 (1): 1–13.

Berlemann, Michael, and Max Friedrich Steinhardt. 2017. Climate change, natural disasters, and migration—a survey of the empirical evidence. *CESifo Economic Studies* 63 (4): 353–385.

Berman, Sheri. 2003. Islamism, revolution and civil society. *Perspectives on Politics* 1 (2): 257–272.

Bernath, Andreas. 2016. *Klimakatastrophen, Vertreibung und Gewalt: Eine makroqualitative Untersuchung sowie eine Einzelfallstudie über den Zusammenhang von umweltbedingten Bevölkerungsbewegungen und gewaltsamen Konflikten.* Hamburg: State and University Library.

Berrebi, Claude, and Jordan Ostwald. 2011. Earthquakes, hurricanes, and terrorism: Do natural disasters incite terror? *Public Choice* 149 (3): 383–403.

Bevan, James. 2008. *Crisis in Karamoja: Armed violence and the failure of disarmament in Uganda's most deprived region.* Geneva: Small Arms Survey.

Bhattarai, Baburam. 1996. 40 point demand. South Asia Terrorism Portal, February 4. https://www.satp.org/satporgtp/countries/nepal/document/papers/40points.htm.

Bhaumik, Subir. 2009. *Troubled periphery: Crisis of India's North East.* New Delhi: Sage.

Biberman, Yelena, and Megan Turnbull. 2018. When militias provide welfare: Lessons from Pakistan and Nigeria. *Political Science Quarterly* 133 (4): 695–727.

Bird, Chris. 1998. Desperate Afghan quake victims await help. ReliefWeb, February 10. https://reliefweb.int/report/afghanistan/desperate-afghan-quake-victims-await-help.

Birkmann, Jörg, Philip Buckle, Jill Jäger, Mark Peeling, Neysa Jacqueline Setiadi, Matthias Garschagen, et al. 2010. Extreme events and disasters: A window of opportunity for change? Analysis of organizational, institutional and political changes, formal and informal responses after mega-disasters. *Natural Hazards* 55 (3): 637–655.

Biswas, Soutik. 2020. Coronavirus: India's pandemic lockdown turns into a human tragedy. BBC News, March 30. https://www.bbc.com/news/world-asia-india-52086274.

Black, Richard, Stephen Bennett, Sandy M. Thomas, and John R. Beddington. 2011. Migration as adaptation. *Nature* 478 (7370): 447–449.

Blattman, Christopher, and Jeannie Annan. 2016. Can employment reduce lawlessness and rebellion? A field experiment with high-risk men in a fragile state. *American Political Science Review* 110 (1): 1–17.

Blattman, Christopher, and Edward Miguel. 2010. Civil war. *Journal of Economic Literature* 48 (1): 3–57.

Bloem, Jeffrey R., and Colette Salemi. 2020. COVID-19 and conflict. *World Development* 140 (1): 105294.

Bob, Clifford. 2005. *The marketing of rebellion: Insurgents, media, and international activism.* Cambridge: Cambridge University Press.

Bobylev, Nikolai. 2011. *Environmental change and migration: Governmental compensation policies to natural disasters victims and urbanization processes.* Bielefeld: CMCD.

References

Boccard, Nicolas. 2021. Analysis of trends in disaster risk. *International Journal of Disaster Risk Reduction* 53 (1): 101989.

Boen, Teddy, and Rohit Jigyasu. 2005. Cultural considerations for post disaster reconstruction post-tsunami challenges. *Asian Disaster Management News* 11 (2): 1–10.

Bollyky, Thomas J., and Chad P. Bown. 2020. The tragedy of vaccine nationalism: Only cooperation can end the pandemic. *Foreign Affairs* 99 (5): 96–109.

Booth, E. D., A. M. Chandler, P. K. C. Wong, and A. W. Coburn. 1991. *The Luzon, Philippines earthquake of 16 July 1990: A field report by EEFIT*. London: Earthquake Engineering Field Investigation Team.

Bose, Sumantra. 2007. *Contested lands: Israel-Palestine, Kashmir, Bosnia, Cyprus, and Sri Lanka*. Cambridge, MA: Harvard University Press.

Boshoff, Henri, Waldemar Vrey, and George Rautenbach. 2010. *The Burundi peace process: From civil war to conditional peace*. Pretoria: Institute for Security Studies.

Bownas, Richard A. 2015. Dalits and Maoists in Nepal's civil war: Between synergy and co-optation. *Contemporary South Asia* 23 (4): 409–425.

Boyle, Michael J. 2009. Bargaining, fear, and denial: Explaining violence against civilians in Iraq 2004–2007. *Terrorism and Political Violence* 21 (2): 261–287.

Brancati, Dawn. 2007. Political aftershocks: The impact of earthquakes on intrastate conflict. *Journal of Conflict Resolution* 51 (5): 715–743.

Brancati, Dawn, Johanna K. Birnir, and Qutaiba Idibi. 2021. *Pax pandemica? The impact of COVID-19 on non-state actor violence*. College Park, MD: Interdisciplinary Laboratory of Computational Social Science.

Branch, Adam. 2005. Neither peace nor justice: Political violence and the peasantry in northern Uganda, 1986–1998. *African Studies Quarterly* 8 (2): 1–31.

Bright, Jonathan, and John Gledhill. 2018. A divided discipline? Mapping peace and conflict studies. *International Studies Perspectives* 19 (2): 128–147.

Brillantes, Alex B., Jr. 1992. The Philippines in 1991: Disasters and decisions. *Asian Survey* 32 (2): 140–145.

Brillantes, Alex B., Jr. 1993. The Philippines in 1992: Ready for take off? *Asian Survey* 23 (2): 224–230.

Brilliant, Franca, Lisa Doughte, Martin Ebube, Jonathan Friedman, Jeanette Harvey, Faye Henderson, et al. 1992. *OFDA annual report 1992*. Washington, DC: U.S. Office of Foreign Disaster Assistance.

Brooke, James. 2010. Russia's heat turns political. VOA (Voice of America), August 11. https://www.voanews.com/a/russias-heat-turns-political-100568959/123733.html.

Broome, Jack. 2021. An end in sight for the Philippines' Maoist insurgency? *The Diplomat*, February 19. https://thediplomat.com/2021/02/an-end-in-sight-for-the-philippines-maoist-insurgency/.

Brzoska, Michael. 2018. Weather extremes, disasters and collective violence: Conditions, mechanisms and disaster-related policies in recent research. *Current Climate Change Reports* 4 (4): 320–329.

Brzoska, Michael. 2019. Understanding the disaster–migration–violent conflict nexus in a warming world: The importance of international policy interventions. *Social Sciences* 8 (6): 167.

Brzoska, Michael, and Christiane Fröhlich. 2015. Climate change, migration and violent conflict: Vulnerabilities, pathways and adaptation strategies. *Migration and Development* 5 (1): 1–21.

Buhaug, Halvard. 2015. Climate–conflict research: Some reflections on the way forward. *Wiley Interdisciplinary Reviews: Climate Change* 6 (3): 269–275.

Buhaug, Halvard, Tor A. Benjaminsen, Espen Sjastaad, and Ole Magnus Theisen. 2015. Climate variability, food production shocks, and violent conflict in sub-Saharan Africa. *Environmental Research Letters* 10 (1): 1–11.

Buhaug, Halvard, Lars-Erik Cederman, and Kristian Skrede Gleditsch. 2014. Square pegs in round holes: Inequalities, grievances, and civil war. *International Studies Quarterly* 58 (2): 418–431.

Bukarti, Bulama. 2020a. A deadly alliance: Coronavirus makes Boko Haram more dangerous than ever. *The Telegraph*, June 7. https://www.telegraph.co.uk/global-health/science-and-disease/deadly-alliance-coronavirus-makes-boko-haram-dangerous-ever/.

Bukarti, Bulama. 2020b. How is Boko Haram responding to Covid-19? Tony Blair Institute for Global Change, May 20. https://institute.global/policy/how-boko-haram-responding-covid-19.

Busygina, Irina. 2012. Threats to critical infrastructure and state responses: The case of the 2010 forest fires in Russia. In *Russian critical infrastructures: Vulnerabilities and policies*, edited by Pynnöniemi, Katri, 57–76. Helsinki: Finish Institute of International Affairs.

Butler, Christopher, and Scott Gates. 2009. Asymmetry, parity, and (civil) war: Can international theories of power help us understand civil war? *International Interactions* 35 (3): 330–340.

Cabral, Sam. 2021. Covid "hate crimes" against Asian Americans on rise. BBC News, May 21. https://www.bbc.com/news/world-us-canada-56218684.

Cafarella, Nicole, ed. 2005. *Mujahideen-e Khalq (MEK) dossier*. New York: Center for Policing Terrorism.

References

Calabrese, John. 2020. Iraq's fragile state in the time of Covid-19. Middle East Institute, December 8. https://www.mei.edu/publications/iraqs-fragile-state-time-covid-19.

Call, Charles T. 2008. The fallacy of the "failed state." *Third World Quarterly* 29 (8): 1491–1507.

Calo-Blanco, Aitor, Jaromír Kovánk, Friederike Mengel, and José Gabriel Romero. 2017. Natural disasters and indicators of social cohesion. *PLOS One* 1 (1): 1–13.

Campbell, John. 2020. Beyond the pandemic, Boko Haram looms large in Nigeria. Council on Foreign Relations, June 11. https://www.cfr.org/in-brief/beyond-pandemic-boko-haram-looms-large-nigeria.

Cappelli, Federica, Valeria Costantini, and Davide Consoli. 2021. The trap of climate change–induced "natural" disasters and inequality. *Global Environmental Change* 70: 102329.

CAREC (Central Asia Regional Economic Cooperation). 2006. *Regional cooperation on disaster management and preparedness*. Urümqi, China: CAREC.

Carter, Timothy Allen, and Daniel Jay Veale. 2013. Weather, terrain and warfare: Coalition fatalities in Afghanistan. *Conflict Management and Peace Science* 30 (3): 220–239.

Casis, Bienvenido. 2008. *Enhancement of the Philippines disaster response capability*. Carlisle, PA: US Army War College.

Cassanelli, Lee V., and Catherine Besteman. 1996. Conclusion: Politics, land, and war in southern Somalia. In *The struggle for land in southern Somalia: The war behind the war*, edited by Catherine Besteman and Lee V. Cassanelli, 201–204. London: Westview Press.

Cassar, Alessandra, Andrew Healy, and Carl von Kessler. 2017. Trust, risk, and time preferences after a natural disaster: Experimental evidence from Thailand. *World Development* 94 (1): 90–105.

Cederman, Lars-Erik, Brian Min, and Andreas Wimmer. 2010. Why do ethnic groups rebel? New data and analysis. *World Politics* 62 (1): 87–119.

Cederman, Lars-Erik, and Manuel Vogt. 2017. Dynamics and logics of civil war. *Journal of Conflict Resolution* 91 (9): 1992–2016.

Cerra, Valerie, and Sweta Chaman Saxena. 2008. Growth dynamics: The myth of economic recovery. *American Economic Review* 98 (1): 439–457.

Çetin, Hakan Cem. 2013. Disaster crises management in Turkey: 1999 Marmara earthquake case. *International Journal of Human Sciences* 10 (2): 628–636.

CFE-DM (Center for Excellence in Disaster Management). 2006. *Indian Ocean earthquake and tsunami emergency update: December 31, 2004*. Ford Island, HI: CFE-DM.

Chandra, Uday. 2014. The Maoist movement in contemporary India. *Social Movement Studies* 13 (3): 414–419.

Chattu, Vijay Kuma, and W. Andy Knight. 2019. Global health diplomacy as a tool of peace. *Peace Review* 31 (2): 148–157.

Chaudoin, Stephen, Zachary Peskowitz, and Christopher Stanton. 2017. Beyond zeroes and ones: The intensity and dynamics of civil conflict. *Journal of Conflict Resolution* 61 (1): 56–83.

Chenoweth, Erica. 2013. Terrorism and democracy. *Annual Review of Political Science* 16 (1): 355–378.

Chernick, Marc. 2001. The dynamics of Colombia's three-dimensional war. *Conflict, Security & Development* 1 (1): 93–100.

Chmutina, Ksenia, and Jason von Meding. 2019. A dilemma of language: "Natural disasters" in academic literature. *International Journal of Disaster Risk Science* 10 (3): 283–292.

Chowdhury, A. Mushtaque R., Abbas U. Bhuyia, A. Yusuf Choudhury, and Rita Sen. 1993. The Bangladesh cyclone of 1991: Why so many people died. *Disasters* 17 (4): 291–304.

Christia, Fotini. 2012. *Alliance formation in civil wars*. Cambridge: Cambridge University Press.

Chung, Eunbin, and Inbok Rhee. 2022. Disasters and intergroup peace in sub-Saharan Africa. *Journal of Peace Research* 59 (1): 58–72.

Clark, Jocalyn. 2015. Pakistan authorities trade blame as heatwave deaths exceed 800. *British Medical Journal* 350 (1): h3477.

CNN. 1998. Thousands feared dead in Afghan quake. May 31. http://edition.cnn.com/WORLD/asiapcf/9805/31/afghan.quake.on/.

Cola, Raoul M. 2003. The needs of children following a disaster: The 1990 earthquake in the Philippines. *Disasters* 17 (3): 248–254.

Collier, Paul, and Anke Hoeffler. 2004. Greed and grievance in civil war. *Oxford Economic Papers* 56 (4): 563–595.

Conrad, Justin, and Kevin Greene. 2015. Competition, differentiation, and the severity of terrorist attacks. *Journal of Politics* 77 (2): 546–561.

Consultative Group on Indonesia. 2006. *Preliminary damage and loss assessment, Yogyakarta and Central Java natural disaster*. Jakarta: BAPPENAS, the Provincial and Local Governments of D. I. Yogyakarta, and the Provincial and Local Governments of Central Java.

Cook, Malcolm. 2021. The Philippines in 2020: Continuity despite crisis. *Southeast Asian Affairs* 47 (1): 237–256.

References

Cools, Sara, Martin Flatø, and Andreas Kotsadam. 2020. Rainfall shocks and intimate partner violence in sub-Saharan Africa. *Journal of Peace Research* 57 (3): 377–390.

Cooper, Christopher, and Robert Block. 2006. *Disaster: Hurricane Katrina and the failure of Homeland Security*. New York: Henry Holt.

Core, Paul. 2009. Burma/Myanmar: Challenges of a ceasefire accord in Karen State. *Journal of Current Southeast Asian Affairs* 28 (3): 95–105.

Cosgrave, John, and Maurice Herson. 2008. Perceptions of crisis and response: A synthesis of evaluations of the response to the 2005 Pakistan earthquake. In *ALNAP seventh review of humanitarian action*, edited by Maurice Herson, John Mitchell, and Ben Ramalingham, 177–224. London: Overseas Development Institute.

Couttenier, Mathieu, and Raphael Soubeyran. 2013. Drought and civil war in sub-Saharan Africa. *The Economic Journal* 124 (1): 201–244.

CRED (Centre for Research on the Epidemiology of Disasters) and UNDRR (UN Office for Disaster Risk Reduction). 2020. *Human costs of disasters: An overview of the last twenty years, 2000–2019*. Brussels: CRED.

Croissant, Aurel. 2007. Muslim insurgency, political violence, and democracy in Thailand. *Terrorism and Political Violence* 19 (1): 1–18.

Cronin, Audrey Kurth, Huda Aden, Adam Frost, and Benjamin Jones. 2004. *Foreign terrorist organizations*. Washington, DC: Congressional Research Service.

Cunningham, David E., Kristian Skrede Gleditsch, and Idean Salehyan. 2013. Non-state actors in civil wars: A new dataset. *Conflict Management and Peace Science* 30 (5): 516–531.

Cuny, Fred. 1983. *Disasters and development*. Oxford: Oxford University Press.

Dalby, Simon. 2020. Bordering sustainability in the Anthropocene. *Territory, Politics, Governance* 8 (2): 144–160.

Daoudy, Marwa. 2020. *The origins of the Syrian conflict: Climate change and human security*. Cambridge: Cambridge University Press.

Das, Debojyoti. 2014. "Majuli in peril": Challenging the received wisdom on flood control in Brahmaputra River Basin, Assam (1940–2000). *Water History* 6 (2): 167–185.

Das, Kumar. 2002. Social mobilisation for rehabilitation: Relief work in cyclone-affected Orissa. *Economic and Political Weekly* 37 (48): 4784–4788.

Das, Partha, Dadul Chutiya, and Nirupam Hazarika. 2009. *Adjusting to floods on the Brahmaputra plains, Assam, India*. Kathmandu: International Centre for Integrated Mountain Development.

Dash, Biswanath. 2002. Lessons from Orissa super cyclone. *Economic and Political Weekly* 37 (42): 4270–4271.

Daw, Mohamed A. 2021. The impact of armed conflict on the epidemiological situation of COVID-19 in Libya, Syria and Yemen. *Frontiers in Public Health* 9 (698): 1–8.

de Bruin, Sophie P., Jannis M. Hoch, Nina von Uexkull, Halvard Buhaug, Jolle Demmers, Hans Visser, et al. 2022. Projecting long-term armed conflict risk: An underappreciated field of inquiry? *Global Environmental Change* 72 (1): 102423.

de Guzman, Arnel, and Tito Craige. 1991. Counterinsurgency war in the Philippines and the role of the United States. *Bulletin of Concerned Asian Scholars* 23 (1): 38–47.

De Juan, Alexander. 2015. Long-term environmental change and geographical patterns of violence in Darfur, 2003–2005. *Political Geography* 45 (1): 22–33.

De Juan, Alexander, Jan H. Pierskalla, and Elisa Schwarz. 2020. Natural disasters, aid distribution, and social conflict—micro-level evidence from the 2015 earthquake in Nepal. *World Development* 126 (1): 1–17.

De Leon, Corazon Alma, and Lina B. Laigo. 1993. Flood relief and rehabilitation in Ormoc: Experiences and insights of administrators. *Philippine Journal of Public Administration* 37 (4): 327–335.

de Montclos, Marc-Antoine, ed. 2014. *Boko Haram: Islamism, politics, security and the state in Nigeria*. Leiden: African Studies Centre.

de Silva, M. W. Amarasiri. 2009. Ethnicity, politics and inequality: Post-tsunami humanitarian aid delivery in Ampara District, Sri Lanka. *Disasters* 33 (2): 253–273.

de Sousa, Ricardo Real Pedrosa. 2014. External interventions and civil war intensity in south-central Somalia (1991–2010). *African Study Notes* 28 (1): 57–86.

Deen, Samar. 2015. Pakistan 2010 floods: Policy gaps in disaster preparedness and response. *International Journal of Disaster Risk Reduction* 12 (1): 341–349.

Deraniyagala, Sonali. 2005. The political economy of civil conflict in Nepal. *Oxford Development Studies* 33 (1): 47–62.

Desportes, Isabella, and Dorothea Hilhorst. 2020. Disaster governance in conflict-affected authoritarian contexts: The cases of Ethiopia, Myanmar, and Zimbabwe. *Politics and Governance* 8 (4): 343–354.

Detges, Adrien. 2016. Local conditions of drought-related violence in sub-Saharan Africa: The role of road- and water infrastructures. *Journal of Peace Research* 53 (5): 696–710.

Detges, Adrien. 2017. Droughts, state-citizen relations and support for political violence in sub-Saharan Africa: A micro-level analysis. *Political Geography* 61 (1): 88–98.

Deutsche Welle. 2008. Hundreds die in Afghan cold. February 11. https://www.dw.com/en/hundreds-die-in-afghan-cold/a-5212436.

References

Diehl, Paul F. 2016. Exploring peace: Looking beyond war and negative peace. *International Studies Quarterly* 60 (1): 1–10.

DiGiuseppe, Matthew R., Colin M. Barry, and Richard W. Frank. 2012. Good for the money: International finance, state capacity, and internal armed conflict. *Journal of Peace Research* 49 (3): 391–405.

Do, Quy-Toan, and Lakshmi Iyer. 2010. Geography, poverty and conflict in Nepal. *Journal of Peace Research* 47 (6): 735–748.

Doocy, Shannon, Eva Leidman, Tricia Aung, and Thomas Kirsch. 2013. Household economic and food security after the 2010 Pakistan floods. *Food and Nutrition Bulletin* 34 (1): 95–103.

Döring, Stefan. 2020. Come rain, or come wells: How access to groundwater affects communal violence. *Political Geography* 76 (1): 102073.

Dove, Michael R., and Mahmudul Huq Khan. 1995. Competing constructions of calamity: The April 1991 cyclone in Bangladesh. *Population and Environment* 16 (5): 445–471.

Drury, A. Cooper, and Richard Stuart Olson. 1998. Disasters and political unrest: An empirical investigation. *Journal of Contingencies and Crisis Management* 6 (3): 153–161.

Dube, Oeindrila, and Juan F. Vargas. 2013. Commodity price shocks and civil conflict: Evidence from Colombia. *Review of Economic Studies* 80 (4): 1384–1421.

Dube, Oeindrila, and Juan Fernando Vargas. 2006. *Resource curse in reverse: The coffee crisis and armed conflict in Colombia*. Bogotá: University de los Andes.

Dubey, Sandeep Kumar. 2013. *Maoist movement in India: An overview*. New Delhi: Manohar Parrikar Institute for Defence Studies and Analyses.

Duncombe, Constance. 2019. Iran, terrorism and the post-9/11 world order. In *Handbook of terrorism and counter terrorism post 9/11*, edited by David Martin Jones, Paul Schulte, Carl Ungerer, and M. L. R. Smith, 240–249. Cheltenham, UK: Edward Elgar.

Dunn, Kevin C. 2004. Uganda: The Lord's Resistance Army. *Review of African Political Economy* 31 (99): 139–142.

Dusa, Adrian. 2022. Critical tension: Sufficiency and parsimony in QCA. *Sociological Methods & Research* 51 (2): 541–565.

Dussaillant, Francisca, and Eugenio Guzmán. 2014. Trust via disasters: The case of Chile's 2010 earthquake. *Disasters* 38 (4): 808–832.

Dutta, Akhil Ranjan. 2014. Civil society's engagement with ULFA in Assam: A historical exploration. *Studies in Indian Politics* 2 (1): 43–54.

Dutta, Uddipan. 2008. *Creating Robin Hoods: The insurgency of the ULFA in its early period, its parallel administration and the role of Assamese Vernacular Press (1985–1990)*. New Delhi: WISCOMP.

Duyvesteyn, Isabelle. 2000. Contemporary war: Ethnic conflict, resource conflict or something else? *Civil Wars* 3 (1): 92–116.

Duyvesteyn, Isabelle. 2017. Rebels & legitimacy; an introduction. *Small Wars & Insurgencies* 28 (4–5): 669–685.

East, Bob. 2013. *Terror truncated: The decline of the Abu Sayyaf group from the crucial year 2002*. Newcastle, UK: Cambridge Scholars.

Eastin, Joshua. 2016. Fuel to the fire: Natural disasters and the duration of civil conflict. *International Interactions* 42 (2): 322–349.

Eastin, Joshua. 2017. Conflict calamities: Natural disasters and the CPP-NPA. *Kasarinlan: Philippine Journal of Third World Studies* 32 (2): 109–138.

Eastin, Joshua. 2018. Hell and high water: Precipitation shocks and conflict violence in the Philippines. *Political Geography* 63 (1): 116–134.

Eastin, Joshua, and Steven T. Zech. 2022. Environmental pressures and pro-government militias: Evidence from the Philippines. *Conflict Management and Peace Science*, online ahead of print, June 28. https://doi.org/10.1177%2F07388942221110128.

Eboh, Camillus. 2021. Around 20% of Nigerian workers lost jobs due to COVID-19. Reuters, September 21. https://www.reuters.com/world/africa/around-20-nigerian-workers-lost-jobs-due-covid-19-stats-office-2021-09-21/.

Eck, Kristine. 2012. In data we trust? A comparison of UCDP GED and ACLED conflict event datasets. *Cooperation and Conflict* 47 (1): 124–141.

The Economist. 2021. Relative peace gives Iraq a chance to build a functioning state. June 19. https://www.economist.com/leaders/2021/06/19/relative-peace-gives-iraq-a-chance-to-build-a-functioning-state.

EESC (European Economic and Social Committee). 1992. *The Ormoc City tragedy of November 5, 1991: An evaluation of the different contributing factors*. Quezon City: European Economic and Social Committee.

El Abdellaoui, Jamila. 2009. *Another crossroad for Burundi: From the FNL to peaceful elections in 2010*. Pretoria: Institute for Security Studies.

El-Batran, Manal, and Christian Arandel. 1998. A shelter of their own: Informal settlement expansion in Greater Cairo and government responses. *Environment and Urbanization* 10 (1): 217–232.

Elhawary, Samir, and Gerardo Castillo. 2008. *The role of the affected state: A case study on the Peruvian earthquake response*. London: Overseas Development Institute.

References

Ember, Carol R., and Melvin Ember. 1992. Resource unpredictability, mistrust, and war: A cross-cultural study. *Journal of Conflict Resolution* 36 (2): 242–262.

Emerald Insight. 1999. Earthquake. *Disaster Prevention and Management* 8 (1): 1–5.

Enia, Jason. 2008. Peace in its wake? The 2004 tsunami and internal conflict in Indonesia and Sri Lanka. *Journal of Public and International Affairs* 19 (1): 7–27.

Enserink, Martin. 2010. Haiti's outbreak is latest in cholera's new global assault. *Science* 330 (6005): 738–739.

Entessar, Nader. 1984. The Kurds in post-revolutionary Iran and Iraq. *Third World Quarterly* 6 (4): 911–933.

Entessar, Nader. 2010. *Kurdish politics in the Middle East*. Lanham, MD: Lexington Books.

Eriksen, Jørgen W., and Tormod Heier. 2009. Winter as the number one enemy? *The RUSI Journal* 154 (5): 64–71.

Espeland, Rune Hjalmar, and Stina Petersen. 2010. The Ugandan army and its war in the north. *Forum for Development Studies* 37 (2): 193–215.

Esteban, Joan, Laura Mayoral, and Debraj Ray. 2012. Ethnicity and conflict: An empirical study. *American Economic Review* 102 (4): 179–204.

Eugenio, Elena A., Lilibeth A. Acosta, Damasa B. Magcale-Macandog, Paula Beatrice M. Macandog, Elaine Kuan-Hui Lin, Jemimah Mae A. Eugenio, et al. 2016. Adaptive capacity of Philippine communities vulnerable to flash floods and landslides: Assessing loss and damage from typhoon Bopha in Eastern Mindanao. *International Journal of Sustainable Development* 19 (3): 279–314.

Evangelista, Matthew. 2002. *The Chechen wars: Will Russia go the way of the Soviet Union?* Washington, DC: Brookings Institution.

Evans, Martin, and John Phillips. 2007. *Algeria: Anger of the dispossessed*. New Haven, CT: Yale University Press.

Eynde, Oliver Vanden. 2018. Targets of violence: Evidence from India's Naxalite conflict. *The Economic Journal* 128 (609): 887–916.

Fair, C. Christine. 2011. Pakistan in 2010: Flooding, governmental inefficiency, and continued insurgency. *Asian Survey* 51 (1): 97–110.

Fair, C. Christine, Patrick M. Kuhn, Neil Malhotra, and Jacob N. Shapiro. 2017. Natural disasters and political engagement: Evidence from the 2010–11 Pakistani floods. *Quarterly Journal of Political Science* 12 (1): 99–141.

Fallesen, Ditte Marie, and Paul Adolfo. 2021. *Impacts of COVID-19 on communities in the Philippines: Results from the Philippines high frequency social monitoring of COVID-19 impacts, round 2: April 8–14, 2021*. Manila: World Bank.

FAO (Food and Agriculture Organization). 1997. Seeds and tools rushed to flood-stricken farmers in Somalia and Myanmar. December 9. https://reliefweb.int/report/somalia/fao-rushes-farm-assistance-rural-flood-victims-somalia-and-myanmar.

FAO (Food and Agriculture Organization). 2005. Food shortages in Burundi deepen as country embraces peace. March 16. https://reliefweb.int/report/burundi/food-shortages-burundi-deepen-country-embraces-peace#:~:text=Following%20Burundi's%20recent%20vote%20for,percent%20more%20than%20last%20year.

Faris, Stephen. 2007. The real roots of Darfur. *The Atlantic Monthly*, April, 2.

Faulkner, Christopher M. 2016. Money and control: Rebel groups and the forcible recruitment of child soldiers. *African Security* 9 (3): 211–236.

Fayutkin, Dan. 2006. Russian-Chechen information warfare 1994–2006. *RUSI Journal* 151 (5): 52–55.

Fearon, James D., and David D. Laitin. 2003. Ethnicity, insurgency, and civil war. *American Political Science Review* 97 (1): 75–90.

Feitelson, Eran, and Amit Tubi. 2017. A main driver or an intermediate variable? Climate change, water and security in the Middle East. *Global Environmental Change* 44 (1): 39–48.

Feldman, Robert L. 2008. Why Uganda has failed to defeat the Lord's Resistance Army. *Defence & Security Analysis* 24 (1): 45–52.

Femia, Francesco, and Caitlin E. Werrell. 2017. An unstable, stable nation? Climate, water, migration and security in Syria from 2006–2011. In *Climate hazard crises in Asian societies and environments*, edited by Troy Sternberg, 1–10. London: Routledge.

Fernandes, Clinton. 2010. East Timor and the struggle for independence. In *The development of institutions of human rights: A comparative study*, edited by Lilian A. Barria and Steven D. Roper, 163–178. New York: Palgrave.

Feyyaz, Muhammad. 2011. Political economy of Tehrik-i-Taliban Swat. *Conflict and Peace Studies Journal* 4 (3): 1–22.

Feyyaz, Muhammad. 2016. The discourse and study of terrorism in decolonized states: The case of Pakistan. *Critical Studies on Terrorism* 9 (3): 455–477.

Feyyaz, Muhammad. 2020. Communication (un)savviness and the failure of terrorism: A case of Pakistani terrorist organizations. *Dynamics of Asymmetric Conflict* 13 (1): 24–46.

Filiu, Jean-Pierre. 2009. The local and global jihad of al-Qa'ida in the Islamic Maghrib. *Middle East Journal* 63 (2): 213–226.

Fischhendler, Itay. 2015. The securitization of water discourse: Theoretical foundations, research gaps and objectives of the special issue. *International Environmental Agreements* 15 (3): 245–255.

References

Fleiss, M., S. Kienberger, C. Aubrecht, R. Kidd, and P. Zeil. 2011. Mapping the 2010 Pakistan floods and its impact on human life: A post-disaster assessment of socioeconomic indicators. *Proceedings of the Annual Geoinformation for Disaster Management Conference* 7 (1): 1–6.

Florea, Adrian. 2020. Rebel governance in de facto states. *European Journal of International Relations* 26 (4): 1004–1031.

Formetta, Giuseppe, and Luc Feyen. 2019. Empirical evidence of declining global vulnerability to climate-related hazards. *Global Environmental Change* 57 (1): 1–9.

Foroughi, Payam. 2002. Tajikistan: Nationalism, ethnicity, conflict, and socioeconomic disparities: Sources and solutions. *Journal of Muslim Minority Affairs* 22 (1): 39–61.

Fortna, Virginia Page, Nicholas J. Lotito, and Michael A. Rubin. 2018. Don't bite the hand that feeds: Rebel funding sources and the use of terrorism in civil wars. *International Studies Quarterly* 62 (4): 782–794.

Franzke, Christian L. E., and Herminia Torelló i Sentelles. 2020. Risk of extreme high fatalities due to weather and climate hazards and its connection to large-scale climate variability. *Climatic Change* 162 (2): 507–525.

Fritz, Charles E., and Harry B. Williams. 1957. The human being in disasters: A research perspective. *Annals of the American Academy of Political and Social Science* 309 (1): 42–51.

Fröhlich, Christiane. 2016. Climate migrants as protestors? Dispelling misconceptions about global environmental change in pre-revolutionary Syria. *Contemporary Levant* 1 (1): 38–50.

Funk, Chris. 2021. *Drought, flood, fire: How climate change contributes to catastrophes*. Cambridge: Cambridge University Press.

Furlan, Marta. 2020. Rebel governance at the time of Covid-19: Emergencies as opportunities for rebel rulers. *Studies in Conflict & Terrorism* 45 (1): 1–24.

FutureLearn. 2021. The Philippines economy and the impact of COVID-19. August 18. https://www.futurelearn.com/info/futurelearn-international/philippines-economy-covid-19.

Gaillard, J. C., Kristinne Sanz, Benigno C. Balgos, Soledad Natalia M. Dalisay, Andrew Gorman-Murray, Fagalua Smith, et al. 2017. Beyond men and women: A critical perspective on gender and disaster. *Disasters* 41 (3): 429–447.

Gaillard, Jean-Christophe, Elsa Clavé, and Ilan Kelman. 2008. Wave of peace? Tsunami disaster policy in Aceh, Indonesia. *Geoforum* 39 (1): 511–526.

Gaillard, Jean-Christophe, Elsa Clavé, Océane Vibert, Azhari Dedi, Jean-Charles Denain, Yusuf Efendi, et al. 2008. Ethnic groups' response to the 26 December 2004 earthquake and tsunami in Aceh, Indonesia. *Natural Hazards* 47 (1): 17–38.

Gaillard, Jean-Christophe, and Jessica Mercer. 2012. From knowledge to action: Bridging gaps in disaster risk reduction. *Progress in Human Geography* 37 (1): 93–114.

Ganapati, N. Emel, Ilan Kelman, and Theodore Koukis. 2010. Analyzing Greek-Turkish disaster-related cooperation: A disaster diplomacy perspective. *Cooperation and Conflict* 45 (2): 162–185.

Ganguly, Rajat. 2001. India, Pakistan and the Kashmir insurgency: Causes, dynamics and prospects for resolution. *Asian Studies Review* 25 (3): 309–334.

Gawande, Kishore, Devesh Kapur, and Shanker Satyanath. 2017. Renewable natural resource shocks and conflict intensity: Findings from India's ongoing Maoist insurgency. *Journal of Conflict Resolution* 61 (1): 140–172.

Gawronski, Vincent, and Stuart R. Olson. 2013. Disasters as crisis triggers for critical junctures? The 1976 Guatemala case. *Latin American Politics and Society* 55 (2): 133–149.

Geddes, Barbara, Joseph Wright, and Erica Frantz. 2014. Autocratic breakdown and regime transitions: A new data set. *Perspectives on Politics* 12 (2): 313–331.

George, Susannah, Azizi Tassal, and Sharif Hassan. 2020. Coronavirus sweeps through Afghanistan's security forces. *Washington Post*, June 25. https://www.washingtonpost.com/world/asia_pacific/afghanistan-coronavirus-security-forces-military/2020/06/24/0063c828-b4e2-11ea-9a1d-d3db1cbe07ce_story.html.

Gerges, Fawaz A. 2016. *ISIS: A history*. Princeton, NJ: Princeton University Press.

Gerszon Mahler, Daniel, Nishant Yonzan, Christopher Lakner, R. Andres Castaneda Aguilar, and Haoyu Wu. 2021. Updated estimates of the impact of COVID-19 on global poverty: Turning the corner on the pandemic in 2021? *World Bank Blogs*, June 24. https://blogs.worldbank.org/opendata/updated-estimates-impact-covid-19-global-poverty-turning-corner-pandemic-2021.

Ghasimi, Reza. 1994. *Tajikistan: A World Bank country study*. Washington, DC: World Bank.

Ghimire, Ramesh, and Susana Ferreira. 2016. Floods and armed conflict. *Environment and Development Economics* 21 (1): 23–52.

Ghimire, Ramesh, Susana Ferreira, and Jeffrey H. Dorfman. 2015. Flood-induced displacement and civil conflict. *World Development* 66 (1): 614–628.

Ghobarah, Ahmed, Murat Saatcioglu, and Ioan Nistor. 2006. The impact of the 26 December 2004 earthquake and tsunami on structures and infrastructure. *Engineering Structures* 28 (2): 312–326.

Giustozzi, Antonio. 2007. *Koran, kalashnikov, and laptop: The neo-Taliban insurgency in Afghanistan*. New York: Columbia University Press.

References

Giustozzi, Antonio. 2019. *The Taliban at war: 2001–2018*. Oxford: Oxford University Press.

Gleditsch, Nils Petter. 1998. Armed conflict and the environment: A critique of the literature. *Journal of Peace Research* 35 (3): 381–400.

Gleditsch, Nils Petter, Peter Wallensteen, Mikael Eriksson, Margareta Sollenberg, and Håvard Strand. 2002. Armed conflict 1946–2001: A new dataset. *Journal of Peace Research* 39 (5): 615–637.

Gleick, Peter. 2014. Water, drought, climate change, and conflict in Syria. *Weather, Climate, and Society* 6 (3): 331–340.

Gohain, Hiren. 2007. Chronicles of violence and terror: Rise of United Liberation Front of Asom. *Economic and Political Weekly* 42 (12): 1012–1018.

Goodhand, Jonathan. 2001. *Aid, conflict and peace building in Sri Lanka*. London: King's College.

Goodhand, Jonathan, and Bart Klem. 2005. *Aid, conflict, and peacebuilding in Sri Lanka 2000–2005*. Colombo: Asia Foundation.

Gossman, Patricia. 2001. Afghanistan in the balance. *Middle East Report* 221 (1): 8–15.

Goyari, Phanindra. 2005. Flood damages and sustainability of agriculture in Assam. *Economic and Political Weekly* 40 (26): 2723–2729.

Grare, Frederic. 2013. *Balochistan: The state versus the nation*. Washington, DC: Carnegie Endowment.

Gray, David H., and Erik Stockham. 2008. Al-Qaeda in the Islamic Maghreb: The evolution from Algerian Islamism to transnational terror. *African Journal of Political Science and International Relations* 2 (4): 91–97.

Grech-Madin, Charlotte. 2021. Water and warfare: The evolution and operation of the water taboo. *International Security* 45 (4): 84–125.

Gretsky, Sergei. 1995. Civil war in Tajikistan and its international repercussions. *Critique: Journal for Critical Studies of the Middle East* 4 (6): 3–24.

Groth, Juliane, Tobias Ide, Patrick Sakdapolrak, Endeshaw Kassa, and Kathleen Hermans. 2020. Deciphering interwoven drivers of environment-related migration—a multisite case study from the Ethiopian highlands. *Global Environmental Change* 63 (1): 102094.

Guha-Sapir, Debarati. 2021. EM-DAT: The international disasters database. Accessed July 27, 2021. www.emdat.be.

Guha-Sapir, Debarati, Benjamin Schlüter, Jose Manuel Rodriguez-Llanes, Louis Lillywhite, and Madelyn Hsiao-Rei Hicks. 2018. Patterns of civilian and child deaths due to war-related violence in Syria: A comparative analysis from the Violation Documentation Center dataset, 2011–16. *The Lancet Global Health* 6 (1): e103–e110.

Gunther, Michael M. 2000. The continuing Kurdish problem in Turkey after Öcalan's capture. *Third World Quarterly* 21 (5): 849–869.

Gupta, Dipak K. 2007. The Naxalites and the Maoist movement in India: Birth, demise, and reincarnation. *Democracy and Security* 3 (2): 157–188.

Gurr, Ted Robert. 1970. *Why men rebel*. Princeton, NJ: Princeton University Press.

Gyves, Cliff, and Chris Wyckoff. 2006. *Algerian Groupe Salafiste de la Predication et le Combat (Salafi Group for Call and Combat, GSPC): An operational analysis*. Monterey: Center for Contemporary Conflict.

Hachhethu, Krishna. 1997. Nepal in 1996: Experimenting with a coalition government. *Asian Survey* 37 (2): 149–154.

Haddad, Mohammed. 2021. Mapping coronavirus anti-lockdown protests around the world. *Al Jazeera*, February 2. https://www.aljazeera.com/news/2021/2/2/mapping-coronavirus-anti-lockdown-protests-around-the-world.

Haer, Roos, Lilli Banholzer, and Verena Ertl. 2011. Create compliance and cohesion: How rebel organizations manage to survive. *Small Wars & Insurgencies* 22 (3): 415–434.

Haer, Roos, and Babak RezaeeDaryakenari. 2022. Disasters and civilian victimization: Exploring the dynamic effect in Africa, 1997–2017. *Journal of Peace Research* 59 (1): 43–57.

Hahn, Gordon M. 2014. *The Caucasus Emirate Mujahedin: Global Jihadism in Russia's North Caucasus and beyond*. Jefferson, NC: McFarland.

Haigh, Richard, Siri Hettige, Maheshika Sakalasuriya, G. Vickneswaran, and Lasantha Namal Weerasena. 2016. A study of housing reconstruction and social cohesion among conflict and tsunami affected communities in Sri Lanka. *Disaster Prevention and Management* 25 (5): 566–580.

Hakuno, Motohiko, Toshifumi Imaizumi, Hiroshi Kagami, Junji Kiyono, Yasutaka Ikeda, Ikuo Towhata, et al. 1997. Preliminary report of the damage due to the Qayen earthquake of 1997, northeastern Iran. *Journal of Natural Disaster Science* 19 (1): 67–81.

Hall, Rosalie Arcala. 2004. Exploring new roles for the Philippine military: Implications for civilian supremacy. *Philippine Political Science Journal* 25 (48): 107–130.

Halvorson, Sarah J., and Jennifer Parker Hamilton. 2010. In the aftermath of the Qa'yamat: The Kashmir earthquake disaster in northern Pakistan. *Disasters* 34 (1): 184–204.

Hamzawy, Amr, and Sarah Grebowski. 2010. *From violence to moderation: Al-Jama'a al-Islamiya and al-Jihad*. Beirut: Carnegie Middle East Center.

Hanif, Un. 2017. Socio-economic impacts of heat wave in Sindh. *Pakistan Journal of Meteorology* 13 (26): 87–96.

Hansen, Stig Jarle. 2013. *Al-Shabaab in Somalia: The history and ideology of a militant Islamist group, 2005–2012*. Oxford: Oxford University Press.

Haque, Afsana, and Sarwar Jahan. 2016. Regional impact of cyclone Sidr in Bangladesh: A multi-sector analysis. *International Journal of Disaster Risk Science* 7 (3): 312–327.

Haque, C. Emdad, and Danny Blair. 1992. Vulnerability to tropical cyclones: Evidence from the April 1991 cyclone in coastal Bangladesh. *Disasters* 16 (3): 217–229.

Hardcastle, Rohan J., and Adrian T. L. Chua. 1998. Humanitarian assistance: Towards a right of access to victims of natural disasters. *International Review of the Red Cross* 38 (325): 589–609.

Hardt, Judith Nora. 2021. The United Nations Security Council at the forefront of (climate) change? Confusion, stalemate, ignorance. *Politics and Governance* 9 (4): 5–15.

Harish, S. P. 2006. Ethnic or religious cleavage? Investigating the nature of the conflict in southern Thailand. *Contemporary Southeast Asia* 28 (1): 48–69.

Harmon, Christopher C. 2020. The Philippines in the face of the New People's Army: Fifty years in the field. In *Routledge handbook of democracy and security*, edited by Leonard Weinberg, Elizabeth Francis, and Eliot Assoudeh, 265–281. London: Routledge.

Harmon, Stephen. 2010. From GSPC to AQIM: The evolution of an Algerian Islamist terrorist group into an Al-Qa'ida affiliate and its implications for the Sahara-Sahel region. *Concerned Africa Scholars Bulletin* 85 (1): 12–28.

Harrowell, Elly, and Alpaslan Özerdem. 2019. Understanding the dilemmas of integrating post-disaster and post-conflict reconstruction initiatives: Evidence from Nepal, Sri Lanka and Indonesia. *International Journal of Disaster Risk Reduction* 36 (5): 1–11.

Hartmann, Betsy. 2014. Converging on disaster: Climate security and the malthusian anticipatory regime for Africa. *Geopolitics* 19 (4): 757–783.

Hashimoto, Takao, and Masakatsu Miyajima. 2002. Relations between building damage and ground conditions in the 1999 Quindío earthquake in Colombia. *Journal of Earthquake Engineering* 6 (3): 315–330.

Hegre, Håvard, Tanja Ellingsen, Scott Gates, and Nils Petter Gleditsch. 2001. Toward a democratic civil peace? Democracy, political change, and civil war, 1816–1992. *American Political Science Review* 95 (1): 33–48.

Helman, David, and Benjamin F. Zaitchik. 2020. Temperature anomalies affect violent conflicts in African and Middle Eastern warm regions. *Global Environmental Change* 63 (1): 102118.

Hendrix, Cullen, and Stephan Haggard. 2015. Global food prices, regime type, and urban unrest in the developing world. *Journal of Peace Research* 52 (2): 143–157.

Hendrix, Cullen S. 2010. Measuring state capacity: Theoretical and empirical implications for the study of civil conflict. *Journal of Peace Research* 47 (3): 273–285.

Hendrix, Cullen S., and Sarah M. Glaser. 2007. Trends and triggers: Climate, climate change and civil conflict in sub-Saharan Africa. *Political Geography* 26 (6): 695–715.

Hendrix, Cullen S., and Idean Salehyan. 2012. Climate change, rainfall, and social conflict in Africa. *Journal of Peace Research* 49 (1): 35–50.

Hendrix, Cullen S., and Idean Salehyan. 2015. No news is good news: Mark and recapture for event data when reporting probabilities are less than one. *International Interactions* 41 (2): 392–406.

Hennings, Anne. 2019. The dark underbelly of land struggles: The instrumentalization of female activism and emotional resistance in Cambodia. *Critical Asian Studies* 51 (1): 103–119.

Herz, John H. 1950. Idealist internationalism and the security dilemma. *World Politics* 2 (2): 157–180.

Heydarian, Richard Javan. 2015. *The quest for peace: The Aquino administration's peace negotiations with the MILF and CPP-NPA-NDF*. Oslo: Norwegian Centre for Conflict Resolution.

Hilhorst, Dorothea, and Rodrigo Mena. 2021. When Covid-19 meets conflict: Politics of the pandemic response in fragile and conflict-affected states. *Disasters*, online ahead of print, September 22. https://doi.org/10.1111/disa.12514.

Hill, Joshua. 2007. Flooding in India leaves 3.5 million homeless. Mongabay, September 11. https://news.mongabay.com/2007/09/flooding-in-india-leaves-3-5-million-homeless/.

Hoffman, Bruce. 2006. *Inside terrorism*. New York: Columbia University Press.

Hoffman, Bruce, and Gordon H. McCormick. 2004. Terrorism, signaling, and suicide attack. *Studies in Conflict & Terrorism* 27 (4): 243–281.

Holden, William N., and R. Daniel Jacobson. 2007. Mining amid armed conflict: Nonferrous metals mining in the Philippines. *The Canadian Geographer* 51 (4): 475–500.

Hollis, Simon. 2018. Bridging international relations with disaster studies: The case of disaster-conflict scholarship. *Disasters* 42 (1): 19–40.

References

Horton, Lynn. 2012. After the earthquake: Gender inequality and transformation in post-disaster Haiti. *Gender & Development* 20 (2): 295–308.

Hossain, Naomi. 2018. The 1970 Bhola cyclone, nationalist politics, and the subsistence crisis contract in Bangladesh. *Disasters* 42 (1): 187–203.

Hosseini, Kambod Amini, Solmaz Hosseinioon, and Zhila Pooyan. 2013. An investigation into the socioeconomic aspects of two major earthquakes in Iran. *Disasters* 37 (3): 516–535.

Housego, Kim. 2003. Toddler rescued from Algerian quake ruins. AP News, May 23. https://apnews.com/29e459992cfa31a8f0d6f0bd60e6ba63.

Howe, Brendan, and Geehyun Bang. 2017. Nargis and Haiyan: The politics of natural disaster management in Myanmar and the Philippines. *Asian Studies Review* 41 (1): 58–78.

Hrishikeshan, K. 2003. Assam's agony: The ULFA & obstacles to conflict resolution. *Faultlines* 12 (2): 29.

Huang, Reyko. 2016. Rebel diplomacy in civil war. *International Security* 40 (4): 89–126.

Huggel, Christian, Annik Raissing, Mario Rohrer, Gilberto Romero, Alfonso Diaz, and Nadine Salzmann. 2015. How useful and reliable are disaster databases in the context of climate and global change? A comparative case study analysis in Peru. *Natural Hazards and Earth System Sciences* 15 (3): 475–485.

Hughes, James. 2001. Chechnya: The causes of a protracted post-Soviet conflict. *Civil Wars* 4 (4): 11–48.

Hultman, Lisa, and Dursun Peksen. 2017. Successful or counterproductive coercion? The effect of international sanctions on conflict intensity. *Journal of Conflict Resolution* 61 (6): 1315–1339.

Hyland, Frank. 2008. Peru's Sendero Luminoso: From Maoism to narco-terrorism. *Terrorism Monitor* 6 (23): 1–3.

Ibrion, Michaela, Mohammad Mokhtari, and Farrokh Nadim. 2015. Earthquake disaster risk reduction in Iran: Lessons and "lessons learned" from three large earthquake disasters—Tabas 1978, Rudbar 1990, and Bam 2003. *International Journal of Disaster Risk Science* 6 (4): 415–427.

ICG (International Crisis Group). 2005. *Southern Thailand: Insurgency, not jihad*. Brussels: International Crisis Group.

Ide, Tobias. 2016. Towards a constructivist understanding of socio-environmental conflicts. *Civil Wars* 18 (1): 69–90.

Ide, Tobias. 2017. Research methods for exploring the links between climate change and conflict. *Wiley Interdisciplinary Reviews Climate Change* 8 (3): 1–14.

Ide, Tobias. 2018. Does environmental peacemaking between states work? Insights on cooperative environmental agreements and reconciliation in international rivalries. *Journal of Peace Research* 55 (3): 351–365.

Ide, Tobias. 2019. The impact of environmental cooperation on peacemaking: Definitions, mechanisms and empirical evidence. *International Studies Review* 21 (3): 327–346.

Ide, Tobias. 2020a. The dark side of environmental peacebuilding. *World Development* 127 (1): 104777.

Ide, Tobias. 2020b. *Natural disasters and political violence: Assessing the intersections*. Stockholm: Global Challenges Foundation.

Ide, Tobias. 2021. COVID-19 and armed conflict. *World Development* 140 (1): 1–6.

Ide, Tobias, Carl Bruch, Alexander Carius, Ken Conca, Geoffrey D. Dabelko, Richard Matthew, et al. 2021c. The past and future(s) of environmental peacebuilding. *International Affairs* 97 (1): 1–16.

Ide, Tobias, Michael Brzoska, Jonathan F. Donges, and Carl-Friedrich Schleussner. 2020. Multi-method evidence for when and how climate-related disasters contribute to armed conflict risk. *Global Environmental Change* 62 (1): 1–8.

Ide, Tobias, Marisa O. Ensor, Virginie Le Masson, and Susanne Kozak. 2021. Gender in the climate-conflict nexus: "Forgotten" variables, alternative securities, and hidden power dimensions. *Politics and Governance* 9 (4): 43–52.

Ide, Tobias, Anders Kristensen, and Henrikas Bartusevičius. 2021. First comes the river, then comes the conflict? A qualitative comparative analysis of flood-related political unrest. *Journal of Peace Research* 58 (1): 83–97.

Ide, Tobias, P. Michael Link, Jürgen Scheffran, and Janpeter Schilling. 2016. The climate-conflict nexus: Pathways, regional links and case studies. In *Handbook on sustainability transition and sustainable peace*, edited by Hans Günter Brauch, Úrsula Oswald Spring, John Grin, and Jürgen Scheffran, 285–304. Dordrecht: Springer.

Ide, Tobias, and Patrick A. Mello. 2022. QCA in international relations: A review of strengths, pitfalls, and empirical applications. *International Studies Review* 24 (1): viac008.

Ide, Tobias, Juan Miguel Rodriguez Lopez, Christiane Fröhlich, and Jürgen Scheffran. 2021. Pathways to water conflict during drought in the MENA region. *Journal of Peace Research* 58 (3): 568–582.

Ide, Tobias, and Jürgen Scheffran. 2014. On climate, conflict and cumulation: Suggestions for integrative cumulation of knowledge in the research on climate change and violent conflict. *Global Change, Peace & Security* 26 (3): 263–279.

IFRC (International Federation of Red Cross and Red Crescent Societies). 1996a. Nepal: Flood relief. Information bulletin no. 1, July 30. https://www.ifrc.org/docs/appeals/rpts96/np001.pdf.

References

IFRC (International Federation of Red Cross and Red Crescent Societies). 1996b. Nepal: Flood relief. Information bulletin no. 3, August 30. http://www.ifrc.org/docs/appeals/rpts96/np003.pdf.

IFRC (International Federation of Red Cross and Red Crescent Societies). 2007a. *Bangladesh: Cyclone Sidr*. Geneva: Information Bulletin 01/2007.

IFRC (International Federation of Red Cross and Red Crescent Societies). 2007b. *Burundi: The lakes are disappearing*. Nairobi: IFRCRCS.

IFRC (International Federation of Red Cross and Red Crescent Societies). 2007c. *Emergency appeal: Peru: Earthquake*. Geneva: IFRC.

IPCC (Intergovernmental Panel on Climate Change). 2018. *Global warming of 1.5 °C: An IPCC special report on the impacts of global warming of 1.5 C above pre-industrial levels and related global greenhouse gas emission pathways*. Geneva: IPCC.

IRI (International Research Institute for Climate and Spciety). 2011. WASP indices. https://iridl.ldeo.columbia.edu/maproom/Global/Precipitation/WASP_Indices.html?bbox=bb%3A-3.09%3A-11.37%3A49.19%3A22.28%3Abb&T=May%202001#tabs-1.

IRIN News. 2006. Burundi: Government sets up food security fund. February 22. https://reliefweb.int/report/burundi/burundi-government-sets-food-security-fund.

Islam, Muinul. 1992. Natural calamities and environmental refugees in Bangladesh. *Refuge* 12 (1): 5–10.

Islam, Rabiul, and Greg Walkerden. 2014. How bonding and bridging networks contribute to disaster resilience and recovery on the Bangladeshi coast. *International Journal of Disaster Risk Reduction* 10 (1): 281–291.

Iyekekpolo, Wisdom Oghosa. 2016. Boko Haram: Understanding the context. *Third World Quarterly* 37 (12): 2211–2228.

Iyengar, Rishi. 2015a. Criticism of Pakistani government intensifies as heat-wave death toll tops 1,000. *Time*, June 25. https://time.com/3935099/pakistan-heat-wave-government-power-cuts-death-toll/.

Iyengar, Rishi. 2015b. Pakistan declares a state of emergency as heat wave death toll soars to nearly 800. *Time*, June 24. https://time.com/3933463/pakistan-heatwave-karachi-sindh-emergency/.

Jabri, Vivienne. 1996. *Discourses on violence: Conflict analysis reconsidered*. Manchester: Manchester University Press.

Jacoby, Tim, and Alpaslan Özerdem. 2008. The role of the state in the Turkish earthquake of 1999. *Journal of International Development* 20 (3): 297–310.

Jadoon, Amira. 2018. Persuasion and predation: The effects of U.S. military aid and international development aid on civilian killings. *Studies in Conflict & Terrorism* 41 (10): 776–800.

Jakarta Post. 2006. Indonesia: Quake victims wait for cash aid. ReliefWeb, August 15. https://reliefweb.int/report/indonesia/indonesia-quake-victims-wait-cash-aid.

Jalali, Ali A. 2001. Afghanistan: The anatomy of an ongoing conflict. *Parameters* 31 (1): 85–98.

Jalali, Rita. 2002. Civil society and the state: Turkey after the earthquake. *Disasters* 26 (2): 120–139.

Jayasekera, Deepal. 1999. Death toll in eastern India cyclone may top 10,000. World Socialist Web Site, November 10. https://www.wsws.org/en/articles/1999/11/cycl-n10.html.

Jennings, Ralph. 2020. Communist rebels fight hard as ever in Philippines as COVID-19 distracts government. VOA, May 15. https://www.voanews.com/a/covid-19-pandemic_communist-rebels-fight-hard-ever-philippines-covid-19-distracts-government/6189326.html.

Jentzsch, Corinna, Stathis N. Kalyvas, and Livia Isabella Schubinger. 2015. Militias in civil wars. *Journal of Conflict Resolution* 59 (5): 755–769.

JICA (Japan International Cooperation Agency). 1992. *Flores Island, Indonesia earthquake of December 12, 1992.* Tokyo: JICA.

Jin, Jian-Min, Peng Bai, Wei He, Fei Wu, Xiao-Fang Liu, De-Min Han, et al. 2020. Gender differences in patients with COVID-19: Focus on severity and mortality. *Frontiers in Public Health* 8 (152): 1–6.

Johnson, Mark S. 1998. The tale of the tragedy of Neftegorsk. *Prehospital and Disaster Medicine* 13 (1): 59–64.

Johnson, McKenzie F. 2021. Fighting for black stone: Extractive conflict, institutional change and peacebuilding in Sierra Leone. *International Affairs* 97 (1): 81–102.

Johnson, McKenzie F., Luz A. Rodríguez, and Manuela Quijano Hoyos. 2020. Intrastate environmental peacebuilding: A review of the literature. *World Development* 137 (1): 105150.

Joshi, Madhav. 2013. Livelihood coping mechanisms, local intelligence, and the pattern of violence during the Maoist insurgency in Nepal. *Terrorism and Political Violence* 25 (5): 820–839.

Jun, Tackseung, and Rajiv Sethi. 2021. Extreme weather events and military conflict over seven centuries in ancient Korea. *Proceedings of the National Academy of Sciences* 118 (12): e2021976118.

Junk, Julian. 2016. Testing boundaries: Cyclone Nargis in Myanmar and the scope of R2P. *Global Society* 30 (1): 78–93.

Justino, Patricia, and Philip Verwimp. 2013. Poverty dynamics, violent conflict, and convergence in Rwanda. *Review of Income and Wealth* 59 (1): 66–90.

Jutila, Matti, Samu Pehkonen, and Tarja Väyrynen. 2008. Resuscitating a discipline: An agenda for critical peace research. *Millennium* 36 (3): 623–640.

Kahl, Colin H. 2006. *States, scarcity, and civil strife in the developing world*. Princeton, NJ: Princeton University Press.

Kalyvas, Stathis N. 2004. Warfare in civil wars. In *Rethinking civil war*, edited by Jan Angstrom and Isabelle Duyvesteyn, 88–108. London: Routledge.

Kalyvas, Stathis N. 2006. *The logic of violence in civil war*. Cambridge: Cambridge University Press.

Kalyvas, Stathis N., and Matthew Adam Kocher. 2007. How "free" is free riding in civil wars? Violence, insurgency, and the collective action problem. *World Politics* 59 (2): 177–216.

Kang, Sung Hoon, and Mark Skidmore. 2018. The effects of natural disasters on social trust: Evidence from South Korea. *Sustainability* 10 (9): 1–16.

Kapur, Roshni. 2021. The Afghan Taliban and Covid-19: Leveraging the crisis or a change of heart? Middle East Institute, April 13. https://www.mei.edu/publications/afghan-taliban-and-covid-19-leveraging-crisis-or-change-heart#_ftn21.

Kapur, Roshni, and Chayanika Saxena. 2020. The Taliban makes the most of Covid-19 crisis in Afghanistan. The Interpreter, April 27. https://www.lowyinstitute.org/the-interpreter/taliban-makes-most-covid-19-crisis-afghanistan.

Katagiri, Nori. 2019. Organized insurgency, lethality, and target selection: Abu Sayyaf Group and Jemaah Islamiyah. *Small Wars & Insurgencies* 30 (3): 518–542.

Katz, Gabriel, and Ines Levin. 2015. The dynamics of political support in emerging democracies: Evidence from a natural disaster in Peru. *International Journal of Public Opinion Research* 28 (2): 173–195.

Kaufman, Stuart. 2001. *Modern hatreds: The symbolic politics of ethnic war*. Ithaca, NY: Cornell University Press.

Kaufman, Stuart. 2011. Symbols, frames and violence: Studying ethnic war in the Philippines. *International Studies Quarterly* 55 (4): 937–958.

Kawata, Y., Y. Tsuji, A. R. Syamsudin, M. Matsuyama, H. Matsutomi, F. Imamura, et al. 1995. Response of residents at the moment of tsunamis: The 1992 Flores Island earthquake tsunami, Indonesia. In *Tsunami: Progress in prediction, disaster prevention and warning*, edited by Yoshito Tsuchiya and Nobuo Shuto, 173–185. Dordrecht: Springer.

Kazim, Hasnain. 2010. Taliban courts Pakistan flood victims: Race to provide aid emerges between West and extremists. Spiegel International, August 16. https://www.spiegel.de/international/world/taliban-courts-pakistan-flood-victims-race-to-provide-aid-emerges-between-west-and-extremists-a-712060.html.

Keefer, Philip, Eric Neumayer, and Thomas Plümper. 2011. Earthquake propensity and the politics of mortality prevention. *World Development* 39 (9): 1530–1541.

Kelman, Ilan. 2006. Acting on disaster diplomacy. *Journal of International Affairs* 59 (2): 215–240.

Kelman, Ilan. 2012. *Disaster diplomacy: How disasters affect peace and conflict.* London: Routledge.

Kelman, Ilan. 2018. Connecting theories of cascading disasters and disaster diplomacy. *International Journal of Disaster Risk Reduction* 30 (B): 172–179.

Kelman, Ilan. 2020. Disaster vulnerability by demographics? *Journal of Population and Sustainability* 4 (2): 17–30.

Kelman, Ilan, Jessica Field, Kavita Suri, and Ghulam M. Bhat. 2018. Disaster diplomacy in Jammu and Kashmir. *International Journal of Disaster Risk Reduction* 31 (1): 1132–1140.

Kelman, Ilan, Jean-Christophe Gaillard, James Lewis, and Jessica Mercer. 2016. Learning from the history of disaster vulnerability and resilience research and practice for climate change. *Natural Hazards* 82 (1): 129–143.

Kepel, Gilles. 2002. *Jihad: The trail of political Islam.* London: I. B. Tauris.

Kfir, Isaac. 2017. Al-Shabaab, social identity group, human (in)security, and counterterrorism. *Studies in Conflict & Terrorism* 40 (9): 772–789.

Khalilzad, Zalmay. 1997. Anarchy in Afghanistan. *Journal of International Affairs* 51 (1): 37–55.

Khalilzad, Zalmay, and Daniel Byman. 2000. Afghanistan: The consolidation of a rogue state. *The Washington Quarterly* 23 (1): 65–78.

Khan, Adeel. 2009. Renewed ethnonationalist insurgency in Balochistan, Pakistan: The militarized state and continuing economic deprivation. *Asian Survey* 49 (6): 1071–1091.

Khan, Kashif Saeed. 2019. Analysing local perceptions of post-conflict and post-floods livelihood interventions in Swat, Pakistan. *Development Policy Review* 37 (S2): O274–O292.

Khan, Muhammad Khalil, and Lu Wei. 2016. When friends turned into enemies: The role of the national state vs. Tehrik-i-Taliban Pakistan (TTP) in the war against terrorism in Pakistan. *Korean Journal of Defense Analysis* 28 (4): 597–626.

Kikuta, Kyosuke. 2019. Postdisaster reconstruction as a cause of intrastate violence: An instrumental variable analysis with application to the 2004 tsunami in Sri Lanka. *Journal of Conflict Resolution* 63 (3): 760–785.

Kingsbury, Damien. 2007. Peace processes in Aceh and Sri Lanka: A comparative assessment. *Security Challenges* 3 (2): 93–112.

References

Kipgen, Ngamjahao, and Dhiraj Pegu. 2018. Floods, ecology and cultural adaptation in Lakhimpur district, Assam. In *Development and disaster management: A study of the northeastern states of India*, edited by Amita Singh, Milap Punia, Nivedita P. Haran, and Thiyam Bharat Singh, 301–318. Singapore: Palgrave Macmillan.

Kirilenko, Anastasia. 2010. As Russian fires rage, forest rangers fume. Radio Free Europe / Radio Liberty, August 9. https://www.rferl.org/a/As_Russian_Fires_Rage_Forest_Rangers_Fume/2122983.html.

Kisekka-Ntale, Fredrick. 2007. Roots of the conflict in northern Uganda. *Journal of Social, Political, and Economic Studies* 32 (4): 421–452.

Klein, Naomi. 2007. *The shock doctrine: The rise of disaster capitalism*. New York: Picador.

Klitzsch, Nicole. 2014. Disaster politics or disaster of politics? Post-tsunami conflict transformation in Sri Lanka and Aceh, Indonesia. *Cooperation and Conflict* 49 (4): 554–573.

Koehnlein, Britt, and Ore Koren. 2022. COVID-19, state capacity, and political violence by non-state actors. *Journal of Peace Research* 59 (1): 90–104.

Koren, Ore. 2018. Food abundance and violent conflict in Africa. *American Journal of Agricultural Economics* 100 (4): 981–1006.

Koren, Ore, and Benjamin E. Bagozzi. 2016. From global to local, food insecurity is associated with contemporary armed conflicts. *Food Security* 8 (5): 999–1010.

Koren, Ore, Benjamin E. Bagozzi, and Thomas Benson. 2021. Food and water insecurity as causes of social unrest: Evidence from geolocated Twitter data. *Journal of Peace Research* 58 (1): 67–82.

Korf, Benedikt, Shahul Habullah, Pia Hollenbach, and Bart Klem. 2010. The gift of disaster: The commodification of good intentions in post-tsunami Sri Lanka. *Disasters* 34 (S1): S60–S77.

Kotwal, Dinesh. 2001. The contours of Assam insurgency. *Strategic Analysis* 24 (12): 2219–2233.

Koubi, Vally. 2019. Climate change and conflict. *Annual Review of Political Science* 22 (1): 18.11–18.18.

Koubi, Vally, Tobias Böhmelt, Gabriele Spilker, and Lena Schaffer. 2018. The determinants of environmental migrants' conflict perception. *International Organization* 72 (4): 905–936.

Koubi, Vally, Quynh Nguyen, Gabriele Spilker, and Tobias Böhmelt. 2021. Environmental migrants and social-movement participation. *Journal of Peace Research* 58 (1): 18–32.

Koven, Barnett S., and Cynthia McClintock. 2015. The evolution of Peru's Shining Path and the new security priorities in the hemisphere. In *Reconceptualizing security* in the Americas in the twenty-first century, edited by Bruce M. Bagley, Jonathan D. Rosen, and Hanna S. Kassab, 189–214. London: Lexington Books.

Kowalewski, Maciej. 2021. Street protests in times of COVID-19: Adjusting tactics and marching "as usual." *Social Movement Studies* 20 (6): 758–765.

Krampe, Florian, Farah Hegazi, and Stacy D. VanDeveer. 2021. Sustaining peace through better resource governance: Three potential mechanisms for environmental peacebuilding. *World Development* 144 (1): 105508.

Kreutz, Joakim. 2012. From tremors to talks: Do natural disasters produce ripe moments for resolving separatist conflicts? *International Interactions* 38 (4): 482–502.

Kugelman, Michael. 2017. Pakistan in 2016: Tensions with neighbors, turmoil at home. *Asian Survey* 57 (1): 33–42.

Kujur, Rajat. 2008. *Naxal movement in India: A profile*. New Delhi: Institute of Peace and Conflict Studies.

Kurosaki, Takashi. 2017. Household-level recovery after floods in a tribal and conflict-ridden society. *World Development* 94 (1): 51–63.

Küstner, Kai. 2010. Pakistani Taliban try to benefit from floods. Deutsche Welle, August 11. https://www.dw.com/en/pakistani-taliban-try-to-benefit-from-floods/a-5891119.

Kustra, Tyler. 2017. HIV/AIDS, life expectancy, and the opportunity cost model of civil war. *Journal of Conflict Resolution* 61 (10): 2130–2157.

Kusumasari, Bevaola, and Quamrul Alam. 2012. Local wisdom-based disaster recovery model in Indonesia. *Disaster Prevention and Management* 21 (3): 351–369.

Kydd, Andrew H., and Barbara Walter. 2006. The strategies of terrorism. *International Security* 31 (1): 49–80.

Laborde, David, Will Martin, Johan Swinnen, and Rob Vos. 2020. COVID-19 risks to global food security. *Science* 369 (6503): 500–502.

Laborde, David, Will Martin, and Rob Vos. 2021. Impacts of COVID-19 on global poverty, food security, and diets: Insights from global model scenario analysis. *Agricultural Economics* 52 (3): 375–390.

Lacina, Bethany. 2006. Explaining the severity of civil wars. *Journal of Conflict Resolution* 50 (2): 276–289.

LADB (Latin American Digital Beat). 1999. Prospects for peace appear dim in Colombia. University of New Mexico, Digital Repository, February 19. https://digitalrepository.unm.edu/notisur/12606/.

LaFree, Gary, Erin Miller, and Sue-Ming Yang. 2013. Terrorism in Indonesia, the Philippines and Thailand, 1970 to 2008. *Security and Peace* 31 (2): 81–86.

References

Lancaster, John. 1994. Grief floods razed town in Egypt. *Washington Post*, November 4. https://www.washingtonpost.com/archive/politics/1994/11/04/grief-floods-razed-town-in-egypt/d32917ca-b36d-4146-9df4-c06ad8cb353e/.

Landis, Steven T. 2014. Temperature seasonality and violent conflict: The inconsistencies of a warming planet. *Journal of Peace Research* 51 (5): 603–618.

Lane, Max. 1991. Philippines 1990: Political stalemate and persisting instability. *Southeast Asian Affairs* 18 (1): 223–239.

Larsson, Oscar L. 2020. The connections between crisis and war preparedness in Sweden. *Security Dialogue* 52 (4): 306–324.

Lawoti, Mahendra. 2009. Evolution and growth of the Maoist insurgency in Nepal. In *The Maoist insurgency in Nepal: Revolution in the twenty-first century*, edited by Mahendra Lawoti and Anup Kumar Pahari, 3–30. London: Taylor & Francis.

Lazarev, Egor, Anton Sobolev, Irina V. Soboleva, and Boris Sokolov. 2014. Trial by fire: A natural disaster's impact on support for the authorities in rural Russia. *World Politics* 66 (4): 641–668.

LeBillon, Philippe. 2001. The political ecology of war: Natural resources and armed conflicts. *Political Geography* 20 (5): 561–584.

LeBillon, Philippe. 2022. Oil and the Islamic State: Revisiting "resource wars" arguments in light of ISIS operations and state-making attempts. *Studies in Conflict & Terrorism* 45 (1): 1–23.

Le Billon, Philippe, and Arno Waizenegger. 2007. Peace in the wake of disaster? Secessionist conflicts and the 2004 Indian ocean tsunami. *Transactions of the Institute of British Geographers* 32 (2): 411–427.

Lebovic, James H., and Erik Voeten. 2009. The cost of shame: International organizations and foreign aid in the punishing of human rights violators. *Journal of Peace Research* 46 (1): 79–97.

Lee, Bomi K., Sara McLaughlin Mitchell, Cody J. Schmidt, and Yufan Yang. 2022. Disasters and the dynamics of interstate rivalry. *Journal of Peace Research* 59 (1): 12–27.

Lee, Harry F. 2018. Internal wars in history: Triggered by natural disasters or socio-ecological catastrophes? *The Holocene* 28 (7): 1071–1081.

Legewie, Nicolas. 2013. An introduction to applied data analysis with qualitative comparative analysis (QCA). *Forum: Qualitative Social Science Research* 14 (3): 1–45.

Leithead, Alastair. 2008. Afghan thaw reveals winter toll. BBC News, February 12. http://news.bbc.co.uk/2/hi/south_asia/7241824.stm.

Leitmann, Josef. 2007. Cities and calamities: Learning from post-disaster response in Indonesia. *Journal of Urban Health* 84 (1): 144–153.

Lekkas, Efthimios L., and Haralambos D. Kranis. 2004. *The Bourmedes-Zemmouri (Algeria) earthquake (May 21, 2003, Mw = 6.8)*. Vancouver, Canada: World Conference on Eearthquake Engineering.

Lemarchand, René. 2009. *The dynamics of violence in Central Africa*. Philadelphia: University of Pennsylvania Press.

Lessing, Benjamin. 2015. Logics of violence in criminal war. *Journal of Conflict Resolution* 59 (8): 1486–1516.

Levy, Ido, and Abdi Yusuf. 2021. How do terrorist organizations make money? Terrorist funding and innovation in the case of al-Shabaab. *Studies in Conflict & Terrorism* 44 (12): 1167–1189.

Lin, Thung-Hong. 2015. Governing natural disasters: State capacity, democracy, and human vulnerability. *Social Forces* 93 (3): 1267–1300.

Lindley, Anna. 2014. Environmental processes, political conflict and migration. In *Humanitarian crises and migration: Causes, consequences and responses*, edited by Susan F. Martin, Sanjula Weerasinghe, and Abbie Taylor, 160–178. London: Routledge.

Linke, Andrew M., Frank D. W. Witmer, John O'Loughlin, J. Terrence McCabe, and Jaroslav Tir. 2018. Drought, local institutional contexts, and support for violence in Kenya. *Journal of Conflict Resolution* 62 (7): 1544–1578.

Lischin, Luke. 2020. Surviving or thriving? COVID-19 and violent non-state actors in the Southern Philippines. New Mandala, September 9. https://www.newmandala.org/surviving-or-thriving-covid-19-and-violent-non-state-actors-in-the-southern-philippines/.

Little, Peter D. 2003. *Somalia: Economy without state*. Oxford: James Currey.

Little, Peter D., Hussein Mahmoud, and D. Layne Coppock. 2001. When deserts flood: Risk management and climatic processes among East African pastoralists. *Climatic Research* 19 (4): 149–159.

Liwanag, Armando. 1991. Reaffirm our basic principles and carry the revolution forward. December 26. http://www.bannedthought.net/Philippines/CPP/1991/Reaffirm BasicPrinciples-AL-911226.pdf.

Loesch, Juliette. 2017. The GPH-MILF peace process in the Philippines to prevent and transform violent extremism in Mindanao. *Journal of Peacebuilding & Development* 12 (2): 96–101.

Lynch, Dov. 2001. The Tajik civil war and peace process. *Civil Wars* 4 (4): 49–72.

Mach, Katharine J., Caroline M. Kraan, W. Neil Adger, Halvard Buhaug, Marshall Burke, James D. Fearon, et al. 2019. Climate as a risk factor for armed conflict. *Nature* 571 (7764): 193–197.

References

Maertens, Ricardo. 2021. Adverse rainfall shocks and civil war: Myth or reality? *Journal of Conflict Resolution* 65 (4): 701–728.

Magen, Amichai. 2018. Fighting terrorism: The democracy advantage. *Journal of Democracy* 29 (1): 111–125.

Magnus, Ralph H. 1998. Afghanistan in 1997: The war moves north. *Asian Survey* 38 (2): 109–115.

Mahadevan, Prem. 2012. The Maoist insurgency in India: Between crime and revolution. *Small Wars & Insurgencies* 23 (2): 203–220.

Mahanta, Nani Gopal. 2005. Politics of peace-making. *Economic and Political Weekly* 40 (1): 25–27.

Mahanta, Nani Gopal. 2013. *Confronting the state: ULFA's quest for sovereignty*. New Delhi: Sage.

Mahdi, Saiful. 2006. *From tsunami pledges to contribution: Who is the most generous?* Banda Aceh: Aceh Institute.

Mahmood, Sara. 2015. Decapitating the Tehrik-i-Taliban Pakistan: An effective counter-terrorism strategy? *Counter Terrorist Trends and Analyses* 7 (6): 24–29.

Mahmud, N. 2000. Flood disasters and displacement: The case of Ormoc City, the Philippines. In *Floods*, vol. 1, edited by Dennis J. Parker, 400–411. London: Routledge.

Mahoney, James. 2010. After KKV: The new methodology of qualitative research. *World Politics* 62 (1): 120–147.

Maizland, Lindsay. 2021. The Taliban in Afghanistan. Council on Foreign Relations, September 15. https://www.cfr.org/backgrounder/taliban-afghanistan.

Maksad, Firas. 2019. Lebanon's year of fire. *Foreign Policy*, October 21. https://foreignpolicy.com/2019/10/21/lebanon-sectarian-protests-forest-fires-self-immolation/.

Makwana, Nikunj. 2019. Disaster and its impact on mental health: A narrative review. *Journal of Family Medicine and Primary Care* 8 (10): 3090–3095.

MAR (Minorities at Risk). 2010. Chronology for Kurds in Iran. July 16. https://web.archive.org/web/20120622215417/http://www.cidcm.umd.edu/mar/chronology.asp?groupId=63007.

Marcus, Aliza. 2007a. *Blood and belief: The PKK and the Kurdish fight for independence*. New York: New York University Press.

Marcus, Aliza. 2007b. Turkey's PKK: Rise, fall, rise again? *World Policy Journal* 24 (1): 75–84.

Marijnen, Esther, Lotje de Vries, and Rosaleen Duffy. 2020. Conservation in violent environments. *Political Geography* 87 (1): 102253.

Marks, Tom. 1993. Maoist miscue II: The demise of the Communist Party of the Philippines, 1968–1993. *Small Wars & Insurgencies* 4 (1): 99–157.

Marshall, Andrew R. C., and Stuart Grudgings. 2013. Desperate Philippine typhoon survivors loot, dig up water pipes. Reuters, November 12. https://www.reuters.com/article/us-philippines-typhoon/desperate-philippine-typhoon-survivors-loot-dig-up-water-pipes-idUSBRE9A603Q20131113.

Martinez, Luiz. 2004. Why the violence in Algeria? *Journal of North African Studies* 9 (2): 14–27.

Martin-Shields, Charles P., and Wolfgang Stojetz. 2019. Food security and conflict: Empirical challenges and future opportunities for research and policy making on food security and conflict. *World Development* 119 (1): 150–164.

Martone, James. 1994. Angry townspeople survey devastation; death toll over 475. AP News, November 4. https://apnews.com/article/ba0faa75aa24b96fb4a6d0d1da21c6c0.

Marx, Axel, and Adrian Dusa. 2011. Crisp-set qualitative comparative analysis (csQCA), contradictions and consistency benchmarks for model specification. *Methodological Innovations Online* 6 (2): 103–148.

Masood, Salman. 2010. In Pakistan, Taliban hint at attacks on relief workers. *New York Times*, August 26. https://www.nytimes.com/2010/08/27/world/asia/27pstan.html.

Masterson, Daniel M. 2010. The devolution of Peru's Sendero Luminoso: From hybrid Maoists to narco-traffickers? *History Compass* 8 (1): 51–60.

Matesan, Ioana Emy. 2020a. Failed negotiations and the dark side of ripeness: Insights from Egypt. *International Negotiation* 25 (3): 463–494.

Matesan, Ioana Emy. 2020b. Grievances and fears in Islamist movements: Revisiting the link between exclusion, insecurity, and political violence. *Journal of Global Security Studies* 5 (1): 44–62.

Matsuoka, Masashi, and Fumio Yamazaki. 2006. *Use of SAR imagery for monitoring areas damaged due to the 2006 mid Java, Indonesia earthquake.* Cambridge: 4th International Workshop on Remote Sensing for Post-Disaster Response, September 25–26.

Matthew, Richard, and Bishnu Raj Upreti. 2018. Disaster capitalism in Nepal. *Peace Review* 30 (2): 176–183.

Maxwell, Daniel, and Merry Pitzpatrick. 2012. The 2011 Somalia famine: Context, causes, and complications. *Global Food Security* 1 (1): 5–12.

Maystadt, Jean-François, and Olivier Ecker. 2014. Extreme weather and civil war: Does drought fuel conflict in Somalia through livestock price shocks? *American Journal of Agricultural Economics* 96 (4): 1157–1182.

Mbaye, Ahmadou Aly. 2020. Climate change, livelihoods, and conflict in the Sahel. *Georgetown Journal of International Affairs* 21 (1): 12–20.

References

McCargo, Duncan. 2006. Thaksin and the resurgence of violence in the Thai South: Network monarchy strikes back? *Critical Asian Studies* 38 (1): 39–71.

McClintock, Cynthia. 1984. Why peasants rebel: The case of Peru's Sendero Luminoso. *World Politics* 37 (1): 48–84.

McDonald, Matt. 2021. *Ecological security: Climate change and the construction of security*. Cambridge: Cambridge University Press.

McDowall, David. 2004. *Modern history of the Kurds*. London: I. B. Tauris.

McFadden, Robert D. 1998. Thousands said to have been killed in Afghan quake. *New York Times*, February 7. https://www.nytimes.com/1998/02/07/world/thousands-said-to-have-been-killed-in-afghan-quake.html.

McKeown, Timothy J. 1999. Case studies and the statistical worldview: Review of King, Keohane and Verba's *Designing social inquiry: Scientific inference in qualitative research*. *International Organization* 53 (1): 161–190.

Mealy, Marisa, and Carol Shaw Austad. 2012. Sendero Luminoso (Shining Path) and the conflict in Peru. In *Handbook of ethnic conflict: International perspectives*, edited by Dan Landis and Rosita D. Albert, 553–583. New York: Springer.

Mehra, Ajay K. 2000. Naxalism in India: Revolution or terror? *Terrorism and Political Violence* 12 (2): 37–66.

Mehrl, Marius, and Paul W. Thurner. 2021. The effect of the Covid-19 pandemic on global armed conflict: Early evidence. *Political Studies Review* 19 (2): 286–293.

Meierding, Emily. 2013. Climate change and conflict: Avoiding small talk about the weather. *International Studies Review* 15 (2): 185–203.

Mello, Patrick A. 2021. *Qualitative comparative analysis: An introduction to research design and application*. Washington, DC: Georgetown University Press.

Mena, Rodrigo, and Dorothea Hilhorst. 2021. The (im)possibilities of disaster risk reduction in the context of high-intensity conflict: The case of Afghanistan. *Environmental Hazards* 20 (2): 188–208.

Menkhaus, Ken. 2006. State collapse in Somalia: Second thoughts. *Review of African Political Economy* 30 (97): 405–422.

Menkhaus, Ken. 2012. No access: Critical bottlenecks in the 2011 Somali famine. *Global Food Security* 1 (1): 29–35.

Meslem, Abdelghani, Fumio Yamazaki, Yoshihisa Maruyama, Djillali Benouar, Abderrahmane Kibboua, and Youcef Mehanic. 2012. The effects of building characteristics and site conditions on the damage distribution in Boumerde's after the 2003 Algeria earthquake. *Earthquake Spectra* 28 (1): 185–216.

MFPED (Ministry of Finance, Planning and Economic Development of Uganda). 2001. *Uganda poverty status report 2001*. Kampala: MFPED.

Miall, Hugh. 2020. *A peace research agenda for the 21st century: Report on an international workshop held in Tokyo, 6–8 December 2019*. Tokyo: Toda Peace Institute.

Michaud, Joshua, Kellie Moss, Derek Licina, Ron Waldman, Adam Kamradt-Scott, Maureen Bartee, et al. 2019. Militaries and global health: Peace, conflict, and disaster response. *The Lancet* 393 (10168): 276–286.

Middeldorp, Nick, and Philippe Le Billon. 2019. Deadly environmental governance: Authoritarianism, eco-populism, and the repression of environmental and land defenders. *Annals of the American Association of Geographers* 109 (2): 324–337.

Milch, Karen, Yuri Gorokhovich, and Shannon Doocy. 2010. Effects of seismic intensity and socioeconomic status on injury and displacement after the 2007 Peru earthquake. *Disasters* 34 (4): 1171–1182.

Miller, Gary J. 2005. The political evolution of principal-agent models. *Annual Review of Political Science* 8 (1): 203–225.

Misra, Udayon. 2009. ULFA: Beginning of an end? *Economic & Political Weekly* 44 (52): 13–16.

Mitchell, Sara McLaughlin, and Elise Pizzi. 2021. Natural disasters, forced migration, and conflict: The importance of government policy responses. *International Studies Review* 23 (3): 580–604.

Mohanty, Lenin. 2010. Super cyclone in Orissa In *Globalization and impact of cyclone on women and children of Orissa*, edited by Lenin Mohanty, 74–103. Bhubaneswar: Utkal University.

Molano, Alfredo. 2000. The evolution of the FARC: A guerrilla group's long history. *NACLA Report on the Americas* 34 (2): 23–31.

Mubarak, Hisham. 1996. What does the Gama'a Islamiyya want? An interview with Tal'at Fu'ad Qasim. *Middle East Report* 198 (1): 40–46.

Mueller, Jason C. 2018. The evolution of political violence: The case of Somalia's Al-Shabaab. *Terrorism and Political Violence* 30 (1): 116–141.

Mukhim, Patricia. 2014. Floods in the north-east: Lack of planning and red tape. *Economic and Political Weekly* 49 (42): 21–23.

Munich RE. 2021. 2020 natural disaster balance. January 7. https://www.munichre.com/en/company/media-relations/media-information-and-corporate-news/media-information/2021/2020-natural-disasters-balance.html.

Murphy, Kim. 1994. 226 killed as floods, fire ravage Egyptian towns: Disaster: Storm waters collapse bridge onto fuel tanks; Contents are set ablaze. Death toll is expected to climb. *Los Angeles Times*, November 3. https://www.latimes.com/archives/la-xpm-1994-11-03-mn-58298-story.html.

References

MWLE (Ministry of Water, Lands and Environment of Uganda). 2002. *Initial national communication on climate change.* Kampala: MWLE.

Myrtinnen, Henri. 2009. East Timor, anti-colonial struggle, 1974 to independence. In *The international encyclopedia of revolution and protest,* edited by Immanuel Ness, 1–5. Hoboken, NJ: John Wiley.

Nabi, Peer Ghulam. 2014. Coordinating post-disaster humanitarian response: Lessons from the 2005 Kashmir earthquake, India. *Development in Practice* 24 (8): 975–988.

Nadiruzzaman, M., and D. Wrathall. 2015. Participatory exclusion—Cyclone Sidr and its aftermath. *Geoforum* 64 (1): 196–204.

Nardulli, Peter F., Buddy Peyton, and Joseph Bajjalieh. 2015. Climate change and civil unrest: The impact of rapid-onset disasters. *Journal of Conflict Resolution* 59 (2): 310–335.

Nauman, Qasim. 2015. Who's to blame for Pakistan's heat wave? Taliban says power companies, government Minister blames India. *IndiaRealTime Blog, Wall Street Journal,* June 26. https://blogs.wsj.com/indiarealtime/2015/06/26/whos-to-blame-for-pakistans-heat-wave-taliban-says-power-companies-government-blames-india/.

NDT Bureau. 2021. Philippines reacts strongly to CCP-NPA announcement of revival of "partisan units." *New Delhi Times,* January 18. https://www.newdelhitimes.com/philippines-reacts-strongly-to-ccp-npa-announcement-of-revival-of-partisan-units/.

Nel, Philip, and Marjolein Righarts. 2008. Natural disasters and the risk of violent civil conflict. *International Studies Quarterly* 52 (1): 159–185.

Nelson, Matthew J. 2010. Pakistan in 2009: Tackling the Taliban. *Asian Survey* 50 (1): 112–126.

Nelson, Travis. 2010. When disaster strikes: On the relationship between natural disaster and interstate conflict. *Global Change, Peace & Security* 22 (2): 155–174.

Nemeth, Stephen, and Brian Lai. 2022. When do natural disasters lead to negotiations in a civil war? *Journal of Peace Research* 59 (1): 28–42.

Nemeth, Stephen C., and Jacob A. Mauslein. 2020. Generosity is a dangerous game: Aid allocation and the risks of terrorism. *Terrorism and Political Violence* 32 (2): 382–400.

The New Humanitarian. 2006. Burundi: Drought kills 120 as thousands flee. Relief Web, January 20. https://reliefweb.int/report/burundi/burundi-drought-kills-120-thousands-flee.

The New Humanitarian. 2008. Government raps emergency response commission as winter death roll rises. February 6. https://www.thenewhumanitarian.org/report

/76600/afghanistan-government-raps-emergency-response-commission-winter-death-toll-rises.

Nieto, W. Alejandro Sanchez. 2008. A war of attrition: Sri Lanka and the Tamil Tigers. *Small Wars & Insurgencies* 19 (4): 573–587.

Nimubona, Julien, Gérard Birantamije, and Joseph Nkurunziza. 2012. The process of security transition in Burundi: Challenges in security sector reform and combatant integration. In *Post-war security transitions: Participatory peacebuilding after asymmetric conflicts*, edited by Véronique Dudouet, Hans J. Giessmann, and Katrin Planta, 143–159. London: Routledge.

Niner, Sarah. 2000. A long journey of resistance: The origins and struggle of the CNRT. *Bulletin of Concerned Asian Scholars* 32 (1): 11–18.

Niner, Sarah. 2019. *Xanana: Leader of the struggle for independent Timor-Leste*. Kew: Australian Scholarly Publishing.

Nordås, Ragnhild, and Nils Petter Gleditsch. 2007. Climate change and conflict. *Political Geography* 26 (6): 627–638.

Norlen, Tova C. 2020. The impact of COVID-19 on Salafi-Jihadi terrorism. *Connections* 19 (2): 11–24.

Norris, Connor. 2008. *Mujahideen-e-Khalq (MEK)*. Sierra Vista, AZ: University of Military Intelligence Fort Huachuca.

Noy, Ilan. 2009. The macroeconomic consequences of disasters. *Journal of Development Economics* 88 (2): 221–231.

Obermeyer, Ziad, Christopher J. L. Murray, and Emmanuela Gakidou. 2008. Fifty years of violent war deaths from Vietnam to Bosnia: Analysis of data from the world health survey programme. *BMJ* 336 (7659): 1482–1486.

O'Brien, McKenzie. 2012. Fluctuations between crime and terror: The case of Abu Sayyaf's kidnapping activities. *Terrorism and Political Violence* 24 (2): 320–336.

O'Donnell, Lynne, and Mirwais Khan. 2020. Leader of Afghan Taliban said to be gravely ill with the coronavirus. *Foreign Policy*, June 1. https://foreignpolicy.com/2020/06/01/afghan-taliban-coronavirus-pandemic-akhunzada/.

O'Hara, Christopher, and Niels Selling. 2012. *Myanmar's ethnic insurgents: UWSA, KNA and KIO*. Stockholm: Institute for Security & Development Policy.

Olawale, Ismael. 2021. *COVID-19 and violent extremism in the Lake Chad Basin*. N'Djamena: United Nations Development Programme.

O'Loughlin, John, Andrew M. Linke, and Frank D. W. Witmer. 2014. Effects of temperature and precipitation variability on the risk of violence in sub-Saharan Africa, 1980–2012. *Proceedings of the National Academy of Sciences* 111 (47): 16712–16717.

References

O'Loughlin, John, Frank D. W. Witmer, and Andrew M. Linke. 2010. The Afghanistan–Pakistan wars, 2008–2009: Micro-geographies, conflict diffusion, and clusters of violence. *Eurasian Geography and Economics* 51 (4): 437–471.

Olson, Richard S., and Vincent Gawronski. 2010. From disaster event to political crisis: A "5C+A" framework for analysis. *International Studies Perspectives* 11 (3): 205–221.

Omelicheva, Mariya Y. 2011. Natural disasters: Triggers of political instability? *International Interactions* 37 (4): 441–465.

Onyeiwu, Stephen. 2021. Nigeria's COVID-19 economic plan has delivered disappointing results: Here's why. The Conversation, October 12. https://theconversation.com/nigerias-covid-19-economic-plan-has-delivered-disappointing-results-heres-why-169417.

Oppenheim, Ben, Nicholai Lidow, Patrick Ayscue, Karen Saylors, Placide Mbala, Charles Kumakamba, et al. 2019. Knowledge and beliefs about Ebola virus in a conflict-affected area: Early evidence from the North Kivu outbreak. *Journal of Global Health* 9 (2): 020311.

Ordinario, Cai. 2020. Job losses to push 3-million Filipinos into poverty. Business Mirror, December 9. https://businessmirror.com.ph/2020/12/09/job-losses-to-push-3-million-filipinos-into-poverty/.

Organski, A. F. K., and Jacek Kugler. 1980. *The war ledger.* Chicago: University of Chicago Press.

Ostovar, Afshon. 2016. *Vanguard of the imam: Religion, politics, and Iran's Revolutionary Guards.* Oxford: Oxford University Press.

Ottmann, Martin. 2017. Rebel constituencies and rebel violence against civilians in civil conflicts. *Conflict Management and Peace Science* 34 (1): 27–51.

Oxford Analytica. 2020. COVID-19 crisis may not benefit Sahelian jihadists. Emerald Insight, May 20. https://doi.org/10.1108/OXAN-DB252722.

Oyero, Kayode. 2020. Boko Haram: COVID-19 affecting equipment production, delivery—DHQ. Punch, November 30. https://punchng.com/boko-haram-covid-19-affecting-equipment-production-delivery-dhq.

Özerdem, Alpaslan. 2006. The mountain tsunami: Afterthoughts on the Kashmir earthquake. *Third World Quarterly* 27 (3): 397–419.

Pakistan Today. 2015. No one ready to own heat-stricken Karachi. June 29. https://www.pakistantoday.com.pk/2015/06/29/no-one-ready-to-own-heat-stricken-karachi/.

Palmer, Blair. 2010. Services rendered: Peace, patronage and post-conflict elections in Aceh. In *Problems of democratisation in Indonesia: Elections, institutions and society*, edited by Edward Aspinall and Marcus Mietzner, 286–306. Singapore: Institute of Southeast Asian Studies.

Palmer, David Scott, and Alberto Bolívar. 2012. *Shining path of Peru: Recent dynamics and future prospects.* Salamanca: Instituto de Iberoamérica.

Panigrahi, Nilakantha. 2003. Disaster management and the need for convergence of services of welfare agencies: A case study of the Super Cyclone of Orissa. *Social Change* 33 (1): 1–25.

Pareeda, Pradeep Kumar. 2002. Towards rebuilding a post-disaster society: A case study of supercyclone-affected coastal Orissa. *Indian Journal of Social Work* 63 (2): 243–262.

Paul, Bimal Kanti. 2009. Why relatively fewer people died? The case of Bangladesh's Cyclone Sidr. *Natural Hazards* 50 (1): 289–304.

Paul, Jomon Aliys, and Aniruddha Bagchi. 2016. Does terrorism increase after a natural disaster? An analysis based upon property damage. *Defence and Peace Economics* 29 (4): 407–439.

Peikar, Farhad. 2008. Deadly Afghan winter brings misery and destruction. CNN, February 15. https://edition.cnn.com/2008/WORLD/asiapcf/02/15/afghanistan.cold/.

Pelling, Mark, and Kathleen Dill. 2010. Disaster politics: Tipping points for the change in the adaptation of socio-political regimes. *Progress in Human Geography* 34 (1): 21–37.

Peregrine, Peter Neal. 2019. Reducing post-disaster conflict: A cross-cultural test of four hypotheses using archaeological data. *Environmental Hazards* 18 (2): 93–110.

Persson, Tove Ahlbom, and Marina Povitkina. 2017. "Gimme shelter": The role of democracy and institutional quality in disaster preparedness. *Political Research Quarterly* 70 (4): 833–847.

Peters, Katie. 2017. *The next frontier for disaster risk reduction: Tackling disasters in fragile and conflict-affected contexts.* London: Overseas Development Institute.

Peters, Katie, and Laura E. R. Peters. 2021. Terra incognita: The contribution of disaster risk reduction in unpacking the sustainability–peace nexus. *Sustainability Science* 16 (4): 1173–1184.

Peters, Laura E. R. 2021. Beyond disaster vulnerabilities: An empirical investigation of the causal pathways linking conflict to disaster risks. *International Journal of Disaster Risk Reduction* 55 (1): 102092.

Peters, Laura E. R., and Ilan Kelman. 2020. Critiquing and joining intersections of disaster, conflict, and peace research. *International Journal of Disaster Risk Science* 11 (1): 555–567.

Petrova, Kristina. 2021. Natural hazards, internal migration and protests in Bangladesh. *Journal of Peace Research* 59 (1): 33–49.

Petrova, Kristina. 2022. Floods, communal conflict and the role of local state institutions in sub-Saharan Africa. *Political Geography* 92 (1): 102511.

Pettersson, Therése, Shawn Davies, Amber Deniz, Garoun Engström, Nanar Hawach, Stina Högbladh, et al. 2021. Organized violence 1989–2020, with a special emphasis on Syria. *Journal of Peace Research* 58 (4): 809–825.

Pfaff, Katharina. 2020. Assessing the risk of pre-existing grievances in non-democracies: The conditional effect of natural disasters on repression. *International Journal of Disaster Risk Reduction* 42 (1): 101337.

Pham, J. Peter. 2011. State collapse, insurgency, and famine in the Horn of Africa: Legitimacy and the ongoing Somali crisis. *Journal of the Middle East and Africa* 2 (2): 153–187.

Pinto, Constancio, and Matthew Jardine. 1997. *East Timor's unfinished struggle—inside the Timorese resistance.* Boston: South End Press.

Plümper, Thomas, Eric Neumayer, and Katharina Gabriela Pfaff. 2021. The strategy of protest against Covid-19 containment policies in Germany. *Social Science Quarterly* 102 (5): 2236–2250.

Polk, William R. 2007. *Violent politics: A history of insurgency, terrorism and guerilla war, from the American Revolution to Iraq.* New York: HarperCollins.

Polo, Sara M. T. 2020. A pandemic of violence? The impact of COVID-19 on conflict. *Peace Economics, Peace Science and Public Policy* 26 (3): 1–13.

Popham, Peter. 1998. Race to reach Afghanistan quake survivors. *Independent*, June 1. https://www.independent.co.uk/news/race-to-reach-afghanistan-quake-survivors-1162408.html.

Porfiriev, Boris. 2015. Climate change as a major slow-onset hazard to development: An integrated approach to bridge the policy gap. *Environmental Hazards* 14 (2): 187–191.

Porfiriev, Boris N. 1996. Social aftermath and organizational response to a major disaster: The case of the 1995 Sakhalin earthquake in Russia. *Journal of Contingencies and Crisis Management* 4 (4): 218–227.

Porfiriev, Boris N. 2012. Managing alleviation of the 1995 Neftegorsk earthquake disaster: A reminiscence. In *Crises in Russia: Contemporary management policy and practice from a historical perspective,* edited by Boris N. Porfiriev and Greg Simons, 83–120. New York: Routledge.

Predo, Canesio. 2010. *Adaptation of community and households to climate-related disaster: The case of storm surge and flooding experience in Ormoc and Cabalian Bay, Philippines.* Singapore: Economy & Environment Program for Southeast Asia.

Pribadi, K. S., and B. W. Soemardi. 1996. Construction management aspect in a massive reconstruction program of earthquake devastated area: Case study of Flores Indonesia. http://www.iitk.ac.in/nicee/wcee/article/11_833.PDF.

Project Ploughshares. 2011. Armed conflicts report: Burundi (1988–2010). Updated February 2011. https://ploughshares.ca/pl_armedconflict/burundi-1988-2010/.

Qazi, Shehzad H. 2010. The "neo-Taliban" and counterinsurgency in Afghanistan. *Third World Quarterly* 31 (3): 485–499.

Quarantelli, Enrico L., and Russell R. Dynes. 1976. Community conflict: Its absence and presence in natural disasters. *Mass Emergencies* 1 (1): 139–152.

Quilty, Andrew. 2020. Afghanistan's unseen Covid crisis. The Interpreter, August 12. https://www.lowyinstitute.org/the-interpreter/afghanistan-s-unseen-covid-crisis.

Quimpo, Nathan Gilbert. 2014. "Revolutionary taxation" and the logistical and strategic dilemmas of the Maoist insurgency in the Philippines. *Journal of Asian Security and International Affairs* 1 (3): 263–287.

Quimpo, Nathan Gilbert. 2016. Oligarchic rule, ethnocratic tendencies, and armed conflict in the Philippines. In *Post-conflict development in East Asia*, edited by Brendan M. Howe, 137–154. London: Routledge.

Quinn, Michael J. 1991. *Philippine insurgencies and the U.S.* Newport, RI: College of Naval Command and Staff.

Radio Free Europe / Radio Liberty. 2010. Why is the death toll tumbling in the north Caucasus? February 10. https://www.rferl.org/a/insurgency-north-caucasus-terrorism-isis/26840778.html.

Ragin, Charles C. 1987. *The comparative method: Moving beyond qualitative and quantitative strategies*. Berkeley: University of California Press.

Ragin, Charles, and Sean Davey. 2017. *fs/QCA [version 3.0]*. Irvine: University of California.

Rahill, Guitele J., N. Emel Ganapati, J. Calixte Clérismé, and Anuradha Mukherji. 2014. Shelter recovery in urban Haiti after the earthquake: The dual role of social capital. *Disasters* 38 (S1): S73–S93.

Rajagopalan, Swarna. 2006. Silver linings: Natural disasters, international relations and political change in South Asia, 2004–5. *Defense & Security Analysis* 22 (4): 451–468.

Rajasingham-Senanayake, Darini. 2009. Transnational peace building and conflict: Lessons from Aceh, Indonesia, and Sri Lanka. *SOJOURN: Journal of Social Issues in Southeast Asia* 24 (2): 211–235.

Raleigh, Clionadh. 2012. Violence against civilians: A disaggregated analysis. *International Interactions* 38 (4): 462–481.

Raleigh, Clionadh, Hyun Jin Choi, and Dominic Kniveton. 2015. The devil is in the details: An investigation of the relationships between conflict, food price and climate across Africa. *Global Environmental Change* 32 (1): 187–199.

References

Raleigh, Clionadh, and Dominic Kniveton. 2012. Come rain or shine: An analysis of conflict and climate variability in East Africa. *Journal of Peace Research* 49 (1): 51–64.

Raleigh, Clionadh, Andrew Linke, Håvard Hegre, and Joakim Karlsen. 2010. Introducing ACLED: An armed conflict location and event dataset. *Journal of Peace Research* 47 (5): 651–660.

Ramana, P. V. 2006. The Maoist movement in India. *Defense & Security Analysis* 22 (4): 435–449.

Ramsay, Kristopher W. 2011. Revisiting the natural resource curse: Natural disasters, the price of oil, and democracy. *International Organization* 65 (2): 507–529.

Ratelle, Jean-François. 2014. The North Caucasus insurgency: Understanding the Chechen rebels in the context of the Caucasus Emirate. In *Chechnya at war and beyond*, edited by Anne Le Huérou, Aude Merlin, Amandine Regamey, and Elisabeth Sieca-Kozlowski, 176–198. Oxon: Routledge.

Razoux, Pierre. 2015. *The Iran-Iraq war*. Cambridge, MA: Harvard University Press.

Reinhardt, Gina Yannitell, and Carmela Lutmar. 2022. Disaster diplomacy: The intricate links between disaster and conflict. *Journal of Peace Research* 59 (1): 3–11.

Renner, Michael, and Zoë Chafe. 2007. *Beyond disasters: Creating opportunities for peace*. Washington, DC: Worldwatch.

Reppert-Bismarck, Juliane. 2003. Hard aftershock hits Algeria quake zone. AP News, May 27. https://apnews.com/02ee3fc5e3410bb3a710aa26fec14243.

Resosudarmo, Budy P., Catur Sugiyanto, and Ari Kuncoro. 2012. Livelihood recovery after natural disasters and the role of aid: The case of the 2006 Yogyakarta earthquake. *Asian Economic Journal* 23 (3): 233–259.

Restrepo, J. I., and H. A. Cowan. 2000. The "Eje Cafetero" earthquake, Colombia of January 25 1999. *Bulletin of the New Zealand Society for Earthquake Engineering* 33 (1): 1–29.

Reuters. 1995. Death toll of 2,000 is feared in quake on Russian island. *New York Times*, May 30. https://www.nytimes.com/1995/05/30/world/death-toll-of-2000-is-feared-in-quake-on-russian-island.html.

Reuveny, Rafael. 2007. Climate change–induced migration and violent conflict. *Political Geography* 26 (6): 656–673.

Richani, Nazih. 2005. The politics of negotiating peace in Colombia. *NACLA Report on the Americas* 38 (6): 17–22.

Richmond, Oliver. 2011. *A post liberal peace*. London: Routledge.

Rigi, Jakob. 2004. Chaos, conspiracy, and spectacle: The Russian war against Chechnya. *International Journal of Anthropology* 48 (1): 143–148.

Rihoux, Benoît, and Charles Ragin. 2009. *Configurational comparative methods: Qualitative comparative analysis (QCA) and related methods.* Thousand Oaks, CA: Sage.

Risse, Thomas, Stephen C. Ropp, and Kathryn Sikking, eds. 2013. *The persistent power of human rights: From commitment to compliance.* Cambridge: Cambridge University Press.

Ritchie, Hannah, Esteban Ortiz-Ospina, Diana Beltekian, Edouard Mathieu, Joe Hasell, Bobbie Macdonald, et al. 2022. Coronavirus pandemic (COVID-19). Our World in Data. https://ourworldindata.org/coronavirus.

Rodolfo, K. S., A. M. F. Lagmay, R. C. Eco, T. M. L. Herrero, J. E. Mendoza, L. G. Minimo, et al. 2016. The December 2012 Mayo River debris flow triggered by Super Typhoon Bopha in Mindanao, Philippines: Lessons learned and questions raised. *Natural Hazards and Earth System Sciences* 16 (12): 2683–2695.

Rodt, Annemarie Peen. 2012. The African Union mission in Burundi. *Civil Wars* 14 (3): 3730392.

Rosauro, Ryan D. 2021. NPA to set up "humanitarian corridor" for passage of COVID shots. Inquirer.Net, February 10. https://newsinfo.inquirer.net/1394141/npa-to-set-up-humanitarian-corridor-for-passage-of-covid-shots.

Ross, Michael. 2004. Does natural resource wealth influence civil war? Evidence from 13 cases. *International Organization* 58 (1): 35–67.

Rossetto, T., N. Peiris, A. Pomonis, S. M. Wilkinson, D. Del Re, R. Koo, et al. 2007. The Indian Ocean tsunami of December 26, 2004: Observations in Sri Lanka and Thailand. *Natural Hazards* 42 (1): 105–124.

Roth, Mitchel P., and Murat Sever. 2007. The Kurdish Workers Party (PKK) as criminal syndicate: Funding terrorism through organized crime, a case study. *Studies in Conflict & Terrorism* 30 (10): 901–920.

Rother, Larry. 1999. Earthquake in Colombia hampered efforts for peace. *New York Times*, February 6. https://archive.nytimes.com/www.nytimes.com/library/world/americas/020699colombia-rebels.html.

Rubin, Barnett R. 1994. The fragmentation of Tadjikistan. *Survival* 35 (4): 71–91.

Rubin, Barnett R. 2000. The political economy of war and peace in Afghanistan. *World Development* 28 (10): 1789–1803.

Ruhe, Constantin. 2021. Impeding fatal violence through third-party diplomacy: The effect of mediation on conflict intensity. *Journal of Peace Research* 58 (4): 687–701.

Rustad, Siri Aas, Håvard Mokleiv Nygård, and Fredrik Methi. 2020. *Are the coronavirus ceasefires working?* Oslo: Peace Research Institute Oslo.

References

Rynning, Sten. 2012. *NATO in Afghanistan: The liberal disconnect*. Stanford, CA: Stanford University Press.

Sagramoso, Domitilla. 2012. The radicalisation of Islamic Salafi jamaats in the North Caucasus: Moving closer to the global Jihadist movement? *Europe-Asia Studies* 64 (3): 561–595.

Saha, Sujan. 2012. Security implications of climate refugees in urban slums: A case study from Dhaka, Bangladesh. In *Climate change, human security and violent conflict: Challenges for societal stability*, edited by Jürgen Scheffran et al., 595–611. Berlin/Heidelberg: Springer.

Sahara Reporters. 2020. COVID-19 worsens Boko Haram crisis in North-East. November 27. http://saharareporters.com/2020/11/27/covid-19-worsens-boko-haram-crisis-north-east.

Saikia, Pahi. 2015. The political economy and changing organisational dynamics of the ULFA insurgency in Assam. In *Ethnic subnationalist insurgencies in South Asia: Identities, interests and challenges to state authority*, edited by Jugdep S. Chima, 41–60. London: Taylor & Francis.

Sakaguchi, Kendra, Anil Varughese, and Graeme Auld. 2017. Climate wars? A systematic review of empirical analyses on the links between climate change and violent conflict. *International Studies Review* 19 (4): 622–645.

Salazar, Lorraine Carlos. 2015. Typhoon Yolanda: The politics of disaster response and management. *Southeast Asian Affairs* 42 (1): 277–301.

Salazar, Miguel Antonio, Arturo Pesigan, Ronald Law, and Volker Winkler. 2016. Post-disaster health impact of natural hazards in the Philippines in 2013. *Global Health Action* 9 (1): 31320.

Salehyan, Idean, and Cullen Hendrix. 2014. Climate shocks and political violence. *Global Environmental Change* 28 (1): 239–250.

Salehyan, Idean, David Siroky, and Reed M. Wood. 2014. External rebel sponsorship and civilian abuse: A principal-agent analysis of wartime atrocities. *International Organization* 68 (3): 633–661.

Salim, A., A. Ahmed, N. Ashraf, and M. Ashar. 2015. Deadly heat wave in Karachi, July 2015: Negligence or mismanagement? *International Journal of Occupational and Environmental Medicine* 6 (4): 249.

Salla, Michael E. 1997. Creating a "ripe moment" in the East Timor conflict. *Journal of Peace Research* 34 (4): 449–466.

Samad, Yunus. 2014. Understanding the insurgency in Balochistan. *Commonwealth & Comparative Politics* 52 (2): 293–320.

Sambanis, Nicholas. 2004. What is civil war? Conceptual and empirical complexities of an operational definition. *Journal of Conflict Resolution* 48 (6): 814–858.

Samii, Cyrus. 2006. Seizing the moment in Kashmir. *SAIS Review of International Affairs* 26 (1): 65–78.

Samuel, Malik. 2021. Boko Haram and COVID-19: Lake Chad Basin's war on two fronts. Institute for Security Studies, June 29. https://issafrica.org/iss-today/boko-har am-and-covid-19-lake-chad-basins-war-on-two-fronts.

Sanchez, W. Alejandro. 2003. The rebirth of insurgency in Peru. *Small Wars & Insurgencies* 14 (3): 185–198.

Sanchez-Silva, Mauricio, Luis E. Yamin, and Bernardo Caicedo. 2000. Lessons of the 25 January 1999 earthquake in central Colombia. *Earthquake Spectra* 16 (2): 493–510.

Santos, Paz Verdades M. 2010. The Communist front: Protracted people's war and counter-insurgency in the Philippines (overview). In *Primed and purposeful: Armed groups and human security efforts in the Philippines*, edited by Soliman M. Santos Jr. and Paz Verdades M. Santos, 17–42. Quezon City / Geneva: South-South Network for Non-State Armed Group Engagement / Small Arms Survey.

Santos, Soliman M., Jr. 2005. *Evolution of the armed conflict on the Communist front*. Manila: Philippine Human Development Network Foundation.

Santos, Soliman M., Jr. 2010. War and peace on the Moro front: Three standard bearers, three forms of struggle, three tracks (overview). In *Primed and purposeful: Armed groups and human security efforts in the Philippines*, edited by Soliman M. Santos Jr. and Paz Verdades M. Santos, 58–90. Quezon City / Geneva: South-South Network for Non-State Armed Group Engagement / Small Arms Survey.

Santos, Soliman M., Jr., and Octavia A. Dinampo. 2010. Abu Sayyaf reloaded: Rebels, agents, bandits, terrorists (case study). In *Primed and purposeful: Armed groups and human security efforts in the Philippines*, edited by Soliman M. Santos Jr. and Paz Verdades M. Santos, 115–138. Quezon City / Geneva: South-South Network for Non-State Armed Group Engagement / Small Arms Survey.

Santos, Soliman M., Jr., and Paz Verdades M. Santos. 2010a. Al-Harakatul Al-Islamiyya, aka Abu Sayyaf Group (ASG). In *Primed and purposeful: Armed groups and human security efforts in the Philippines*, edited by Soliman M. Santos Jr. and Paz Verdades M. Santos, 364–378. Quezon City / Geneva: South-South Network for Non-State Armed Group Engagement / Small Arms Survey.

Santos, Soliman M., Jr., and Paz Verdades M. Santos. 2010b. Communist Party of the Philippines and its New People's Army (CPP-NPA). In *Primed and purposeful: Armed groups and human security efforts in the Philippines*, edited by Soliman M. Santos Jr. and Paz Verdades M. Santos, 261–278. Quezon City / Geneva: South-South Network for Non-State Armed Group Engagement / Small Arms Survey.

Sato, Jin. 2010. Matching goods and people: Aid and human security after the 2004 tsunami. *Development in Practice* 20 (1): 70–84.

Scanlon, Eric. 2018. Fifty-one years of Naxalite-Maoist insurgency in India: Examining the factors that have influenced the longevity of the conflict. *Asian Journal of Peacebuilding* 6 (2): 335–351.

Scartozzi, Cesare M. 2021. Reframing climate-induced socio-environmental conflicts: A systematic review. *International Studies Review* 23 (3): 696–725.

Schaffar, Wolfram. 2021. An authoritarian reaction to COVID-19 in the Philippines: A strong commitment to universal health care combined with violent securitization. In *The populist radical right and health national policies and global trends*, edited by Michelle Falkenbach and Scott L. Greer, 181–192. Cham, Switzerland: Springer.

Scheffran, Jürgen, Michael Brzoska, Jasmin Kominek, P. Michael Link, and Janpeter Schilling. 2012a. Climate change and violent conflict. *Science* 336 (6083): 869–871.

Scheffran, Jürgen, Michael Brzoska, Jasmin Kominek, P. Michael Link, and Janpeter Schilling. 2012b. Disentangling the climate-conflict-nexus: Empirical and theoretical assessment of vulnerabilities and pathways. *Review of European Studies* 4 (5): 1–15.

Schneider, Carsten Q., and Claudius Wagemann. 2010. Standards of good practice in qualitative comparative analysis (QCA) and fuzzy-sets. *Comparative Sociology* 9 (3): 397–418.

Schneider, Carsten Q., and Claudius Wagemann. 2012. *Set-theoretic methods for the social sciences: A guide to qualitative comparative analysis*. Cambridge: Cambridge University Press.

Schneider, Saundra K. 2018. Governmental response to disasters: Key attributes, expectations, and implications. In *Handbook of disaster research*, edited by Havidán Rodríguez, William Donner, and Joseph E. Trainor, 551–568. Cham, Switzerland: Springer.

Schuck, Christoph. 2016. Peacebuilding through militant Islamist disengagement: Conclusions drawn from the case of Al-Gama'a al-Islamiyya in Egypt. *Peacebuilding* 4 (3): 282–296.

Schuck, Christoph. 2021. How Islamist is the Abu Sayyaf Group (ASG)? An ideological assessment. *Asian Security* 17 (1): 105–118.

Schulze, Kirsten E. 2003. The struggle for an independent Aceh: The ideology, capacity, and strategy of GAM. *Studies in Conflict and Terrorism* 26 (4): 241–271.

Schulze, Kirsten E. 2007. From the battlefield to the negotiating table: GAM and the Indonesian government 1999–2005. *Asian Security* 3 (2): 80–98.

Schulze, Kirsten E. 2009. The AMM and the transition from conflict to peace in Aceh, 2005–2006. In *The European Union and human security: External interventions and missions*, edited by Mary Martin and Mary Kaldor, 12–34. London: Routledge.

Selby, Jan, Omar S. Dahi, Christiane Fröhlich, and Mike Hulme. 2017. Climate change and the Syrian civil war revisited. *Political Geography* 60 (1): 232–244.

Selby, Jan, and Clemens Hoffmann. 2014. Beyond scarcity: Rethinking water, climate change and conflict in the Sudans. *Global Environmental Change* 29 (1): 360–370.

Selby, Jan, and Mike Hulme. 2015. Is climate change really to blame for Syria's civil war? *Guardian*, November 29. www.theguardian.com/commentisfree/2015/nov/29/climate-change-syria-civil-war-prince-charles.

Sen, Amartya. 1983. *Poverty and famines: An essay on entitlement and deprivation*. Oxford: Oxford University Press.

Serres, Philippe. 2000. The FARC and democracy in Colombia in the 1990s. *Democratization* 7 (4): 191–218.

Seter, Hanne. 2016. Connecting climate variability and conflict: Implications for empirical testing. *Political Geography* 53 (1): 1–9.

Shah, Aqil. 2016. Pakistan in 2015: Fighting terror, Pakistan army style. *Asian Survey* 56 (1): 216–224.

Shah, Aqil, and Bushra Asif. 2015. Pakistan in 2014: Democracy under the military's shadow. *Asian Survey* 55 (1): 48–59.

Sharifi, Ayyoob, Dahlia Simangan, and Shinji Kaneko. 2021. Three decades of research on climate change and peace: A bibliometrics analysis. *Sustainability Science* 16 (4): 1079–1095.

Sharifi, Shoaib, and Louise Adamou. 2018. Taliban threaten 70% of Afghanistan, BBC finds. BBC News, January 31. https://www.bbc.com/news/world-asia-42863116.

Sharma, Deepti. 2015. The Kashmir insurgency: Multiple actors, divergent interests, institutionalized conflict. In *Ethnic subnationalist insurgencies in south Asia: Identities, interests and challenges to state authority*, edited by Jugdep S. Chima, 17–40. London: Taylor & Francis.

Sharma, Riya. 2021. The impact of COVID-19 on poverty in Afghanistan. The Borgen Project, July 7. https://borgenproject.org/the-impact-of-covid-19-on-poverty-in-afghanistan/.

Sheikh, Mona Kanwal. 2016. *Guardians of God: Inside the religious minds of the Pakistani Taliban*. Delhi: Oxford University Press.

Shire, Mohammed Ibrahim. 2022. More attacks or more services? Insurgent groups' behaviour during the COVID-19 pandemic in Afghanistan, Syria, and Somalia. *Behavioral Sciences of Terrorism and Political Aggression* 14 (1): 1–24.

References

Shola, Akinyetun Tope, Hungevu Erubami Paul, Salau Jamiu Adewale, Bakare Tope Oke, and Ahoton Aihonsu Samuel. 2021. Coronavirus disease (Covid-19) pandemic and violent extremism in Nigeria: The two-faced agony. *African Journal of Terrorism and Insurgency Research* 2 (1): 69–87.

Siddiqi, Ayesha. 2013. The emerging social contract: State–citizen interaction after the floods of 2010 and 2011 in southern Sindh, Pakistan. *IDS Bulletin* 44 (3): 94–102.

Siddiqi, Ayesha. 2014. Climatic disasters and radical politics in southern Pakistan: The non-linear connection. *Geopolitics* 19 (4): 885–910.

Siddiqi, Ayesha. 2018. Disasters in conflict areas: Finding the politics. *Disasters* 42 (S2): S161–S172.

Siddiqi, Ayesha, and Jose Jowel P. Canuday. 2018. Stories from the frontline: Decolonising social contracts for disasters. *Disasters* 42 (S2): S215–S238.

Siddique, Qandeel. 2010. *Tehrik-E-Taliban Pakistan: An attempt to deconstruct the umbrella organization and the reasons for its growth in Pakistan's north-west*. Copenhagen: DIIS.

Sidel, John T. 2014. The Philippines in 2013: Disappointment, disgrace, disaster. *Asian Survey* 54 (1): 64–70.

Sidel, John T. 2015. The Philippines in 2014: Aquino fights back. *Asian Survey* 55 (1): 220–227.

Silva, Kalinga Tudor. 2009. "Tsunami third wave" and the politics of disaster management in Sri Lanka. *Norsk Geografisk Tidsskrift—Norwegian Journal of Geography* 63 (1): 61–72.

Sindre, Gyda Marås. 2010. From political exclusion to inclusion: The political transformation of GAM. In *Aceh: The role of democracy for peace and reconstruction*, edited by Olle Törnquist, Stanley Adi Prasetyo, and Teresa Birks, 215–256. Jakarta: PCD Press.

Singh, Bikash. 2008. Central govt's response to Assam floods discriminatory, alleges ULFA. *Economic Times*. Last updated September 4. https://economictimes.indiatimes.com/news/politics-and-nation/central-govts-response-to-assam-floods-discriminatory-alleges-ulfa/articleshow/3442075.cms?from=mdr.

Siroky, David, Carolyn M. Warner, Gabrielle Filip-Crawford, Anna Berlin, and Steven L. Neuberg. 2020. Grievances and rebellion: Comparing relative deprivation and horizontal inequality. *Conflict Management and Peace Science* 37 (6): 694–715.

Slettebak, Rune T. 2012. Don't blame the weather! Climate-related natural disasters and civil conflict. *Journal of Peace Research* 49 (1): 163–176.

Smith, Benjamin. 2009. *Land and rebellion: Kurdish separatism in comparative perspective*. Ithaca, NY: Cornell University.

Smith, Craig S. 2003. Quake demolishes confidence in Algerian rulers. *New York Times*, May 30. https://www.nytimes.com/2003/05/30/world/quake-demolishes-confidence-in-algerian-rulers.html.

Snedden, Christopher. 2013. Kashmir: Placating frustrated people. In *Diminishing conflicts in Asia and the Pacific: Why some subside and others don't*, edited by Edward Aspinall, Robin Jeffrey, and Anthony Regan, 237–249. London: Routledge.

Solomon, Hussein. 2014. Somalia's Al Shabaab: Clans vs Islamist nationalism. *South African Journal of International Affairs* 21 (3): 351–366.

Sorens, Jason. 2011. Mineral production, territory, and ethnic rebellion: The role of rebel constituencies. *Journal of Peace Research* 48 (5): 571–585.

Sorokin, Pitrim A. 1942. *Man and society in calamity*. New York: Dutton.

Souleimanov, Emil. 2011. The Caucasus Emirate: Genealogy of an Islamist insurgency. *Middle East Policy* 18 (4): 155–168.

South, Ashley. 2008. Burma after the cyclone: Making a disaster out of a cyclone. *The World Today* 64 (4): 25–27.

South, Ashley. 2011. *Burma's longest war: Anatomy of the Karen conflict*. Amsterdam: Burma Center Netherlands.

South Asia Terrorism Portal. 2018. Purba Banglar Communist Party (PBCP). https://www.satp.org/satporgtp/countries/bangladesh/terroristoutfits/PBCP.htm.

Sowers, Jeannie L., Erica Weinthal, and Neda Zawahri. 2017. Targeting environmental infrastructures, international law, and civilians in the new Middle Eastern wars. *Security Dialogue* 48 (5): 410–430.

SPA (Saudi Press Agency). 2010. Dagestan announces state of emergency in 26 districts. August 24. https://www.spa.gov.sa/812549.

Spagat, Michael, Andrew Mack, Tara Cooper, and Joakim Kreutz. 2009. Estimating war deaths: An arena of contestation. *Journal of Conflict Resolution* 53 (6): 934–950.

Sperling, James, and Mark Webber. 2012. NATO's intervention in the Afghan civil war. *Civil Wars* 14 (3): 344–372.

Srivastava, Mukesh Kumar, and Arundhati Sharma. 2010. Democratic experience in South Asia: Case study of Nepal. *International Journal of South Asian Studies* 3 (2): 399–410.

Staniland, Paul. 2013. Kashmir since 2003: Counterinsurgency and the paradox of "normalcy." *Asian Survey* 53 (5): 931–957.

START (Study of Terrorism and Responses to Terrorism). 2015. Al-Gama'at Al-Islamiyya (IG). January. https://www.start.umd.edu/baad/narratives/al-gamaat-al-islamiyya-ig.

References

START (Study of Terrorism and Responses to Terrorism). 2018. Global terrorism database. https://www.start.umd.edu/gtd.

Steckley, Marylynn, and Brent Doberstein. 2011. Tsunami survivors' perspectives on vulnerability and vulnerability reduction: Evidence from Koh Phi Phi Don and Khao Lak, Thailand. *Disasters* 35 (3): 465–487.

Steed, Brian. 2019. *ISIS: The essential reference guide*. Santa Barbara, CA: ABC-CLIO.

Stoddard, Abby, Paul Harvey, Monica Czwarno, and Meriah-Jo Breckenridge. 2019. *Aid worker security report 2019*. London: Humanitarian Outcomes.

Strand, Arne, Kristian Berg Harpviken, and A. W. Najimi. 2000. *Afghanistan: Current humanitarian challenges*. Bergen: Chr. Michelsen Institute.

Streich, Philip A., and David Bell Mislan. 2014. What follows the storm? Research on the effect of disasters on conflict and cooperation. *Global Change, Peace & Security* 26 (1): 55–70.

Subedi, D. B. 2013. From civilian to combatant: Armed recruitment and participation in the Maoist conflict in Nepal. *Contemporary South Asia* 21 (4): 429–443.

Sulistiyanto, Priyambudi. 2001. Whither Aceh? *Third World Quarterly* 22 (3): 437–452.

Sundberg, Ralph, and Erik Melander. 2013. Introducing the UCDP Georeferenced Event Dataset. *Journal of Peace Research* 50 (4): 523–532.

Suykens, Bert, and Aynul Islam. 2015. *The distribution of political violence in Bangladesh (2002–2013)*. Brussels: Conflict Research Group.

Swee, Eik Leong. 2015. On war intensity and schooling attainment: The case of Bosnia and Herzegovina. *European Journal of Political Economy* 40 (1): 158–172.

Szakonyi, David. 2011. *You're fired! Identifying electoral accountability in a competitive authoritarian regime*. Washington, DC: George Washington University.

Tariq, Maliha. 2013. Conflict in Balochistan: Natural resources and the way forward. *Strategic Studies* 33 (3/4): 23–40.

Taucer, Fabio, John Alarcon, and Arup Emily So. 2007. *2007 August 15 magnitude 7.9 earthquake near the coast of central Peru*. Luxembourg: Joint Research Centre.

Tayag, Jean C., and Sheila I. Insauriga. 1993. Organizational response to the July 1990 Luzon earthquake. *Philippine Journal of Public Administration* 37 (4): 375–394.

Taydas, Zaynap, Jason Enia, and Patrick James. 2011. Why do civil wars occur? Another look at the theoretical dichotomy of opportunity versus grievance. *Review of International Studies* 37 (5): 2627–2650.

Taylor, Lewis. 2017. Sendero Luminoso in the new millennium: Comrades, cocaine and counter-insurgency on the Peruvian frontier. *Journal of Agrarian Change* 17 (1): 106–121.

Terpstra, Niels. 2020. Rebel governance, rebel legitimacy, and external intervention: Assessing three phases of Taliban rule in Afghanistan. *Small Wars & Insurgencies* 31 (6): 1143–1173.

Tezcür, Güneş Murat. 2015. Violence and nationalist mobilization: The onset of the Kurdish insurgency in Turkey. *Nationalities Papers* 43 (2): 248–266.

Than, Tin Maung Maung. 2009. Myanmar in 2008: Weathering the storm. *Southeast Asian Affairs* 36 (1): 195–222.

Thomalla, Frank, and Hanna Schmuck. 2004. "We all knew that a cyclone was coming": Disaster preparedness and the cyclone of 1999 in Orissa, India. *Disasters* 28 (4): 373–387.

Thomas, Timothy L. 1995. EMERCOM: Russia's emergency response team. *Low Intensity Conflict and Law Enforcement* 4 (2): 227–236.

Thruelsen, Peter Dahl. 2010. The Taliban in southern Afghanistan: A localised insurgency with a local objective. *Small Wars & Insurgencies* 21 (2): 259–276.

Thurston, Alyssa Mari, Heidi Stöckl, and Meghna Ranganathan. 2021. Natural hazards, disasters and violence against women and girls: A global mixed-methods systematic review. *BMJ Global Health* 6 (4): e004377.

Timberman, David G. 1991. The Philippines in 1990: On shaky ground. *Asian Survey* 31 (2): 153–163.

Tishkov, Valery. 1997. Political anthropology of the Chechen war. *Security Dialogue* 28 (4): 425–437.

Tominaga, Yasutaka, and Chia-yi Lee. 2021. When disasters hit civil wars: Natural resource exploitation and rebel group resilience. *International Studies Quarterly* 65 (2): 423–434.

Törnquist, Olle. 2010. Democracy in Aceh: Diagnosis and prognosis. In *Aceh: The role of democracy for peace and reconstruction*, edited by Olle Törnquist, Stanley Adi Prasetyo, and Teresa Birks, 73–170. Jakarta: PCD Press.

Toromade, Samson. 2021. Buhari begs for French support to crush Boko Haram, COVID-19. Pulse, May 18. https://www.pulse.ng/news/local/buhari-begs-for-french-support-to-crush-boko-haram-covid-19/sqq0j8x.

Toya, Hideki, and Mark Skidmore. 2014. Do natural disasters enhance societal trust? *Kyklos* 67 (2): 255–279.

Trinn, Christoph, and Thomas Wencker. 2021. Integrating the quantitative research on the onset and incidence of violent intrastate conflicts. *International Studies Review* 23 (1): 115–139.

Tunçer-Kılavuz, Idil. 2011. Understanding civil war: A comparison of Tajikistan and Uzbekistan. *Europe-Asia Studies* 63 (2): 263–290.

Tunçer-Kılavuz, Idil. 2019. Success or failure in the peace processes of Aceh and Sri Lanka: A comparative study. *Terrorism and Political Violence* 31 (4): 712–732.

Uddin, Ala. 2016. Dynamics of strategies for survival of the indigenous people in southeastern Bangladesh. *Ethnopolitics* 15 (3): 319–338.

Uddin, Nasir. 2008. Living on the margin: The positioning of the "Khumi" within the sociopolitical and ethnic history of the Chittagong Hill Tracts. *Asian Ethnicity* 9 (1): 33–53.

UN (United Nations). 2015. *Sendai Framework for Disaster Risk Reduction, 2015–2030*. New York: UN.

UN (United Nations). 2020. UN secretary-general calls for global ceasefire to focus on ending the COVID-19 pandemic. https://www.un.org/en/academic-impact/un-sec retary-general-calls-global-ceasefire-focus-ending-covid-19-pandemic.

Ünal, Mustafa Coşar. 2012. *Counterterrorism in Turkey: Policy choices and policy effects toward the Kurdistan Workers' Party (PKK)*. Oxon, UK: Routledge.

UNCU (UN Coordination Unit). 1998. UNCT Somalia Monitor 5 to 14 April 1998. April 17. https://reliefweb.int/report/somalia/unct-somalia-monitor-5-14-april-1998.

UNDESA (UN Department of Economic and Social Affairs). 2015. SDG 11: Make cities and human settlements inclusive, safe, resilient and sustainable. https://sdgs .un.org/goals/goal11.

UN DHA (UN Department of Humanitarian Affairs). 1994. Egypt—floods Nov 1994 UN DHA situation reports 1–4. Relief Web, November 4. https://reliefweb.int/report /egypt/egypt-floods-nov-1994-un-dha-situation-reports-1-4.

UN DHA (UN Department of Humanitarian Affairs). 1996. Nepal—floods situation report no. 1, 26 July 1996. https://reliefweb.int/report/nepal/nepal-floods-situation -report-no-1-26-july-1996.

UNDP (United Nations Development Programme). 2021. *Findings from the assessment of the socioeconomic impact of COVID-19 on Iraq's vulnerable populations*. Bagdad: UNDP.

UNDP (United Nations Development Programme). 2022. *New threats to human security in the Anthropocene: Demanding greater solidarity*. New York: UNDP.

UN General Assembly. 2016. *Report of the open ended intergovernmental expert working group on indicators and terminology relating to disaster risk reduction*. New York: United Nations.

UNICEF (United Nations International Children's Emergency Fund). 2022. *Are children really learning? Exploring foundational skills in the midst of a learning crisis*. New York: UNICEF.

UN OCHA (United Nations Office for the Coordination of Humanitarian Affairs). 1998. Report of the UNDAC Mission (10 February to 6 March 1998) following the earthquake of 4 February, 1998 in Rustaq, Afghanistan. Relief Web, March 10. https://reliefweb.int/report/afghanistan/report-undac-mission-10-february-6-march-1998-following-earthquake-4-february.

UN OCHA (United Nations Office for the Coordination of Humanitarian Affairs). 2000. Independent evaluation of expenditure of DEC India cyclone appeal funds: Volume 1 and volume 2. November 11. https://reliefweb.int/report/india/independent-evaluation-expenditure-dec-india-cyclone-appeal-funds-volume-1-and-volume-2.

UN OCHA (United Nations Office for the Coordination of Humanitarian Affairs). 2013. Philippines: Typhoon Bopha situation report no. 19 (as of 12 February 2013). Relief Web, February 13. https://reliefweb.int/report/philippines/typhoon-bopha-situation-report-no-19-12-february-2013.

UN OCHA (United Nations Office for the Coordination of Humanitarian Affairs). 2019. Humanitarian appeals. https://www.unocha.org/media-centre/news-updates/humanitarian-appeals.

UNSCN (United Nations System Standing Committee on Nutrition). 2003. *Refugee nutrition information system RNIS 42—summary*. Geneva: UNSSCN.

UN Security Council. 2021a. *8864th meeting: Maintenance of international peace and security; climate and security*. New York: United Nations.

UN Security Council. 2021b. *Thirteenth report of the Secretary-General on the threat posed by ISIL (Da'esh) to international peace and security and the range of United Nations efforts in support of Member States in countering the threat*. New York: UN Security Council.

UN Women. 2020. *COVID-19 and ending violence against women and girls*. New York: UN Women.

UPI. 1996. Nepal floods, landslides kill 54. July 21. https://www.upi.com/Archives/1996/07/21/Nepal-floods-landslides-kill-54/1883837921600/.

Upreti, Bishnu Raj. 2004. *The price of neglect: From resource conflict to Maoist insurgency in the Himalayan kingdom*. Kathmandu: Bhrikuti Academic Publications.

USAID. 2006. Burundi: Complex emergency situation report #2. July 19. https://reliefweb.int/report/burundi/burundi-complex-emergency-situation-report-2-fy-2005.

Uyangoda, Jayadeva. 2005. Ethnic conflict, the state and the tsunami disaster in Sri Lanka. *Inter-Asia Cultural Studies* 6 (3): 341–352.

Valentino, Benjamin A. 2014. Why we kill: The political science of political violence against civilians. *Annual Political Science Review* 17 (1): 89–103.

Valinejad, Afshin. 1997. 2,000 killed, 5,000 hurt as 7.1 quake hits Iran. *Los Angeles Times*, May 11. https://www.latimes.com/archives/la-xpm-1997-05-11-mn-57844-story.html.

References

van Acker, Frank. 2004. Uganda and the Lord's Resistance Army: The new order no one ordered. *African Affairs* 103 (412): 335–357.

Vandeginste, Stef. 2009. Power-sharing, conflict and transition in Burundi: Twenty years of trial and error. *Africa Spectrum* 44 (3): 63–86.

van de Voorde, Cécile. 2005. Sri Lankan terrorism: Assessing and responding to the threat of the Liberation Tigers of Tamil Eelam (LTTE). *Police Practice and Research* 6 (2): 181–199.

Van Leeuwen, Matjis, and Gemma Van der Haar. 2016. Theorizing the land–violent conflict nexus. *World Development* 78 (1): 94–104.

van Weezel, Stijn. 2019. On climate and conflict: Precipitation decline and communal conflict in Ethiopia and Kenya. *Journal of Peace Research* 56 (4): 514–528.

van Wyk, Jo-Ansie. 2017. Joseph Kony and the Lord's Resistance Army. In *Violent non-state actors in Africa: Terrorists, rebels and warlords*, edited by Caroline Varin and Dauda Abubakar, 225–250. Cham, Switzerland: Palgrave Macmillan.

Varma, Navarun, and Arabinda Mishra. 2017. Discourses, narratives and purposeful action—unravelling the socio-ecological complexity with the Brahmaputra basin in India. *Environmental Policy and Governance* 27 (3): 207–228.

Vasquez, Tim. 2011. The Russian inferno of 2010. *Weatherwise* 64 (2): 20–25.

Venturini, Gabriella. 2012. Disasters and armed conflict. In *International disaster response law*, edited by Andrea de Guttry, Marco Gestri, and Gabriella Venturini, 251–266. Dordrecht: Springer.

Venugopal, Rajesh, and Sameer Yasir. 2017. The politics of natural disasters in protracted conflict: The 2014 flood in Kashmir. *Oxford Development Studies* 45 (4): 424–442.

Verhoeven, Harry. 2011. Climate change, conflict and development in Sudan: Global Neo-Malthusian narratives and local power struggles. *Development and Change* 42 (3): 679–707.

Vesco, Paola, Matija Kovacic, Malcolm Mistry, and Mihai Croicu. 2021. Climate variability, crop and conflict: Exploring the impacts of spatial concentration in agricultural production. *Journal of Peace Research* 58 (1): 98–113.

Vestby, Jonas. 2019. Climate variability and individual motivations for participating in political violence. *Global Environmental Change* 56 (1): 114–123.

Villaveces, Juanita. 2003. Why peace processes fail or move forward? Negotiations in Colombia with FARC and AUC (1998–2003). *Economía Serie Documentos* 35 (8): 1–30.

Vinci, Anthony. 2006. An analysis and comparison of armed groups in Somalia. *African Security Review* 15 (1): 75–90.

Vinci, Anthony. 2007. Existential motivations in the Lord's Resistance Army's continuing conflict. *Studies in Conflict & Terrorism* 30 (4): 337–352.

Visser, H., S. de Bruin, A. Martens, J. Knoop, and W. Ligtvoet. 2020. What users of global risk indicators should know. *Global Environmental Change* 62 (1): 102068.

Vivekananda, Janani, Martin Wall, Florence Sylvestre, and Chitra Nagarajan. 2019. *Shoring up stability: Addressing the climate and fragility risks in the Lake Chad region*. Berlin: adelphi.

von Uexkull, Nina. 2014. Sustained drought, vulnerability and civil conflict in sub-Saharan Africa. *Political Geography* 43 (1): 16–26.

von Uexkull, Nina, and Halvard Buhaug. 2021. Security implications of climate change. *Journal of Peace Research* 58 (1): 3–17.

von Uexkull, Nina, Mihai Croicu, Hanne Fjelde, and Halvard Buhaug. 2016. Civil conflict sensitivity to growing-season drought. *Proceedings of the National Academy of Sciences* 113 (44): 12391–12396.

Vu, Tuong, and Patrick van Orden. 2020. Revolution and world order: The case of the Islamic State (ISIS). *International Politics* 57 (1): 57–78.

Walch, Colin. 2014. Collaboration or obstruction? Rebel group behavior during natural disaster relief in the Philippines. *Political Geography* 43 (1): 40–50.

Walch, Colin. 2018a. Disaster risk reduction amidst armed conflict: Informal institutions, rebel groups, and wartime political orders. *Disasters* 42 (S2): S239–S264.

Walch, Colin. 2018b. Weakened by the storm: Rebel group recruitment in the wake of natural disasters in the Philippines. *Journal of Peace Research* 55 (3): 336–350.

Walker, Martin. 2000. The Turkish miracle. *The Wilson Quarterly* 24 (4): 72–143.

Wang, Chunlei, Dake Wang, Jaffar Abbas, Kaifeng Duan, and Riaqa Mubeen. 2021. Global financial crisis, smart lockdown strategies, and the COVID-19 spillover impacts: A global perspective and implications from Southeast Asia. *Frontiers in psychiatry* 12: 643783.

Warner, Jason, and Stephanie Lizzo. 2021. The "Boko Haram disaggregation problem" and comparative profiles of factional violence: Challenges, impacts, and solutions in the study of Africa's deadliest terror group(s). *Terrorism and Political Violence*, online ahead of print, May 27. https://doi.org/10.1080/09546553.2020.1860950.

Wasiak, Anna. 2014. Why now? Typhoon Haiyan and the peace agreement between the Philippine government and the Moro Islamic Liberation Front. *Revista "Cuadernos Manuel Giménez Abad"* 1 (7): 199–248.

Webersik, Christian. 2005. Fighting for the plenty: The banana trade in southern Somalia. *Oxford Development Studies* 33 (1): 81–97.

References

Wegren, Stephen. 2011. Food security and Russia's 2010 drought. *Eurasian Geography and Economics* 52 (1): 140–156.

Weigand, Florian. 2017. Afghanistan's Taliban—legitimate Jihadists or coercive extremists? *Journal of Intervention and Statebuilding* 11 (3): 359–381.

Welthungerhilfe. 2008. Cold snap in Afghanistan: Welthungerhilfe provides blankets, boots and food for 50,000 people. ReliefWeb, January 18. https://reliefweb.int/report/afghanistan/cold-snap-afghanistan-welthungerhilfe-provides-blankets-boots-and-food-50000.

Welton, George. 2011. The impact of Russia's 2010 grain export ban. *Oxfam Policy and Practice: Agriculture, Food and Land* 11 (5): 76–107.

Welzer, Harald. 2012. *Climate wars: What people will be killed for in the 21st century.* Cambridge: Polity Press.

Werrell, Caitlin E., Francesco Femia, and Troy Sternberg. 2015. Did we see it coming? State fragility, climate vulnerability, and the uprisings in Syria and Egypt. *SAIS Review of International Affairs* 35 (1): 29–46.

West, Ben, and Lauren Goodrich. 2010. Power struggle among Russia's militants. RANE Worldview, August 19. https://worldview.stratfor.com/article/power-struggle-among-russias-militants.

Westfall, Sammy. 2021. As most students return to classrooms, schools in some countries have been shuttered for 18 months straight. *Washington Post*, September 13. https://www.washingtonpost.com/world/2021/09/13/global-school-reopening-18-months/.

WFP (World Food Programme). 1998. World Food Programme reports dramatic drop in Somalia harvest. March 3. https://reliefweb.int/report/somalia/world-food-programme-reports-dramatic-drop-somalia-harvest.

WFP (World Food Programme). 2004. *Budget increase to protracted relief and recovery operation: Uganda 10121.0.* Rome: World Food Programme.

Whitehead, Margaret, David Taylor-Robinson, and Ben Barr. 2021. Poverty, health, and Covid-19. *BMJ* 372 (1): n376.

The White House. 2015. Remarks by the President at the United States Coast Guard Academy Commencement. May 20. https://obamawhitehouse.archives.gov/the-press-office/2015/05/20/remarks-president-united-states-coast-guard-academy-commencement.

Wilder, Andrew. 2010. Aid and stability in Pakistan: Lessons from the 2005 earthquake response. *Disasters* 34 (S3): 406–426.

Wilhelmsen, Julie. 2005. Between a rock and a hard place: The Islamisation of the Chechen separatist movement. *Europe-Asia Studies* 57 (1): 35–59.

Williams, Brian Glyn. 2020. Islamic State calls for followers to spread coronavirus, exploit pandemic and protests. The Conversation, June 23. https://theconversation.com/islamic-state-calls-for-followers-to-spread-coronavirus-exploit-pandemic-and-protests-136224.

Winsemius, Hessel C., Brenden Jongman, Ted I. E. Veldkamp, Stephane Hallegatte, Mook Bangalore, and Philip J. Ward. 2018. Disaster risk, climate change, and poverty: Assessing the global exposure of poor people to floods and droughts. *Environment and Development Economics* 23 (3): 328–348.

Wirtz, Angelika, Wolfgang Kron, Petra Löw, and Markus Steuer. 2014. The need for data: Natural disasters and the challenges of database management. *Natural Hazards* 70 (1): 135–157.

Wischnath, Gerdis, and Halvard Buhaug. 2014. Rice or riots: On food production and conflict severity across India. *Political Geography* 43 (1): 6–15.

Wisner, Ben. 2017. "Build back better"? The challenge of Goma and beyond. *International Journal of Disaster Risk Reduction* 26 (1): 101–105.

Wisner, Ben, Piers Blaikie, Terry Cannon, and Ian Davis. 2004. *At risk: Natural hazards, people's vulnerability and disasters*. London: Routledge.

Wittig, Katrin. 2016. Politics in the shadow of the gun: Revisiting the literature on "Rebel-to-Party Transformations" through the case of Burundi. *Civil Wars* 18 (2): 137–159.

Wood, Reed M., and Thorin M. Wright. 2016. Responding to catastrophe: Repression dynamics following rapid-onset natural disasters. *Journal of Conflict Resolution* 60 (8): 1446–1472.

Woodward, Susan L. 2007. Do the root causes of civil war matter? On using knowledge to improve peacebuilding intervention. *Journal of Intervention and Statebuilding* 1 (2): 143–170.

World Bank. 1993. *Memorandum and recommendation of the president of the International Bank for Reconstruction and Development to the executive directors on a proposed loan in an amount equivalent to US$42.1 million to the Republic of Indonesia for Flores Earthquake Reconstruction Project*. Washington, DC: World Bank.

World Bank. 1999. *Marmara earthquake assessment*. Washington, DC: International Bank for Reconstruction and Development.

World Bank. 2018. *Republic of Burundi: Addressing fragility and demographic challenges to reduce poverty and boost sustainable growth*. Washington, DC: World Bank.

World Bank. 2022. World Bank open data. https://data.worldbank.org/.

World Bank and GFDRR (Global Facility for Disaster Reduction and Recovery). 2016. Tajikistan. https://www.gfdrr.org/sites/default/files/Tajikistan.pdf.

References

Wucherpfennig, Julian, Nils W. Metternich, Lars-Eric Cederman, and Kristian Skrede Gleditsch. 2012. Ethnicity, the state, and the duration of civil war. *World Politics* 64 (1): 79–115.

Xu, Jiuping, Ziqi Wang, Feng Shen, and Yan Tu. 2016. Natural disasters and social conflict: A systematic literature review. *International Journal of Disaster Risk Reduction* 17 (1): 38–48.

Yamada, Seiji, and Absalon Galat. 2014. Typhoon Yolanda/Haiyan and climate justice. *Disaster Medicine and Public Health Preparedness* 8 (5): 432–435.

Yamada, Seiji, Ravindu P. Gunatilake, Timur M. Roytman, Sarath Gunatilake, Thushara Fernando, and Lalan Fernando. 2006. The Sri Lanka tsunami experience. *Disaster Management and Response* 4 (2): 38–48.

Yee, Dakila Kim P. 2018. Violence and disaster capitalism in post-Haiyan Philippines. *Peace Review* 30 (2): 160–167.

Youngman, Mark. 2019. Broader, vaguer, weaker: The evolving ideology of the Caucasus Emirate leadership. *Terrorism and Political Violence* 31 (2): 367–389.

Zamarro, Gema, and María J. Prados. 2021. Gender differences in couples' division of childcare, work and mental health during COVID-19. *Review of Economics of the Household* 19 (1): 11–40.

Zartman, I. William. 2000. Ripeness: The hurting stalemate and beyond. In *Internal conflict resolution after the Cold War*, edited by Paul Stern and Daniel Druckman, 225–250. Washington, DC: National Academy Press.

Zeccola, Paul. 2011. Dividing disasters in Aceh, Indonesia: Separatist conflict and tsunami, human rights and humanitarianism. *Disasters* 35 (2): 308–328.

Zenn, Jacob. 2021. Boko Haram's factional feuds: Internal extremism and external interventions. *Terrorism and Political Violence* 33 (3): 616–648.

Zhou, Yanqiu Rachel. 2022. Vaccine nationalism: Contested relationships between COVID-19 and globalization. *Globalizations* 19 (3): 450–465.

Zürcher, Christoph. 2016. What do we (not) know about development aid and violence? A systematic review. *World Development* 98 (1): 506–522.

Zyck, Steven A. 2012. How to lose allies and finance your enemies: The economisation of conflict termination in Afghanistan. *Conflict, Security & Development* 12 (3): 249–271.

Index

Note: Page numbers in *italics* indicate figures, tables, and boxes.

Abu Sayyaf Group (ASG), 129–131, 129n99
Aceh, Indonesia, 4–5, 8, 35, 37, 86–89, 112–114. *See also* Free Aceh Movement (GAM)
Aceh Monitoring Mission, 114
Adivasis, 62
Afghanistan, 102–107, 103n66, 103n68, 105n70, 182, 187–191
African Union Mission to Somalia (AMISOM), 97n57, 99
Agency, 202
Agricultural
  collapse, 98, 99, 109
  conflict intensity, 11–12
  costly signal, 34
  dependence, 50, 51, 159–161, 163, 216
  economy, 77, 98, 106
  land, 66, 69, 75, 93, 109
  livelihoods, 63, 64, 93, 95, 99, 111, 118
  opportunity, 30
  overlap, 51
  sector, 64, 118, 130, 158, 160, 197
  state weakness, 31
Aid. *See also individual cases*
  conflict dynamics, 158–159
  conflict intensity, 11–12, 14

costly signal, 35
grievances, 26
image cultivation, 36–37
opportunity, 30–31
QCA, 52
state of knowledge, 9–10
Aideed, Mohammad Farrah, 95
Algeria, 107–108
al-Qaeda, 60, 129, 184, 188, 192
Al-Shabaab, 31, 97–100, 98n58, 151–152, 192
Andhra Pradesh, 62–65
Anocracies, 7, 7n8, 164
Apurimac–Ene River Valleys (VRAE), 123, 124
Arab Spring, 11, 184
Armed conflict
  communication, 152–155
  data reliability, 144, 144n2
  de-escalation, 166–173
  disaster types, 155–158
  escalation, 166–173
  motive, 145–146
  opportunity, *142*, *145*, 145, 147–148
  strategy, 147–152
Armed conflict intensity, 5, 23, 49, 141, 208, 214–215
Armed Conflict Location and Event Data Project (ACLED), 96, 108

Armed Islamic Group (GIA), 107
Assam, 65–67, 65nn13–14, 67nn17–18, 109–110
Australia, 180n4
Autocratic Regime Dataset, 50

Baluchistan Liberation Army (BLA), 120–121, *165*
Bangladesh
 battle-related deaths, *46*
 Chittagong Hill conflict, 55–57, 153
 communication, 155
 COVID-19 pandemic, 178
 Cyclone Bhola, 1
 Cyclone Sidr and the Maoist insurgency, 78–81, 151–152
 escalation or de-escalation after a disaster, 168, 171
 grievances, 27
 migration, 27
Bangsamoro Islamic Freedom Movement, 131
Bargaining theory, 169
Barre, Siad, 95, 97
Battle-related deaths, 41, 41n5, *46–47*
Boko Haram, 4, *182*, 191, 192–196
Burundi, 81–84, 82nn38–39

Cases, sample of, 39–41, *42–43*, *44*, *46–47*
Caucasus Emirate, 134, 134n108, 135
Causal conditions and theoretical expectations
 adverse impacts on conflict parties, 51–52
 agricultural dependence, 50
 capable state, 54
 conflict parties, impact on, 53
 democracy, 50–51
 overlap, 51
 overview, 48–49
 poverty, 49–50
 rebel dependence, 53
 two-stage QCA, *49*
 unfair distribution, 52
 weak rebels, 53–54
Charles III (king), 4
Chechen-Ingush Autonomous Soviet Socialist Republic (CI-ASSR), 131–132
Chechnya, 131–133, 131n102, 133n105
Chile, 180n4
China, 1, 9, 37, 91, 177, 179, 180
Chittagong Hill Tracts People's Coordination Association (JSS), 56. *See also* JSS/SB
Citizens Armed Forces Geographical Units (CAFGUs), 68, 70
Civil war, definition of, 15
Climate change
 armed conflict dynamics, 19–20
 armed conflict intensity, 141, 143
 climate-conflict linkages, 13
 Darfur conflict, 8
 disaster-conflict research, 6
 security implications, 7, 207–208
 state fragility and insurgents, effect on, 175
 strategy, 148
 Syrian civil war, 4, 8, 10, 135
 violence-as-communication approach, 214
Cold spell, 15, 41, 106–107, 155
Colombia (1999), 6.1-magnitude earthquake, 57–60
Communication, 22, 23, 33–38, 152–155, 157n8, 201
Communist Party of India (Marxist-Leninist), 62
Communist Party of the Philippines (CPP), 67–70, 126, 196. *See also* CPP/NPA; New People's Army (NPA)
Communist Popular Democratic Party (CPDP), 102
Conflict bias, 143–144
Conjunctural causation, 45

Index

Constraints
  Bangladesh, 80
  causal conditions/theoretical expectations, 51
  communication approach, 23
  conflict dynamics, 157, 159
  constraints, 32–33
  COVID-19 pandemic, 180, 195, 199, 202–203
  de-escalation, 171
  empirical argument, *175*, 176
  Indonesia, 88, 89, 112
  Kashmir, 86
  key findings, 208–209
  Pakistan, 94
  pathway, 148–150, *150*, 172–173
  Russia, 135
  Somalia, 96, 97, 100
  strategic, 80, 86, 100
  strategy, 151
Costly signal
  armed conflict dynamics and disaster impacts, *145*
  armed conflict escalation, de-escalation, and continuation, 140–141
  Bangladesh, 57, 153
  causal conditions and theoretical expectations, 50–52
  Colombia, 59
  communication, 153–155
  conflict (de-)escalation, 23
  conflict dynamics, disaster impact on, 163
  disaster types and conflict dynamics, *156*, 157n13
  empirical argument, overview of, *175*
  escalation or de-escalation after a disaster, 168
  key findings and implications, 206, 209
  Nepal, 119
  new theoretical approach, 214
  overview, 33–35

  Pakistan, 121
  Sri Lanka, 73
  Thailand, 137
COVID-19 disaster, 177–205
CPN-Maoist (CPN-M), 118–119
CPP/NPA, 67–70, 125–129, 140, 149, 182, 196–200, 203
CPP/NPA and the Philippine government, conflict between, *182*, 196–200
Cyclone
  Andhra Pradesh and Orissa, 62–65
  Bhola, 1
  Bopha, 130
  Gorky, 55–57, 153, 155, 207
  Nargis, 37, 53, 89–92
  Sidr, 78–81, 151–152

Dalits, 62, 118
Data collection and analysis, 41, 43–48
Data reliability, 144, 144n2
Democracy
  Boko Haram insurgency, 191
  Burundi, 81–84
  causal conditions, 50–51, 54
  conflict (de-)escalation, 20, 176
  conflict dynamics, 158, 163–164, 164nn15–16
  COVID-19, 180
  CPP/NPA, 196
  Myanmar, 90
  Nepal, 117
  QCA, 43
Democratic Kayin Buddhist Army (DKBA), 90
Disaster
  conflict research, emergence of, 5–8
  defined, 15, 39
  impact on individuals, groups, and societies, 1–5
  sociology, 5–8
  trends, 3
  types and conflict dynamics, 155–158, *156*

Disaster diplomacy
  conflict bias, 143
  conflict dynamics, 146
  costly signal, 34
  COVID-19 pandemic, 199
  disaster-conflict research, 7
  Kashmir, 85
  key findings, 206, 207
  solidarity, 28–29
Disaster governance, 30, 207
Disaster risk reduction (DRR), 4, 50, 61, 143, 151, 214, 216
Disaster vulnerability, 82, 142–143, 160–165
Drought
  agricultural dependence, 50
  Bangladesh, 27
  Burundi, 81–84, 157
  conflict dynamics, 163
  conflict prevalence, 170
  costly signal, 34
  Darfur, 8
  disaster, type, 155
  Ethiopia, 1, 205
  grievances, 27
  image cultivation, 36
  India, 1
  Kenya, 205
  Nigeria, 4
  opportunity, 30
  Russia, 134–135
  Somalia, 97–100, 151, 152, 205
  state of knowledge, 10, 11, 12
  Syria, 4, 8, 205
  Uganda, 76–78, 147–148
Duterte, Rodrigo, 196–197, 199

Earthquake
  Afghanistan, 102–105, 140, 146
  Algeria, 107–108, 141
  Colombia, 57–60, 169, 210
  disaster-conflict research, 6, 7
  grievances, 25, 26
  Haiti, 1, 30
  Indian Ocean, 7, 71–72, 136
  Indonesia, 86–89, 110–114, 140
  Iran, 114–117, 140
  Kashmir, 84–86, 146, 151, 153
  Nepal, 9
  Pakistan, 120–121
  Peru, 123–124, 141
  Philippines, 67–70, 146, 167
  Russia, 131–133
  Sri Lanka, 71–73
  Tajikistan, 167
  Thailand, 136
  Turkey, 101–102, 146, 173
Earthquakes
  Boumerdès, 107–108, 141
  Flores, 110–112, 140
  Luzon, 70, 125, 146
  Manjil-Rudbar, 114–116
  Marmara, 101–102, 153
  Qayen, 116–117, 140
  Quindío, 169, 210
  Rustaq, 103, 140
  Sakhalin Island, 131–133, 140
  Yogyakarta, 113, 140
Egypt, 60–62, 145, 162, 209
#EndSARS protests, 202
Ethiopia, 1, 95, 97, 99, 205

Federally Administered Tribal Areas (FATA), 92, 92n48
Flood
  Agricultural dependence, 50
  Assam, 65–67, 109–110, 141, 165, 209
  China, 1
  classification of, 155–157
  Colombia, 205, 210
  Egypt, 60–62, 209
  India, 205
  motive, 145
  Nepal, 117–119
  Pakistan, 30, 92–94
  Philippines, 125–126, 167

Index

Somalia, 95–97
Tajikistan, 74–76, 167
Food insecurity
   Assam (India) (2007), 109
   Boko Haram insurgency, 193, 195
   conflict dynamics, 161
   CPP/NPA and the Philippine government, 199
   India, 64
   Pakistan (2010), 93
   Philippines (2012), 130
   Somalia (2010–2011), 98
   Uganda, 76–78
Free Aceh Movement (GAM), 87–89, 87n45, 112–114, 114n79, 154, 172

GDP loss, 79, 83–84, 124, 173
Gender identities, 213
Georeferenced Event Dataset (GED), 59. *See also* UCDP-GED
Global Terrorism Database, 131, 131n101
Grievances
   agricultural dependence, 50
   aid, 52
   Boumerdès earthquake, 107–108
   Boko Haram insurgency, 191, 195
   capable state, 54
   conflict dynamics, *145*, 162, 163, 164, 164n15
   conflict parties, impact on, 53
   COVID-19 pandemic, 181, 196
   CPP/NPA and the Philippine government, 196
   democracy, 50
   disaster, after the, 21, 24
   disaster impacts on conflict dynamics by disaster type, *156*
   discussion, 201–202
   empirical argument, *175*
   escalation or de-escalation after a disaster, 170, 171
   foundation, setting the, 4–19
   future research, 213, 214
   image cultivation, 35
   key findings/implications, 206, 208–212
   motive, 145–146
   overlap, 51
   overview, 25–27
   pathway, 145–146, 157
   poverty, 49
   unexplained cases, conflict escalation, *169*
   unfair distributions, 52
   weak rebels, 53
Guterres, António, 4

Haiti, 1, 30
Hazard. *See also individual cases*
   cases, 39
   COVID-19, 177
   democracy, 50
   external shocks, 210
   setting the foundation, 6, 9–10, 14–15, 19
Heat wave
   Baluchistan, 121–122
   cases studied, *42–43*
   classification of, 155–156
   Pakistan, 148
   Punjab, 121–122
   Russia, 134
   Sindh, 121–122
Hizb-ul-Mujahedeen, 84
Holy Spirit Movement (HSM), 76
Hutu, 81–83, 81n37

Image cultivation
   communication approach, 153–154, 157, 157n13
   Indonesia, 88–89
   Kashmir, 86
   Myanmar, 92, 154, 154n9, 171
   overview, 35–37
   Pakistan Taliban, 94

Image cultivation (cont.)
    PKK, 102
    rapid-onset disasters, 172
    Russia, 135
    slow-onset events, 157n13
    Turkey, 173
India. *See also individual cases*
    battle-related deaths, *46*
    cases, sample of, 39n1, 41, *42*
    communication, 152, 153, 153n8
    conflict dynamics, 162, 165
    conflict escalation, 170, 171n18, 172
    COVID-19, 178, 179, 180
    drought, 1
    floods, 205, 209
    motive, 146
    strategy, 147, 151, 152
Individual greed, 20–21
Indonesia, 86–89, 110–112, 112–114, 113n78
Intergovernmental Panel on Climate Change (IPCC), 7
Internally displaced people (IDP), 77, 78
International Disaster Database (EM-DAT), 40, 40n3, 77n30, 79n34
International Security Assistance Force (ISAF), 105, 106, 190n11
Iran, *46*, 102, 103, 114–116, 116–117, *165*
Islamic Courts Union (ICU), 97
Islamic Group (IG), 60–62, 60nn5–6
Islamic Salvation Front, 107
Islamic State (IS), 183–187, 186n8, 192–194

Jama'at al Tawhid wal Jihad (JTJ), 183–184
Jamaats, 134
Jama'atuAhlis Sunna Lidda'awati Wal-Jihad (JAS), 191, 191n14, 192, 194
Jammu and Kashmir state (J&K), 84
Jana Andolan movement, 117

Janajuddha Faction (PBCP-J), 79–81, 152
Jihad, 187
JSS/SB, 56, 57
Jumma, 55

Karen National Union (KNU), 89–91
Karen National Union–Peace Council (KNU-PC), 90
Karen Nation Liberation Army, 90
Kashmir
    battle related deaths, *46*
    communication logic, 172
    COVID-19 pandemic, 215n5
    cross-border constraints, 84–86, 84nn42–43
    de-escalation, 171n18, 172
    disaster governance, 207
    earthquake, 119, 120
    floods, 205
    motive, 146
    strategy, 151–155
Kenya, 96, 99, 180n4, 205
Key findings and implications
    climate change and security, 207–208
    dynamics and intensity of armed conflict, 208–209
    external shocks, 209–210
    grievances and opportunities, 209
    perceptions, norms, and discourses, 210–211
    research methods, 211–212
Kurdish, 100–102, 102n64, 114–116, 154, *165*, 173
Kurds, 100

Lahkar-e-Toiba, 84, 86
Liberal Movement (LM), 116
Liberation Tigers of Tamil Eelam (LTTE), 71–73, 153, 154, 157, 170, 211
Logical minimization, 45, 48
Lord's Resistance Army (LRA), 76–78, 76n27, 76n29

Index

Maoist
  Bangladesh (2007), 78–81
  CPN-Maoist (CPN-M), 118–119
  Maoist Communist Centre (MCC), 64
  Maoist Communist Party of Nepal–Unity Center (CPN-UC), 118
  Maoist Communist Party of Peru, 123
  Maoist CPP, 67
  Philippines, 57
Migration
  Assam, 109
  Bangladesh, 55–56
  climate change, 143
  country-level disasters, 40
  disaster-migration-grievances pathway, 31
  grievances, 26–27, 27n2
  Pakistan, 120
  Philippines, 129
  research methods, 211, 214
  state of knowledge, 9, 10
Mooryaan, 97
Moro Islamic Liberation Front (MILF), 129, 129n98
Motivations, 11, 17, 21, 24, 176, 201
Motive, 20, 21, 23, 25, 80, 110, 205–206
Mujahedin, 102, 187
Mullahs, 187, 188
Myanmar
  battle-related deaths, *46*
  casualties, 153n8
  communication approach, 153, 172
  image cultivation, 37, 154, 171
  Karen conflict after Cyclone Nargis, 89–92

National Council for Defense of Democracy–Forces for the Defense of Democracy (CNDD-FDD), 81–84
National Council of the Maubere Resistance (CNRM), 110n74, 111
National Liberation Forces (FNL), 81, 110n74

National Resistance Army (NRA), 76–78, 76n28
Naxalite conflict, 62–65
Naxalite insurgents, 62–65, 165, 205
Nepal, 9–10, 117–119
New People's Army (NPA), 67–70, 125, 126, 127–129, 127n94. *See also* CPP/NPA
Nigeria, 182–183, 192–193
Non-State Actor dataset, 53–54
Northern Alliance, 103–105
North-West Frontier Province (NWFP), 92

Öcalan, Abdullah, 100, 102, 102n65
Offensive Jihadism, 183
Omar, Mohammad, 103, 104, 188
Operation Enduring Freedom, 105
Operation Iron Fist, 78
Operation Zarb-e-Azb, 121n87
Opportunity/opportunities
  Algeria, 107–108
  Andhra Pradesh and Orissa, 62–65
  armed conflict risk, 209
  armed conflicts, 2, 14
  Assam, 65–67, 109–110
  Bangladesh, 57
  cease-fires and peace talks, 216
  climate-related disasters, 208
  collective action resources, 29
  Colombia, 59–60
  communication, 154
  conflict de-escalation, 14, 24
  conflict dynamics, 16, 157, 157n13, 162
  conflict escalation, 140–141, 176
  conflict intensity, 5, 217
  COVID-19 pandemic, 178, 194, 195, 196, 203
  CPP/NPA, 28n95
  de-escalation, 37, 171, 206
  after the disaster, 29–32
  disaster-conflict research, 6
  disaster diplomacy, 28

Opportunity/opportunities (cont.)
  empirical argument, *175* (*see also individual cases*)
  escalation or de-escalation, 168–169
  FARC, 59
  food insecurity, 161
  grievances, 24, 209
  image cultivation, 35
  Indonesia, 112
  IS, 184, 186, 201
  key findings, 206, 208
  MEK, 117n82
  motive, 145
  Nepal, 119
  Nigeria, 202
  Pakistan, 121
  Philippines, 67–70, 129
  poverty, 49
  preoccupation of the security forces, 216
  PWG, 64
  Sri Lanka, 73
  strategic opportunities, 31
  strategy, 147–148, 152, 209
  strategy-based approaches, 22
  Tajikistan, 75
  Thailand, 137
  Turkey, 102
  violence as form of communication, 214
  weather conditions, 22
Organisation for Economic Co-operation and Development (OECD), 164
Orissa, 62–65, 65–67

Pahari, 55
Pakistan, *47*, 92–94, 93n50, 119–121, 121–122, 122nn88–89
Pakistani Inter-Services Intelligence (ISI), 65, 154
Pakistani Taliban / Tehrik i-Taliban Pakistan (TTP), 92–94, 94n51, 121–122

Panchayat system, 117
Party for the Liberation of Hutu People (PALIPEHUTU), 81–84
Party for the Liberation of Hutu People–National Liberation Forces (PALIPEHUTU-FNL), 157, *173*
Pashtun, 103, 103n67
Patani, 135–137, 136n111
Peace Force (SB), 56. *See also* JSS/SB
People's Consultative Group (PCG), 109
People's Mujahideen Organisation (MEK), 116–117, 117n82, 140
People Surge movement, 128
People's War Group (PWG), 62–65, 62n9, *165*, 170
Peru, 123–124
Philippines, 11, 17, 41, 140, 144n2, 146, 149, 157, 180n4
  Communist rebellion in, 18
  conflict de-escalation, 67–70, 125–126
  COVID-19 and conflict, 196–200
  earthquake-related opportunities, 67–70
  military, 69, 70, 131
  super typhoon, 127–129
  typhoon and conflict escalation, 129–131, 130n100
Plan Colombia, 59
Political Geography, 7
PolityIV dataset, 50
Post-conflict peace building, 213–214
Post-Tsunami Operational Management Structure (P-TOMS), 73
Poverty
  causal conditions and theoretical expectations, 49–50, 51
  conflict dynamics, 158, 159, *159*, 160–161, *160*, 163
  COVID-19 disaster, 178, 179
  CPP/NPA and the Philippine government, 196, 197
  practice and policy, lessons for, 216

Index

Practice and policy, lessons for, 214–216, 215nn5–6
Purbo Banglar Communist Party (PBCP), 78–80

Qualitative comparative analysis (QCA)
  causal conditions and theoretical expectations, 48–49
  conclusion, 211
  overview, 14, 43–45, 43n7, *44*, *161*
  results, interpreting, *161*
  two-stage QCA, visualization of, *49*
Quindío, 59

Rapid Action Battalion (RAB), 80
Rapid-onset disasters, 9, 17, 31, 149, 155–158, 172, 206
Rapid-onset events, 41, 155, 156, 156n10, 157, 157n11
Rebel governance, 27, 151
Red Cross, 82n39, 118, 190
Relative deprivation, 20, 209
Republic of Kurdistan, 114
Republic of Mahabad, 114
Revolutionary Armed Forces of Colombia (FARC), 57–59, 124
Revolutionary Front for an Independent East Timor (FRETILIN), 110–112, 110n74
Revolutionary Guards (Iran), 116
Ripeness theory, 33
Rondas campesinas, 123
Russia, 131–133, 133–135, 134n109. *See also* Soviet Union
Rwanda, 3

Salafism, 183
Salafist Group for Preaching and Combat (GSPC), 107–108
Saudi Arabia, 96, 102, 103n66, 178
Sendero Luminoso (Shining Path), 123–124, 123nn90–91
Sharia, 92, 191
Sinhalese, 71, 73

Slow-onset disasters, 41, 147, 155–158, *156*
Slow-onset events, 155, 156–157, 158
Solidarity
  agricultural dependence, 50
  Bangladesh, 79, 80
  Chechen, 131
  conflict dynamics, 25, 146, 157
  costly signal, 34–35
  COVID-19, 187, 202
  de-escalation, 16
  image cultivation, 35–37
  Indonesia, 89, 113
  key findings, 206
  Myanmar, 91
  overlap, 51
  Pakistan, 94, 122, 129
  post-disaster, 49–50, 176
  poverty, 49–50
  solidarity, 27–29, 28n3
  Sri Lanka, 72
  state of knowledge, 9
  Turkey, 102
Somalia, 95–97, 95nn52–53, 96n55, 97–100, 98nn59–60
Somali National Alliance, 95
Southern Bloc Guerrilla (SBC), 57. *See also* Revolutionary Armed Forces of Colombia (FARC)
Soviet Union, 6, 102, 132n104, 187
Sri Lanka
  civil war, 8
  communication, 155
  conflict dynamics, 157, 162, 163, 164n15
  conflict escalation, 170–171
  conflict parties' perceptions, 210–211
  costly signal, 25
  disaster governance, 207
  disaster-related grievances, 145
  motive, 145
  opportunity, 31
  state of knowledge, 11
  wave of violence, 71–73

State weakness, 6–7, 10, 21–22, 31, 53, 149, 163
Storm. *See also* Cyclone; Tsunami; Typhoon
  armed conflict risks, 4
  Bangladesh, 27, 29
  constraints, 32
  grievances, 25, 26
  image cultivation, 36
  India, 63–64
  Myanmar, 90
  Philippines, 125–128, 130–131
Strategy, 21–22, *147*, 147–152, *150*, 201
Surrendered ULFA (SULFA), 65–66
Syria
  drought, 8, 205
  Islamic State, 184–185
  Kurdistan Workers Party, 100
  life expectancy, 2
  state of knowledge, 11
  strategy, 149

Tajikistan, 74–76, 74n24
Taliban (Afghanistan)
  COVID-19 cases, *182*
  COVID-19 pandemic, 189–191, 201–203, 215
  GDP loss, 189
  monthly battle-related deaths, *182*
  1998, 102–105
  2008, 105–107
  overview, 187–191, 188nn10–12
  September 11, 2001, 188
Tehreek-e-afaz-e-Shariat-e Mohammadi (TNSM), 92, 92n49
Thailand, 135–137
Threat multiplier, 208n2
Transnational Federal Government (TFG), 97, 99, 100
Truth table, 45, 45n9
Truth table analysis, 159, *160*, 166, 166n17, *168*, *172*

Tsunami
  Aceh, 88–89, 114
  classification of, 155–156
  costly signal, 153, 155
  disaster-conflict research, 5, 7, 8
  East Timor, 111–112
  Flores Island, 111
  image cultivation, 27, 88–89
  Indian Ocean, 155
  Indonesia, 5, 87
  motive, 145
  opportunity, 30, 31
  solidarity, 146
  Sri Lanka, 71–72, 73, 145
  state of knowledge, 11–12
  Thailand, 135–137
Turkey, *46*, 100–102, 145, 146, 152–153, *153*
Tutsi, 81, 81n37
Twitter, 213
Typhoon. *See also* Cyclone
  Bopha, 125, 130–131, 141
  conflict dynamics, 157
  Haiyan, 127–129, 146, 157
  Philippines, 127–129, 129–132, 196
  strategy, 149
  Uring, 125

UCDP-GED, 41, 41n5, 70, 96, 101, 101n63, 110, 181
Uganda, 76–78, 77n30
Uganda People's Democratic Army (UPDA), 76
United Islamic Front for the Salvation of Afghanistan (UIFSA), 103–105
United Liberation Front of Assam (ULFA), 65–67, 109–110, 141, *165*
United Nations Commission on Human Rights, 36
United Somali Congress (USC), 95, 96n54, 210
United States, 102, 105, 192
United Tajik Opposition (UTO), 74–75

Index

Unit of analysis, 39, 39n1
UN Peacekeepers, 82, 82n40
UN Security Council, 4, 7, 207
Uppsala Conflict Data Program (UCDP), 2, 15, 40

Vaccine nationalism, 179
Violence-as-communication approach, 22–24, 33–34, 154, 162, 214
Vulnerability. *See also* Disaster vulnerability
　conflict dynamics, 17, 174
　costly signal, 34
　definition of, 15–16
　disaster-conflict research, 7
　disaster prevention, 15
　disaster vulnerability, 160–165
　effect of aid on, 52
　external shocks, 209–210
　Sri Lanka, 72
　trends in disasters, 2, 4, 14
　Uganda, 77

World Food Programme, 118
World Health Organization (WHO), 177

Xenophobia, 180